The Politics of Africa:

Dependence and Development

Dalhousie African Studies Series
General Editor: John Flint

The Politics of Africa:

Dependence and Development

Edited by Timothy M. Shaw and Kenneth A. Heard

Africana Publishing Company
A Division of Holmes & Meier, New York
Dalhousie University Press

First published in the United States of America 1979 by
Africana Publishing Company
a Division of Holmes & Meier Publishers, Inc.
30 Irving Place
New York, N.Y. 10003

Library of Congress Cataloging in Publication Data

Main entry under title:

Politics of Africa.

   (Dalhousie African studies series)
   Papers selected from the third and fourth
conferences of the Canadian Association of African
Studies, held at Carleton University, Ottawa, and
Dalhousie University, Halifax, in Feb. 1973 and
1974.
   Includes index.
   1. Africa—Politics and government—1960–
—Addresses, essays, lectures. 2. Africa—
Economic conditions—1945–   —Addresses, essays,
lectures. 3. Africa—Foreign relations—Addresses,
essays, lectures. 4. Economic assistance in Africa
—Addresses, essays, lectures. I. Shaw,
Timothy M. II. Heard, Kenneth A. III. Canadian
Association of African Studies. IV. Series.
DT30.P54   320.9'6'03   78-15215
ISBN 0-8419-0378-6
ISBN 0-8419-6389-1 pbk.

Printed in Great Britain by
J. W. Arrowsmith Ltd., Bristol BS3 2NT

088527

Contents

Foreword   vii

Notes on the contributors   ix

Part 1. *Uneven Development and Class Formation*   1

  Chapter 1. Robin Cohen

            The Making of a West African Working Class   5

  Chapter 2. Henry Cooperstock

            Some Methodological and Substantive Issues
in the Study of Social Stratification in Tropical
Africa   23

Part 2. *Dependent Development*   39

  Chapter 3. Jan Jelmert Jørgensen

            Structural Dependence and the Move to the
Left: The Political Economy of the Obote
Regime in Uganda   43

  Chapter 4. Joel W. Gregory

            Underdevelopment, Dependence, and Migration in Upper Volta   73

  Chapter 5. Roger Leys

            Lesotho: Non-Development or Underdevelopment. Towards an Analysis of the
Political Economy of the Labour Reserve   95

Part 3. *Political Change and Participation*   131

  Chapter 6. John Cartwright

            The Limits to Leadership: Sierra Leone Under
the Margais   135

  Chapter 7. Richard Hodder-Williams

            Support in Eastern Africa: Some Observations
from Malaŵi   153

Chapter 8. Douglas G. Anglin
Zambia and the Southern African Liberation
Movements: 1964–1974   183

Part 4. *Aid to Africa: Interdependence or Dependence?*   217
Chapter 9. Gerald K. Helleiner
Aid and Dependence in Africa: Issues For
Recipients   221
Chapter 10. Kenji Okuda
Canadian Government Aid: A Critical
Assessment   247

Part 5. *Africa and International Politics*   265
Chapter 11. David H. Johns
Diplomatic Exchange and Interstate Inequality
in Africa: An Empirical Analysis   269
Chapter 12. James Mayall
The Implications For Africa of the Enlarged
European Economic Community   285
Chapter 13. John F. Clark
Patterns of Support for International
Organisations in Africa   319
Chapter 14. Timothy M. Shaw
The Actors in African International Politics   357

Index   397

Foreword

This collection of fourteen original essays is intended to be both a review and overview of current theoretical and empirical research on Africa. It is one result of the annual conferences organised by the Canadian Association of African Studies; all these chapters originated as papers presented at the Association's third or fourth conferences held at Carleton University, Ottawa, and Dalhousie University, Halifax, in February 1973 and 1974. They represent a selection from the exciting research currently being undertaken in Canada and elsewhere on the impact of political change and development in Africa. They cover a wide range of case studies, from Lesotho and Uganda to Upper Volta and Sierra Leone, and examine national, continental and global politics. The contributors also deal, more or less explicitly, with a group of theoretical issues, from class formation and types of development strategies to foreign aid and the characteristics of African international relations. We hope that this collection will appeal both to the particular and general interests of Africans and Africanists.

We are especially grateful to our contributors for their patience in the face of the delays that seem to beset publications of this kind and for their willingness to revise their essays in the light of the constraints that we have had to impose. The very successful conferences from which these papers derive owed much to the organising abilities of Lynn Mytelka of Carleton and Bala Pillay of Dalhousie respectively. The Faculty of Graduate Studies, the Department of Political Science, the Centre for Foreign Policy Studies and the Centre for African Studies of Dalhousie University have given valuable support and provided essential services for the conferences and the preparation of the manuscript for this book. We are particularly appreciative of the careful and timely editorial assistance provided by George Braden and the

quick and accurate typing services of Doris Boyle, Marlene
Brooks, Judy Campbell, Ann Deane, Lorna Cross, Wilhelmina
Ross and Claudia Rocheleau. Finally, we are both very indebted
for the love and indulgence of our families in tolerating all the
absences involved in bringing this publication to press.

Timothy M. Shaw and Kenneth A. Heard
Halifax, August 1977

Notes on the Contributors

Douglas G. Anglin is Professor of Political Science at Carleton University, Ottawa, Canada and was Vice-Chancellor of the University of Zambia from 1965 to 1969. Among his many publications on African international relations are: 'Confrontation in Southern Africa: Zambia and Portugal', *International Journal* (1970); 'Zambia and the recognition of Biafra', *African Review* (1971); 'The politics of transit routes in land-locked Southern Africa', in Cervenka, ed., *Land-locked Countries of Africa* (1973); 'Britain and the use of force in Rhodesia', in Fry, ed., *Freedom and Change: essays in honour of Lester B. Pearson* (1975); 'Zambia and Southern African "détente"', *International Journal* (1975); and 'Zambian disengagement from Southern Africa and integration with East Africa 1964–1972: a transaction analysis', in Shaw and Heard, eds., *Cooperation and Conflict in Southern Africa: papers on a regional subsystem* (1976).

John Cartwright is Associate Professor of Political Science at the University of Western Ontario, London, Canada. Among his publications on West African politics are *Politics in Sierra Leone 1947–1967* (1970); 'Some constraints upon African political leadership', *Canadian Journal of African Studies* (1977); and *Political leadership in Sierra Leone* (1978).

John F. Clark was a Lecturer in Political Science at the University of Florida, Gainesville, Florida and is currently Legislative Assistant for Congressman John W. Jenrette in the US House of Representatives. He is author of several papers on African international politics and organisations, including: 'National attributes associated with dimensions of support for the United Nations' (with O'Leary and Wittkopf), *International Organization* (1971);

and 'Africa's Role in International Organizations', African Studies Association Conference (1974).

Robin Cohen is Senior Lecturer in Sociology at the University of the West Indies, St Augustine, on leave from the Department of Sociology, at the University of Birmingham, England and an associate of its Centre for West African Studies. Among his several publications on politics and class in Africa are: 'Class in Africa: analytical problems and perspectives', in Miliband and Saville, eds., *The Socialist Register, 1972; Labour and politics in Nigeria* (1974); and 'African peasants and resistance to change: a reconsideration of sociological approaches' (with Caroline Hutton) in Oxaal *et al.*, eds., *Beyond the Sociology of Development* (London, 1975); he is editor with Richard Sandbrook of *The Development of An African Working Class: studies in class formation and action* (1975).

Henry Cooperstock is Professor of Sociology at the University of Toronto, Toronto, Canada.

Joel W. Gregory is Assistant Professor of Demography at the University of Montreal, Montreal, Canada. His publications include: 'Development and in-migration in Upper Volta' in Amin ed., *Modern Migration in Western Africa* (1974); and 'Population and development in Africa: the persistence of the conventional wisdom' (with Victor Piche) *Journal of Modern African Studies* (1976).

Kenneth A. Heard is Professor, and Past-Chairman, of the Department of Political Science, Dalhousie University, Halifax, Nova Scotia and a member of its Centre for African Studies; he previously lectured at the University of Natal. His publications include: *Political Systems in Multi-racial Societies* (1962); and *General Elections in South Africa, 1943–1970* (1974). He is also co-editor with Timothy M. Shaw of *Cooperation and Conflict in Southern Africa: papers on a regional subsystem* (1976).

Gerald K. Helleiner is Professor of Political Economy at the University of Toronto, Canada. He has published extensively on the problems of economic development, including: *Peasant Agriculture, Government and Economic Growth in Nigeria* (1966); *Inter-*

national Trade and Economic Development (1972); 'Socialism and economic development in Tanzania', *Journal of Development Studies* (1972); 'Manufactured exports from less developed countries and multinational firms', *Economic Journal* (1973); and 'The less developed countries and the international monetary system', *Journal of Development Studies* (1974). He is editor of *A World Divided: the less developed countries in the international economy* (1976).

Richard Hodder-Williams is Lecturer in Politics at the University of Bristol, Bristol, England. Among his many publications on the politics of Southern Africa are: 'Malawi's decade under Dr. Banda: the revival of politics', *Round Table* (1973); 'Dr. Banda's Malawi', *Journal of Commonwealth and Comparative Politics* (1974); and 'Afrikaners in Rhodesia: a partial portrait', *African Social Research* (1974).

David H. Johns is Professor of Political Science at San Diego State University, San Diego, California. Among his several publications on continental relations in Africa are: 'The normalisation of intra-African diplomatic activity', *Journal of Modern African Studies* (1972); 'Diplomatic activity, power and integration in Africa', *Sage International Yearbook of Foreign Policy Studies Vol. 3* (1975); and 'The foreign policy of Tanzania', in Aluko, ed., *The Foreign Policies of African States* (1977).

Jan Jelmert Jørgensen is Research Associate at the Centre for Developing Area Studies, and Sessional Lecturer in Sociology at McGill University, having previously been a Research Fellow at the International Peace Research Institute, Oslo, Norway and at the Centre for Foreign Policy Studies, Dalhousie University, Halifax, Canada. He has published papers on Africa's political economy, including 'Multinational corporations and the indigenisation of the Kenyan economy', in Widstrand (ed.) *Multinational Firms in Africa* (1975); and 'Domestically-oriented production as an anti-domination strategy: the case of Ghana and Kenya', in Gleditsch and Jørgensen (eds), *Theories of Dominance and Dependency Structures* (1975). He has done field work in Uganda, Kenya, and Ghana and is author of *The Modern History of Uganda* (forthcoming).

Roger Leys is Research Fellow in Political Science at the University of Copenhagen, Denmark. Among his publications on underdevelopment in Africa are: 'A theoretical approach to the problems of African land-locked states' (with Pedersen), in Cervenka, ed., *Land-locked Countries of Africa* (1973); and 'South African gold mining in 1974: "the gold" of migrant labour', *African Affairs* (1975).

James Mayall is Senior Lecturer in International Relations at the London School of Economics and Political Science, England. Among his many publications on African international politics are: 'Malawi's foreign policy', *The World Today* (1970); *Africa: the cold war and after* (1971); 'The Malawi–Tanzania boundary dispute', *Journal of Modern African Studies* (1973); and 'African unity and the OAU: the place for a political myth in African diplomacy', in *Year Book of World Affairs, Vol 27* (1973). He is also an editor (with Watt and Navari) of *Documents on International Affairs, 1963* (1972).

Kenji Okuda is Professor of Economics at Simon Fraser University, Burnaby, British Columbia, Canada. He has acted as economic consultant in Uganda and Lesotho through the Canadian International Development Agency.

Timothy M. Shaw is Associate Professor of Political Science and Director, Centre for African Studies at Dalhousie University, Halifax, Nova Scotia, Canada. His publications on African politics include: 'Uganda under Amin: the costs of confronting dependence', *Africa Today* (1973); 'The Organisation of African Unity: prospects for the second decade', *International Perspectives* (1973); 'African States and international stratification: the adaptive foreign policy of Tanzania', in Ingham, ed., *Foreign Relations of African States* (1974); 'Southern Africa: cooperation and conflict in an international subsystem', *Journal of Modern African Studies* (1974); 'Discontinuities and inequalities in African international politics', *International Journal* (1975); 'Zambia: dependence and underdevelopment', *Canadian Journal of African Studies* (1976); and 'Zambia's foreign policy', in Aluko, ed., *The Foreign Policies of African States* (1977).

Part 1 Uneven Development and Class Formation

Studies of African politics have been transformed in the last five years and have begun to adopt a new and more critical 'paradigm'. During the first decade of Africa's recaptured independence, political scientists concentrated on the problems of nation-building, the military, mobilisation, modernisation and ethnicity. In Africa's second decade the focus has shifted to class-formation, inequalities, one-party systems, and state capitalism. The problems of development in Africa have increased rather than decreased in the first decade of formal independence. Neither aid, regional integration, political order, or socialist rhetoric have solved the problems of development; rather, international and internal inequalities have tended to grow. Conflict rather than cooperation, underdevelopment rather than development, characterise contemporary African politics.

In response to the elusiveness of development and the inappropriateness of established modes of analysis, students of Africa have begun to adopt a new approach to the understanding of African politics. This new paradigm is more critical and controversial than the old orthodoxy. Its origins lie in radical European scholarship rather than in American behavioural social science; it has also incorporated the centre-periphery model of Scandinavian scholars and the dependence theory of Latin American intellectuals. It is consistent with the mode of analysis that deals with global as well as local relations and with the interrelations of international and internal inequalities. This new 'school' of African politics' also revives the traditions of political economy and political history in Africa, often within the 'neo-Marxist' genre. It presents an African-oriented response to the impact of dependence comparable with the new African historiography which places more emphasis on resistance to colonialism than on collaboration and tries to escape from earlier imperialist perspectives.

This is exemplified by Chapter 1 in which Cohen is critical of African history written from an imperial, ruling-class perspective. He suggests five alternative types of African history which would advance class analysis from pre-colonial to contemporary times. This typology serves to introduce his own work on the working classes of West Africa. His analysis of the organisation, action and consciousness of workers in Africa indicates that class is not merely a contemporary phenomenon but has a long vintage; he appeals for 'another kind of African history'.

In Chapter 2, Cooperstock proposes a mode of analysis of social stratification which differentiates among the several types of core-periphery relations and of state-class relations in Africa. He suggests that in addition to the peasantry, four classes are emerging in Africa: the political-administrative elite, the bourgeoisie, the petty-bourgeoisie, and the proletariat. His review of the burgeoning literature on class formation in Africa uses examples drawn from the case of Kenya. Cooperstock points to the need for a distinctively African theory of social conflict and change, one that will incorporate patron–client relations into patterns of group development. He concludes by suggesting that class conflict is likely to follow from the inability of clients to satisfy patrons; when the initial benefits of *uhuru* have been redistributed and exhausted, the disadvantaged will begin to demand structural change rather than patronage.

These two chapters provide a useful theoretical base for the case studies in Part 2 on Dependent Development, which examine the impact of uneven growth on the political economy of three African states.

Note

1. This new, critical approach to African politics is best represented in its several varieties by: Samir Amin, *Neo-colonialism in West Africa*, Penguin, 1973; Giovanni Arrighi and John S. Saul, *Essays on the Political Economy of Africa*, Monthly Review Press, New York, 1973; E. A. Brett, *Colonialism and Under-development in East Africa*, Heinemann, 1972; Justinian Rweyemamu, *Under-development and Industrialisation in Tanzania: a study of perverse capitalist industrial development*, Oxford University Press, Nairobi 1973; Basil Davidson,

Can Africa Survive? Arguments Against Growth Without Development, Little, Brown, Boston 1974; Colin Leys, *Underdevelopment in Kenya: the political economy of neo-colonialism*, University of California, Berkeley 1974; Richard Harris, ed., *The Political Economy of Africa*, Schenkman, Cambridge, Mass. 1975; Peter C. W. Gutkind and Immanuel Wallerstein, eds., *The Political Economy of Contemporary Africa*, Sage, Beverly Hills 1976; Peter C. W. Gutkind and Peter Waterman, eds., *African Social Studies: a radical reader*, Heinemann, 1977; and Irving Leonard Markovitz, *Power and Class in Africa*, Prentice-Hall, Englewood Cliffs 1977.

Robin Cohen

1   The Making of a West African Working Class

1. What Kind of African History?

One of the more persistent illusions about the writing of African history is that we are in the process of achieving some kind of satisfactory symmetry in the presentation of the Africans' point of view as against that of the imperialist powers. Colonial history, seen solely in terms of the expansion of Europe, has long been denounced as ethnocentric, insulting or derogatory. The redress was seen to lie in developing schools of African history, firmly based in Africa, which presented a contrasting and opposing view to that of the imperialist historians. Some European historians working in Africa made notable contributions to the development of this perspective, but much of the ongoing work has been taken up by African historians themselves. Within the USA, the increased black consciousness led to a reinforcement of the new concern and in particular, an interest in the contributions of translantic blacks in the growth of African nationalism.

The contrast between the two perspectives is rather more superficial than perhaps might be adduced at first sight. In essence the bulk of historical writing from 'the Africans' point of view' bears an uncomfortably close reciprocal image to imperialist history. 'Our warfare was as sophisticated in techniques and stratagems as European warfare.' 'We too had our captains and kings, our merchant princes, military heroes and royal houses.' 'Our great states rivalled Europe's in sophistication, wealth and administrative complexity.' 'Our thought, customs, values, dress, religion and languages are as good as or superior to those that the European powers brought with them.' Such assumptions underpin the very fabric of current African historiography, but the terms of the dialectic are those set by an elitist European perspective and built round an almost conditioned response to it. Where, in the conventional historic scenarios, is the woman, the slave, the foot soldier, the hunter, the fisherman, the herdsman, the wage earner and above all the rural producer? Such *dramatis personae* provided the surplus value and labour power which built the fortress of Zimbabwe and the great states of the Western Sudan.

Of course it caricatures the work of recent scholars to say that they are engaged totally in writing ruling-class history. Useful work has been done by economic historians and anthropologists, by geographers and others whose discipline requires some understanding of productive activities. The early, rather uncritical canonisation of the westernised elite has given way at some places to a greater interest in collaboration by elites across the colour line. Then too, a certain amount of interest has recently been shown in agricultural and labour history. It is nonetheless notable that we have had no significant interpretation and critical justification of the mainstream of African historiography by a practising historian. Presuppositions that the subject matter and ideological content of African history need no further analysis have prevailed, while an ideological counter-position has remained dormant or been contained within an overt Marxist or new leftist perspective.

For African historians who have been closely involved in the creation of nationalist mythologies, conversion to a Marxist perspective is, to put it mildly, unlikely. Nonetheless a reappraisal of the dominant modes of historical explanation and description may begin in a more limited way. Such a reorientation could take three forms: (*a*) A movement away from the analysis of what the Mensah Sarbahs, Africanus Hortons and Holy Johnsons *said* to what the bulk of the populace *did* in their daily lives; (*b*) The espousal of a greater interest in the broader social effects of oppression and exploitation perpetuated by colonial and indigenous rulers alike; (*c*) The greater use of tools of analysis derived from the social sciences rather than a mechanical adherence to formalised rules of historical method; or more concretely, a discarding of what might be crudely termed 'bourgeois objectivity' in favour of a reconstruction of reality seen from the perspective of dispossessed and hitherto ignored social groups.

2. Analysing Class Formation

The study of class formation in Africa has suffered from the perpetuation of the 'Merrie Africa' myth – as Hopkins calls the tendency for uncritical celebration of the African past, and the exaggeration of the degree of communal solidarity in pre-industrial societies.[1] It would be sterile to extensively rebut notions emanating from certain western observers and African writers and politicians alike, that Africa is, or was, composed of a set of classless societies.[2] Instead, I simply assert that the process of class formation was obscured by the ideological hegemony of the dominant school of African history. The real problem lies not in the supposed non-existence of classes, but in how one might best analyse their character. Five theoretical points of departure are discussed below.

(a) Locating the 'classical' classes

This style of analysis is represented best perhaps, among contemporary writers, by the English social historian, E. P. Thompson, and in the African context, by orthodox Marxists such as Jack Woddis. The evolutionary assumptions of the Marxist hagiography are present in that the implicit assumption exists that one particular mode of production (the 'capitalist') is predominant, will become predominant, or is already of sufficient centrality to locate the classes classically described by Marx. 'Process' and 'becoming,' emphasised as critical changes in pro-ductive forces, are seen to give rise to changes in productive relations – changes which result ultimately in the reproduction of classes in a comparable, if not totally similar form, to those con-fronting Marx and Engels in the nineteenth century. Action, organisation and the development of a class ideology congeal, though in an uneven manner, to create, for example, a working-class identity. Thompson expresses the style elegantly in his *Making of the English Working Class* (from which the title of this chapter is obviously derived):

> The working class did not arise like the sun at the appointed time. It was present at its own making . . . The finest-meshed sociological net cannot give up a pure specimen of class, any

more than it can give us one of deference and love. The relationship must always be embodied in real people and in a real context ... [and in another place] The working class made itself as much as it was made.[3]

One of the classical classes – the working class – can, I believe, be successfully described by employing a methodology of this kind, though it is far from clear that other elements in the social structure are amenable to this kind of treatment. The perspective 'fits' precisely because the determining factor is the transformation of the labour component in collective and other modes of production into the sale of labour-power, i.e. the process of turning labour into a commodity to be bought, sold or controlled in the market place. Who is doing the buying (though of vital concern in looking at other class interests) is of secondary importance to the central fact that the appropriation of the surplus value of labour-power takes place. Obvious behavioural manifestations of class solidarity (though not less obvious ones like the extent of alienation, machine-breaking etc.) are easily subject to the historian's craft, who can plot a succession of more or less self-conscious class-based acts by the investigation of data relating to strikes, man-days lost, demonstrations, industrial accident rates, etc. The very nature of the data in other words confers legitimacy on the style of analysis.

(b) Objectifying subjective attitudes

In this class of explanation I would include survey research based on the administration and coding of schedules, but reserve for a somewhat different treatment evaluations of ideologies held or supposedly held by corporate groups like 'the peasants', 'the lumpenproletariat', etc. The methodology used rests essentially on the analysis of expressed attitudes or images of the stratification order.

Often the data of particular interest to *class* analysis are submerged in a wider sociological investigation which may concern, for example, attitudes to housing, education, social welfare, employment opportunities, perception of traditional norms and sanctions, etc. For the historian an additional problem arises in the usual lack of a time series in presenting similar or comparable data.

The most important results from a perspective of this kind are those which suggest an 'ideological barrier' to the expression of 'objective' class interests, for example, looking at the extent of adherence to patron-client relationships which cross-cut or even obscure the identification of a class interest. A sophisticated treatment of clientalism and personalism in politics can demonstrate that such relationships are themselves subject to a broader process of social differentiation rooted in material conditions.[4] Nonetheless, perceptions ('objectified' by survey methods) that are in conflict to a class model of society are important in that as Ossowski has remarked: 'An intellectual scheme that is rooted in the social consciousness may within certain limits withstand the test of reality.'[5]

But the limits are clear and real. The relativistic nature of survey evidence (i.e. its utter dependence on time and circumstance) can give us little guide to past behaviour and attitudes (because memory is selective and defective) and cannot tell us how a different situation will be responded to – where once again we may be forced back into defining a reality parallel or incongruent to the respondents' own construction of their reality.

(c) Delineating subterranean classes

This is a difficult perspective to define in precise terms as its proponents may evince fringe Marxist, phenomenological or anarcho-syndicalist views. What these elements hold in common is a great stress on 'sudden insight' and 'spontaneous' reactions engendered by dramatic shifts in the character and intensity of the exploitative relationship. Groups 'leap forward' – driven by myth or ideology (which are not necessarily distinct categories) into a political realisation of their interests.

In the context of Africa the most important intellectual figure who expresses this perspective is Fanon. Like Sorel and some anarcho-syndicalists, he believed that oppressive class relationships could be overturned by a conscious act of political will galvanised from a blend of memory, fantasy, belief and immediate experience. Class formation is not, then, as in the original Marxist view I have identified, associated with a slow aggregative process of productive relations moving into harmony with productive forces – but on the contrary in the total resolution of their contradiction by a head-on confrontation. Though extremely vague in its scientific assumptions, historical evidence – slave revolts, popular participation in the Jihads, peasant rebellions and political action undertaken by lumpen elements – confirms that even previously unorganised groups do on rare occasions have the capacity to seize the political initiative and undertake class action *for* themselves. Groups and strata that are only with difficulty described as classes of themselves can *become* if only for short moments, classes for themselves. To this statement must immediately be added a qualification. If objective class interests and experience do not pervade the group as a whole, class-based acts cannot represent anything but a temporary manifestation. The general rule in Africa is that class action undertaken by 'under classes' has been arrested or diverted – partly no doubt because of the failure of political will, but also because of the strengths of conservative communal ties and the diffuse and limited character of the contradictions introduced by capitalist and imperialist penetration.

(d) Embedding classes in the metropolitan/satellite relationship

From our point of view this style of analysis is important in that it breaks down dichotomous presentations of African *v.* European interests and sets local societies within the context of a world political economy. The class structure is then part and parcel of an international division of labour (and resources) which has to be defined in terms of each corporate socio-economic group's relationship to the overall structure of domination. In terms of our present interest in the growth of a working class, the labour aristocracy thesis propounded by G. Arrighi and J. Saul is to be seen in the light of their concern to identify the structural consequences of the metropolitan/satellite link. In their view, the working class (or at least that part of it that is not a semi-proletarianised peasantry) has been progressively inducted into those local classes that are tightly bound to the external estate. In exchange for their (comparatively) privileged status and economic position they renounce any claims to being a leading revolutionary class. If revolutionary activity is to be undertaken, it will have to be undertaken by classes or strata who are less structurally involved in the preservation of the *status quo*.[6] I am not concerned to evaluate this thesis here – but merely to illustrate how the adoption of a particular theoretical point of departure can shift a basic interpretation of similar historical data into a particular direction.

(e) Defining African modes of production and the relationship of classes thereto

One of the most fruitful growth areas in the Marxist, particularly French Marxist, literature has been the reconsideration of Marx's original definitions of the various modes of production. The social organisation of production in pre-colonial West Africa was, as Hopkin's recent economic history confirms, much too varied to be encompassed by the categories 'primitive' or 'communal'. Nor is Marx's sub-variant, the Asiatic mode, exactly thick on the ground in Sub-Saharan Africa.

If, however, suitable categories can be agreed on, both in the context of pre-colonial modes and those contemporaneous with the introduction of the imperialist nexus, a considerably more subtle and telling class analysis may be devised. Different agents and different agencies were used to enforce the neo-imperial order – some of which challenged local power-wielders by making obsolete their control over anachronistic modes of production. Other ruling groups were located in more adaptive modes, which meant they could perpetuate older forms of social control over production, exchange and distribution.

The evolution of superior taxonomies does not however, as a group of French Marxists have realised, provide the dynamic and causative features that are necessary to a creative Marxism (I refer here to the work of Terray, Meillassoux, Coquéry-Vidrovitch and Amin). Much discussion has therefore ranged on the question of the 'articulation' of modes of production. The word is perhaps unfortunate in that it may be misunderstood simply as 'the expression of' whereas it is used most frequently to mean the 'grafting onto' or the 'coupling together' of two or more modes of production. It is, I suggest, a marked feature of West African societies, that no clear social formation exists, *or needs to exist* in order to successfully serve the interests of the external estate. (A social formation is, with Amin, defined as 'a *concrete* structure, organised and characterised by a *dominant* mode of production which forms the apex of a complex set of subordinate modes').[7] The external estate can extract sufficient surplus value from peasant producers, wage labourers, etc. not to make essential the total destruction of indigenous modes of production. One may alternatively argue that the external estate is incapable of following any other course. The net result is, however, a kind of equipoise where indigenous modes of production can survive in some areas in a more or less intact form even though the external modes dominate the overall structure. Depending on how a society is seen at a given moment of time, ancillary notions such as a 'decaying mode', a 'mixed mode' or a 'marginal mode' can be employed, all of which conceptions critically affect any discussion of class formation. The proletariat itself becomes a product of the juxtaposition of different modes of production and may represent the advent, though not the total hegemony, of a mode introduced and cemented by the imperial experience.

3. Organisation, Action and Consciousness

By now the reader must wonder whether a kilo of methodology must precede every gram of fact. But I must crave his indulgence a little further before moving on to some illustrative material. For we have to know what historical questions are thought of as significant, particularly by those working in the tradition described as approach (*a*) above. Here I can do no better than cite at some length John Iliffe's introduction to his article on the dockworkers of Dar es Salaam:

> First, the history of a labour movement must be based on a history of work, and the most profound source of change in such a movement is the changing nature of the work in which men are engaged. Second, organisation and group consciousness among workers are created by workers themselves . . . Industrialisation or a colonial economy creates only *workers.* If these workers then come to feel solidarity among themselves, become conscious of forming a group with special common interests, and organise to advance these interests, then the workers are agents in this process creating their own group consciousness and organisation in response to their common status. Further, at all stages in this process

there is an interplay between consciousness and action. Men work together, share common experiences, and realise that they have common interests. By acting together to advance these interests, they learn the need for unity. This growing consciousness enables them to act more effectively, and shared experience of successful action in turn intensifies group consciousness.[8]

Whether or not we are specifically concerned with a labour movement as such or interested more broadly in the growth of a wage labour group, it is clear that we need to devote some attention to a history of work in West Africa. We know something about how labour supplies were procured by the colonial administrators and that this process often took violent forms – *prestation*, forced labour, hut taxes, etc. It is also possible to get some data on comparative wage rates. But little is known about the conditions and hours of work in the Public Works Department or the Railway. How were the workers housed, fed and clothed? What was their normal working life and their life-span? Virtually nothing has been done to establish these basic social facts of existence, to map the landscape of a daily routine, and the life opportunities of a labourer. The data for undertaking such a study are not easily recoverable. West Africa didn't have its Mayhew or Engels (as Victorian England did), but some possibilities nonetheless exist. To take but a small example found in the Nigerian Archives. In 1938 the Commissioner of Labour proposed to establish a small committee 'to keep under continuous review the conditions under which labour is employed in Lagos'. The representative of John Holt and Co. (no less) dutifully reported on a survey he had carried out on four houses. In one, at the rear of a barber's shop there was a building 10 × 20 yd (9 × 18 m) consisting of 13 rooms, each about 12 ft (3·5 m) square. In the house lived 26 adults and 15 children. The men were casual labourers, motor drivers and cycle repairers, each paying 5 shillings per month in rent (this represented about one-quarter of an unskilled wage labourer's pay). In another house, made of bamboo, the rooms were in 'a filthy condition with cooking pots strewn all over'. 'The overcrowding and the condition of the house was appalling.' In spite of these observations, the representative of John Holt asserted that 'the inhabitants appeared happy, healthy and contended [a typist's error no doubt] with their lot'. Though difficult to retrieve from the variety of sporadic archival sources, such information *is* available for the scholar who wishes to recreate the flavour of the common man's lot. It may also be suggested that the very tangible advances made in the techniques of using oral history may also be employed in reconstructing the history of work and daily existence as well revamping old legends and African cosmologies.

While we can derive little comfort from the dearth of studies written about Iliffe's first concern, there has been rather more attention devoted to the early growth of group consciousness and action by the wage labour force. (I impose an arbitrary cut-off date of 1945 as meaning 'early'; thereafter the literature becomes too diverse to allow the simple inferences I draw below.) None, perhaps, of the studies so far undertaken has entirely successfully plotted the interplay of consciousness and action, or devoted much attention to the amplification effect of shared experience and successful action that Iliffe's introduction highlights. Some evincive data may, however, be noted:

(a) Organisation

Organising of the wage and salary earners was both more widespread and took place at an earlier date than has previously been adduced. Hughes and Cohen have shown in their work on Lagos that in addition to the Railway Workers' Union, the Nigerian Union of Teachers and the Civil Service Union, several others, including three railway unions, were organised in the period *before* 1938 when the trade union ordinance was passed giving the legal incentive to organise.[9] In the Gold Coast, a Mechanics Committee petitioned the Governor in 1918, and Railway Associations were formed in Sekondi (1923). Though initially elitist in character, subsequent organisations (particularly the Gold Coast Railways African Workers' Union formed in 1934) embraced all grades of workers. In addition, the ubiquitous I. T. A. Wallace Johnson had dealings with the Gold Coast Motor Car Workers' Union in 1933 and 1934. In Sierra Leone at least six well-established unions (including unions in the War Department and those organising maritime workers and seamen) existed before 1938. In the Gambia, a general workers' union was in existence at an early stage, the Bathurst Trade Union being formed in 1929. The organisation of workers took place at a later date in French West Africa; repressive legal sanctions deterred overt organisation until after the Second World War. After that period, union organisation at the higher levels was distorted by the connection with the metropolitan unions, though Chris Allen has done much to correct the erroneous view that African initiatives and demands were subordinated to the whims of the metropolitan unions.[10]

In noting a few details of early organisation, I have been careful to distinguish economic organisations specifically set up to defend the interests of workers from political bodies like the Nigerian Labour Party (1930) or the West African Youth League (1938)

Table 1.1 Strikes and Labour Unrest in Nigeria: 1897–1939[9]

Strike action		Proletariat	
	Salariat	Skilled	Semi/Unskilled
1. *Public sector*			
Railways	x — — — — x — — — — x		
	x — — — — xx — — — xx		
		x	x
Coal mines			xxxx
Public Works Department		x — — — — x	
			x
Marine Department		x — — — — x	
Printing Department		x	
Government Hospital			x
Government canoemen			x
2. *Private sector*			
Bus drivers		x	
Docks and Marine		x	xx
Produce labourers			x
3. *Labour unrest*			
Civil Service	x		
Police		x	
Railway		x	

Summary: Twenty strikes by employees, 15 in the public sector. One strike involved nearly all wage earners. One strike among salariat only. Four strikes involved skilled workers only, while 4 involved skilled and semi/unskilled labour acting together. Ten strikes involved semi/unskilled labour only. In addition, there were 3 incidents of serious unrest in the public sector, 1 among the salariat and 3 among the skilled workers.

which espoused their cause. If we widen the definition of organisation to include such bodies and include also the development of informal and loosely structured temporary bodies set up, for example, during strikes or in the course of presenting grievances, the extent of organisation becomes much greater. That an organisation is active only sporadically or usually in abeyance does not of course mean that it is ineffective in coping with the demands of a particular situation.

(b)   Action

The extent of at least one form of action, namely strike action, is increasingly becoming available for scrutiny. Detailed studies of at least two major early strikes (those of Lagos in 1897 and the rail strikes in Sierra Leone in 1919) have been published,[11] while an examination of archival material and press accounts turns up example after example of smaller-scale action. Nigeria and the Gold Coast are somewhat easier to document. Hughes and Cohen's data on strike action and labour unrest in Nigeria in the period 1897–1939 are summarised in Table 1.1 (p. 15).

In the Gold Coast, a wide range of industrial disturbances occurred before 1945, a fact which belies the often-repeated claim that it was not before the 1950 positive action campaign that the wage earners were able to assert their group interests. I have compiled on p. 17 a list of strikes and labour unrest in the Gold Coast between 1918–40.

Strike action and major demonstrations of labour unrest represent only the more obvious behavioural manifestations of worker protest. It is much more difficult, and may be impossible, to document the full extent of minor expressions of workers' grievances. This would involve a discussion of short stoppages and walk-outs, petitions, machine-breaking, go-slows, industrial sabotage, accident rates, etc. It is worth noting that whereas in western industrial societies these phenomena have provoked intensive investigation by industrial sociologists interested in the extent of alienation, similar manifestations of dissatisfaction by African workers (where they are noted at all) are simply dismissed as confirming European stereotypes regarding 'lazy' or 'feckless' Africans or discussed in terms of the economists' euphemism of 'low commitment' to the industrial ethic.

Table 1.2 Strikes and Labour Unrest in the Gold Coast: 1918–40[12]

1918	Labour unrest among artisans and engineers at Takoradi.
1918	Strike at Sekondi workshops apparently organised by the Railway Mechanics Committee.
1918/19?	Strike in Public Works Department (Accra).
1918/19?	Strike amongst miners in Kumasi.
1921	'Several hundred workers' in the Railway and Public Works Department went on strike.
1925	Strike at Prestea Mine.
May 1930	Unrest amongst construction workers in Takoradi.
1930	Unrest among lower-paid workers and engine drivers on the railway who agitated for an effective union.
Sept. 1930	Strike at Prestea Mines 'attended by some violence, the mine being picketed and "blacklegs" assaulted and beaten'. The strike was provoked by racialist whites in the management and resulted in the wounding of eight miners.
Nov. 1931	Major strike in Sekondi and Takoradi with all the railway workers (5 000) involved. Sympathy strikes in other industries in Takoradi.
May 1939	A strike for one week organised by the Gold Coast Railway African Workers' Union. The union made representations to the Governor who conceded most of their demands. The management sabotaged the agreement and the strike spread geographically to Kumasi and Tarkwa. During the course of the strike there were several marches, a running battle with the police and a sympathy strike by postal workers.
1939	The Labour Department for that year mentions several strikes other than the one above, including strikes by Shell Petrol workers and employees on a rubber plantation.
1940	Widespread dissatisfaction and numerous incidents which amounted eventually (in the Labour Department's own phrase) to 'a partial general strike'.

(c) *Consciousness*

Were workers conscious of their corporate interests and group identity? To what extent did consciousness pervade all sections of the work force, salariat, skilled and unskilled alike? To what extent were workers able to express a solidarity which differed from or was not dependent on the middle class whose own interests impelled them towards the creation of an anti-colonial front? To answer these questions fully it would be essential to have testimony which stemmed directly from workers or workers' organisations themselves. Few data of this kind exist. A content analysis of workers' petitions, evidence presented by union officials to infrequent commissions of inquiry, one or two rule books and some newspaper reportage is of some use. But we are not in the fortunate position, that, say, E. P. Thompson was in, where there is a wealth of ephemeral literature produced by workers describing the situation they found themselves in. Instead we have for the most part to *infer* consciousness from action. This involves basically an in-depth investigation of the issues that galvanised the workers into self-expression, a full discussion of the course of strike action, an assessment of the extent of participation across all grades of labour, and an analysis of the degree to which middle-class elements represented, 'cooled-out' or permeated worker organisations.

To suggest that we are in a position to undertake such an investigation at this stage would be premature, but, on the limited evidence cited, we can at least advance a number of hypotheses. First, that the work relationship itself is a more important determinant of an African worker's social role than is frequently portrayed. Despite simultaneous attachments to patron-client networks and communal loyalties, the worker was able, at a very early stage of involvement in wage employment, to conceptualise the character of his exploitation, organise to defend his position and strike to advance or protect his interests. Second, that there does seem to be a growth of a reasonably homogeneous corporate identity which approximates a class consciousness. More speculatively one may advance the view that working class consciousness was invaded and colonised by the African bourgeoisie and all but disappeared from sight during the post-1945 nationalist period. This led to the misguided historical assumption that it didn't exist, was of marginal importance or could easily be subordinated to the will of the indigenous ruling groups. Many post-colonial African governments are discovering this error to their cost. Third, that worker organisations, though sporadic, on occasions successfully managed to mobilise a wide range of workers for a limited tactical end. Fourth, that the degree of consciousness amongst the workers was itself not sufficiently intense for the working class to become the 'general representative' of their societies. As Marx wrote in *Zur Kritik der Hegelschen Rechtsphilosophie* of nineteenth-century German classes 'there is lacking the generosity of spirit which identifies itself if only for a moment, with the popular mind, that genius which pushes material force to political power, that revolutionary daring which throws at its adversary the defiant phrase, *I am nothing, and I should be everything.*'

4. Conclusion

This chapter has largely been interpretative rather than substantive but I hope it has laid down the outlines of how a subject of this kind could be tackled. I must, however, press this disclaimer further – even in terms of the interpretative framework I have used. Section 3 of this chapter took as its theoretical point of departure only one of the five possible frameworks outlined in section 2. I do not think theoretical eclecticism is unlimited and in fact consider that, at this stage of our understanding, the analytical structure I have used is likely to yield the most fruitful results. But at the same time there are clear limitations that inhere in this approach. A West African working class was being made at a particular time in a particular place – in the context of the superimposition of an imperialist order which crucially distinguishes the African experience from that of Europe. To explore this macro-situation it is necessary to understand the metropolitan/satellite relationship and the juxtaposition of the imperial and internal modes of production. Further, the incomplete and sporadic character of working-class formation means that the matrices of interpenetration and alliance (in short the dialectic) between the working class and other components of the West African social structure, needs to be marked out. So while little enough has been accomplished, much more remains to be done by the historian who wishes to write another kind of African history.

Notes

A Note on Sources

In addition to the following notes, it might be helpful to interested scholars to note a few sources for the study of labour history. Archival material in the form of government reports, official circulars, etc. are available in the Gambia, Liberia, Sierra Leone, Ghana and Nigeria. I understand (though I have not worked there) that the Dahomey archives also have some relevant material. In addition the Macaulay Papers in Ibadan University Library contain a file on trade-union matters, while the Institute of African Studies at Legon has some items of interest including a memoir by I. T. A. Wallace-Johnson. Chris Allen's article on 'Union-Party Relationships in French West Africa' contains a number of references to obscure or ephemeral items. Ousmane's magnificent fictional re-creation of the Dakar railway strike (1947–48), *God's Bits of Wood*, London, 1970, should also be mentioned if only to identify a book whose lucidity and vividness is unlikely to be attained by mere academics. Departments of Labour were not established until the late 1930s or after the war, so the items sought in archives may be found in such diverse places as company or government department (particularly the Railways') reports, discussions of sanitary inspection, town planning and public works and occasional reports on destitution and pauperage. Newspaper material is particularly rich in Sierra Leone (where I would draw attention to the publication of *The Artisan* and *The Commonwealth* in the 1880s) and in Nigeria. Research in the Public Records Office (UK) can reveal some information on bodies like the League Against Imperialism and the Red International of Labour Unions which maintained some contact with African union-ists. Investigation of the various International Seamen's Unions is also likely to yield some results. Two unpublished theses of particular interest are A. B. Akpan, 'The African Policy of the Liberian Settlers 1841–1932: Study of the Native Policy of a Non-Colonial Power in Africa', Ph.D. thesis, University of Ibadan, 1968, and O. Oyemakinde, 'A History of Indigenous Labour on the Nigerian Railway', Ph.D. thesis, University of Ibadan, 1971. Finally, I would repeat my plea for the application of oral history in this field.

1. A. G. Hopkins, *An Economic History of West Africa*, Longman, London, 1973, pp. 9–11, 293.
2. For some discussion of this, however, see R. Cohen, 'Class in Africa: analytical problems and perspectives' in R. Miliband and J. Saville, eds., *The Socialist Register 1972*, Merlin Press, London, 1972, pp. 231–4.
3. E. P. Thompson, *The Making of the English Working Class*, Penguin, 1968, pp. 9–16.
4. See G. Williams, 'Class, Politics and the State in Nigeria', unpublished paper, Institute of Commonwealth Studies, London, p. 4.
5. S. Ossowski, *Class Structure in the Social Consciousness*, Routledge and Kegan Paul, 1963, p. 38.
6. G. Arrighi and J. S. Saul, *Essays on the Political Economy of Africa*, Monthly Review Press, London and New York, 1973, chs. 2, 3 and 5.
7. S. Amin, 'Underdevelopment and dependence', *Journal of Modern African Studies*, x, 4, 1972, pp. 503–22.
8. J. Iliffe, 'A history of the dockworkers in Dar es Salaam', *Tanzania Notes and Records*, 71, 1970.
9. A. Hughes and R. Cohen, 'Towards the Emergence of a Nigerian Working Class: The Social Identity of the Lagos Labour Force 1897–1939', occasional

paper, Faculty of Commerce and Social Science, University of Birmingham, series D., no. 7, 1971.

10. C. Allen, 'Union party relationships in francophone West Africa: A critique of "téléguidage" interpretations', in R. Sandbrook and R. Cohen, eds., *The Development of an African Working Class: Studies in Class Formation and Action*, Longman, London, 1975.

11. A. G. Hopkins, 'The Lagos strike of 1897: An exploration in Nigerian labour history', *Past and Present*, 35, 1966, pp. 133–55; H. Conway, 'Labour protest activity in Sierra Leone', *Labour History*, 15, 1968, pp. 49–63.

12. The major source for the information given in Table 1.2 is L. A. Lacey's M.A. thesis, 'A History of Railway Unionism in Ghana', Institute of African Studies, University of Ghana. See also S. D'Aguilar Crookshank, *The PWD on the Gold Coast*, Dunstable and Watford, London 1924; *Gold Coast Enquiry ... into the Wounding of Eight Africans at Prestea on 15th September 1930*, Government Printer, Accra 1930; and *Labour Department Annual Reports (1938 onwards)*.

Henry Cooperstock

2 Some Methodological and Substantive Issues in the Study of Social Stratification in Tropical Africa

Studies of social stratification in the industrial societies of the west can hardly be said to have achieved even a modicum of general agreement at the level of interpretation.[1] Even those who follow a common general orientation disagree among themselves, functionalists as well as Marxists and Weberians.[2] While these differences stem partly from the varied purposes of the research-ers as well as from disparate ideological positions,[3] they also result from the fact that the empirical referents themselves cover a great range of times and places and are ever in flux.

As we turn from the older, industrially developed nation-states of the West to the new states of tropical Africa, most of which have been independent for scarcely more than ten years, we encounter an incomparably greater complexity and fluidity in the configurations of stratification systems. The development of new forms of colonialism, the rise of an African political and adminis-trative elite in the place of the colonial regimes, the breakneck pace of diverse and distinctive urbanising processes, the jux-taposition of cash-cropping with traditional forms of subsistence agriculture in the rural areas, the persistence of a dazzling array of colonial patterns of stratification superimposed on precolonial ones, the continuing loyalties of kinship, locality, and ethnic group, and, above all, the interplay among these processes, serve to discourage all but the most reckless from attempting to apply any one paradigm to African stratification systems.

Yet, in the face of this great complexity, what alternative is there to engaging in a certain measure of simplification by select-ing from the myriad of interpenetrating forces several elements which appear to offer some promise of helping one to understand the emerging contours of social stratification in Africa? This chapter proposes to examine some of these elements.

Three caveats are in order, however, before proceeding further. First, because the overriding condition which characterizes patterns of stratification in Africa is great fluidity,[4] the analyst is enjoined to keep on the lookout for transitional phenomena. Among the objects of study in this connection would be the viability of military elites in the structure of state power and the continuing though diminished presence of expatriates in senior civil service positions.

The second reminds us that the shape of stratification systems in sub-Saharan Africa, as elsewhere outside the industrial West, is profoundly influenced by the neo-colonial character of economic development. The subordination of African states to the requirements of the world economy represents the familiar pattern of the 'development of underdevelopment',[5] which results in the distortion of class formation in the peripheral states.

However, while it is true, as Wallerstein has said, that 'the primary contradiction' is 'between the interests organized and located in the core countries and their local allies on the one hand, and the majority of the population on the other',[6] it would be a grave error if the inference were drawn that the developing patterns of stratification in the periphery are nothing more than a mere reflection of that relationship. The formation of classes in the peripheral states and the internal political consequences which ensue, while crucially conditioned by the world economy, are just as decisively fashioned by the pre-existing history and social structure of these societies, and this fact is important in terms of its impact on the political realm and the range of inequality as well as of its independent effects on centre-peripheral relations.

Miliband makes this point in his discussion of the role of the state in the peripheral countries. Noting the need for studies of political power in these societies, he tells us that

> It is clearly not good enough to say that these countries, insofar as they are particularly prey to imperialism, are 'run' from the metropolitan centers. . . . At the very least, matters must be declared to be rather more complex than that . . .[7]

The fact is that the relationship between centre and periphery is not everywhere the same. Tanzania, for example, has renounced the path of capitalist development and attempted to extricate itself from dependence on the industrial West, while Kenya has committed itself to capitalism and has steadfastly maintained its economic ties to the metropole. Differences such as these are to be explained not only by the variations which have occurred in the external relations of these countries, but also by their distinctive internal features, including pre-colonial ones. In terms of the significance of these differences for the development of classes, one would expect the divergent policies of Tanzania and Kenya to have quite different consequences; for instance, the prospects for the growth of a bourgeoisie are clearly not the same in the two countries.

The third caveat requires a more extended discussion. It has to do with Marx's oft-quoted distinction between a class-in-itself and a class-for-itself, the former being merely an aggregate of persons in similar economic circumstances or occupying a common position in relation to productive property, and the latter a class-conscious, cohesive group with its own culture and ideology, organised politically to engage in class conflict.[8] Some have argued that this distinction implies a clear dichotomy: a category of persons in society either is or is not a class on the basis of the criteria set forth by Marx. Sandbrook, for example, has echoed this position:

> Social class shapes the attitudes and actions of its members only to the extent that individuals occupying similar economic roles recognize their common interests vis-à-vis an antagonistic grouping. Without this inter-relation of classes, a class represents nothing more than a category imposed by the observer.[9]

A softer variant of this interpretation is to insist on an unspecified level of class-consciousness. R. H. Jackson, for example, begins a recent article as follows:

> To have sociological meaning social classes must be recognized categories in the social outlook of a society's population. . . . [T]o better understand how collective interests are formed and articulated in a political system and to know which groups benefit and which do not from the exercise of public authority . . . a system of social stratification must be more than a mere ranking of groups according to

some externally-imposed criterion such as, for instance, the possession of wealth.[10]

It should be apparent, however, that social classes never arrive fully formed as historical actors. While we can leave the task of determining what Marx *really* meant to the theologians, the concepts of class-in-itself and class-for-itself, if they are to have any heuristic value, can surely be seen as ideal-typical polar opposites, joined by a continuum along which it is at least theoretically possible to locate a given case. If there is any validity to this view, we are led in any empirical investigation to seek answers to quite specific questions. When large numbers of rural migrants come to Nairobi, we may wish to inquire, among other things, about their residential patterns and hence about their interconnectedness, the ethnic loyalties which circumscribe communications networks, the shared attitudes, the frustrations and resentments, and the modes of presenting and accommodating grievances. In short, we undertake the search for the conditions under which a class-in-itself is transformed over the course of time into a class-for-itself, recognising all the while that in any particular instance this transformation is problematic.

An extreme but arguable form of this proposition is that it is even useful to describe the development of a statistical aggregate, such as the increase in the numbers of persons working for wages in various branches of industry, so long as the matter is not allowed to rest there. Changes of this kind, in so far as they create the necessary preconditions for class formation, provide at least partial clues to this process, though additional data are required and counteracting tendencies must be weighed before it is possible to speak of a class as a political actor. Robin Cohen has put the matter well:

> ... [W]e would make a plea for a minimalist definition of class; one that recognizes the incomplete and embryonic character of class formation and development on the one hand, but that nonetheless attempts to derive a meaningful frame of reference for explaining a class-based action on the other.[11]

With these caveats in mind, the rest of this paper will attempt an exploratory discussion of four categories in the social structure of tropical Africa with a view to confronting, for each of these, some of the methodological and substantive problems involved in studying class formation. My intention here is largely pro-grammatic, with a view to shaping the contours of my own future research and stimulating an exchange of ideas with colleagues who share similar interests. The four categories to be considered are: (*a*) the political-administrative elite; (*b*) the bourgeoisie; (*c*) the petit-bourgeoisie; and (*d*) the proletariat. The peasantry will be touched on only in passing, not because this stratum is not of overwhelming importance – indeed it is – but because limitations of space render it extremely difficult to deal even briefly with the great complexity of the issues involved.[12] It should be abundantly clear, however, that any attempt to delineate an African pro-letariat must come to grips with the various subdivisions of the peasantry.

The Political-Administrative Elite

The political-administrative elite stands at the apex of the social structure, towering over all the rest of society. Even those who deny the applicability of the concept of classes to tropical Africa acknowledge the existence of an elite, though they differ in their specifications as to who is to be included in its boundaries.[13] Chodak and Cohen use such terms as 'political class' and 'ruling elite' in a manner reminiscent of Mosca to suggest that this cate-gory should be limited to those who hold power in the central government, that is, the top government and party leaders, including, in some cases, senior military officers.[14] P. C. Lloyd and R. H. Jackson, on the other hand, cast their nets more widely. Lloyd includes not only politicians, but also higher level employees in the bureaucracies, university graduates, pro-fessionals, and others, closely knit together in informal networks, and Jackson considers civil servants, parastatal officials, pro-fessors, university students, and 'generally all other persons who enjoy public employment involving some exercise of authority, actual or potential' and sharing a Western life style, as belonging to the elite.[15]

As any scheme of classification can only be justified in terms of its theoretical purposes, one way of confronting the problem of whom to include in the elite is to establish the cutting points with reference to the locus of political and economic power. With this in mind, the views expressed by Chodak and by Cohen are helpful in that they limit this stratum to those leaders of party and government who are in control of the state machinery, especially in the one-party states of Africa. Not only do these men exercise control over the principal resources of the nation; they also define the relations of their countries with the world economy and are the principal beneficiaries of the external estate. Furthermore, in their competition for power, they are in a strategic position to mobilise and articulate tribal sentiments and to represent the interests of ethnic constituencies.

Yet another dimension of the power of this group has been described by Sandbrook, who has noted that the pyramid of patron-client networks, so vital to political control in these states and subsuming ethnic loyalties, reaches right to the very top, with the men at the centre in full command of such resources as 'jobs in the public sector, licenses, government contracts, government loans, and development funds'.[16] I shall return to the significance of both ethnicity and of patron-client networks for social stratification later in this chapter.

How are we to understand the position of this elite in the social structure? Certainly it is clear that it is not a ruling class in the Marxist sense in that it does not own the means of production, though it exercises a considerable measure of control over these through such means as I have described above as well as through the parastatal corporations. Even as a political elite, however, it has distinctive features, for there is a significant difference between most African political elites and those of the West. While in Europe wealth and status have usually led to power, in Africa power is often followed by wealth and status.[17] Members of the political-administrative elite are in a position to utilise their offices and their connections with the financial and business community to increase their wealth by such means as the acquisition of land, small industries, and monopolistic control over certain sectors of trade,[18] and in some cases through outright corruption in the awarding of contracts. The power of the elite thereby becomes a source of economic stratification through the *embourgeoisement* of its members.[19]

While the inclusion of individuals below the political elite can only serve to obscure the enormous gap between the power of this group and all others in the society, the role of the bureaucratic elite should also be placed in perspective. Possessing a distinctive subculture and cohesiveness of its own, this group consists of highly educated professionals and specialists in the civil service whose function it is to keep the machinery of government and of parastatal corporations oiled and in working order. Despite their considerable capacity for sabotage, they are nonetheless, as Chodak has observed, 'a stratum of clients who individually depend on patrons in the higher rank'.[20]

A sub-category of the bureaucratic elite that deserves particular attention because of its special connections with the external estate is the group which Cohen has termed the 'intendant class'. It includes the various bureaucrats and supervisory personnel whose purpose it is to operate or facilitate foreign aid and investment programmes, cultural exchanges, training projects, and the like. Cohen sees this group as especially conservative because of its function of serving the interests of the external estate in 'a more rational system of exploitation, namely that of neo-imperialism'.[21]

Thus dividing the political-administrative elite into a political elite at the pinnacle of power and a bureaucratic elite as its subordinate staff serves to sort out some of the component parts of the upper reaches of the social structure in African societies, not only from the observer's point of view but also, presumably, in terms of meaningful distinctions that are made by the actors themselves. Taken together, these two groups constitute a national elite in most of the independent states of Africa and are recognised as such by the members of these societies.

The Bourgeoisie and Petit-Bourgeoisie

As soon as we begin to consider other strata in the population, however, it becomes much more difficult to speak of national classes. In Kenya, for example, there are few signs of the growth of an African haute bourgeoisie. Large businesses in that country are owned mainly by expatriates, and no very large industrial firms are owned by Africans.[22] The significance of this fact may be seen in a few statistics concerning large non-agricultural business establishments in Kenya. In 1971, of a total of 23 437 business establishments, 1 048 (or 4·5 per cent) had 50 or more employees, but of the 323 983 employees in all business firms, 236 175 (or 72·9 per cent) were in these large establishments.[23]

In most other contemporary African countries, the situation is much the same: an African big bourgeoisie in the private sector simply does not exist. Whether such a class will emerge from the petit-bourgeoisie remains an open question. Chodak believes they are becoming more important and that they 'will take over sooner or later when the European and Asian entrepreneurs are gone'.[24] Jackson, on the other hand, raises some very real doubts about the outcome. The Africanisation of international firms, he points out, has generally meant the creation of an African salaried corps 'usually without genuine managerial power within the foreign-controlled enclave'.[25] The alternative pattern of nationalisation or joint ownership of such businesses by African governments has also resulted in the growth of a salaried corps.[26] Whichever policy is followed, the likelihood that a true African haute bourgeoisie will develop is minimised, though we can expect some variability in this respect from country to country. The limited evidence at hand would seem to indicate that Jackson is close to the mark in his assessment of the future of an African bourgeoisie. He says,

> Instead of the emergence of a confident, independent and effective business class in many tropical African countries we appear to be witnessing the development of mercantilist economies in which government, by shoring up questionable African businesses and attempting to do the entrepreneur's job for him, enhances its own power and promotes economic unification under public auspices. The host in this symbiotic relationship – the state and its functionaries – often constitutes the only national business class.[27]

This is not to say that an African business class is entirely absent, but the men in this class operate much smaller firms, each with a few employees. On the basis of indirect evidence, Leys states that in Kenya they consist of traders and transporters, many of whom have taken advantage of the departure of Asians to extend their business interests, and of civil servants, professionals, and politicians who have invested in property. They constitute a petit-bourgeoisie rather than a haute bourgeoisie. The 'really rich probably number no more than one or two thousand'.[28]

In Kenya, in the late 1960s, the government took steps to protect the markets of African traders through various programmes of public assistance, including licensing, exclusive distributorships, and publicly guaranteed commercial credit, but it did so in a manner that could only serve to complement foreign capital rather than replace it with African-owned firms. As Leys points out,

> ... the effect of granting the conditions in which African traders could make profits and begin to accumulate capital was to bind them tightly to the established foreign suppliers and to the state, making them into highly dependent clients, not entrepreneurs. ... In the most successful – that is to say, the most thoroughly protected – cases, they could best be regarded as being an extension of the parastatal system, receiving a commission on turnover instead of a salary, a new and politically powerful element in the petit-bourgeoisie to be provided with a share of the national surplus.[29]

Below these, operating on yet a smaller scale, are those traders who are rooted in purely local markets, a large proportion of whom are also dependent upon farming, augmenting their incomes from their small farms by operating retail shops with the help of family members.[30]

The Proletariat

As we turn to consider the urban proletariat, we find considerable agreement in the interpretations of different observers. Arrighi and Saul divide the wage-workers into two strata, a lower stratum who are only partly proletarianised because they depend for their subsistence on ties to their families on the land, and an upper stratum whose incomes are sufficient to enable them to sever their connections with the peasantry.[31] The lower stratum they consider a part of the peasantry, while the more affluent workers are identified with the elites and sub-elites in the bureaucracies and are looked upon as an aristocracy of labour.[32]

Jackson agrees that most wage earners in urban Africa are tied to their rural base, and, as they can return to this base in difficult times, they are not fully responsive to appeals to class solidarity or class conflict, as were their counterparts during the rise of the European working class.[33] True proletarians, says Jackson, 'are still practically unknown in tropical Africa'.[34] Chodak agrees, observing that the working class is very small in sub-Saharan Africa.[35]

Leys' analysis is rather more complex but still in general agreement. On one important point, however, there is a substantial difference between Leys' interpretation and that of Arrighi and Saul. The latter portrayed an undifferentiated lower stratum working in the towns who were basically tied to the land and therefore to the peasantry. Leys, however, commenting on the results of a study of urban wage-workers in Nairobi, subdivides this group into those who were sufficiently well off to maintain a relationship with their rural home bases, and those who could not. Leys argues that, 'It was the economically weak, who could not afford to maintain an active interaction of visits, gifts, etc., who appeared most urban-based.[36] On the basis of this limited and indirect evidence, Leys states:

> The conclusion which these data suggest is that a true pro-letariat in Kenya could develop from those who work in town but have neither enough land, nor large enough incomes, to maintain close ties with their rural home area.[37]

But Leys qualifies this conclusion. Typically, he points out, the economically depressed urban worker cannot afford to keep his wife and family in town. Though he owns no land, his wife

> will almost always have one or more small plots to cultivate on land belonging to relatives or old family friends. So long as this can continue, the men who are the most natural candidates to constitute a true proletariat are those whose families are of necessity most closely bound to the land.[38]

In view of this state of affairs, Leys submits that, 'It makes as much sense to talk of the peasantization of wage employment as to speak of the proletarianization of the peasantry . . .'[39]

Still, one may hypothesise that it is precisely in such a stratum that feelings of discontent and resentment can be expected to

arise. Tied to the urban centres because they have no land, unable
to bring their wives and families to live with them because they are
too poor, earning wages that are substantially lower than those of
the upper stratum of workers who live in the cities with their
families, these workers would appear to be eminently qualified to
become true proletarians.

The available data direct us to look to certain industries rather
than others for possible evidence of discontent and the growth of
a class-conscious proletariat. If we examine earnings in the formal
sector in Kenya in 1971, we find considerable variation in the
proportions of persons earning low wages by urban standards,
casual employees excluded. The percentages earning less than
200 Kenya shillings per month, and the numbers of persons on
which these percentages are based, are shown in Table 2.1.[40]

Table 2.1

	Per cent	Base N
Mining and quarrying	35·4	1 961
Manufacturing	20·1	83 148
Building and construction	11·8	21 705
Electricity and water	6·7	3 915
Commerce	18·9	42 448
Transport and communications	13·7	41 266
Services	41·9	227 680
ALL INDUSTRIES	30·9	422 123

Furthermore, in mining and quarrying, electricity and water,
services, and in all industries combined, most of those earning
under 200 sh. were in fact earning under 150 sh. per month. We
have of course no warrant for drawing reliable conclusions about
the pervasiveness of feelings of discontent or of the development
of class consciousness from such data alone. To do so, we would
also require information on the role of the trade unions in each of
the industries, variations in opportunities for communication
among workers, the ethnic composition of the work force in
major locations, attitudes expressed and actions taken, and so on,
but, as I have already indicated earlier, the hard data do at least
provide us with some preliminary clues.

Patron-Client Networks

Any model of social stratification in tropical Africa must come to terms with the reality of ethnicity and of patron-client relations. There can be little doubt that the classic Marxist analysis of class structure in the European context is seriously confounded by this reality. Sandbrook and Jackson have both argued that the particularistic loyalties of tribe, clan, and village, and the network of patron-client relations, have significantly attenuated the development of trans-ethnic classes.[41] In the face of the human problems thrown up by urbanisation and development, of jobs, housing, and welfare, the pattern is for the weak to look to the strong for protection and a helping hand, and for the men of power to receive political support in return. Any tendencies for trans-ethnic classes to develop are thereby weakened. Instead of a national peasantry, for example, we find multiple, sub-national peasantries dependent upon patron-client relations to articulate their interests. 'By stressing the practical advantages of personal contacts', says Jackson, 'patron-client politics reduce the chances for collective action whether of a class or a strictly communal nature, for that matter'.[42]

The point is well taken. It serves, quite rightly, to discourage the facile application of Western models of social stratification to tropical Africa. On the other hand, the choice is not between an interpretation of African social structures in class terms and one that stresses ethnic solidarities and patron-client networks, for it is likely that both influences are at work. Stratifying processes may well be in motion alongside the continuing resilience of the particularistic politics of patron-client networks, though the specific mix of the two realities have to be assessed for each country.

There may also be a serious limit to the capacity of patron-client networks to serve their functions. The very legitimacy of these networks depends, after all, on certain reciprocities. Clients will deliver their loyalty only if their patrons can in turn deliver, or are believed to be in a position to deliver in the future, certain desired goods and services. If, however, the patrons fail to reciprocate in this manner, the very basis of these relationships may be threatened, resentments may grow, and new loyalties, including class identities which cut across ethnic solidarities, may develop. The poorer urban worker without land to fall back upon, for example, and secondary school leavers unable to find urban jobs to which they feel their education entitles them, may feel ill-served by the existing arrangements.[43]

The soft spot in the otherwise powerful system of patron-client networks would then be their inability to serve the needs of significant segments of the population. If there are simply not enough jobs for school leavers, if wages are low in particular sectors of the economy, if there is insufficient housing for all in the urban centres, then the needs of clients thus affected will be left unmet. It is in structural situations such as these that we can expect to encounter elements of incipient class formation and a corresponding adaptation of patron-client networks. We shall have to look to the empirical data for signs of such tendencies.

Postscript (26 August 1977)

Since this paper was written, there have been indications in Kenya, to take a specific case, of a possible erosion of trust in traditional patron-client relationships. In March 1975, J. M. Kariuki, a highly popular member of the Kenya legislature and a leading critic of corruption and of the enrichment of the elite, was assassinated. Kariuki had inveighed against the failure to redistribute land equitably and against the amassing of very large tracts of prime farmland by men in positions of power in the government. Students staged demonstrations and workers were prevented from marching in memory of the slain legislator. Two months later, following further student demonstrations, the University of Nairobi was closed indefinitely. In June, a parliamentary investigating committee charged that there had been a cover-up of Kariuki's murder and urged the dismissal of several senior security and police officers who were believed to have been implicated. A government motion to discredit the investigation was defeated, indicating that the government had in fact lost its parliamentary majority, an unprecedented development in this one-party state in which every member of the legislature is required to be a member of the ruling party. Growing disenchantment with President Kenyatta was reported because of the alleged illegal accumulation of great fortunes by members of his family. The correspondent for the *New York Times* wrote in

October 1975 that 'The increasingly politicized and well-informed public is less willing to forgive, and certainly will not ignore, reports of [Kenyatta's] family's doings.'[44] Two legislators critical of the government were placed in detention that October, and another, identified with these two, was detained in May 1977.

These and similar developments, taken by themselves, do not add up to a breakdown of trust in the patron-client network. Much depends on whether the patrons are still able to dispense valued patronage to sufficient numbers of clients so strategically located in the ethnic and class structures of Kenyan society as to offset the disaffection of other aggrieved groups. If, however, the Kenya elite are widely seen as arrogating to themselves the wealth of the land and the fruits of development, then the efficacy of patron-client relationships may be seriously compromised. The extent to which this has occurred will probably be reflected in the struggle which seems likely to occur over the succession to the Presidency.

Notes

This chapter is a revised version of a paper presented at the annual conference of the Canadian Association of African Studies at Dalhousie University, Halifax, Nova Scotia, 27 February–2 March 1974. The research for this paper was supported by a grant from the Canada Council.

1. The best treatment of differences in interpretation of social stratification from the standpoint of the sociology of knowledge is still Stanislaw Ossowski, *Class Structure in the Social Consciousness*, Routledge and Kegan Paul, London, 1963. Interesting attempts to bridge the differences between competing theories of stratification are to be found in Ralf Dahrendorf, *Class and Class Conflict in Industrial Society*, Routledge and Kegan Paul, London, 1959, and Gerhard E. Lenski, *Power and Privilege*, McGraw-Hill, New York, 1966.

2. Robert M. Marsh comments on this point in 'Evolution and revolution: two types of change in China's system of social stratification', in Leonard Plotnicov and Arthur Tuden, eds., *Essays in Comparative Social Stratification*, University of Pittsburgh Press, 1970, p. 149.

3. There is considerable agreement that vertical social stratification is to be distinguished from ranking or differentiation and that the notion of inequality among strata is essential to the definition, but here the consensus ends.

4. Cohen emphasises the fluidity of class relationships in Africa in 'Class in Africa: analytical problems and perspectives', in Ralph Miliband and John Saville, eds., *Socialist Register*, Merlin Press, London, 1972, p. 243.

5. Andre Gunder Frank, *Capitalism and Underdevelopment in Latin America,* Monthly Review Press, New York, 1967, pp. 3–20.

6. Immanuel Wallerstein, 'Class and class-conflict in contemporary Africa', *Canadian Journal of African Studies,* vii, 3, 1973, p. 380.

7. Ralph Miliband in *Monthly Review,* xxvi, 2, June 1974, p. 66.

8. *The Eighteenth Brumaire of Louis Bonaparte,* transl. Daniel De Leon, Charles H. Kerr, Chicago, 1907, p. 71.

9. Richard Sandbrook, 'Patrons, clients, and factions: new dimensions of conflict analysis in Africa', *Canadian Journal of Political Science,* 5, March 1972, p. 107.

10. R. H. Jackson, 'Political stratification in tropical Africa', *Canadian Journal of Political Science,* 5, March 1972, p. 381.

11. Cohen, 'Class in Africa', p. 252.

12. For an insightful discussion of the role of the peasantry in Kenya, see Colin Leys, 'Politics in Kenya: the development of peasant society', *British Journal of Political Science,* I, July 1971.

13. See, for example, P. C. Lloyd, 'Introduction', in P. C. Lloyd, ed., *The New Elites of Tropical Africa,* O.U.P., 1966, pp. 7–10, and Jackson, 'Political stratification in tropical Africa', p. 393.

14. Szymon Chodak, 'Social stratification in sub-Saharan Africa', *Canadian Journal of African Studies,* vii, 3, 1973, p. 411, and Cohen, 'Class in Africa', p. 248.

15. Lloyd, *The New Elites,* pp. 4ff. and 33f., and Jackson, 'Political stratification in tropical Africa', p. 343.

16. Sandbrook, 'Patrons, clients, and factions', *passim.* Quotation on p. 109.

17. Cohen makes this important point in 'Class in Africa', p. 247.

18. Colin Leys, 'The limits of African capitalism: the formation of the mono-polistic petty-bourgeoisie in Kenya', in *Developmental Trends in Kenya,* proceedings of a seminar held at the Centre of African Studies, University of Edinburgh, 28–29 April 1972, pp. 1–24.

19. On this point see Jackson, 'Political stratification in tropical Africa', p. 393, and Cohen, 'Class in Africa', p. 248. There are of course many cases in the West, especially in the United States, even at the very summit, of politicians using their positions to acquire wealth, but this fact does not diminish the difference between Africa and the West in the usual temporal sequence between power and wealth.

20. Chodak, 'Social stratification in sub-Saharan Africa', p. 414.

21. Cohen, 'Class in Africa', p. 249.

22. Leys, 'Politics in Kenya', p. 313.

23. Republic of Kenya, Ministry of Finance and Planning, *Statistical Abstract* 1972, Table 78(a) and (b), pp. 84–9.

24. Chodak, 'Social stratification in sub-Saharan Africa', p. 415.

25. Jackson, 'Political stratification in tropical Africa', p. 389.

26. *Ibid.*

27. *Ibid.,* p. 391. The most complete study thus far of the difficulties faced by African businessmen is that by P. Marris and H. C. A. Somerset, *African*

Businessmen: a study of entrepreneurship and development in Kenya, Routledge and Kegan Paul, 1971.

28. Leys, 'Politics in Kenya', p. 313.
29. Leys, 'The limits of African capitalism', p. 8.
30. Leys, 'Politics in Kenya', p. 312.
31. Giovanni Arrighi and J. S. Saul, 'Nationalism and revolution in sub-Saharan Africa', in Ralph Miliband and John Saville, eds., *Socialist Register*, Merlin Press, 1969, pp. 158f.
32. *Ibid.*, p. 159.
33. Jackson, 'Political stratification in tropical Africa', p. 388.
34. *Ibid.*, p. 387.
35. Chodak, 'Social stratification in sub-Saharan Africa', p. 415.
36. Leys, 'Politics in Kenya', op. cit., p. 315, citing Marc H. Ross, 'Politics and urbanisation: two communities in Nairobi', unpublished Ph.D. dissertation, Northwestern University, 1968, Table 3.1, p. 70.
37. Leys, 'Politics in Kenya', p. 315.
38. *Ibid.*, p. 316.
39. *Ibid.*
40. Republic of Kenya, *Statistical Abstract* 1972, Table 232(d), p. 227.
41. Sandbook, 'Patrons, clients, and factions', and Jackson, 'Political stratification in tropical Africa'.
42. Jackson, 'Political stratification in tropical Africa', p. 392.
43. For an illuminating discussion of this problem see J. E. Anderson, 'The rationality of the school leaver: Africa's teenage problem', in *Developmental Trends in Kenya*, pp. 109–49.
44. *New York Times*, 17 Oct. 1975, 1.

Part 2　Dependent Development

The elusiveness of development and stability in Africa has led to a search for explanations of the perpetuation of underdevelopment and instability. Many of the analyses of Africa's characteristic pathology centre on the concept of 'dependent development'. The three case studies in this Part all focus on the tenuousness and tensions of Africa's independence in an international system typified by stratification and inequality. These cases reflect both the different political economies and histories of the three states examined and the different emphases of the authors. Nevertheless they all point to the need to take into account the impact of external dependence on the rate and direction of social and economic development.

Jørgensen (Ch. 3) presents a major reinterpretation of Uganda's political economy in his study of the evolution of its structural dependence. His analysis of the politics of race, ethnicity and property constitutes the backdrop to the economic and authoritarian rule of President Amin. The incumbent coalition of a Baganda political and administrative elite, a European and Asian commercial elite, and a non-Baganda military elite constrained the 'commanding heights strategy' of Obote's 'move-to-the-left' and prevented it from restructuring Uganda's economy away from external dependence and towards domestic requirements. Obote retreated from any confrontation with these established elites and their external associates; and consequently Uganda's economy served to satisfy foreign demands rather than basic internal needs. General Amin has since overthrown many of the existing relationships of structural dependence which Obote hesitated to challenge, but whether he can effectively restructure the economy of Uganda in the manner needed to achieve genuine economic independence and the satisfaction of basic needs is highly problematic.

Jørgensen writes in the tradition of critical political science; Gregory (Ch. 4) has adopted and modified dependence theory from the perspective of a demographer. He focuses on the impact of migration on a dependent society and suggests that such processes are characteristic of a neocolonial type of 'development'. His analysis of the political economy of migration points to the considerable costs of economic inequalities. He also indicates how the export of primary commodities and the establishment of new industries reinforce rather than reduce dependency. Although the relationships between emigration, underdevelopment and dependency have become more complex over time, Upper Volta reveals continuities based on its dependent status and role in the global economy; it has not yet begun to overcome its location at the periphery of the periphery.

Leys (Ch. 5), like Jørgensen, writes in the tradition of radical political science, especially the critical scholarship of Scandinavian social science. He concentrates on the political economy of Lesotho as a labour reserve; its major function as a dependent economy is to provide migrant workers rather than primary products or markets. Like Jørgensen and Gregory, Leys presents an analytic framework based on a critical reading of the literature on modernisation and development; this leads him to a revisionist history of Lesotho and to a serious evaluation and critique of its 'development' strategy. He rejects the notion of a dual economy but rather prefers to investigate the 'proletarianisation' of labour in Lesotho.

Lesotho has become more and not less, dependent on income from labour migration to South Africa since independence. Leys argues that its characteristic 'non-development' is due to the nature of the class structure and the distribution of political power in Lesotho. The identity and poverty of the Basotho were both shaped by dramatic changes in the geo-politics of Southern Africa in the nineteenth century. Political conflict and repression in Lesotho, according to Leys, is an inevitable result of the impossible position of the present ruling elite. This elite came to power because the 'proletarian' migrant labour force supported it. However, it has become the uncomfortable mediator between demands of the labour force and the mine-owners of South Africa; it is compromised in the widening class conflict of Southern Africa.

These three chapters all reveal the dilemmas posed by dependent development and the insights derived from critical analysis. Dependence clearly conditions the development prospects and internal structures of the three countries examined, although each of them has distinctive historical and sociological features. All three authors focus on small states, but their mode of analysis and cautionary findings are of relevance for most African states. They may be usefully contrasted with the essays contained in Part 3.

Jan Jelmert Jørgensen

3   Structural Dependence and the Move to the Left: The Political Economy of the Obote Regime in Uganda

The purpose of this chapter is, first, to define structural dependence and to describe how the phenomenon of structural dependence manifested itself in Uganda in the 1960s, and, second, to analyse critically the attempts of the Obote regime to transform the inherited structure of economic dependence from the time of formal political independence in October 1962 to the overthrow of the regime by the military in January 1971. It will be argued that the strategy chosen by the Obote regime in pursuing the goal of transforming political independence into economic independence was marred by two faulty assumptions: the one about the class nature of the political and administrative cadres in Uganda; the other about the structure and mechanisms of dependence in Uganda.

The first assumption was that the Uganda Peoples' Congress (UPC) was a party of the masses and that the Africanised administrative bureaucracy could be transformed into an instrument to serve the needs of the people in fighting ignorance, disease and poverty. This assumption neglected the fact that the UPC's own base and that of the administrative cadres lay within the domestic coalition which had supported and benefited from the dependent pattern of development during the colonial occupation.

The second assumption was that the structure of the Ugandan economy could be redirected from a dependent orientation to a more equal interdependent relationship with the capitalist world economy through piecemeal reforms – diversifying sources and types of foreign 'aid', increasing import substitution and expanding state control of the economy. By ignoring the need for an integrated domestic economy with interdependent economic sectors, the Obote regime's piecemeal reforms merely served to perpetuate Uganda's subordinate role in the vertical international division of labour. Building an integrated domestic economy would have required income redistribution and internally-oriented development planning based on domestic human needs. Instead, the Obote regime for the most part continued the colonial pattern of externally-oriented planning based on external demands of the capitalist world system and domestic demands of the urban state salariat.

1. The Structural Dependence of Uganda's Economy

(a) The concept of structrual dependence

The focus of this study is the internal or domestic dynamics of dependence conditioned by the subordinate position of Uganda in relation to the world economy. The world economy is dominated by the capitalist mode of production and is characterised by a vertical international division of labour. Historically this vertical international division of labour emerged as a consequence of the expansion of the European mercantilist-capitalist system from the sixteenth century onward to societies at unequal levels of economic and military strength. The militarily weaker societies of Asia, Latin America and Africa (the 'periphery') became both figuratively and often literally the hewers of wood and drawers of water for the military stronger societies of Europe and later North America and Japan (the 'centre'). Yet the division of the world into centre and periphery[1] was more complex than an external process by which a system of exploitation was forcibly imposed on a passive subjugated colonial people.

As can be seen in the case of Uganda, domestic factors were also important in the process of transforming an *un*developed economy into an *under*developed economy. The structural dependence of Uganda in relation to the world economy was established in the period 1888-1920 as a result of the *interaction* between a *domestic* political coalition and *external* factors.[2] In defining dependence I accept the definition given by dos Santos:

> By dependence we mean a situation in which the economy of certain countries is conditioned by the development and expansion of another economy to which the former is subjected.[3]

In other words, because of the unequal political, military and economic relationships between a dependent economy and the dominant external economy, the structure of the former is shaped as much or more by the requirements of the external economy as by its own domestic needs. Not only is the domestic economy shaped by the interaction with a more powerful external economy, but the domestic political economy is also shaped by this process. Indeed, the economic side of dependence would be impossible to maintain without the existence of what Boden-heimer has termed the 'infrastructure of dependency'[4] or the domestic configuration of strata, institutions and mechanisms which supports and is in turn supported by external factors.

Thus both the economy and the political relationships of an underdeveloped nation are conditioned by the dynamics of interaction with the external economy. This dependence is reflected in the structure of both the economy and the political relationships of the underdeveloped country. The economy consists of the pattern of production and distribution of goods and services; the political economy of the pattern of social and political relations engendered by the economic pattern. However, the relationship between the political economy (the superstructure) and the economy (the mode of production, in the case of Uganda the peripheral-capitalist mode of production) is not deterministic but rather dialectic; each can modify as well as reinforce the other.

(b) The structural dependence of Uganda's economy in the 1960s

Uganda's economy in the 1960s exhibited a variety of structural characteristics which reflected and reinforced Uganda's dependence on the capitalist world system. Six of these structural characteristics are reviewed in this section as being especially noteworthy, though the list is by no means exhaustive.

The first such structural characteristic of dependence was the lack of interdependence between sectors of the domestic economy and the consequent extent to which the external trading sector, rather than indigenous industry, was called upon to transform raw materials into producer goods and consumer goods. Economic growth in Uganda as measured by changes in Gross Domestic Product was more closely linked to the vagaries of weather and external commodity prices than to the level of domestic investment in immediately preceding years.[5] Throughout the 1960s agriculture accounted for 25 per cent of Gross Domestic Product, and the subsistence or non-monetary sector, a further 30 per cent, making a total of 55 per cent.[6] Moreover, the rural sector accounted for over 90 per cent of population and employment. Agricultural exports accounted for 80 per cent of total exports. Mining, manufacturing, construction and electricity combined contributed only 10 per cent to the Gross Domestic Product. Furthermore, aside from preliminary processing of commodity exports (cotton ginning, coffee processing and copper smelting), most manufacturing was of the import-substitution variety which relied heavily on imported raw materials and machinery and thus contributed only marginally to the integration of the domestic economy. Since trade rather than domestic industry transformed raw materials into finished products, employment opportunities which accompany processing remained overseas.

A second, and closely related, characteristic of the Ugandan economy was the commodity composition of trade. Exports consisted of a few agricultural and mineral raw materials, namely coffee, cotton, tea and copper, all subject to frequent erratic price fluctuations in the world market. In 1968 raw materials accounted for 84·4 per cent of Uganda's total exports.[7] Conversely, imports consisted largely of manufactured consumer goods and producer goods required to sustain the extraction of raw materials including agricultural commodities. This pattern of trade had remained virtually unchanged for over fifty years.

Thirdly, Uganda's lack of technological autonomy resulted in the leakage of the benefits of multiplier effects and backward linkages to overseas suppliers of machinery when major investment projects were undertaken.[8] Because of its unintegrated domestic economy and lack of technological autonomy, increased investment in Uganda was more likely to lead to increased employment in the industrialised nations which supplied equipment and know-how than in Uganda.[9]

Fourthly, the structure of Uganda's economy at the time of independence in 1962 was characterised by the paucity of indigenous control of key sectors of the economy. Foreign firms and non-citizens controlled most commercial banks, all insurance companies, import and export houses, construction firms, mining operations, distribution of petroleum, wholsesale trade, the larger retail shops and most industry.[10]

A fifth structural characteristic of dependence was the gross asymmetry in the trading relationship between Uganda and its main trading partner, the United Kingdom. In 1968 Uganda's total trade with the United Kingdom represented 21·9 per cent of Uganda's total trade with all nations combined. By contrast this same volume of trade represented only 0·1 per cent of the United Kingdom's trade with all nations combined. Thus this flow of trade was far more important to Uganda than to the United Kingdom. The ratio of the United Kingdom's total trade with all nations to Uganda's total trade with all nations was of the order of 90 to 1, which gives a rough indication of the relative trading strength of the two nations in the world market.[11]

Finally, contrary to all the discussion of Uganda's need for foreign capital, data from the Bank of Uganda for the period 1966-70 show that the sum total of factor income (interest, dividends, royalties and profits) and private capital flow (long term and short term) was negative in all of these years, averaging an annual net *outflow* of U.Sh. 160 million, or more than the average annual *inflow* of foreign 'aid' which was U.Sh. 118 million per year in the course of the same period, most of it in the form of low-interest long-term loans which eventually had to be repaid.[12] At no point in the five-year period did the net foreign investment (new investment minus disinvestment) offset the outflow of factor income due to previous foreign investment. All in all, Uganda was a net exporter of capital during the period 1966-70.[13] The problem in a structurally dependent economy is generally not one of a *shortage* of capital, as is commonly supposed, but a lack of *indigenous control* of the accumulation and allocation of surplus value.[14]

2. Structural Dependence and the Economic Policy of the Obote Regime

Whereas the overall economic goal of the Obote regime – transforming political independence into economic independence, as espoused by Kakonge at the 1962 UPC delegates' conference[15] – was basically sound, execution of strategy to reach that goal revealed two faulty assumptions: the one about the class nature of the political and administrative cadres in Uganda; the other about the structure and mechanisms of dependence in Uganda. I do not wish to argue that the transformation of the Ugandan economy from its external orientation to self-reliance would be easy or accomplished in a short span of time. The range of choices available to the Obote regime was limited by the structure of the economy and by the political and social base of the regime consisting of the UPC and the state salariat. Both the economy and the political and social base of the regime were conditioned by the interaction of domestic and external factors during the period of British colonial rule. While history does not determine the future, it does determine the present, or starting point, and thereby limits the range of possibilities for the future by closing off certain options.

As a result of the incorporation of the Ugandan economy into the capitalist world market at the turn of the century, the option facing the Obote regime was not a *tabula rasa* choice between absolute economic dependence and absolute economic independence *vis-à-vis* the international economic system; nor was there a *tabula rasa* choice between capitalism and socialism. Instead, there was a choice between *continuing* to support the 'inherited' structure of dependence and *beginning* to build an integrated economy thereby creating the possibility for building socialism.[16]

(a) The social and political base of the Obote regime

The social and political base of the Obote regime was itself conditioned by the structural dependence of Uganda. The regime consisted of the ruling political party, the UPC, and its allies plus the Africanised civil service (the state salariat). The alliance of the UPC with other elements in the infrastructure of dependence shifted over the course of the 1960s from an initial alliance in 1962-64 with the Buganda Kingdom salariat and Baganda capitalist farmers embodied in the Kabaka Yekka political party and its patron, Kabaka Edward Mutessa II, to an unstable grand alliance of political notables in 1964-66 which emasculated opposition parties in the National Assembly as their leaders crossed to join the UPC, and finally to an alliance with the Army in the period 1966-71, which ended when the Army found the UPC to be both stingy and expendable.

Although the origins of Obote's political party, the UPC, can be traced back to the first economic protest movement of the 1920s,[17] it never had the populist backing of the largely Baganda capitalist farmers who had been a key element in the Bataka Association of the 1920s, the 1946-48 Uganda African Farmers Union, the Bataka Party (1945-48), the 1959 Uganda National Movement, and the Kabaka Yekka (KY) Party (1961-67). In terms of its own base the UPC owed more to the urban trade-union movement, the anti-Buganda sentiments of northern Uganda, the modern educated Baganda professionals represented by those sections of the United National Party which joined the UPC after 1961, and teachers and civil servants whose orientation was more urban than rural. The UPC, despite failing to obtain Baganda farmer support, was able to strike an alliance with the populist Kabaka Yekka party in the period 1962-64 on the basis of promises to respect the autonomy of the traditional Buganda hierarchy and, indeed, to elevate the Kabaka to the position of President of all Uganda. The UPC-KY alliance ensured victory over the Democratic Party led by Benedicto Kiwanuka in the 1962 elections and ensured that A. Milton Obote became the Prime Minister of Uganda at Independence.

Even in northern Uganda, such as in Obote's home constituency in Lango, the UPC was not particularly egalitarian or peasant-based. Although more non-Westernised in language, symbols and values than the administrative cadres in Lango who represented the state apparatus, the Lango local political elite in the UPC tended to be the 'big men' – traditional political leaders, businessmen and professionals. They were not 'common men', though through 'hospitality and generosity' (*noblesse oblige*) they formed a patron–client link between the common man in the countryside and the party headquarters in Kampala.[18]

The UPC members of Parliament elected in 1962 differed only marginally from Kabaka Yekka members and Democratic Party members in terms of their occupational backgrounds.[19] Among its elected M.P.s, the UPC could count a larger proportion who had been involved in trade unions or growers' cooperatives and a slightly larger proportion who had been employed as salesmen or clerks. The Democratic Party's elected members had a somewhat larger proportion who listed teaching as a former occupation than did the other two parties. The Kabaka Yekka M.P.s could count a larger proportion of professionals amongst themselves – law, medicine, journalism and accountancy – than the other two parties. Yet there were also striking similarities: in all three parties a large proportion of M.P.s were former teachers or members of the civil service.

The fact that the UPC had more in common with the urban administrative cadres, which now was no longer exclusively Baganda, than with the rural peasant growers was reflected in the economic policies of the Obote regime to the extent that in real terms national income was redistributed from peasant growers in the rural areas to the administrative cadres and 'labour aristo-cracy' in the urban centres. The UPC became increasingly a party of urban interests serving the bureaucratic cadres, the educated middle class and unionised skilled labour, to the neglect of growers in rural areas and unskilled labour.

On the other hand, the leadership of the UPC demonstrated a shrewd understanding of the ethnic aspects of the matrix of political and economic interests inherited from the British colonial era, particularly the nature of such alliances as that between the British and Baganda, and between the British and the non-African commercial strata. Over the period 1962–70, the Obote regime attacked these coalitions with vigorous rhetoric and piecemeal reforms, which obscured the fact that its own base lay within the relatively privileged urbanised educated strata which had benefited from Uganda's pattern of dependent development. Failing to expand its base to rural areas and unwilling or unable to attack the privileges of its urban base, the UPC gradually fell back on the empty rhetoric of the mass party backed by the reality of support from the Army, the Special Forces and the General Service Unit.

The Africanised salariat of the post-colonial state not only had its own class and organisational interests to protect but also sought to emulate the living standards and goals of the departing Euro-pean administrative cadres.[20] The standard operating procedures of the bureaucratic apparatus embodied the caution and conser-vatism of the colonial era appropriate for the maintenance of a dependent colonial economy, but markedly unsuited for dramatic transformation of the structure of the Ugandan economy towards meeting domestic human needs.

Transition from colonial rule to formal political independence required the Ugandanisation of the state salariat to 'consolidate Uganda's independence'[21] or, more accurately, to legitimise neo-colonialism. Yet Ugandanisation posed a dilemma both in terms of income distribution and in terms of educational curriculum. Paying newly promoted Africans anything less than the salaries of departing Europeans would have smacked of racial discrimination.[22] On the other hand, paying the European wage would establish an enormous wage differential between Africans in the higher levels of the public service and ordinary African workers and peasants. Faced with this dilemma, both the British colonial regime and the Obote regime opted for the latter alternative of 'equal pay for equal work', which in effect only removed the racial basis of inequality between the salariat and the producing strata.

Thus in the 1960s higher civil servants received annual incomes of U.Sh. 36 000 or more, *plus* free or subsidised housing, *plus* use of a government car or a subsidised car loan.[23] By comparison, in the same period the minimum wage of unskilled workers was only U.Sh. 1 800 per annum. Over one-half of the employed labour force earned no more than this minimum wage.[24] In rural areas where 95 per cent of the population lived, 93 per cent of graduated taxpayers reported annual incomes in 1969 of less than or equal to U.Sh. 2 000.[25] Surveys have shown that even in the relatively prosperous coffee areas of the Buganda region, most rural family-units in 1962–63 earned an average of U.Sh. 1 730 per year including the value of subsistence product.[26] Therefore, even excluding the value of fringe benefits, higher civil servants earned salaries twenty times the wages or income of the majority of peasants and workers in Uganda.[27]

Focusing on a slightly lower salary scale of U.Sh. 12 000 per annum or almost seven times what most peasants and workers earned, one finds the following changes in the period 1964–69. This echelon, comprising 3·9 per cent (607) of the administrative branch of the state sector in 1964, earned a total salary equal to 11·6 per cent of total wages paid to all males in the administrative branch of the state sector. By 1969, 9·6 per cent (1 716) of the administrative branch of the state sector earned at least U.Sh.

12 000 per annum, their total salary equalling 26·0 per cent of total wages paid to all males employed in the administrative branch. Thus the size of this privileged group almost tripled in absolute terms, more than doubled in relative terms, and almost tripled its share of total wages and salaries within the administrative branch.[28] The higher echelons of the state salariat fared very well under the Obote regime.

Turning to the educational aspects of Ugandanisation of the salariat, one finds that rapid expansion of the educational system to meet the administrative manpower requirements of Ugandanisation took priority over changing the curriculum of the educational system to meet the changing needs of politically independent Uganda. The number of senior secondary schools admitting Africans was increased from nineteen schools serving 3 153 students in 1958 to seventy-two schools serving 35 924 students in 1969.[29] But this revolutionary expansion was not matched by revolutionary changes in curriculum, which remained basically British-colonial in its orientation, designed to produce capable administrative cadres who scorned both manual labour and entrepreneurial activity and who lacked technical and engineering skills.

As Obote himself admitted in 1969:

we have not moved very far from the results of the educational investments which the British wanted to get when they introduced formal education in Uganda.[30]

In the same speech Obote argued that the other alternative, that of delaying Ugandanisation of the salariat until the educational system could be made more responsive to Uganda's needs, would have been even more unacceptable since Uganda could not afford to entrust the implementation of new policies to a civil service composed largely of expatriates. Yet the results achieved by the Africanised salariat in implementing Obote's policies were always contingent on the African salariat protecting its prerogatives. The serious effects of rapid expansion of education for the sake of Ugandanisation without regard for curriculum content were perceptively predicted by Ehrlich in 1963:

In the narrow sense, therefore, education in Uganda has become a machine for the production of a class of white-collar workers, and a highly rewarded elite of professional workers who will rule the masses of the peasants who produce the cash crops which remain the basis of the economy. Paternalism remains, but the paternalists are being Africanized.[31]

When the Obote regime did finally attempt to reduce the prerogatives and privileges of the salariat in 1969–70, the salariat viewed the moves not only as a threat to their class interests but as a threat to their inherited standards of maintaining equality with the departing Europeans.[32]

Thus the assumption that the UPC was a party of the masses and that the Africanised salariat could be transformed into an instrument to serve the needs of the people was a faulty assumption. The base of the UPC and that of the administrative cadres lay within the domestic coalition which had supported and benefited from the dependent pattern of development in the colonial period. When any conflict of interest arose in terms of what action to take, both the UPC and the salariat would be more responsive to their own largely urban-class interests than to the long neglected interests of the peasant growers and migrant labourers in rural areas and of unskilled workers in urban areas.[33]

(b) The 'commanding heights' strategy of the Obote regime

The Obote regime sought to direct the control of the modern economic sector through a 'commanding heights' strategy which involved increasing state control of key firms and key institutions such as major industries, financial intermediaries and marketing structures. Consolidating Uganda's independence required Ugandanisation of the civil service. Winning economic independence and building socialism required increasing state control of the economy. However, while increasing state control of the economy and other Fabian socialist reforms might contribute to building socialism in a nation with an integrated economy such as Great Britain, the same strategy would be insufficient in a dependent economy which was not integrated at the domestic level. The failure to recognise the need for an integrated economy with interdependent economic sectors responsive to domestic needs constituted the second faulty assumption underlying the economic policy of the Obote regime.

In other words, Obote tried to control the commanding heights of an unintegrated economy which was structurally dependent on the international economic system for the transformation of its raw materials into producers' goods and consumer goods. In and of itself state control of the economy could not transform the structure from a dependent to a more independent and self-reliant orientation. Control of the commanding heights of a dependent economy would not in itself further the cause of economic independence. At best it could be a first step or means of building economic independence and socialism; at worst it could be a cosmetic 'changing of the guard' leading to state-controlled neo-colonialism – the Africanisation of dependence.

How could state control of the commanding heights of the Ugandan economy have been used as a means to building economic independence and socialism? First of all, lack of effective demand is one of the barriers to industrialisation in Uganda. The base of effective demand could be broadened by a policy of income-redistribution which would increase the purchasing power of people in lower income levels, people in rural areas. The consumption pattern of low income persons is more compatible with goods that can be produced locally from local raw materials than is the import-intensive and technologic-ally-intensive consumption pattern of high income groups in the cities who demand a life-style equivalent to the middle class in industrialised nations. Production would thereby become more responsive to domestic needs than to externally stimulated wants of urban elites. Secondly, as an interim measure attempts could be made to increase the degree of raw material processing per-formed in Uganda. To some extent this was carried out, although tremendous tariff and market access barriers exist to any under-developed nation's attempts at increasing the degree of pro-cessing done within its own borders unless this processing is controlled by multinational corporations.[34] Thirdly, again as an interim measure and one full of pitfalls, some industries could be established on the basis of import-substitution. However, once again these industries all too often tend to be controlled, directly or via management contracts, by multinational corporations who use imported rather than local raw materials. Moreover, one may question the wisdom of engaging, in import substitution before attacking the problem of income redistribution and the related problem of the urban elite's imported pattern of consumption. Import-substitution as a strategy for industrialisation relies on foreign trade and existing luxury patterns of consumption rather than rational planning based on low-income needs to identify viable domestic industrial projects.[35] Fourthly, the Uganda government should have undertaken an input–output analysis of the economy, regardless of the fact that everyone 'knows' that such an analysis would reveal the lack of domestic inter-industry linkages.[36] Such an analysis would point out areas in which new industries could be established to increase domestic links, increase the use of local raw materials and increase the utilisation of by-products from existing industries.

Development of a more integrated domestic economy would have to be linked with expansion of the regime's base to rural areas to make politically feasible such radical measures as income redistribution and restructuring of consumption patterns to fit local needs of the majority of citizens and local resources rather than import-intensive consumption patterns of an urban elite. Restructuring the domestic economy would require restructuring the political economy.

In contrast to such a strategy of domestically oriented development planning the Obote regime continued for the most part the colonial pattern of externally oriented development planning. In spite of lip service to the importance of domestic savings, domestic investment and domestic effort, the general orientation and expectation was that Uganda's economic salvation would come from abroad in the form of increased demand or increased prices for export commodities, in the form of foreign aid (preferably aid without 'strings')[37] and in the form of massive private foreign investment. Development plans were drawn up as much for the purpose of attracting foreign aid and foreign investment as for the purpose of outlining domestic goals and priorities.[38]

At another level criticism has been directed at the tactics used by the Obote regime in pursuing its 'commanding heights' strategy, notably the nationalisation policy popularly known as the Nakivubo pronouncement of 1970. Critical articles, such as that by Gershenberg,[39] have argued that the nationalisation policy of the Obote regime was haphazard and ill-conceived – haphazard in that the eighty or so firms originally scheduled to be nationalised were not always the largest firms in an industry nor even the most solvent firms, and ill-conceived in the sense that management rights continued to be vested in the former owners through management contracts.

As has already been argued, the major defect of the 'commanding heights' strategy of the Obote regime was that it failed to consider the wider context of the dependent structure of the Ugandan economy. Therefore, control of the commanding heights or key industries, financial intermediaries and marketing structures of the dependent economy would not in itself further the cause of economic independence.

Subject to this important *caveat* and recognising that the Nakivubo list of firms to be partially nationalised did contain some errors and omissions, the list was nevertheless consistent with a 'commanding heights' strategy.

If a regime is faced with limited political resources in the form of popular support and technical expertise, then it makes sense to deploy those resources in a way which will maximise their effect. In such a case it would be important to seek control of the most important, the most dynamic, and the most modern firms in the economy. It would also be wise to employ the tactic of *leverage* by for example controlling 60 per cent of x plus y firms rather than 100 per cent of merely x firms. Once controlling interest was in state hands, the regime could in future enlarge its share ownership without necessarily resorting to new decrees and encountering fresh opposition. Given the inherited shortage of managers and technicians, a case could even be made for *temporarily* allowing the partially nationalised firms to continue under the old managers through management contracts until such time as sufficient numbers of local citizens became available to replace them.

What constitutes the commanding heights of an economy is determined by the structure of that economy. To a large extent the commanding heights of most structurally dependent economies are controlled by foreigners and their domestic allies. Multinational corporations follow their own 'commanding heights' strategy. As one international banker aptly summarised it:

We like to look at the flow of funds in a particular country and economy, and then try to figure out how do we get in between those flow [sic] of funds to capture them for the benefit of our clients all over the world.[40]

'Our clients' refers of course to the multinational corporation clients of the multinational banks rather than to ordinary citizens in a particular country whose primary function is to serve as a source of deposits for lending to multinational firms.[41]

In Uganda in 1963 foreigners and non-citizen Asians controlled commercial banks, insurance companies, import and export houses, construction, mining, wholesale trade, importation and distribution of petroleum, major retail shops and much of industry. For their part Ugandan citizens at least nominally controlled the following: the state, including both political and administrative structures; agricultural production, with the exception of sugar and some tea and coffee estates; most small retail shops and most small-scale transport firms. The state in turn controlled coffee and cotton marketing, the production and distribution of electricity, as well as a major industrial and plantation holding group, the Uganda Development Corporation (UDC).

Throughout the 1960s the parastatal sector was expanded by the Obote regime.[42] It is necessary to note that the partial nationalisation policy announced by Obote in 1970 did not constitute much of a sharp break with past policy but rather a new stage in implementation of a long-established policy of expanding state control of the economy and Ugandan control of the state salariat. Moreover, it is also important when discussing continuity to note that many of the parastatal corporations – the Uganda Development Corporation, the Uganda Electricity Board, the Lint Marketing Board, the Coffee Marketing Board, and the East African Community parastatal corporations – had been established under colonial rule to serve British imperial interests.

The 1970 partial nationalisation sought to place majority control of the following sectors into the hands of the state: all commercial banking, all petroleum distribution, the import-export trade, and much manufacturing and bus transport. Most controversy has centered around the choice of manufacturing firms to be partially nationalised. Was the list really haphazard, a product of more or less random choice? Or is it possible to detect a strategy in the choice of manufacturing firms to be partially nationalised?

This chapter argues that there was a clear pattern of partial nationalisation of the larger firms in the more important manufacturing groups in terms of contribution to Gross Domestic Product; in short, the list was consistent with a 'commanding heights' strategy for Uganda.

The focus will be on the nine sub-sectors of manufacturing which together accounted for 82 per cent of manufacturing value added in Uganda in 1967.[43] These nine sub-sectors were the following: sugar refining and tobacco manufacture; brewing and distilling; textiles and rope; sawmills and woodmills; pulp, paper and printing; refining animal and vegetable fats and oils; cement and similar products; iron and steel, basic industry; and transport repair and cycle parts. The total value added of these nine sub-sectors was U.Sh. 251 777 000, or 82 per cent of total value added in manufacturing.[44]

Although data were not available for calculating the distribution of value added by size of firm, it was possible to compute distribution of gross output by size of firm. Firms with 100 or more employees accounted for only 11·5 per cent of all manufacturing firms, yet accounted for 64·3 per cent of total gross output in manufacturing.[45] Because of economies of scale, the distribution of value added would presumably be skewed even more dramatically in the direction of large firms. Furthermore, my argument assumes that what is true for the manufacturing sector as a whole is also more or less valid for the nine sub-sectors listed in the previous paragraph.[46]

Within the nine sub-sectors which accounted for four-fifths of total value added in manufacturing there were a total of 38 firms employing 100 or more persons. Had the Nakivubo pronouncement been fully implemented,[47] the Ugandan government, public bodies and parastatal bodies would have had majority control or full control of thirty of these large firms.[48] Thus through control of the majority of the largest firms in the most important sectors of manufacturing, the Obote regime would have had sufficient leverage to control the commanding heights of manufacturing in Uganda. Therefore, the nationalisation policy of the Obote regime was not as haphazard as it might have seemed at first sight and was indeed consistent with a 'commanding heights' strategy of increasing state control of key sectors of the economy.

(c) Income distribution and the urban elite

Mazrui has argued that 'the gap between the elite and masses in East Africa is much narrower than it is in developed countries'.[49] Whatever may be the validity of this assertion in terms of cultural gaps, in terms of social origins, in terms of the alleged levelling effects of extended families, and so forth, the fact remains that in terms of income not only was there an enormous gap between the urban elite and the rural masses in Uganda, but that this gap actually widened during the Obote regime. As pointed out in the discussion of the social and political base of the Obote regime, the UPC had more in common with the administrative salariat, the urban professionals and unionised skilled labour than with the rural peasant growers. The party's urban bias was reflected in the economic policy of the Obote regime to the extent that national income in relative terms was re-distributed further from rural areas to urban centres, from peasant growers to the salariat, the professionals and the 'labour aristocracy'. However, in no sense did the 'labour aristocracy' consist of the entire working class.[50] The majority of workers continued to earn subsistence wages which did not keep pace with the rise in prices, wages which were roughly equivalent to the total cash and subsistence income of the majority of rural peasant families.

Except where otherwise noted, comparisons in this section are based on the three-year average 1960–62, which includes the date of Independence and the start of the Obote regime, and the three-year average 1967–69.[51] Computing peasants' share in the national income of Uganda poses some problems. The only precise figures are those compiled by the marketing boards on payments to growers for coffee and cotton. In the period 1960–62 these averaged U.Sh. 441·2 million; in the period of 1967–69 they averaged U.Sh. 554·7 million. In addition estimates of subsistence product are available. The estimated annual average subsistence product for 1960–62 was U.Sh. 1 345 million; and for 1967–69, U.Sh. 2 086 million. There remains the problem of estimating other cash income from such activities as petty trading and cultivation of food crops such as plantain (matoke), groundnuts, sim-sim for sale to urban areas, and minor cash crops such as tea and tobacco. I arbitrarily assumed that cash income from other sources did not exceed cash income from coffee and cotton.[52] On the basis of this assumption total peasants' income, including subsistence product averaged U.Sh. 2 227·4 million in the 1960–62 period and U.Sh. 3 195·4 million in the 1967–69 period.[53] As a share of total national disposable income, the peasant growers' share declined from 50·2 per cent of the total in 1960–62 to 43·6 per cent in 1967–69. In terms of African rural income per capita, the absolute increase from U.Sh. 305 per capita per annum in 1960–62 to U.Sh. 355 in 1967–69 represented an average annual increase of 2·3 per cent which lagged behind the annual inflation rate of 4 per cent. On the basis of these calculations and assumptions it would appear that rural incomes declined in real terms under the Obote regime.

Computing wage labour's total share in the national income of Uganda is a fairly simple task, if one ignores the exclusion of domestic servants and most migrant agricultural labourers from official statistics. The average total wage bill was U.Sh. 334·5 million in 1960–62 and U.Sh. 783·3 million in 1967–69. As a share of total national disposable income, this represented an increase from 7·5 to 10·7 per cent of annual national disposable income. The average annual wage per employee increased from U.Sh. 1 505 in 1960–62 to U.Sh. 2 978 in 1967–69, an average annual increase of 10·1 per cent, or well ahead of the annual inflation rate in that relatively stable period. However, this increase was not evenly distributed among employees. In both periods three-fifths of all employees earned the bare minimum wage which ranged from U.Sh. 720 to U.Sh. 1 200 in non-urban areas to U.Sh. 1 800 per annum in urban areas.

The true labour aristocracy consisted of those earning at least U.Sh. 6 000 per annum or U.Sh. 500 or more per month, or over three times the minimum wage. The size of this labour aristocracy increased from approximately 8 000 (or 4 per cent) of the reported labour force in 1964 to approximately 23 600 (or 9 per cent) in 1969, despite increasing unemployment. Total employment in Uganda failed to increase as fast as the rate of increase in population. Nonetheless, the size of the labour aristocracy tripled in this period. Moreover, the average earnings of this labour aristocracy increased at a rate faster than the rate of increase in total national income. Thus the relatively rich became richer while others lagged behind.

This analysis excludes self-employed professionals, non-salaried owners of firms, and directors of firms, many of whom presumably fared much better than the labour aristocracy.

By allowing the redistribution of income from the rural areas to the national bourgeoisie in urban centres, the UPC protected and enriched its political base.

(d) Obote's economic policy and the contradiction between Buganda and Uganda

As a result of their alliance with the British colonial state, the Baganda political-administrative cadres were among the first Africans to enjoy such fruits of colonialism as education and admission to the civil service. Although restricted from entering large-scale commerce, the Baganda were able to parley the benefits of the *mailo* land system of 1900 and the major land reforms of 1927–28 into entry to the professions, medicine, law, teaching, transport, petty trade, education for children, and large-scale farming using migrant labour. The traditional Baganda political elite represented by the Kabaka, the royal family of Buganda, and appointed chiefs, the modern educated Baganda professionals, and the Baganda capitalist farmers owed their relatively privileged position among Africans in Uganda to the colonial alliance between the Baganda and the British. While they resented the racial restrictions of the colonial period, at heart many Baganda were Anglophiles who viewed Independence with mixed emotions. On the one hand, they could no longer count on British support to remain first among equals in their relations with other Ugandans. On the other hand, the coming of Independence gave the opportunity of ensuring that Ugandan-isation of the salariat would be largely a process of replacing the British by Baganda, who were better qualified than other Africans in education and administrative experience. But more importantly, Independence presented the opportunity of using state power to remove the barriers which continued to favour the European and Indian commercial strata and prevented the emergence of a strong Baganda commercial class during the colonial era. Baganda commercial power could in turn be used to strengthen further the political power of the Bagandan bour-geoisie *vis-à-vis* other Ugandans.

In the section on the political base of the UPC it was noted that one major strand differentiating the UPC from its predecessor, the Uganda National Congress, was the absence of large-scale Baganda farmer support and the presence in the UPC of anti-Buganda elements from northern Uganda who resented the sub-imperialism of the Baganda in the colonial period. The Obote regime recognised that an economic policy which merely sought to shift economic control from foreigners to Ugandan citizens could be expected to operate in favour of creating a powerful Baganda bourgeoisie, since the Baganda, as a result of the pre-existing structure, possessed a head start in terms of skills, experience and resources. Therefore, a policy which sought to redress the ethnic imbalance of the political economy of the colonial period would also have to check the further commercial (and political) expansion of the Baganda bourgeoisie.

One way to check Baganda commercial expansion would be to have the state rather than individuals control the commanding heights of the economy. However, the contradiction implicit in this tactic was that while non-Baganda had a preponderant influence within the UPC, Baganda professionals were in a better position to fill the administrative positions in a state-controlled economy. There was, in other words, a danger that even a 'commanding heights' strategy would aggrandise the power of the Baganda.

As Kasfir has observed, this potential problem of ethnic rivalry within the higher civil service was defused by the very pace of Ugandanisation. Although the number of Baganda in the higher civil service increased from 23 in December 1961 to 105 in March 1967, in relative terms their share of Africanised posts decreased from 46·9 per cent to 35·6 per cent.[54] This share was still twice as large as Baganda share in the African population, yet the trend indicated that the Obote regime was succeeding in making the salariat more representative, regionally and ethnically.

While the 'commanding heights' strategy of the Obote regime was a subtle means of checking, at least temporarily, the Bagandanisation of the commercial strata, the Obote Revolution of 1966 attacked directly the institutional basis of Baganda supremacy embodied in the federalism of the 1962 Constitution. The political implications of the events of 1966 have been discussed elsewhere by others.[55] In this section it is only necessary to relate the Obote

Revolution to the economic policy of the Obote regime within the framework of Uganda's structural dependence. On the one hand, there is no doubt that the events of 1966 imposed a great cost on the Obote regime in terms of loss of legitimacy among many Baganda, in terms of sheer financial cost, in terms of delay of implementation of economic reforms, and last but not least in terms of having to base political survival of the regime on the open use of the Army, the military arm of the salariat. On the other hand, it is also apparent that Obote viewed the constitutional prerogatives of the Baganda aristocracy as the 'immediate enemy' in the struggle to consolidate Uganda's independence, build economic independence, and reduce ethnic and regional disparities. Thus the Common Man's Charter of 1969 was as much an attempt to cast the events of 1966 within the coherent framework of a Move to the Left strategy which required the political elimination of 'feudal' elements which had been 'bought to serve the interests of foreigners',[56] as an attempt to outline future economic policy.

Rather than viewing 'the Buganda question' as a problem which overshadows other contradictions in Uganda such as class and economic structure, one can view the problem of the contradiction between Buganda and the rest of Uganda, including the events of 1966, as part of the problem of dismantling the inherited infrastructure of dependence which had supported and benefited from the dependent development of Uganda's economy. To this extent Obote's revolution of 1966 was strategically correct. However, at the same time the Obote regime chose to ignore the fact that the largely urban middle-class base of the UPC also lay within the inherited infrastructure of dependence. Moreover, the tactics chosen to liquidate the Baganda political hierarchy and to block Baganda takeover of the state and economy earned Obote the emnity of not only the traditional Baganda aristocracy and urban middle class, but also of the capitalist farmers of rural Buganda who correctly perceived that the end of Buganda autonomy would eventually also require the state's abolition of the economic basis of Buganda supremacy – the *mailo-kibanja* land tenure system.[57] Lack of mass support in rural areas for the Obote regime, combined with the decision to subject Buganda to virtually indefinite military occupation under a 'state of emergency', placed the survival of the Obote regime increasingly in the hands of the third element of the collaborative coalition of colonial occupation, the military, headed by Major-General Idi Amin.

(e) Summary

Both the economy and political economy of Uganda were transformed in the period 1888–1920 into a dependent relationship within the international capitalist system. This transformation could not have succeeded and could not have been sustained without the collaboration of domestic elements within Uganda. The main structural feature of Uganda's dependent economy was the lack of an integrated domestic economy with inter-industry linkages responsive to local needs. The growth and development of the Ugandan economy were conditioned by the demands of the external world market. Furthermore, Uganda had to rely on foreign trade rather than local industry for the transformation of local raw materials into manufactured producers' goods and consumer goods.

The Obote regime sought to transform political independence into economic independence through a 'commanding heights' strategy of increasing state control of key sectors of the economy and through a policy of restoring ethnic balance among Ugandans by attacking the institutional base of Baganda privilege. The economic policy of the Obote regime was deficient in two crucial aspects. First, it ignored the fact that both the UPC and the salariat were also rooted in the coalition which had benefited from collaboration with British imperialism and were thus more representative of the interests of urban strata rather than rural commodity producers. This urban bias was reflected in the income redistribution from rural to urban strata which took place under the Obote regime. Secondly, the 'commanding heights' strategy ignored the fact that state control of a dependent economy could not in itself transform the structure of that economy to meet the needs of the people of Uganda.

Transforming Uganda's economy from a dependent structure responsive to the external demands of the world market to an integrated economy responsive to domestic needs and resources would have required, first of all, a broadening of the political base of the regime to include peasant growers, migrant labourers and unskilled workers, and secondly a coherent plan for developing an integrated economy responsive to local human needs and based on local technology and resources. Such an economic transformation would also have required an egalitarian redistribution of income to broaden the base of effective demand for locally produced goods and an end to the regime's practice of favouring urban areas at the expense of rural areas.

Notes

This chapter can also be identified as PRIO publication no. 27-33 (1974) from the International Peace Research Institute, Oslo. Fieldwork was supported by grants from the Centre for Developing Area Studies, McGill University, and the Norwegian Agency for International Development. Portions of the chapter appeared earlier as the author's contribution to a joint paper with Timothy M. Shaw entitled 'International Dependence and Foreign Policy Choices: The Political Economy of Uganda', presented to the Canadian Association of African Studies, Ottawa, Feb. 1973.

  1. Wallerstein makes a strong argument that the capitalist world economy must be viewed as tri-modal, consisting not only of core states and peripheral areas but also of semi-peripheral countries which have a distinct and necessary function within the world economy above and beyond that of being mere sub-imperialist 'go-betweens'. See Immanuel Wallerstein, *The Modern World-System: Capitalist Agriculture and the Origins of the European World-Economy in the Sixteenth Century*, Academic Press, New York, 1974, pp. 349–50. During Uganda's colonial period South Africa, India, Japan and even Kenya functioned as semi-peripheral territories with economic interests in Uganda somewhat independent of and antagonistic to British imperial interests, particularly in the fields of finance, cotton industry and textiles.
  2. Although the domestic coalition changed over time, its basic elements included the following:
     (a) Baganda administrative cadres and capitalist farmers whose political and economic power was aggrandised by the British, who gave them preferential access to territory, to possession of land, to the labour-power of migrants, to education and to political institutions including the salariat of the colonial state;
     (b) an African military force recruited largely fron non-Baganda ethnic groups; and
     (c) the Asian and European commercial strata who were protected from African competition by the colonial state. The basic elements of the external environment were the imperialism of free trade within British hegemony and later British political overrule which integrated Uganda into the capitalist world system as a producer of raw materials and consumer of imported manufactured goods. The link between imperialism and Uganda's domestic political economy has been touched upon

by many writers, the most neglected of which are perhaps Ramkrishna Mukherjee, *The Problem of Uganda: a study in acculturation*, Akademi-Verlag, Berlin, 1956; and Ignatius K. Musazi, 'Strikes and disturbances in Uganda; Their origins and results', in *Labour Problems in Uganda*, Milton Obote Foundation, Kampala, 1966. The most recent works on the subject include Mahmood Mamdani, *Politics and Class Formation in Uganda*, Monthly Review Press, New York and London, 1976; and J. J. Jørgensen, *The Modern History of Uganda*, Croom Helm, London, and Africana, New York (forthcoming).

3. T. dos Santos, 'The structure of dependence', *American Economic Review: Papers and Proceedings*, lx, 2, May 1970, p. 231.

4. S. Bodenheimer, 'Dependency and imperialism: The roots of Latin American underdevelopment', *Politics and Society*, i, 3, May 1971, p. 335.

5. Two economists (Faaland and Dahl) who did attempt to find correlations between investment and output in Uganda were forced to conclude: 'Thus we have unsuccessfully run regressions between our time series [1955–1965] of GDP and capital stock, absolute levels and incremental values, lagged and not lagged, with or without population as a supplementary variable, etc.' See Just Faaland and Hans-Erik Dahl 'The economy of Uganda', in *Trade Prospects and Capital Needs of Developing Countries*, UNCTAD Secretariat, United Nations, New York, 1968, p. 249.

6. Data in this paragraph are derived from the following sources: Uganda, *Background to the Budget 1970–71*; and Uganda, *Statistical Abstract* for the years 1965, 1969 and 1970.

7. Uganda's percentage of raw material commodity concentration in exports is far higher than for industrialised nations which are also reputed to be dependent on exports of raw materials. For example, in the same year the top three raw material commodity exports of Canada (wood and pulp, wheat, and iron) accounted for only 18·3 per cent of total exports; and the top three raw material commodity exports of Norway (aluminium, fish, and wood and pulp) also accounted for only 18·3 per cent of total exports. Based on data from the United Nations *Yearbook of International Trade Statistics*, United Nations, New York, 1971.

8. Briefly stated, multiplier effects are secondary, tertiary, etc. increases in demand generated by an investment. Backward linkages are the 'up-stream' firms (firms providing producer goods and raw materials) which could be established to supply a firm in the 'down-stream' stage of a production process.

9. Uganda's total imports of capital goods in 1968 were U.Sh. 305·4 million or 46·4 per cent of the total estimated fixed capital formation in that year (US $1·00 = 7·14 U.Sh.). Based on data in Uganda, *Statistical Abstract 1970*, pp. 23, 27 and 90. The domestic content of fixed capital investment is largely in the form of wages to labourers working on investment projects. Of these wages a significant percentage would be spent on imported consumer goods. Thus one could conservatively estimate that over half of any secondary demand or multiplier effects of investment in Uganda are transmitted or 'leaked' overseas. See also Meir Merhav, *Technological Dependence, Monopoly*

and Growth, Pergamon Press, Oxford, 1969, p. 30. For an opposing view discounting the importance of such leakage effects, see H. Myint, 'The gains from international trade and the backward countries', *Review of Economic Studies*, xxii, 1954–55, pp. 129–42.

10. The clearest non-dogmatic exposition of the importance of who controls centres of production and trade in terms of consequent allocation of benefits of gains in productivity can be found in H. W. Singer, 'The distribution of gains between investing and borrowing countries', *American Economic Review: Papers and Proceedings*, xl, May 1950, pp. 473–85.

11. Similar calculations of the relative importance of the main trading partners were carried out for five other underdeveloped nations (Kenya, Tanzania, Ghana, Nigeria and the Ivory Coast) and for six industrialised nations (the United States, Canada, Norway, the United Kingdom, Japan and France). Some industrialised nations such as Canada had a higher concentration of trade with their major trading partner (70·4 per cent) than did Uganda (21·9 per cent), but the statistic which clearly separated the underdeveloped African nations from the industrialised nations was the ratio of total trade of a focus nation's trading partner to the total trade of the focus nation. In the case of Uganda this ratio was 90:1. The *lowest* ratio for the five other underdeveloped African nations was that of the Ivory Coast with a ratio of 19:1. By way of contrast the *highest* ratio for any of the six industrialised nations was only 2·8:1. Both Canada and Japan had this ratio. In other words the industrialised nations had a more balanced trading power *vis-à-vis* their respective major trading partners than did the underdeveloped African nations. Based on data in United Nations, *Yearbook of International Trade Statistics 1969*.

12. Data from Bank of Uganda, *Quarterly Bulletin* 2, Sept. 1970, p. 45, and *Quarterly Bulletin* 3, Mar. 1971, p. 21; and from Uganda, *Plan III* (1972), p. 125.

13. The obverse of this phenomenon is that industrialised nations such as the United States are net importers of capital from the rest of the world, despite claims about foreign investment and foreign 'aid' flowing to under-developed nations. See Michael Hudson, 'A financial payments-flow analysis of US international transactions: 1960–68', *The Bulletin*, 61–63, Institute of Finance, New York University Graduate School of Business Administration, March 1970; and Harry Magdoff, 'The American empire and the US economy', in Robert I. Rhodes, ed., *Imperialism and Underdevelopment*, Monthly Review Press, New York, 1970, pp. 18–44.

14. With minor exceptions these six features of structural dependence are equally characteristic of Uganda's economy in the mid-1970s. The one exception is the fourth characteristic, the paucity of indigenous control of key sectors of the economy. Indigenisation of control increased under both the Obote and Amin regimes. It remains to be seen whether indigenisation will by itself lead to the development of a more integrated economy at the structural level.

15. See the message by John Kakonge, then Secretary-General of the UPC, in

the pamphlet printed for the UPC Second Annual Delegates Conference, Mbale, 4–6 August 1962, p. 5.

16. The earliest statement of the UPC's socialist goals occurred in Obote's announcement on 7 January 1964 that Uganda was to 'follow a socialist line of development': *Uganda Argus*, 8 Jan. 1964. As might be expected given the political base of the UPC, this announcement was greeted with resistance and scepticism within the party.

17. The genealogy of the UPC is fairly complex, but its main strands can be summarised. The UPC was founded in 1960 as the result of a merger between Obote's wing of the Uganda National Congress (UNC) and the Uganda People's Union, an anti-Buganda coalition of northern politicians. Obote's UNC and Musazi's UNC had split in 1959. The original UNC was founded in 1952. The founders included such political activists as I. K. Musazi, who had been involved in the founding of the Uganda Motor Drivers' Association (1938), the Uganda Transport and General Workers' Union (1946), the Uganda African Farmers' Union (1946–48), the Federation of Partnerships of Uganda African Farmers (1950), and following the break with Obote in 1959 the Uganda National Movement. The Baganda farmer-trader elements of the UNC of 1952 could also trace a lineage back to the Bataka Party (1945–48) which included the activists Spartas Mukasa, Joseph Kivu and James Miti. Joseph Kivu and Spartas Mukasa had been involved with Musazi in the founding of the Uganda Motor Drivers' Association, whereas James Miti had been active in the original Bataka Association (1920s) which played a key role in agitation which led to the land tenure reform of 1927–28. Sources of information for this brief genealogy include: David Apter, *The Political Kingdom in Uganda*, 2nd edition, Princeton University Press, 1967, pp. 181–233, 301–48; Donald Anthony Low, *Political Parties in Uganda, 1949–62*, Athlone Press, University of London, 1962; Musazi, 'Strikes and Disturbances in Uganda; their origins and results'; E. Mutesa, *Desecration of My Kingdom*, Constable, London, 1967; F. W. Welbourn, *Religion and Politics in Uganda: 1952–62*, East African Publishing House, Nairobi, 1965; and R. C. Pratt, 'Nationalism in Uganda', *Political Studies*, ix, 2, 1961, pp. 157–98.

18. F. M. Dahlberg, 'The emergence of a dual governing elite in Uganda', *Journal of Modern African Studies*, ix, 4, Dec. 1971, pp. 618–25.

19. Based on data compiled by the author using E. G. Wilson, ed., *Who's Who in East Africa, 1965–66*, Marco Publishers Ltd, Nairobi, 1966. Most members of Uganda's Parliament listed two, three or four occupations in their biographies.

20. See also Ahmed Mohiddin, 'Changing of the guard', *Mawazo*, ii, 4, Dec. 1970, pp. 19–28; and Peter Anyang-Nyongo, 'The civil servant in Uganda', *East Africa Journal*, vii, 4, Apr. 1971, pp. 9–19.

21. As Obote observed, education in Uganda both in the colonial period and after independence was geared first and foremost to meet Uganda's *administrative* manpower requirements – in the first instance to consolidate British rule and in the second instance to consolidate Uganda's indepen-

dence by Africanising the salariat: A. Milton Obote, 'Policy proposals for Uganda's educational needs', *Mawazo*, ii, 2, Dec. 1969, pp. 3–9.

22. Up until 1953, not only were senior civil service posts generally reserved for Europeans, but any African or Asian making the grade was paid only three-fifths of the salary of a European doing the same job. See Edouard Bustin, 'L'Africanisation des cadres administratifs de l'Ouganda', *Civilisations*, ix, 2, 1959, p. 135.

23. At the exchange rate of US $1·00 = 7·1428 U.Sh. the salary alone amounted to US $5 040 per annum.

24. Uganda, *Statistical Abstract 1965*, p. 94; and Uganda, *Statistical Abstract 1970*, p. 106. Official statistics exclude the large number of migrant labourers from Rwanda, Burundi and the Sudan who work for capitalist African farmers (usually Baganda) for even lower wages.

25. Uganda, *Plan III: The Third Five-Year Plan* (1972), pp. 93–4.

26. Results of survey of low-income or 'Stratum I' cultivators in Buddu, Bulemezi, Busiro and Kyagwe counties of Buganda. Stratum I cultivators were defined as cultivators 'with not more than 1½ acres under coffee and cotton' and were estimated to comprise 50 to 70 per cent of all cultivators in Buganda: Uganda, *The Patterns of Income and Expenditure of Coffee Growers in Buganda 1962–63*, Statistics Division, Ministry of Planning and Economic Development, Entebbe, mimeo., Jan. 1967, p. 2 and Appendix II.

27. In 1969 the number of male African civil servants earning more than U.Sh. 36 000 per annum was 172. This figure includes only those working in administrative posts for the central government. It excludes, for example, managers of state corporations: Uganda, *Statistical Abstract 1970*, p. 106.

28. Data are available for African males only: Uganda, *Statistical Abstract 1965*, p. 94; and Uganda, *Statistical Abstract 1970*, p. 106.

29. Uganda, *Statistical Abstract 1965*, p. 100; and Uganda, *Statistical Abstract 1970*, p. 112.

30. Obote, 'Policy proposals for Uganda's educational needs', p. 4. Also A. G. G. Gingyera-Pinycwa, 'Political Development and Ideological Void: Uganda under Apolo Milton Obote', paper presented to the International Political Science Association World Congress, Montreal, August 1973.

31. Cyril Ehrlich, 'Some social and economic implications of paternalism in Uganda', *Journal of African History*, iv, 2, 1963, p. 285.

32. The reduction in privileges for the salariat involved the elimination of state guaranteed car loans and a change from annual to biennial salary increases: A. Milton Obote, 'Communication from the Chair of the National Assembly', 20 Apr. 1970, reprinted in Obote, *The Common Man's Charter With Appendices*, Government Printer, Entebbe, 1970, pp. 23–9. The suspension of state guaranteed car loans had an immediate impact on motor car sales in Kampala with dealers reporting a decline in sales of one-third to one-half: Godfrey Kalibala, 'Car loan reaction', *Uganda Argus*, 9 Oct. 1970, p. 3.

33. Rural areas were not totally neglected, however. There were, for example, programmes for providing water boreholes in rural communities and for building rural health dispensaries.

34. The tariff and other barriers to increased processing of exported raw materials from underdeveloped nations are discussed in Helge Hveem, 'The global dominance system: notes on a theory of global political economy', *Journal of Peace Research*, x, 4 1973, pp. 319–40.

35. Subject to these limits, the Obote regime did achieve success in some areas of import substitution, notably cotton piece goods, synthetic fabrics, clothing and footwear, cigarettes and tobacco, alcoholic beverages, and corrugated iron sheets for roofing.

36. Astoundingly, one of the few references to inter-industry linkages the author found in speeches by members of the Obote regime used the development of such intermediate-goods linkages in glass, asbestos cement pipes, paper bags and manufactured metals as evidence of untapped potential for *foreign* investors! See L. Kalule-Settala, Minister of Finance, *Budget Speech*, 15 June 1966, p. 5. Such attitudes ignore the need for Ugandan control of inter-industry linkages.

37. See reports of speeches by: A. M. Obote, *Uganda Argus*, 11 May 1964, 14 June 1966, and 8 Dec. 1966; by Foreign Minister Sam Odaka, *Uganda Argus*, 23 Nov. 1966, and 25 Oct. 1968; by the Minister for Economic Planning, J. M. Okae, *Uganda Argus*, 12 Dec. 1970. See also the discussion of tied foreign aid in Uganda, *Work for Progress: The Second Five-Year Plan, 1966–71* (1966).

38. The external orientation of planning was used as justification for not publishing details of projects in the First Five-Year Plan on grounds that the local details would be of minor interest to potential overseas donors: A. M. Obote (Debate on the First Five-Year Plan), National Assembly of Uganda, *Official Proceedings*, 11 July 1963.

39. I. Gershenberg, 'Slouching towards socialism: Obote's Uganda', *African Studies Review*, xv, 1, April 1972, pp. 79–95.

40. G. A. Costanzo, director of both First National City Bank of New York and Grindlays Bank, 40 per cent of whose shares are owned by City Corp, as quoted in H. E. Heinemann, US bankers survey a multinational horizon', *New York Times*, 26 Apr. 1970, Financial Section, p. 22.

41. The expatriate banks in East Africa (notably Grindlays, Barclays and Standard Bank) opened vast networks of rural branches in the 1950s and 1960s. Many of these 'upcountry' branches were in themselves unprofitable, but, as a London banker pointed out to the author (interview, London, 22 Nov. 1973), within the overall operations of the banks the rural branches were important sources of deposits to be lent to customers in urban areas. This was confirmed by confidential data on advances/deposits ratios for rural versus urban branches, made available to the author by expatriate officials of several banks in East Africa. The depositors in rural areas were mainly the African growers, traders, and local salariat. The borrowers in urban areas were mainly multinational firms, non-citizen firms and the state. The argument that the benefits of such pooling of capital from rural areas to be lent in urban areas eventually trickle back to the rural areas in the form of jobs and agricultural investment ignores the point that the control of accumulation and allocation of capital remains in the hands of foreign firms and higher functionaries of the salariat in the urban areas.

42. The following are some of the state corporations established by the Obote regime, for the dual purpose of expanding state control of the economy and increasing the pool of jobs to be awarded by patronage: the National Housing Corporation (1964); upgrading of the Uganda Savings and Credit Bank to become the Uganda Commercial Bank (1965); National Insurance Corporation (1964); Bank of Uganda (central bank, 1966); National Trading Corporation (1966); Dairy Industry Corporation (1967); the Produce Marketing Board (1968); Apolo Hotel Corporation (1968); and the Export and Import Corporation (1970).

43. In defining manufacturing, I excluded the following activities: cotton ginning, coffee processing, construction, mining, and the generation of electricity.

44. Calculations based on data from Uganda, *Survey of Industrual Production 1967*, Statistics Division, Ministry of Planning and Economic Development, Entebbe, 1969.

45. The total number of firms with *ten* or more employees in 1967 was 400; their total gross output was U.Sh. 1 114 131 000 (approximately US $156 million).

46. In 1967 there were a total of 46 manufacturing firms with 100 or more employees. The 9 sub-sectors under discussion contained 38 (or four-fifths) of these large firms.

47. The implementation of the semi-nationalisation of manufacturing firms was delayed by lengthy negotiations over terms of compensation and was finally interrupted by the 1971 coup.

48. Based on data compiled from information in the Companies (Government and Public Bodies Participation) Bill 1970; Uganda, *Survey of Industrial Production 1967*; and Uganda, *Directory of Establishments 1967*.

49. Ali A. Mazrui, 'Social distance and the transclass man' in his *Cultural Engineering and Nation-Building in East Africa*, Northwestern University Press, Evanston, 1972, p. 159.

50. I define the 'labour aristocracy' as consisting of employees earning at least three times the minimum wage or three times what the majority of workers earn, rather than merely asserting that all workers or workers employed by multinational firms are somehow automatically a privileged class in East Africa. Arrighi appears to use too broad a definition of 'labour aristocracy' in his article 'International corporations, labour aristocracies, and economic development in tropical Africa', in Rhodes, ed., *Imperialism and Under-development*, pp. 220–67.

51. The calculations on which this section is based are derived from data from the following sources:
    (*a*) Payment to growers, 1960–62: Uganda, *Statistical Abstract 1965*, p. 40;
    (*b*) Payment to growers, 1967–69: Uganda, *Statistical Abstract 1970*, p. 42;
    (*c*) Estimate of subsistence product, 1960–62: 1961 figures in Uganda, *Background to the Budget 1970–71*, p. 4;
    (*d*) Estimate of subsistence product, 1967–69: Uganda, *Plan III*, p. 52;
    (*e*) Estimate of other cash income for peasants: two-times cash crop income from coffee and cotton;

(*f*) National disposable income based on data from Uganda, *Background to the Budget 1970–71*; and *Plan III*, p. 52;

(*g*) Estimate of rate of inflation during the 1960s: Uganda, *Plan III*, p. 38;

(*h*) Estimate of population growth: Uganda, *Plan III*, p. 69;

(*i*) Estimate of African rural population: Uganda, *Plan III*, pp. 69, 71 and 100;

(*j*) Cash wages of employees, 1960–62: Uganda, *Statistical Abstract 1965*, p. 93;

(*k*) Cash wages of employees, 1967–69: Uganda, *Statistical Abstract 1970*, p. 105.

52. This assumption is supported by surveys of coffee-growing districts in Buganda, where income from coffee and cotton constituted 65 per cent of total cash income of the entire sample, and 50 per cent of total cash income of low income growers: Uganda, *The Patterns of Income and Expenditure of Coffee Growers in Buganda 1962–63*, Appendix VI. The problem remains whether this relationship holds in cotton-growing areas and in areas outside Buganda.

53. Thus the formula for total peasants' income was as follows: subsistence income plus two-times cash income from sale of coffee and cotton. ʲ

54. Nelson Kasfir, 'Cultural sub-nationalism in Uganda', in Victor Olorunsola, ed., *The Politics of Cultural Sub-Nationalism in Africa*, Anchor Books, Garden City, New York, 1972, p. 127.

55. See: M. Crawford Young, 'The Obote revolution', *Africa Report*, xi, 6, June 1966, pp. 8–14; Special Correspondent, 'The Ugandan army: nexus of power', *Africa Report*, xi, 6, December 1966, pp. 37–39; E. Mutesa, *Desecration of My Kingdom*, Constable, London, 1967; A. Milton Obote, 'The footsteps of Uganda's revolution', *East Africa Journal*, v, 10, October 1968, pp. 7–13; and the free verse account in Akena Adoko, *Uganda Crisis*, African Publishers, Kampala, 1970.

56. See, for example, Obote, *Common Man's Charter* (1970), article 15, and the frequent references to 'feudal elements', 'feudalism', and 'feudalists' in other articles, all clearly directed at supporters of Buganda separatism and the Kabakaship.

57. Jørgensen, *The Modern History of Uganda.*

Joel W. Gregory

4 Underdevelopment, Dependence and Migration in Upper Volta[1]

In at least two ways Upper Volta is not a 'typical' African country. First, the quantity of Voltaic migration is massive.[2] Second, Upper Volta is among the poorest African countries.[3] Yet migration and poverty are not unique to Upper Volta. For example, Chad, Mali, and Niger share many problems with Upper Volta; in southern Africa, the problems of Botswana, Lesotho, and Swaziland may be parallel.

1. Definitions

(a) *Development*

The meaning of development is the subject of a wide-ranging debate. This debate focuses on a discussion of strategies.[4] It is frequently assumed that there is agreement about goals, and that the real question is how to achieve them. In fact, the lack of agreement about strategies may reflect a deeper, inarticulated disagreement about the goals of development.

A popular conception of the goal of development, with which many would agree, is that development is the change by which poor countries become more like rich ones. This definition underlies the conventional wisdom and is based on three assumptions:

1 development is primarily a measure of wealth;
2 to develop is to become more like rich countries;
3 it is poor countries that require development.

Beginning with goals of development rather than the means of achieving it, Dudley Seers provides an alternative definition. He says that development should lead to the 'realisation of the potential of the human personality'. He suggests three criteria for development. First is food, and/or the money to buy it; this furnishes energy and good health, and an interest in things besides food. Second is a job; to depend on someone else's productivity negates self-respect. Third is equality of income.[5] These characteristics can be restated and expanded to the following four criteria: adequate and nutritious food; good health; sufficient and satisfying employment; and equality of wealth. Essentially these four criteria are a statement of development goals. Once defined they can also be used to evaluate development strategies. In fact, these criteria suggest that the relationship between goals and strategies is very close.

The redefinition implies the rejection of the three assumptions which underlie the conventional wisdom about development. First, development is not primarily a measure of wealth; while an increase in income is part of the development process in most countries, its achievement is not sufficient (and sometimes not necessary) for development. Second, to develop is not to become more like rich societies; rather to develop is to satisfy certain human needs. Third, it is not only poor countries that need to develop; the inability of rich societies to achieve some or many of these goals is well known.

(b) Dependence

Dependence is the result of an unequal relationship, where the weaker of the two parties is dominated by the stronger.[6] Self-reliance is the opposite of dependence. A country seeking self-reliance within the international system attempts to minimise external domination of politics, the economy, and culture. Within a country, self-reliance implies a dispersion of power and benefits among the entire population, rather than a concentration among the elite. Self-reliance, however, does not imply isolation. Interdependence is the relationship between self-reliant parties. Interdependence differs from dependence in that each party has more or less equal control over its own affairs. This equality permits cooperation rather than exploitation.

One useful explanation of dependence is the centre-periphery model. The centre of the system is dominant; the periphery is subordinate. Johan Galtung distinguishes the centre of the Centre from the periphery of the Centre, as well as the centre of the Periphery from the periphery of the Periphery.[7] Internal and international forms of dependence can be seen as part of the same system. Class or regional inequalities within a country are the domestic forms of the rich-poor inequalities of the international system. At the centres of both the Centre and the Periphery are concentrated the rich and the elites; at the peripheries are the poor and the masses.

Another difference between the Centre and the Periphery is the origin of demand. At the Centre, demand has evolved historically from a demand for necessities to a demand for consumer durables. At the Periphery, demand originates externally, through foreign capital expended at the Periphery, through foreign wages paid to expatriates in the Periphery economy, and through the income of the national elite.[8]

To see dependence as a system with four sub-sectors, however, is a conceptual over-simplification. In reality, there are a series of 'nested' and interconnected dependent relationships. Internationally, for example, Upper Volta functions as the periphery of the Periphery; Ivory Coast and Ghana function as the centre of the Periphery; France is the centre of the Centre; with perhaps Italy and Spain functioning as the periphery of the Centre. In addition to countries, there are other international actors, including multinational corporations (operating from the centre) and international labour migrants (from the periphery). Within each country, there are centres and peripheries, defined primarily in spatial terms (urban versus rural, North versus South). In other words, dependence is not only internal as well as international but also it can characterise political, economic, and cultural relations between geographical units, classes, and sectors.

Historically, two important types of dependence have been colonialism and neo-colonialism. Most of the societies of the Third World have experienced both forms of dependence, and Upper Volta is no exception. Colonialism is defined as an international dependence system, composed of both independent countries (the Centre) and colonies (the Periphery). Political decisions are made at the Centre. Material and human resources are used for the benefits of the elites of the Centre, with some limited benefits for the masses of the Centre. Cultural values of the Centre are imposed on the periphery.

Neo-colonialism is defined as a dependence system made up almost exclusively of independent countries. The intermediate role of neo-colonial elites (located at the centre of the Periphery) is of great importance. Political decisions are made within each country by the elites, with varying constraints imposed on the Periphery. The material and human resources of the Periphery are exploited for the benefit of the elites of the Centre. Substantial economic benefits are received by the elites of the Periphery for maintaining and running their part of the system; if the economic benefits are large, some will 'trickle down' to the masses of the Centre and perhaps even some to the masses of the Periphery. Some cultural values of the Centre are held by the Periphery. The elites of the Periphery are profoundly affected by the conflicts between the value system of the Centre and that of the Periphery. Values held by the elites in the Periphery affect political decisions in the Periphery and the way in which the material and human resources of the Periphery are used.

(c) Migration

Two factors cause changes in the distribution of population: migration and differential rates of natural increase. In this study, only the first is discussed in detail.

Two spatial forms of migration are of greatest importance in this study: international migration from what is now Upper Volta to Ivory Coast and Ghana, and internal migration within Upper Volta. Migration from Upper Volta to Ivory Coast and Ghana originates primarily in rural Upper Volta; destinations are in both rural and urban areas. While migration within Upper Volta occurs in all possible spatial combinations – rural–rural, rural–urban, urban–rural, urban–urban – the rural–urban movement is the focus of this study.

To minimise conceptual confusion, Tables 4.1–4.3 and Fig. 4.1 are presented as a basis for discussion. Table 4.1 summarises the static forms of development, dependence, and population distribution. The most noteworthy aspect of this Table is the fact that no value is assigned to a particular level of migration and urbanisation; they are neither inherently desirable nor inherently undesirable.[9] Yet migration and urbanisation can have positive implications, to the extent that they serve development and self-

Table 4.1   Static Forms of Development, Dependence, and Population Distribution

Phenomena	Characteristics	Possible states	Values
Development	Food Health Employment Wealth	Underdeveloped to Highly developed	Undesirable Desirable
Dependence	Decision-making Resource use Culture, values	Highly dependent to Self-reliant	Undesirable Desirable
Population distribution	Migration Rate of natural increase	Predominantly rural to highly urbanised	Neutral Neutral

reliance, and negative implications, to the extent that they serve underdevelopment and dependence.

Tables 4.2 and 4.3 outline two dynamic aspects of the analytical framework, the processes of development and of increasing self-reliance. Table 4.2 summarises changes that would lead to a more

Table 4.2   Changes Leading Towards a More Developed Status

Character-istics	Qualitative changes	Quantitative changes	Changes in distribution
Food	Improved nutritional content	More food	More equitably distributed according to need
Health	Improved health and improved health services	More health services	Services more equitably distributed according to health needs and population distribution
Employment	Increased satisfaction	More employment opportunities	More equitably distributed, according to population distribution
Wealth	—	—	More equally distributed

Table 4.3   Changes Leading Towards More Self-reliant Status

Characteristics	Changes
Decision-making	More participation at the periphery, more dispersed
Resource use	Increased use at periphery, benefits more dispersed throughout the periphery
Culture, values	More consistent with value system of the periphery or increasingly generated from the periphery

developed status; Table 4.3 summarises changes leading to a more self-reliant status.

Finally Figure 4.1 summarises another dynamic aspect of the analytical framework; the interrelationship of development, dependence, and migration. Conceptually, both positive and negative feedback are possible. For example, an increase in the quantity of jobs can cause either an increase or a decrease in migration, depending primarily on the location of the jobs. The form of the Figure emphasises the fact that none of the three phenomena is conceived as an independent or a dependent variable. Each phenomenon acts upon the other two phenomena, and in turn is acted upon by them. The Figure, however, suggests one important qualification. The role of migration (we are not speaking of pre-colonial migration, but rather of 'modern' migration) is far more limited than the role of development and dependence. Both development and dependence are acted upon and act upon phenomena outside the system described here; migration, on the other hand, is a function of underdevelopment, dependence, and

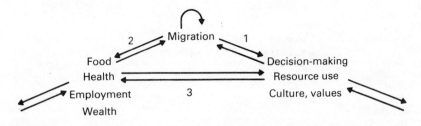

Figure 4.1   Interrelationship of Development, Dependence, and Migration

earlier migration. Underdevelopment is a function of dependence, migration, and 'other' phenomena (not specified here). Likewise, dependence is a function of underdevelopment, migration and 'other' phenomena. In one sense the arrows in this Figure are misleading, because they appear to operate simultaneously. While all the relationships represented by the arrows may be operating at the present time, they have not all operated continuously and simultaneously since 1896 (the date of the French 'conquest' of Upper Volta, and the beginning of the period studied here).

2. Feedback Mechanism 1: Migration and Dependence

In Upper Volta it is necessary to understand the historical and political origins of migration. French colonial policy assigned a special role to Upper Volta within French West Africa. With a relatively large and densely-settled population, with few known natural resources, with no sea-coast, with undependable and sparse rainfall, Upper Volta was used as a labour reservoir for 'development' projects in more promising parts of the colony (Ivory Coast in particular).[10]

As early as 1896, the colonial administration began taxing the Voltaic people, with substantial increases imposed over the next few years. These taxes were collected in francs rather than in kind or in cowries.[11] Initially taxes were seen simply as a source of revenue. In fact, however, many Voltaics were obliged to emigrate in order to earn the necessary cash. By the end of the First World War labour requirements in the coastal areas of West Africa were larger. In order to meet this demand forced labour was practised in French West Africa from 1919 to 1946.[12] Annually, chiefs of Voltaic villages provided men to work for a specific period of time to meet quotas established by the colonial administration.[13] As a result of these two colonial policies, taxation and forced labour, migration was a social and economic institution by the end of the Second World War.[14] More recently, neo-colonialism has replaced colonialism *per se*. Neo-colonialism was made possible by the creation of an African elite during the latter part of the colonial era. The maintenance of the elite class is one reason for the concentration of job and income opportunities in the cities of

Upper Volta. The doubling of the number of salaried jobs in Ouagadougou between 1962 and 1970 (discussed in detail in section 3) reflects the economic importance of the growing bureaucracy. The concentration of wealth makes Ouagadougou and other administrative centres in Upper Volta increasingly attractive destinations for the migrant leaving rural Upper Volta.

As indicated earlier, neo-colonialism operates through a series of 'nested' dependence relationships. The rural population is dominated by an urban elite; a poor country is dependent on her richer neighbours for the provision of employment and for the transportation of imports and exports; and both the Voltaic and the coastal economies are dominated by European economic interests. The rural areas of Upper Volta are at the extreme periphery of a monetised economic system, and migration is an attempt to move towards the centre of activity. For the Voltaic villager three alternative destinations are available: Ivory Coast, Ghana, and the cities of Upper Volta. What appears to the Voltaic villagers to be the 'Centre', however, is really the centre of the Periphery of an international economic system, focused outside Africa. Abidjan, Accra, and Ouagadougou all serve as points of contact between the Centre and the Periphery.

In terms of economic resources, Upper Volta is tied to her neighbours and to France. In the 1960s, between 50 and 65 per cent of annual Voltaic exports went to Ivory Coast and Ghana, and between 13 and 26 per cent to France. By contrast the largest quantity of annual imports, between 44 and 54 per cent, came from France, and a lesser amount from her coastal neighbours, between 15 and 22 per cent.[15]

In terms of foreign aid France plays an equally important role in Upper Volta's economic affairs. From 1959 to 1971 an average of approximately $6·4 million were annually invested in Upper Volta through *Fonds d'aide et de coopération* (FAC). Between 1968 and 1971 an additional $4·2 million were annually invested in Upper Volta in other forms of French aid. This represents the bulk of bilateral aid, with investments by FED (multilaterial aid from the European Economic Community) nearly equalling those made by FAC during the 1960s.[16]

The domination of Voltaic trade and aid by France has direct implications for migration. To the extent that foreign economic activities are concentrated in cities rather than dispersed (discussed in detail in section 3) the job and income structure is unbalanced. With the exception of two new agricultural processing plants in Banfora, for example, all industries are located in the three largest cities, Ouagadougou, Bobo-Dioulasso, and Koudougou.[17] Elsewhere I have calculated that a substantial majority of expenditures during the *1967–70 Plan Cadre* were made in the two largest cities.[18] In addition the four largest categories of imports in the 1960s were products heavily consumed by the urban, cash sector; machinery, textiles, transport materials and supplies, and petroleum products.[19]

Briefly, then, neo-colonialism in Upper Volta has been a major cause of economic imbalance, characterised by a concentration of monetised economic activities in the cities of Upper Volta and in Ivory Coast and Ghana. This imbalance is a major cause of out-migration from rural Upper Volta. Migration, in turn, reinforces the economic imbalance. When migrants are predominantly in the 15 to 29 years age-groups, as in Upper Volta,[20] the receiving area is importing a factor of production for which it did not pay. Great flexibility is added to the labour force of the receiving area, as the migrant group, by definition, is mobile. Due to the low incomes of the sending area, the migrant group is usually willing to accept low pay.[21]

Meanwhile, the sending area is losing a part of its labour force, frequently during the migrants' most productive years. For Upper Volta, as demonstrated historically, losing a part of her labour force is losing her richest factor of production. The sending area can become involved in a spiral of migration, dependence, and poverty. A productive portion of the labour force leaves, placing a heavier burden on the old people and the children, who are less productive. A fall in productivity and output forces more people to leave to provide for the remaining people, and so on.[22] While this downward spiral seldom reaches catastrophic proportions, the dependence burden of sending areas is frequently far greater than that of the receiving areas.[23]

Another aspect of dependence is the status of the individual migrant. The individual Voltaic migrant moves from a 'self-reliant' to a dependent status. As land is held collectively by villagers, every Voltaic participates in the ownership of the means of production (as a bare minimum capital, in the form of tools, is involved).[24]

By migrating to cash employment in the Ivory Coast, Ghana, and the cities of Upper Volta, the individual changes his status. In terms of class analysis, migration is the principal process by which Africa is being proletarianised.[25] If a Voltaic migrant finds a job, he is likely to find low-paying employment. Voltaic emigrants to Ivory Coast and Ghana overwhelmingly are members of the lowest stratum of the proletariat, while those who migrate to Upper Volta's two largest cities have only a slightly greater opportunity to enter middle and upper level occupations.[26]

In addition to political and economic dependence, cultural dependence is related to migration. European ways of doing things have frequently been favoured while African ways have been denigrated. For example, the Voltaic civil service is limited to graduates of European style schools. Graduates of the Centres for Rural Education, which teach agriculture and literacy skills, do not have access to jobs in the civil service.[27] Thus schooling serves as a filter, letting only those exposed to European ways of thinking and behaviour pass into the elite.

An insightful study of migration and cultural dependence was made by Jean Hochet, a social psychologist. For many young Voltaics, he claims, there is a lack of social and psychological security. Before colonialisation the family head was the focus of solidarity and authority. He had both spiritual and material authority. Increasingly, these roles are being assumed by the church, government, and private business. Youth are frequently obliged to make value judgements about which authority is 'better'. Money is central to the conflict between value systems: money for taxes, money for dowries, money for prestige. Migration by a young villager is a means of 'resignation and flight in the face of a life style which does not correspond to a more or less conscious ideal . . . of man and his future'.[28]

Migration is a cause as well as a result of cultural dependency. Migrants return to their villages with values and habits not particularly geared to development needs. The purchase of certain consumer goods (clothes and cloth, radios, bicycles) uses a substantial portion of many migrants' savings. Taxes consume another portion. Investments by returning migrants are rare.[29] A new mentality is frequently observed in the returning migrant, characterised by prestige consumption and a lack of respect for elders.[30]

3. Feedback Mechanism 2: Migration and Underdevelopment

Migration is both a result and a cause of the inability of Upper Volta to raise her level of development substantially, as measured by the four criteria of food, health, employment, and income equality.

The most noticeable aspect of this relationship is the link between employment and migration.[31] As discussed in section 2, migration is a function of difference between the opportunity structures of (1) rural Upper Volta; and (2) Ivory Coast, Ghana, and the cities of Upper Volta. Historically the development of jobs in the monetary sector has been spatially concentrated away from the 94 per cent of the Voltaic population which is rural. At the beginning of the twentieth century, virtually all salaried employment found by Voltaics was in Ivory Coast and Gold Coast. At present, cash employment is increasing in Upper Volta, but it is heavily concentrated in urban areas.[32]

The standard analysis of labour migration is that it is a rational adjustment to economic development, and serves the sending as well as the receiving area.[33] In terms of providing adequate and satisfying jobs for everyone, it is questionable if such a process is rational. The urban sector in Upper Volta is unable to generate employment for all those who migrate there. According to the data available for Ouagadougou and Bobo-Dioulasso, during the past ten years the ratio of jobs to job seekers has risen only once above one in three.[34] In Ivory Coast the situation may be worse. In 1969, for example, some 10 000 unemployed persons demonstrated against the government, demanding that Europeans and Voltaics be removed from the top and the bottom of the employment ladder respectively.[35]

Voltaic underdevelopment has produced a highly unbalanced spatial pattern of economic opportunity resulting in out-migration from rural areas. In turn, this out-migration may be reducing the potential of Upper Volta to generate adequate and satisfying employment within the rural sector. At least one observer has noted that the agricultural skills learned by the Mossi in Ghana are not appropriate to the soils, climate, and land tenure of Upper Volta.[36] Furthermore, the absence of substantial numbers of young males from the agricultural labour force undoubtedly decreases the potential for rural development.[37]

The relationship between employment and migration is closely tied to the relationship between the distribution of wealth and migration. A concentration of cash employment in urban Upper Volta and in Ivory Coast and Ghana means a concentration of wealth in these same places. In 1970 per capita Gross Domestic Product in Upper Volta was estimated to be 14 890 Fr.CFA (approximately $60).[38] In the wage sector an average of 223 217 Fr.CFA was reported for 1970,[39] some eighteen times greater than per capita product. While this is a comparison of extremes, it does serve as an index of the enormous income difference between the urban middle and upper class and rural Voltaics. Certainly this fact reinforces the motivation of those migrating to find a job and to find a higher income.

According to various studies of Voltaic migration, economic motives are of considerable importance. The data available stress the importance of economic motives for men and family reasons (marriage, following husband) for women. Among the Mossi, the emphasis on economic motives for migration is so strong, that one study found all respondents gave economic reasons for their migration.[40]

Inequality of income opportunities may encourage migration; migration to urban areas may cause other inequalities. Particularly in terms of services, it has been observed that an increase in urban population strains the government's ability to provide adequate services.[41] The provision of urban services is frequently at the expense of rural services. A 'demonstration effect' is at work. Since colonial times certain services (water, electricity, schools, hospitals, paved streets, etc.) have been provided in urban areas. Urban residents, including the newly arrived, now expect these services, at least in some minimum form. In Upper Volta the concentration of these services is easily observed: the city-wide availability of electricity in only the four largest cities; the availability of piped water in only some of the largest cities; and the concentration of secondary schools, hospitals, and clinics in major urban centres.[42] These services are not mentioned here as an index of development; rather they are capital-intensive means of providing amenities, which absorb large portions of available development funds, and which are concentrated in a few urban areas away from 94 per cent of the population. The growth of cities through in-migration further exaggerates demand for these services, spreading even thinner the provision of services in rural areas, widening the urban–rural gap. Some would claim that this inequality in itself is a cause for migration.

4. Feedback Mechanism 3: Dependence and Underdevelopment

Some of the effects of dependence on underdevelopment and *vice versa* have already been suggested in sections 2 and 3. For example, the relationship between external economic ties and the spatial pattern of investments has already been discussed. How European attitudes about development have permeated African ways of thinking has already been considered.

During the colonial period little effort was made to build up food production, health services, and employment opportunities in Upper Volta. Upper Volta was a labour reservoir, and nothing more. The development of Ivory Coast was made possible by this supply of cheap labour. At the time of Independence, therefore, Upper Volta was relatively poor in terms of industries, cash crops, social services, and economic infrastructure as compared with her neighbours to the south. Yet colonialism and migration had exposed Voltaics to Western technology and materialism, creating a mentality of underdevelopment.

Since Independence, the government has sought to carve out a larger economic role for Upper Volta, in both the rural sector and the 'modern' sector. In order to do so, Upper Volta has actively sought investments, advisers, and managers from the rich countries of the West.

In the rural sector, for example, development strategy is implemented through a series of Rural Development Offices (ORDs). Seven of the ten functioning ORDs are linked to foreign technical 'companies'. There are two reasons for this system of 'intervention'. First the ORDs need technical advice, as Upper Volta has an extremely limited number of agronomists, agricultural engineers, agricultural economists, rural sociologists, etc. Secondly, the ORDs need financing, and the technical assistants are part of the aid package. Each company is represented by at least one expatriate technical assistant in a top position in the central office of the individual ORDs.

One of the companies giving technical aid, the CFDT (la

Compagnie Française pour le Développement des Textiles), is particularly suspect in terms of its self-serving policies. Two opposing interests are in direct conflict: the desire of the Office of Rural Development to make the ORDs self-financing and the desire of the CFDT to make a profit on cotton. All farmers must sell to the CFDT. Direct exportation by the producer is not allowed; direct sale by the producer to the textile factory is not allowed. Teams from the CFDT, assisted by government civil servants, come to every village between November and January, and weigh and buy cotton. At that time the farmer is paid, and the CFDT agent is present to collect on debts incurred during the previous agricultural season. In at least one region most farmers are pleased with the system (having known no other) and find cotton to be the first important source of cash income in their area.[43]

Yet the Office of Rural Development sees processing and marketing by the ORDs as essential to eventual self-financing. Both the government of Upper Volta and the Voltaic farmers, therefore, are in an awkward position. Cotton is a source, one of the only sources for the present, of cash income.[44] CFDT provides technical personnel, makes administrative investments, extends credit, and makes certain investments in infrastructure in order to increase cotton production. Yet, in reality the Voltaic government subsidises these operations through the use of Voltaic personnel (extension agents, primarily) to popularise cotton-growing practices and to aid in the collection and purchase of all cotton for the company.

As practised at present, cotton production may hinder other agricultural activities. The CFDT advises that cotton should be planted between June 15 and July 15, yet this is the time when other agricultural activities are at their peak, including the planting of food crops for self-consumption.[45] If cotton production were important enough, by itself, to support family needs, then this consideration would not be important. But as long as the farmer is obliged to produce both food and cotton, the time distribution of labour activities is very important.

Development strategy for the modern sector is also causing an increase in Voltaic economic dependency. The large-scale technological bias of industrial development, the capital-intensive projects being undertaken, and the quantities of imported capital

goods being consumed by industry all cause increased dependence. In theory, development policy stresses the 'Voltaic' role in
industrial growth: the use of Voltaic primary materials, the training of Voltaic personnel. At the same time, however, foreign
investment is to be encouraged by a liberal capital-transfer policy
and investment code.

On the basis of total investments, it is possible to calculate a
crude measure of the foreign role in the industrial sector. The
government of Upper Volta and the Banque Nationale de
Développement (BND) own 50·9 per cent of the stock in twenty
major industrial enterprises; French companies and individuals
own 39·9 per cent; the other 9·2 per cent of stock is held by
companies and individuals elsewhere, or is unspecified. On the
other hand, 51·0 per cent of annual production (for the fifteen
enterprises for which production is given) is generated by the
French share of the industrial sector, with only 25·1 per cent being
generated by the Voltaic share.[46] In other words, while there is a
large 'public' participation in the industrial sector, foreign private
interests are very significant. Data on profits are unavailable.

Over time the industrial sector is not becoming any less dependent. Of the major industries established between 1966 and 1972,
(and including the expansion of existing industries) approximately 57 per cent of the investments were made through the
BND and the government of Upper Volta.[47] Yet, the government
of Upper Volta may be underwriting a disproportionate amount
of industrial investment relative to the benefits coming to Upper
Volta. For example, the value-added in the manufacturing sub-
sector for Upper Volta in 1965 was 32·2 per cent; the value-added
for manufacturing in 1970 was 30·6 per cent.[48] During a period
when public expenditures were accounting for nearly 60 per cent
of new industrial investments, the relative value-added in Upper
Volta did not increase. Admittedly value-added is far from a
perfect indicator of 'benefits' accruing to Upper Volta. Yet, it
indicates a consistent level of dependence on imported inputs.

Two examples illustrate the mechanisms by which industrial
'development' maintains dependency. VOLTELEC, the only
electric company, has been owned by the Voltaic government
since 1966. VOLTELEC accounts for two-thirds of the publicly-
owned industry in Upper Volta, and for one-third of public
investments in the industrial sector. This company generates all

its electricity with diesel fuel which is imported over a railway owned by a French company, and is purchased from European and American companies. Most of the administrative and technical personnel are French. Stated simply, Voltaic ownership does not guarantee a redirection of expenditures or effective control. Between 1966 and 1970, in fact, the value-added in Upper Volta for the energy sub-sector fell from 60 to 51 per cent.[49]

The activities of the Société Sucrière de Haute-Volta (SOSUHV), a sugar refinery, provide a second example of increasing dependence through industrial growth. In principle, SOSUHV falls into a preferential category: it is a company which processes an agricultural product which can be grown in Upper Volta. A cane-plantation has been established. The land for this plantation was taken from villagers and given to the company. Some of these farmers have moved to the nearby town of Banfora, and now work as agricultural labourers for the company. Apparently, the possibility of teaching farmers to raise sugar cane on their own land, or organising a cooperative to cultivate on a larger scale were not considered. In the short run, some residents of the Banfora region are undoubtedly happy to have wage employment on the plantation. Yet, the potential integration of industry with agriculture has been short-changed. A company enclave has been created, with the company all but shutting off opportunities for participation by Voltaic farmers, except as wage-labour on company land.

5. Summary and Conclusions

The historical pattern of Voltaic migration can be divided into three phases. Early Voltaic emigration was caused primarily by Upper Volta's dependent, colonial status. With the end of the Second World War, emigration became more a function of Voltaic underdevelopment than a function of her dependence. This underdevelopment had been caused by her dependence and by migration itself. Migration, in turn, fed on itself, and contributed to spatial patterns of underdevelopment and dependence. With independence, a third stage of migration – urbanisation – was begun. Employment opportunities in the cities and towns of Upper Volta began a rapid growth, increasing their ability to compete with Ghana and Ivory Coast as destinations for migration. This phase of migration is again characterised by migration contributing to the spatial patterns of underdevelopment and dependence.

Schematically, these phases are shown in Figure 4.2. Obviously, this scheme is oversimplified, but it provides a basic illustration of the changing pattern of the relationship of migration, development, and dependency over time.

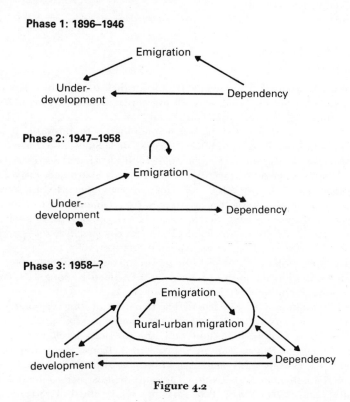

Phase 1: 1896–1946

Emigration

Under-development ← Dependency

Phase 2: 1947–1958

Emigration

Under-development → Dependency

Phase 3: 1958–?

Emigration

Rural-urban migration

Under-development ← Dependency

Figure 4.2

In considering the future, two basic facts must be kept in mind. First, over 90 per cent of the population of Upper Volta is rural. Second, in many ways Upper Volta is a sub-region of the larger geographic, economic, and cultural region of West Africa. Thus, the future of migration must be thought about not only in terms of the past, but also in terms of the present low level of urbanisation and the high levels of intra-regional and rural–urban migration. The same two facts affect the way we think about the future of development and self-reliance. If food, health, employment, and equality of wealth are to be provided for the people of Upper Volta, the fact that most of them live in rural areas affects both the choice and the location of development activities. The fact that Upper Volta is part of a larger geographic, economic, and cultural unit suggests both constraints and potential for development efforts. In relocating decision-making and resource use at the periphery and in building on the value of the periphery, these two factors are crucial.

Notes

1. I would like to thank the following people for their useful criticism of earlier versions of this study: Robert Beauregard, Richard Curtain, William Goldsmith, Rukudzo Murapa, and D. Ian Pool.

2. Quantitative documentation of Voltaic migration is found in the following censuses and sample censuses: RHV, Service de la Statistique, *Enquête démographique par sondage en RHV, 1960–1961*, INSEE Paris and Secrétariat d'Etat aux Affaires Etrangères, 1970; RHV, Service de la Statistique, *Enquête démographique par sondage en RHV, 1960–1961, les émigrations*, INSEE Paris and Secrétariat d'Etat aux Affaires Etrangères, 1972; Ghana, Census Office, *1960 Population Census of Ghana*, Accra, 1964, vol. III, pp. 99–136; République de Côte d'Ivoire, Ministère du Plan, *Côte d'Ivoire, population, études régionales 1962–1965 – synthèse*, Imprimerie National, Abidjan, 1967, pp. 143–56.

3. 1971, Upper Volta was one of fifteen African countries among the twenty-five least developed countries named by the United Nations. UN, General Assembly, resolution 2768 (XXVI), 18 Nov. 1971.

4. See, for example: Carl K. Eicher, 'The dynamics of long-term agricultural development in Nigeria', *Journal of Farm Economics*, xlix, 5, Dec. 1967, pp. 1158–70; K. B. Griffin, 'Reflections on Latin American development', xviii, 1, *Oxford Economic Papers*, Mar. 1966, pp. 1–18; J. Irons, 'How to squeeze the farmer successfully', *The Journal of Developing Areas*, iv, 2, Jan. 1970, pp. 153–6; Timothy and Leslie Nulty, 'Pakistan: the busy bee route to development', *Trans-Action*, viii, 4, Feb. 1971, pp. 18–26; and P. P. Streeten, 'The frontiers of development studies', *Journal of Development Studies*, iv, 1, Oct. 1967, pp. 2–24.

5. Dudley Seers, 'The meaning of development', *International Development Review*, 11, Dec. 1969, pp. 2–3.

6. While the concept of dependence can be applied to individuals, its use in this study is limited to groups of people. Dependence helps explain relationships between countries, regions, sectors, etc.

7. Johan Galtung, 'Structural theory of imperialism', *Journal of Peace Research*, vii, 2, 1972, pp. 81–118, and 'Dependency', paper presented at meetings of the Canadian Association of African Studies, Feb. 1973.

8. Samir Amin, *Accumulation on a World Scale*: *A Critique of The Theory of Underdevelopment*, Monthly Review Press, New York, 1974.

9. This is rarely the orientation of writers on modernisation, social change and development. A similar sentiment, however, is expressed eloquently by Fatouma Agnes Diarra, a Nigerian sociologist. 'Migration is not itself a misfortune. Migration is bad when it alienates and oppresses a people. Migration is acceptable or desirable when it permits the process of an "emancipating modernization" at the same time that it permits inter-ethnic and international contact in the spirit of African solidarity.' 'Les relations entre les hommes et les femmes et les migrations des Zarma'. Conference on Migration in Africa, IDEP/IAI, Dakar, Mar.–Apr. 1971, p. 34, reprinted in S. Amin (ed.), *Modern Migrations in Western Africa*, OUP, International African Institute, 1974, pp. 226–38.

10. Elliott P. Skinner, 'Labour migration among the Mossi of the Upper Volta', in Hilda Kuper, ed., *Urbanization and Migration in West Africa*, University of California Press, Berkeley and Los Angeles, 1965, p. 63.

11. *Ibid.*, pp. 62–3.

12. Georges Sanogoh, 'Les migrations Voltaiques', *Notes et documents Voltaiques* 4, Jan–Mar. 1971, pp. 3–5; A. Songre, J.-M. Sawadogo and G. Sanogoh, 'Réalities et effets de l'émigration massive des Voltaiques dans le contexte de l'Afrique Occidentale', in Amin, ed., *Modern Migration in Western Africa*, pp. 384–406.

13. R. Deniel, *De la savane à la ville*, Aubier-Montaigne, Paris, 1968, pp. 44–5.

14. Skinner, 'Labour migration', p. 66.

15. Le Secrétariat du Comité Monétaire de la Zone Franc, *La Zone Franc en 1966 . . . 1970*, Paris, 1967 to 1971.

16. RHV, Ministere du Plan, Direction du Plan et des Etudes de Développement, *Investissements financés en Haute-Volta par les fonds d'aide et de coopération de la République Française, 1959–1971*, Ougadougou, 1972, pp. 3–4. République Française Direction de la Documentation, 'La République de Haute-Volta' *Notes et Etudes Documentaires* (3818–3819), Sept. 1971, p. 63.

17. See EDIAFRIC, *L'industrie Africaine en 1970*, vol. II, Paris, 1970, pp. 359–61.

18. Joel W. Gregory, 'Development and in-migration in Upper Volta', in Amin, ed., *Modern Migration in Western Africa*, pp. 305–20.

19. Le Secrétariat du Comité Monétaire, *La Zone Franc en 1966 . . .*

20. RHV, Service de la Statistique, *Enquête démographique* (1970) vol. 1, p. 159.

21. G. LeCour Grandmaison, 'Migrations et croissance économique en Côte d'Ivoire', Montreal, Oct. 1969, 14; Jacques Hauser, 'Les grands problèmes du continent: 4, la traite des travailleurs', *Jeune Afrique*, 525, 26 Jan. 1971, pp. 55–61; and Madeleine Trebous, *Migration and Development*: *The Case of Algeria*, OECD, Paris, 1970, pp. 202–4.

22. Richard W. Stephens, *Population Pressures in Africa South of the Sahara*, Washington, D.C.: Department of Sociology, George Washington University, 1968, p. 20.

23. RHV, Service de la Statistique, *Recensement démographique Ouagadougou, 1961–1962, résultats définitifs*, INSEE and Secrétariat d'Etat aux Affaires Etrangères, Paris, 1964, p. 15.

24. For a discussion of land tenure and work habits among the Mossi see R. Christophe Sawadogo, *Etude d'une coopérative agricole en milieu rural, la société coopérative du lac Bam*, unpublished mémoire de maîtrise, University of Paris, 1970, pp. 51–2. For a survey of practices among major ethnic groups in Upper Volta see R. Verdier, 'Problèmes fonciers Voltaiques', *Penant* 74, Apr.–June 1964, pp. 263–9.

25. The literature on this subject is incomplete; many works refer to the question of African class formation in passing. Most observers see some class consciousness developing although they differ widely as to the extent. See among others: Abdoulaye Bara Diop, *Initiations Africaines, XVIII, société Toucouleur et migration*, IFAN, Dakar 1965; Walter Elkan, *Migrants and Proletarians*, OUP, Nairobi, 1960; Marie-Hélène le Divelec, 'Les nouvelles classes sociales en milieu urbain: le cas du Senegal et celui du Nigeria du Nord', *Civilisations* 17, 1967, pp. 240–53; Philip Mayer, 'Migrancy and the study of Africans in towns', *American Anthropologist*, lxiv, 3, June 1962, pp. 576–92; and Pierre Verneuil, 'L'exploitation des paysans à Madagascar et la formation du sous-développement dans l'agriculture', Paris, n.d., mimeo.

26. Peter A. Cornelisse, 'Aspects économiques de la migration en Afrique de l'Ouest: étude de deux pays', *Notes et Documents Voltaiques* 5, Apr.–Jun 1972, pp. 32–56; RHV, Service de la Statistique *Enquête démographique . . . les émigrations* (1972) p. 93; and RHV, Ministère de Travaux Publics et Société Centrale pour l'Equipement du Territoire, *Etude socio-economique de Bobo-Dioulasso*, SEDES, Paris 1969 pp. 49 and 69.

27. Elsewhere I have discussed schooling in detail. See 'Urbanization and Development Planning in Upper Volta: The Education Variable', in Robert A. Obudho and Salah S. H. El-Shackhs eds., *Urbanization, National Development and Regional Planning in Africa*, Praeger, New York 1973, pp. 130–42.

28. Jean Hochet, *Origines psycho-sociologiques de l'exode rural des jeunes en Haute-Volta*, CDPP, Ouagadougou 1963, *passim*.

29. In rural Upper Volta one does not observe buildings constructed or machinery purchased by returned migrants or with the money sent by migrants. This observation is consistent with earlier studies, including Hans Panofsky, 'The significance of labour migration for the economic welfare of Ghana and the Voltaic Republic', *Bulletin of the Inter-African Labour Institute* 7, July 1970, pp. 30–44. This is in contrast to rural improvements made by migrants in other parts of Africa; see, for example, E. Dussauze-Ingrand, 'L'émigration Sarokollaise du Guidimaka', Conference on Migration in Africa, IDEP/IAI, Dakar, Mar.–Apr. 1972, reprinted in Amin, ed., *Modern Migration in Western Africa*, pp. 239–57.

30. Deniel, *De la savane*, pp. 152–5 and Jean Hochet, *Inadaptation et délinquance juvenile en Haute-Volta*, CVRS, Ouagadougou, 1967, pp. 56–9.

31. The relationship between migration and unbalanced employment structure is widely discussed in development literature. For Africa, the following works are among the more provocative: Ralph E. Beals, Mildred B. Levy and Leon N. Moses, 'Rationality and migration in Ghana', *The Review of Economics and Statistics*, xlix, 4, Nov. 1967, pp. 480–6; Elliot J. Berg, 'Back-

ward-sloping labour functions in dual economies – the Africa case', *Quarterly Journal of Economics*, lxxv, 3, Aug. 1961, pp. 468–92; Carl K. Eicher, 'Tackling Africa's employment problems: agriculture offers the best prospects for absorbing labour, but present policies must change', *Africa Report*, xvi, 1, Jan. 1971, pp. 30–3; E. M. Godfrey, 'Labour-surplus models and labour-deficient economies: the West African case', *Economic Development and Cultural Change*, xvii, 3, Apr. 1969, pp. 382–91; and J. K. Hart, 'Migration and the opportunity structure: a Ghanaian case study', in Amin, ed., *Modern Migration in Western Africa*, pp. 321–42.

32. Ministère du Travail, Direction du Travail, *Statistique 1961* and *1970*, Ouagadougou, 1963 and 1971.

33. See, for example: Elliot J. Berg, 'The economics of the migrant labour system', in Kuper, ed., *Urbanization and Migration*, pp. 160–81; and Hans W. Singer, 'Brief note on unemployment rates in developing countries', *Manpower and Unemployment Research in Africa*, 3, Apr. 1970, p. 2.

34. This is a very limited measure of unemployment as it includes only jobs and job-seekers registered at the national employment office. RHV, *Statistique 1961* and *1970*.

35. Michael A. Cohen, 'The "sans-travail" demonstrations: the politics of frustration in Ivory Coast', *Manpower and Unemployment Research in Africa*, 5, Apr. 1972, p. 22.

36. P. C. Lloyd, *Africa in Social Change*, Penguin, Baltimore, 1967, p. 95.

37. G. LeCour Grandmaison, 'Migration et croissance', pp. 17–8; D. Ian Pool, 'The development of population policies', *Journal of Modern African Studies*, ix, 1, may 1971, p. 17; and Elliott P. Skinner, 'Labour migration and its relation to socio-cultural change in Mossi society', *Africa*, xxx, 4, Oct. 1960, p. 398. For a theoretical discussion of the unconventional idea that out-migration is not economically rational for the rural sector see R. Albert Berry and Ronald Soligo, 'Rural-urban migration, agricultural output and the supply price of labour in a labour-surplus economy', *Oxford Economic Papers*, New Series, xx, 2, July 1968, pp. 230–49.

38. RHV, Ministère du Plan, Direction du Plan et des Etudes du Développement, *La situation de l'économie Voltaique à l'issue de Premier Plan*, Ouagadougou, 1971.

39. RHV, *Statistique 1970*.

40. Skinner, 'Labour migration among the Mossi', p. 66.

41. A. Mabogunje, *Urbanization in Nigeria*, Africana Publishing Company, New York, 1968, especially pp. 315–17.

42. EDIAFRIC, *L'industrie*, pp. 359–61. RHV, Office des postes et télécommunications, *Répertoire officiel des téléphones 1972*, Imprimerie Presses Africaines, Ouagadougou, 1972.

43. Oumarou Dao, 'Culture cotonnière et développement agricole dans la région de Hounde', *Notes et Documents Voltaique*, 2, July–Sept. 1969, pp. 18–27.

44. The price for first choice cotton paid by the CFDT to the farmer has steadily falled from 34 Fr.CFA/kilogram in 1964 to 30 Fr. in 1970. Second choice has fallen from 30 to 28. Soumana Traore, *Systèmes fonciers et problematiques de*

développement rural en Haute-Volta, unpublished mémoire, first year, doctorat de troisième cycle, University of Paris I, 1971, p. 31.

45. Dao, 'Culture cotonnière', p. 5.
46. République Française, *Notes et Etudes*, pp. 24–31; EDIAFRIC, *L'industrie Africaine en 1970*, Vol. II, pp. 351–82; and *Annuaire des entreprises et organismes d'outre-mer*, 1967, Renemoreaux, Paris, 1967; *Guid'Ouest Africain*, Yvetot, 1971, pp. 161–212.
47. *Ibid.*
48. RHV, Plan Cadre 1967–1970, vol. II, Paris, 1968, pp. 115, 137–8; and RHV, *La situation de l'économie*, annex II, pp. 7–11.
49. See notes 47 and 48.

Roger Leys

5 Lesotho: Non-Development or Underdevelopment. Towards an Analysis of the Political Economy of the Labour Reserve

This chapter is intended as a re-examination of current analyses in the social sciences about Lesotho and, by extension, has some relevance to the analysis of the political economy of all those regions of Africa that Samir Amin has characterised as labour reserves (i.e. the primary characteristic of the dominant capitalist mode of production in southern Africa).[1] By insisting that migrant labour – which at any given time involves about 45 per cent of Lesotho's adult male population in working in the Republic of South Africa – is the key to understanding Lesotho's current predicaments, one is not saying anything new. Lesotho's dependence on migrant labour to the Republic of South Africa has existed for 100 years and has been noted by many.

> The guiding principle (of colonial rule) was that the territories exist to supply the requirements of the Union's labour markets, without any claim for reciprocal benefits and regardless of the effects on the vitality, the tribal organization or the economic conditions of the territories themselves.[2]

Furthermore, the work of social scientists and planners in Lesotho today does reveal a fundamental awareness of the dependence of Lesotho on the economy of South Africa. But much of this work tends to adopt a passive stance *vis-à-vis* the basic premises of imperialism, the dynamics of historical underdevelopment and the formulation of alternative development strategies which do not take current market relationships as given. In this sense, the stance of social science is apologetic.

A basic trait of current analyses of Lesotho is the use of a type of circular reasoning. For example, that the pressure of population on land leads to soil erosion which increases the pressure of population on land. This form of reasoning is frequently used to 'explain' Lesotho's dependent status. Certainly, at one level, such explanations are true. Soil erosion in Lesotho is horrific, gulleys (dongas) can grow 10 yards (9 m) a year, and this increases population pressure on the available arable land that is left.[3] That such explanations fail to give an historical and genetic understanding of how this situation arose and what is its inner dynamic will be regarded by many as an irrelevant objection. The only relevant criteria are those which can be used to assess the degree to which such studies illuminate current realities. In a word, they tell it as it really is. But, at another level, such analyses obscure what they purport to illuminate.[4] This is the level at which such explanations are used as a basis for policy-making, for defining plan targets and, even, outlining development strategies. These tasks are inherently political. Not in the banal sense that they are the tasks of the 'politicians' but in the sense that these tasks require assessing alternatives. They involve asking why did this situation come about and not another one. What is the dynamic of this process? What can be done to stop it and, above all, who can do the stopping?

Social analysts cannot do the stopping but they can provide some ammunition. About Lesotho, specifically, three key questions emerge:

1. What are the historical circumstances that ensured the dominance of external markets for labour, commodities and capital? Does such analysis identify key points of leverage?

2. How does capital in the 'core' areas of economic growth – in the case of Lesotho primarily the mining industry of the Republic of South Africa – ensure the conditions for its expanded reproduction? Will, for example, the use of an increasingly capital-intensive technology coupled with the xenophobia that apartheid ideology generates bring about an increasing marginalisation of the Basotho?

3. How can the size of Lesotho's surplus – generated by migrant labour but largely accumulated as capital in the Republic and to overseas shareholders – be calculated? What are the consequences of this calculation for measuring the opportunity cost of migrant labour and the cost to Lesotho of providing the social overhead capital – in education, infrastructure and administration, etc., by which this labour power is reproduced?

The chapter that follows is divided into four sections. The first section contains comments on the general frame of reference for the Marxist analysis of a labour reserve economy. The second section gives a brief background to the current situation of Lesotho, especially the economy. The third section contains an empirical critique of current 'non-development' interpretations of Lesotho and the fourth section attempts an analysis of the 'underdevelopment'[5] of the political economy of Lesotho within the political economy of southern Africa and a short comment on current perspectives.

1. The Marxist Analysis of a Labour Reserve Economy: From Pre-Capitalism to the Dominance of the Capitalist Mode of Production

In raising the question of why labour ever began to migrate from Lesotho to the Republic of South Africa, we cannot avoid encountering two colliding traditions of analysis. According to what I will term the apologetic tradition, the transition from pre-capitalism to dominant capitalism is explained by those factors that engender capitalist development. The question – why did labour migrate to the Republic? – is according to this analysis not very meaningful. The question, in the dualist tradition of analysis, is answered by reference to the automatic pull of the growth poles on the subsistence sector. The peasant in the subsistence sector, on the basis of a rational calculation of his economic choices, finds the opportunity costs of labour in the modern sector lower than the opportunity costs of labour in the traditional, subsistence sector. The more so if, as Lewis has argued, there is a surplus of labour in the subsistence sector.[6] Hence the question: why does the Mosotho peasant migrate? translates into the question: why does the Mosotho peasant behave rationally?

But according to the Marxist tradition of analysis, the transition to capitalism requires one basic condition – the creation of a labour market. Hence a process by which the Basotho begin to sell their labour on the market, a process of proletarianisation, must be set in motion. Marxism does not argue that, in an encounter with capitalism, pre-capitalist modes of production are inherently inferior. The process of primitive accumulation and the way in which – usually by political violence – capitalist dominance is achieved has to be historically specified. On theoretical grounds there is no case for the argument that capitalism would *automatically* pull labour out of the subsistence sector. It is, indeed, theoretically possible to argue that pre-capitalist production is more 'efficient' than capitalist. The rewards to the factors of production are simply different. In essence, the problem facing capitalism is that it is impossible to break into the closed circle of peasant and artisan without recourse to non-economic means.[7] A further point, extremely relevant to southern Africa, is that if a capitalist market incentive is applied to African pre-capitalist society and to the extended type of agriculture practised by British and Boer, then there are no grounds for assuming that white will 'triumph' over black unless there is recourse to political violence (and historical experience suggests that, without violence, black societies could compete successfully with white).[8]

(a)   The critique of dualism[9]

A presumption of this chapter is that readings of underdevelopment which emphasise the 'non-development' characteristic of the political economy of underdevelopment rest, explicitly or implicitly, on a dualist model of economic growth. The dualist model is explicitly descriptive but implicitly prescriptive. Current social science readings of Lesotho purport to describe the predicaments facing the Basotho in a totally objective fashion. However, the dualist assumption of a pristine traditional sector with surplus labour which finds opportunities through migration (*a*) is belied by the economic history of South Africa's modern sector which has been characterised by a shortage of cheap black labour at the price South African capital was willing to pay and able to enforce given their political power, and (*b*) treats the emergence and dynamic of migrant labour as a structural characteristic in the political economy of southern Africa, i.e. as a natural phenomenon in the sense that it obeys strictly 'economic' laws. Nothing could be further from reality. Historical experience shows that it is the creation of a political structure – labour recruiting organisations, the establishment of black labour reserves, the direction of the labour supply and the suppression of trade unions and political organisations of black workers – that gives rise to the migrant labour.

However, the difference between the type of approach offered to the study of labour migration by Lewis, Houghton and the dualists on the one hand and such Marxist analysts as Arrighi and Amin on the other cannot be seen in isolation. It is intimately related to a more fundamental conflict between Marxism and bourgeois social science. Is there a fundamental and irreconcilable conflict between Marxist and bourgeois social science? Given that the fundamental purpose of Marxist analysis is not to describe reality but to change it, Marxist analysis is inherently revolutionary. Theory and analysis is a weapon in the organisational, cultural and military liberation struggle. Bourgeois social science emerges out of that situation which is the subject of analysis. Bourgeois theory and models have, in this context, an ideological function in terms of legitimising the structure of exploitation and oppression (however disparate and seemingly pluralist).

On the other hand, it is clear that the revolutionary struggle is in need of information that comes from a very eclectic set of sources. Marx himself made extensive use of highly eclectic information in *Capital*. Hence, the position of the self-proclaimed Marxist who rejects the body of bourgeois research on the basis of *his or her* revolutionary intentions is clearly absurd. And, at a more profound level, it is hard to locate an epistemological break in Marx's own writings.[10]

But the question of reconcilability obviously goes deeper than the somewhat trite observation that Marx and Engels were historians. The process by which a given set of ideas achieves hegemony and then recedes is, in essence, not determined by thought but by struggle. This was true of Marx as it is of the rise of national and class liberation forces in the world today. Ten years ago, the ideas of modern functionalism – of modernisation and political development – had such an hegemonic position in bourgeois social science. These ideas were clearly American in origin and their strength reflected not merely the strength of imperialism as such but the strength of American political and military power within the imperialist system. The dominant position of the US in the imperialist bloc is today under challenge from a variety of internal and external revolutionary forces. And it is this challenge that has shaken the hegemony of functionalist ideas, not the scholastic critique of any number of Marxists who emerged *deus ex machina* in this period.[11] As a consequence of this crisis, the hegemony of US social and political science is undergoing a crisis. The years of facile optimism about modernisation and political development are a thing of the past and the methodology which gave rise to this thinking is also under attack. For this reason a body of literature is emerging which gives a trenchant critique to such ideas as modernisation and political development – their ideological and ethnocentric assumptions, theoretical inadequacy and inefficacy as a policy guide.[12] The reactions of bourgeois social science to this crisis and the critique it has generated have been many and varied. Some have abandoned any claim to theoretical generality and retreated into case and area studies. Others are engaged in a frantic effort to resurrect a new 'science' of political economy that will borrow some of the terminology of Marxism and yet strip it of its historical materialism and its revolutionary objectives. The result is frequently a hotch-potch of unrelated 'concepts', 'variables' and 'models' that serve scholars little purpose other than to divert their and their students' attention from substantial issues.

And yet it is the existence of this crisis that does enable us to operate with a kind of 'epistemological threshold'[13] in which we are no longer so easily diverted by the charms of scholasticism – be it bourgeois or Marxist. We are both more able in this situation to give a sober measurement to the adequacy of existing social 'science' to explain reality when we are unencumbered by the methodological baggage of current social science literature and we are forced to ask ourselves the purpose and meaning of our own work. Were this not so there would be no way of evaluating the current interpretations of reality on and within Lesotho or anywhere else. And were it not so, there would be no point to the exercise.

(b) Proletarianisation in the labour reserve economy

The point of departure for the analysis of the political economy of the labour reserve in Lesotho is the process of proletarianisation, the creation and the dynamic of wage labour. We are fortunate here in being able to draw upon the scientific work of a penetrating study of this process in another labour reserve economy in southern Africa, that of Arrighi on the proletarianisation of the African peasantry in Rhodesia.[14] Since the framework and concepts in this analysis of underdevelopment in Lesotho will be closely related to those of Arrighi it will be useful to summarise his arguments and basic concepts.

In his analysis of the proletarianisation of the African peasantry in Rhodesia, Arrighi has argued that the supply of African labour to the European farms and plantations was not, when considered historically, primarily determined by wage rates but rather should be seen as a set of structural changes in which:

1. In the first stage – 1903–22 – a set of 'non-economic' mechanisms such as land appropriation and the imposition of taxation raised the 'effort price' of African participation in the peasant economy.

2. In the second stage – 1922–45 – a process of self-sustained underdevelopment had been set in motion. In the period an increasing supply of labour is offered on the market without a corresponding increase in wages. The momentum of this process is sustained by a number of 'vicious circle' factors – soil erosion for example.

The broad conclusion of Arrighi's analysis is that

While before 1922 African participation in the labour market did not increase in periods of falling real wages, after that year it always increased irrespective of whether real wages were falling, rising or remaining constant.[15]

Three elements in Arrighi's analysis further illuminate the process of proletarianisation in Lesotho:

1. The wages of migrant workers were determined not by market mechanisms but by the custom of the subsistence wage.

Market mechanisms were largely discarded in the determination of wages and the real wage came to be customarily fixed at a level that would provide for the subsistence of a *single* worker while working in the capitalist sector and a small margin to meet the more urgent of the cash income requirements of his family who continued to reside in the peasant sector.[16]

For a more general analysis of the conditions governing the development of underdevelopment in southern Africa this point would need elaboration. The establishment of such a 'subsistence' wage in the colonial period is not simply the result of a quaint historical tradition. The physical reproduction of the family unit requires both food crops and cash crops.

2. Arrighi argues that the term 'subsistence requirements' is not to be understood in an exclusive, physiological sense and that a part of the process of the distortion of the Rhodesian economy was the substitution of demands that would be satisfied within the subsistence sector by demands that could only be satisfied within the capitalist sector. While in the short-run, in periods of falling real income this consumption can be cut back, in the long-run the result is that African people would be compelled to sell their labour time in order to satisfy their *subsistence* requirements. Arrighi describes this process as the transformation of 'discretionary' cash requirements into 'necessary' requirements.

3. The process of self-sustained underdevelopment which occurred after 1922 was precipitated by a slump in cattle and maize prices. There followed a sharp increase in labour migration which set in motion a 'vicious circle' or 'cumulative evil' since

> the future ability of the Africans who had migrated to obtain their cash requirements through the sale of produce was, of course, jeopardised.[17]

The very reliance of the household economy on cash remittances from migrant labour meant that it was essential to retain extended family ties at all costs. This peculiar type of economy in which the migrant earnings subvent the production of the household plot which, in turn, subvents the wages of the migrant, requires that the social relationships of the family have to be defended at all cost – even when this defence appears irrational to agricultural advisers and others concerned with the problem of soil erosion and the vicious circle of immiseration in the peasant economy.

(c) The structural and opportunity-costs of migrant labour

In attempting to assess the 'costs' and 'benefits' of migrant labour in West Africa, Samir Amin in a recent paper relates the problem squarely to the nature of the labour market.[18] He regards it as characteristic of apologetic and marginalist economic thought to regard the existing distribution of the factors of production – labour and capital[19] – as given. Amin insists that in Senegal the existing distribution of labour and capital is the result of the development strategy of the colonial period which enforced peanut production for export. An alternative development strategy based on the development of intensive, irrigated agriculture of rice and market produce is precluded by the requirements of international capitalism. Hence development policies directed towards the extension of the peasant crop are not, for Senegal, either more or less 'rational'. Whether they are rational or not depends on the underlying development strategy.

> There is no 'economic rationality' in itself, independent of the point of view on which it is based. What is rational from Senegal's point of view – the exploitation of the Fleuve – is not so from the point of view of the world system, because self-sufficient economies based on this alternative would have difficulty in 'reimbursing' capital which would then appear as real aid. On the other hand, what is irrational from Senegal's point of view – the extension of peanut agriculture – is perfectly rational from the point of view of the world system. Because of the deterioration of the terms of exchange, from which Senegal cannot escape as a result of its export-based economy (peanuts must be exported): what is 'unfortunate' for this country, will be 'beneficial' for the world system and it is this that determines its choice.[20]

Amin further attempts a cost-benefit analysis of the migration of labour from the West African interior to the coast. This analysis is not based on the existing distribution of the factors of production. This would not be possible since current development strategy does not provide capital and hence employment opportunities in the West African interior. Amin's analysis contrasts current remittances from the labour of migrants (estimated at US $18 million a year) with estimates of the profits made by coastal planters from the labour of migrants (approximately $75 million).

Amin's conclusion is that the whole export-oriented foreign capital basis of the economy of the labour reserve must be called into question before an estimate can be made of the costs and benefits of migrant labour. But a major problem with this type of analysis is that it does not, *ipso facto*, reveal how this export orientation can be 'called in to question'. Who, in brief, can stop it? The answer to this question lies in an historical examination of how this export domination emerged, what perpetuates it and of the forces opposed to it.

2. Background to Lesotho's Economy

Lesotho is an arid, land-locked mountain kingdom of some 30 340 square kilometres. It is situated in the middle of South Africa's most mountainous region, the Drakensberg Mountains, that rise to a height of nearly 12 000 feet (3 657 m). To the east and south the land falls away sharply to Natal and the Cape Province and, to the west, more gently to the Caledon river which marks the boundary between Lesotho and the Orange Free State. Although Lesotho lies within the temperate zone, its altitude – over 5 000 feet (1 524 m) at the lowest points on the Caledon river border – gives it an erratic climate. In the winter the mountains are snow-covered and the winds howl through the mountain passes; and in the summer, the sun scorches the bare, eroded earth.

The total population of the kingdom of Lesotho is estimated at some 1 100 000. Of the active male labour force, perhaps 225 000, it is estimated that at any one time, some 150 000 are working across the border in the Republic of South Africa.[21] Five out of every six adult males in paid employment are migrant workers in the Republic so, in this respect, Lesotho is an almost perfect example of the labour reserve economy. Basotho workers in the Republic are concentrated in the mining industry where Basotho are famed for their physical toughness.

Lesotho is one of the poorest countries in the world and a rough estimate of gross national product per capita is US $100. Infant mortality is estimated at 106 per 1 000 live births.[22] Exactly what percentage of the population live in poverty is difficult to estimate and depends on the definition of poverty. A poverty datum line study for the city of Maseru estimated that in 1972–73, only 40 per cent of Maseru households were above the poverty line.[23] And the proportion for rural households is certainly far higher since living costs are higher but fewer are in wage employment.

Most of the population of Lesotho are rural and raise crops – maize and sorghum in the lowlands and wheat and beans in the foothills and mountains – but the income that can be gained from agriculture is so low that crop cultivation can only provide a means of livelihood for those with extensive flocks of cattle, sheep and goats. This predicament applies to the vast majority of the population, to those with an independent cash income – predominantly from migrant labour. Furthermore there is evidence that agricultural production is, per head of population, declining as the pressure of population on existing arable land (and only 13 per cent of this mountainous country is suitable for crop cultivation) increases.[24] Ecologically, Lesotho is declining rapidly.[25] One result of this is that, despite the efforts to encourage industrial development, the World Bank Report estimates

in real terms total GDP per capita has fallen slightly over the last decade or so, but this decrease has been compensated by an increase in remittances from migrant workers. GNP per capita, therefore, may have remained stable at $100.[26]

The British Protectorate of Basutoland became the Independent kingdom of Lesotho in 1966 under a minority party rule, that of the Basutoland National Party with its leader, Chief Leabua Jonathan, as Prime Minister. In 1970, Jonathan conducted what amounted to a *coup d'état* by declaring a state of emergency when the results of a remarkably open and fair election showed a clear victory for the opposition party, the Basuto Congress Party.[27]

Lesotho is a near-perfect example of 'flag-independence'. Economically, Lesotho is a hostage of the Republic of South Africa. Politically, Chief Jonathan and his government can and do make noises against apartheid (governed partly by the extent to which it suits the white regime in Pretoria to show their tolerance by permitting this militancy). But, economically, Lesotho is totally dependent on imports from the Republic and on the earnings of Basotho migrants in the Republic.

Since Independence in 1966, the government has made efforts to diversify the economy and to bring about industrial development. The spearhead of these activities has been the Lesotho

National Development Corporation (LNDC). Between 1967 and 1972 the LNDC is estimated to have provided 20 million rand (US $1=R0·86). The LNDC engages in both joint ventures and in outright ownership. A candle factory, a carpet and weaving factory, a pottery and other small workshops have been constructed but their output is so small and the numbers employed so few that their total effect on output and employment has been very limited.[28] The greatest expansion has taken place in the tourist trade, especially the Holiday Inn hotel and gambling casino.

Lesotho's hopes for spectacular economic development previously hinged on the Oxbow Scheme – a plan to dam the Malibamatso river (one of the sources of the Orange River) and to sell hydro-electric power to the Republic. But negotiations with the Republic failed to agree on a price for power that would make the scheme economically viable for Lesotho, and today the scheme is in abeyance. Current schemes for irrigation and power are based on the domestic market and the objective of self-sufficiency.

Table 5.1 Deferred Pay Plus Remittances. January 1963–July 1974[30] (yearly totals in Rands)

1963	1964	1965	1966	1967	1968
1 721 868	1 850 431	2 199 546	2 148 309	2 162 984	2 141 885

1969	1970	1971	1972	1973	Jan.–July 1974
2 703 377	3 956 460	4 708 150	5 818 175	8 642 610	6 050 395

Despite these efforts, Lesotho's dependence on the earnings of migrant workers has increased rather than decreased since independence. A main reason for this is that with the rise of the price of gold and the growing shortage of black goldminers in the Republic, wages on the mines have risen considerably in the last two years (from a starting shift rate of R0·70 in 1972 to a starting shift rate of R1·60 in 1974) and it is estimated that migrant workers bring home more than R60 million annually.[29] The rate of growth of Lesotho's earnings from migrant labour has been spectacular as the figures in Table 5.1 illustrate.

A calculation by Michael Ward indicates that migrant remittances alone represent an increasing proportion of Gross Domestic Product – from 11 per cent in 1966–67 to 18 per cent in 1970–71.[31] These percentages clearly underestimate the real return to Lesotho since they do not include cash and goods that the miners bring home with them. One estimate of the financial return to Lesotho from migrant workers for a 12-month period (1972–1973) gave the following[32]

Deferred pay (1972 figure)	R3 420 000
Remittances	R5 820 000
Cash in hand	R2 820 000
Goods in hand	R3 850 000
Total	R15 910 000

As one of the poorest twenty countries that are member states of the United Nations, Lesotho receives priority in multilateral assistance. A wealth of multilateral and bilateral assistance projects exists. Some, such as the Thaba Bosiu Rural Development Project (TBRDP) designed to achieve substantial improvements in agricultural output in the lowlands and foothills of the Maseru district are relatively large (TBRDP will have an outlay of over $8 million in under five years) and others very small. But the net benefit of these projects is difficult to assess. On the one hand, they provide a trickle of jobs, cash and credit. On the other hand they have a direct financial cost: they also tend to increase Lesotho's dependence on external market forces and give rise to a wealthy expatriate community of 'experts', centred in the capital city, Maseru, and commuting frequently to white South Africa, which makes a very visible and obvious source of privilege and inequality.

But however these projects are viewed, few assume that they can, in themselves, make a substantial contribution to alleviating poverty and decreasing Lesotho's economic dependence on the Republic. Lesotho is, and for the foreseeable future will be, a labour reserve of the Republic of South Africa. To understand how this dependence came about and what factors sustain it is crucial to any discussion of development and underdevelopment in Lesotho.

3. 'Non-Development' Interpretations of Lesotho – A Critique

(a) Interpretations of Lesotho's economy

Firstly we will attempt a brief evaluation of current social science analyses of Lesotho's development and potential. The reason for this critique is, let us hope, motivated less by a desire for academic point-scoring than to reveal the ideological frame of reference of this critique and the role it plays in deflecting attention from the real sources of exploitation in Lesotho – the sectors of South African capital that employ Basotho labour, especially the gold-mining industry, the South African white regime which receives considerable income from the gold-mining industry and the international capital invested there.

Economic analysts of Lesotho are agreed on two principal points. One is that the economy is dependent on South Africa which 'provides' five out of every six jobs. The other is that no alternative strategy than a continuance of this dependence is conceivable in the near future. There are, of course, variations and nuances within this broad agreement. Some interpretations feel no need to explain why Lesotho is underdeveloped and tend to advocate a strategy of ever closer links between Lesotho and the Republic of South Africa.[33] Other explanations account for the absence of industrialisation by reference to colonial neglect and to the 'pull' on production factors of South African industrial growth.[34] But, by and large, both explanations offer the same solution. An active government policy requires the modernisation of the economic structure and the traditional values and attitudes that inhibit growth. By doing so the 'traditional' sector, the subsistence economy, will disappear. But the relationship between migrant labour and the perpetuation of the subsistence economy is not considered. That 'traditionalism' exists is taken for granted. But why it persists after a hundred years of wage labour in the Republic is, in this type of analysis, not explained at all.

(b) Industrial development: spatial and social dualism

A penetrating analysis of industrial development strategy for Lesotho has been made by Selwyn.[35] While this analysis is only preliminary it deserves intensive study. Selwyn's analysis is based on three types of dualism: spatial, sectoral and social. The starting point for his analysis is that Lesotho's economy cannot be studied in isolation but only as a part of the wider study of the South African economy as a whole. Selwyn emphasises the factors that tend to drain off both labour and capital from Lesotho to the 'core' areas of growth in the Republic. Analysing the market for Basotho labour in the Republic, Selwyn puts forward the cautious hypothesis that Lesotho can benefit from the anomaly that, although she is part of the labour market of the Republic, she is not subject to the job-reservation policy as practised in South Africa. Hence, in theory, Lesotho could supply skilled labour at a price below that required for white, skilled labour. But Selwyn also analyses the impediments to such a strategy. Some of these impediments are part of the very backwardness and traditionalism of Lesotho – the lack of entrepreneurship, the absence of credit and financial institutions for investing in Lesotho, lack of management skills and of information as to market possibilities in the Republic. These impediments Selwyn attributes to sectoral dualism: in brief, that Lesotho is part of the subsistence sector of the dual economy of southern Africa as a whole. This spatial and sectoral dualism is exacerbated by social dualism – the apartheid policies of the Republic which *in effect* treat black Basotho workers with exactly the same degree of discrimination as black South Africans are treated.

This analysis provides a useful descriptive paradigm but contains central flaws as soon as it is used to 'explain' the absence of industrialisation. Here Selwyn argues that

> unskilled labour wages have been kept down not only by the existence of a pool of unemployed but also by the weak bargaining position of African workers resulting from discriminatory legislation.[36]

But how was this pool of unemployed created and what undermined the surplus-generating capacity of the Basotho people? The existence of labour surplus – the reserve army of the unemployed – is treated in the dualist analysis as a cause of the low wages paid in the modern sector. But, and this is a point we will explore later, the history of capitalist development in South Africa, particularly in the gold mining industry, is a history of a chronic shortage of black labour.[37] The crux of the matter is that the dualist analysis – while insisting on its descriptive character – develops a model of underdevelopment according to which the low wages paid in the modern sector are brought about by low opportunity costs in the traditional sector. *But it is the structural character of wage labour that is the root of low wages in both 'modern' and 'traditional' sectors.*

(c) 'Non-development' interpretations of migrant labour

Few analyses have attempted to come to grips with the problem of why labour began to migrate from Lesotho to the Republic. Leistner has an interesting analysis that concentrates on recruitment of Basotho by the Chamber of Mines (formerly, the Transvaal and Orange Free State Chamber of Mines).[38] This indicates that in 1904 the number of migrant workers in the gold mines was only 2 300 – a figure which rose slowly to 20 900 in 1930, and then more rapidly to 50 000 by the outbreak of the Second World War. Leistner's general explanation for this steady growth is the pull on production factors of South Africa's industrial development. The explanation for the rapid increase in the rate of migration after 1930 is partly the effect of a serious drought which led to widespread famine in Lesotho and partly the world economic crisis which led to a catastrophic fall in Lesotho's earnings from exports of maize, wool and mohair. Leistner also argues that a considerable part of the 'migrant' labour has, historically, been emigrant labour. By computing a natural population increase of 1·7 per cent per annum in the period 1936–56 and then comparing the census figures of *de jure* population for 1936 with those of 1956, Leistner estimates that at least 140 000 Basotho have been permanently absorbed in South Africa – a brawn and brain drain of incredible magnitude for a country with a population, in this period, of under three-quarters of a million.

In considering the economic implications of migrant labour, Williams also looks briefly at its historical development. He points out that

The institution of migrant labour flowing from Lesotho to South Africa is familiar to all and actually pre-dates the formal British annexation of Lesotho to Cape Colony in 1871. Writing in 1861 one of the first two missionaries to Lesotho

'stated that the country of the Basotho furnished the Cape
Colony every year with a great many workers who easily
found employment owing to the confidence inspired by their
reputation'. By 1892, 30 000 Basotho were working in South
African mines and on the Port Elizabeth railway.[39]

Table 5.2, used by Williams, shows the growth of migrant labour
for the period 1911–66.

Table 5.2. Basuto Migrants, 1911–66[39]

Year	Male	Female	Total	% of total *de jure* population
1911	21 658	2 972	24 630	5·8
1921	37 827	9 314	47 141	8·7
1936	78 604	22 669	101 273	15·3
1946	95 000	32 000	127 000	18·5
1956	112 000	41 992	154 782	19·5
1960	—	—	206 424	23·2
1964	—	—	164 000	—
1966	97 529	19 744	117 273	12·0

There is fairly widespread agreement that the migrant labour
system has extremely damaging effects on the economic and social
structure of Lesotho. These effects range from the concern,
especially of the missionaries, for the spiritual values, sexual and
mental health of the migrants and of their families in Lesotho,[40] to
that of anthropologists who have pointed out that village life is
crippled by the migrant labour system. Sandra Wallman, a leading authority on the Basotho,[41] argues that 'non-development' is
a function of three mutually-interrelated factors: poverty, migration and ideology. The pressure of population on land forces
the peasant to look for work outside the borders of Lesotho.
Migration disrupts the family and the wider organisation of
chieftainship. Furthermore the migrant's experience in cities like
Johannesburg and general contact with urban culture creates
expectations and wants that village life cannot satisfy. The
ideology or cultural climate of village engenders apathy. The
village and its mores are denigrated by the young migrant as not
'semate' (smart). Agriculturalists and economists have also stressed the damaging effects on cultivation and the care of livestock of

a society where the vast majority of the active male labour force cannot participate fully in rural development.[42]

The interpretations of the origin and dynamic of migrant labour are apologetic and ethnocentric. A closer look at the historical underdevelopment of Lesotho in the last thirty years of the nineteenth century reveals, as we shall see in the next section, that conscious and deliberate efforts were made to produce a labour reserve economy by applying a variety of 'non-economic' measures similar to those used in Rhodesia to the north. Furthermore, the concentration on migration after 1900 is misleading in two respects. Firstly, it ignores the fact that labour migration was endemic in this period and that, as census figures suggest, the proportion of the total *de jure* populations who were migrants was almost certainly as high in the 1880s as it was in the 1920s. What is also misleading is the use of the period immediately after the Boer War as a base line for measuring the rate of increase in labour migration. The figures for pass returns issued in 1901–02 were:[43]

Object of journey	No. of individuals
To work at the Kimberley, Jagersfontein and Cape coal mines	2 427
Farm and domestic labour	3 920
Employed by Army	8 847
Other purposes	27 549
Total	42 549

This total was exceedingly low compared with the average figure for pass returns in the last quarter of the nineteenth century and this is even commented on by the Resident Commissioner in the 1901–02 Basutoland Colonial Report: 'No deductions can be drawn from these figures, as they are merely the result of the disorganised circumstances of the year.' By 'disorganised circumstances' he clearly referred to the Boer War which had stopped production in the mining industry.

Turning to the crucial period of the depression in the world market and the years of drought in the early thirties, Leistner has argued that these factors had been largely responsible for the dramatic increase in migrant labour. The financial crisis that these events provoked, gave rise to a Commission of Enquiry (the Pim Report),[44] which provided some invaluable data with which to assess these arguments (see Table 5.3).

Table 5.3. Return of Passes Issued to Basotho to Enter the Union[44a]

Year	Labour			Total (Mining)	Agriculture	Railway Const.	Total Labour*	Grand Total†
	Gold	Coal	Diamonds					
1921	—	—	—	33 853	12 301	2 082	69 079	118 271
1922	—	—	—	23 947	11 578	2 032	57 663	117 192
1923	—	—	—	26 358	15 613	794	76 202	109 396
1924	—	—	—	32 002	14 834	862	88 627	130 468
1925	—	—	—	22 912	13 194	233	79 592	110 882
1926	—	—	—	34 504	19 217	659	95 864	134 769
1927	13 309	1 854	9 697	24 860	9 507	173	57 947	118 140
1928	15 490	764	9 269	25 523	7 353	284	53 878	111 840
1929	18 995	694	9 016	28 705	13 483	449	74 762	112 126
1930	21 571	572	6 383	28 526	12 778	185	64 787	113 022
1931	24 162	254	2 434	26 850	12 099	—	66 751	103 706
1932	25 542	47	62	25 751	12 678	—	58 057	96 067
1933	25 731	72	—	25 803	15 237	—	51 856	109 507

* Includes figures of passes issued for miscellaneous labour.

† Includes figures of passes issued for visiting in the Republic.

It is interesting to compare Table 5.3's figures of pass returns with data about exports of Lesotho's two principal products, wool and mohair, in the same period shown in Table 5.4.

There is no clear correlation between export earnings on wool and mohair and variations in the numbers of labour passes issued. Such a correlation might have been expected if production for export and migrant labour are regarded as alternative sources of cash earnings. The jump in recruitment between 1925 and 1926 may, however, have been caused by the poor returns for wool and mohair in 1925. In sum, neither the arguments suggesting a 'gradual' growth in labour migration, nor the arguments for the rapid increase in labour migration as caused by the recession in world prices are supported by the available evidence. Further, the concentration on the growth of mining and industrialisation in South Africa as the prime cause of labour migration from Lesotho in the twentieth century tends to neglect the substantial amount

Table 5.4. Lesotho's Exports 1921–33[44b]

Year	Wool		Mohair	
	quantity (lb)	value (£)	quantity (lb)	value (£)
1921	12 826 772	211 981	2 330 066	63 756
1922	12 829 330	377 333	2 326 367	104 833
1923	10 264 894	513 644	2 001 564	119 646
1924	11 577 384	715 665	2 455 950	183 076
1925	11 721 411	469 315	1 958 877	119 285
1926	12 131 574	427 047	2 156 603	121 098
1927	12 906 789	508 687	2 132 907	139 226
1928	12 726 153	610 750	1 921 189	139 484
1929	12 937 198	436 083	1 961 746	94 352
1930	9 729 169	156 601	942 725	21 837
1931	9 325 140	98 304	1 241 743	21 442
1932	11 832 391	105 435	1 033 863	10 136
1933	9 864 043	196 146	1 926 180	26 697

and extent of labour migration in the nineteenth century. We need another way of understanding the dynamics of labour migration from Lesotho to the Republic.

(d) 'Non-development' and political development

Most interpretations of political development in Lesotho are closely allied to the 'non-development' or 'vicious circle' form of explanation. They tend to involve a circularity by which development strategies and political constellations are explained by the absence of a meaningful alternative. Studies of Lesotho's political development frequently emphasise that, almost alone in sub-Saharan Africa, Lesotho is a homogeneous nation – its people speak one language, have no significant ethnic minorities[45] and have been united politically for over a hundred years. The history of Lesotho in the twentieth century has been dominated by one major threat, that of incorporation into the Republic of South Africa. In fact the Act of Union, which unified South Africa's four provinces made specific provision for the possible future incorporation of Lesotho and the other two High Commission Territories (Swaziland and Botswana) into the Union and, to a large extent, the British geared their colonial administration around such an eventual incorporation. And yet, despite the massive nature of this threat and the overwhelming presence of South Africa in Lesotho, modern politics in Lesotho have been bitter and divisive.

According to Weisfelder, one of the foremost authorities on the politics of Lesotho, the explanation of this paradox is to be sought in a deep conflict within the society as to the nature of the Basotho nation and its position in southern African and world affairs.[46] The Basutoland National Party (BNP) which came in power – on a minority vote and because the opposition was split – in 1966 formed the first government with Chief Leabua Jonathan as Prime Minister. The BNP is buttressed by the Catholic church and supported by a majority of the principal chiefs. It tends towards a definition of Basotho identity in a close, southern African context and has in the past, though less so today, accepted the need for a dialogue with the white regime in Pretoria. By contrast, the opposition Basuto Congress Party (BCP) is a 'grievance' party – with strong support among the Protestants and among the mineworkers and the intelligentsia. Far from conceptualising Basotho identity in terms of the present power structure within southern Africa, the BCP takes a more active Pan-Africanist stance (the party is, in origin, closely related to the African National Congress of South Africa although it also has had strong ties to the Pan-African Congress). In a recorded interview with the BCP leader, Ntsu Mokhehle, Weisfelder notes that when asked to imagine the role of Lesotho as a separate political entity within a liberated South Africa, Mokhehle saw no need for the continuance of a separate Lesotho political entity.[47]

On Friday, 30 January 1970, while election results were coming in that indicated a clear victory for the opposition BCP, Chief Jonathan declared a state of emergency and seized power. BCP leaders were detained and attempts were made to crush the BCP by physical force (although Chief Jonathan kept up negotiations with Mokhehle until the British restored aid that had been cut off after the coup).[48] Jonathan finally persuaded a number of prominent BCP members to accept nomination to the National Assembly. This was rejected by Mokhehle and the majority of the BCP's executive committee. Since the state of emergency in 1970 there has been a decidedly authoritarian trend in Lesotho politics. In January 1974 supporters of the BCP launched armed attacks on a number of police posts. In the raids and retaliation a considerable number of people were killed. Mokhehle fled into exile in Zambia.

A key thrust of Weisfelder's argument is that the BCP could not offer a realistic alternative to the policies advocated by the BNP. While a BCP victory might have led to a more militant stance *vis-à-vis* South Africa, the BCP had no alternative domestic policy and would have had to accept continuance of the labour reserve as the essential, long-term structural characteristic of Lesotho's role within the wider economy of southern Africa. Given the structural nature of contemporary labour migration there is no development strategy open to Lesotho other than a policy of ameliorating the worst features of the present situation.

But these differing conceptions of Lesotho's politics and role in African affairs are not merely the result of 'ideological' factors but have their roots in different classes and strata that Lesotho's historical development has given rise to. And since the key social formation in Lesotho is that of migrant labour it is essential to understand its history and dynamic in order to come to grips with political development in Lesotho.

(e) Lesotho's current development plan and strategy

During the colonial period no serious efforts were made to develop a comprehensive planning framework for Lesotho. Within different government departments plans were made for such problems as soil conservation but no clear strategy as to the long-run development of the territory was articulated. After Independence a Central Planning and Development Office was set up and the First Five Year Development Plan 1970/71–1974/75 produced. Given the absence of firm statistical data the planners worked under great difficulties. An even greater problem was the fact that the government apparatus was fundamentally geared to the maintenance of law and order and the collection of taxes. While machinery could be set up for developing new functions it was extremely difficult for the planners to come to grips with the fundamental 'function' of the economy of Lesotho – the provision of cheap labour to the mines and farms of the Republic. This process was and is (as of the time of writing) handled by the licensed recruiting agencies who pay taxes to government and submit returns to the Department of Labour but, essentially, operate independently of the planning machinery. Hence the main functions of the planning office have been: (*a*) to attempt to coordinate the activities of such Ministries and Departments as Agriculture, Health, Education, etc.; (*b*) to set up organisations such as the Lesotho National Development Corporation to deal with such new activities as industrial development; and (*c*) perhaps most important of all, to deal with bilateral and multilateral assistance projects. But, in essence, the prime economic function of Lesotho – that of a labour reserve of South Africa – is not a main function of the planning office.

There is also a certain ambivalence in this first plan as to the costs and benefits of migrant labour. In the introduction to the plan, Chief Jonathan, the Prime Minister, states that 'Lesotho is becoming a reservoir of unskilled, cheap labour for South Africa with little hope of creating an indigenous base for economic development'.[49]

While the plan emphasises the negative consequences of migrant labour it does see some positive aspects as 'The Basotho are getting used to working for money and for improved standards of living'.

One of the key targets of the plan is, by industrialisation, to lessen Lesotho's dependence on migrant labour. This envisages the creation of 10 000–15 000 new jobs in the non-agricultural sector during the plan period. In this way, it is hoped that, in the long run, the problem of migrant labour will wither on the vine.

For the next five years this policy concentrates on the annual increase of the labour force, which (estimated at an average of 4 000 males and 2 000 females) seems to be in line with the expected annual increase in the employment opportunities in the country. This will provide an indirect solution to Lesotho's almost entire present dependence on uncertain employment opportunities outside the country. If the annual increase in labour can be absorbed in relatively sound employment opportunities in the country, the relative importance of this problem will be gradually reduced, in the long run, to such an extent that it will eventually cease to be a major problem. Moreover, the continuous expansion of domestic employment opportunities will stimulate a repatriation flow.[50]

But even the figure of 10 000 to 15 000 new jobs has proved to be unrealistic. It is estimated that in fact 3 000 to 4 000 new jobs have been created in the first three years of the planning period,[51] in effect only some 15 to 20 per cent of the increase in the labour force in this period. And as we have seen, Lesotho's economic dependence on the earnings of migrant labour has increased rather than decreased in the plan period.

It will be interesting to see what proposals are contained in the new development plan for 1974/75–1978/79. Essentially four kinds of changes are possible:

1. An even more imaginative and expansive policy *vis-à-vis* industrialisation, which would include such schemes as a brewery and more concentration on the processing of Lesotho's agricultural and livestock production.
2. A more labour-intensive policy of industrialisation (but this is limited by the need to be competitive with South African industry in terms of the common market area).
3. A greater concentration on agricultural development, particularly livestock for which prices have risen considerably and which Lesotho's high altitude and relative absence of disease favours.
4. A total re-thinking of Lesotho's strategy *vis-à-vis* migrant labour. And it is clearly in this area, given Lesotho's dependence on labour migration, that radical and far-reaching changes could be made.

4. The Analysis of the Political Economy of Underdevelopment in Lesotho

(a) *The establishment of the British Protectorate*

The very existence of the kingdom of Lesotho is a tribute to the heroic struggle of the Basotho against imperial aggression. The nation as such was founded by Chief Moshweshwe who gathered around him the remnants of bands broken by the Zulu Empire and the northward drive of British and Boer. He established his headquarters on the flat and almost impregnable mountain plateau of Thaba Bosiu and fought off challenges by Africans, Boer and British. While the skill of his warriors, mounted on

Basotho ponies, played an important part in this defence, of even greater importance was the skill of Moshweshwe and his French Protestant advisers, particularly the missionary Eugene Casalis, in cultivating British friendship and insinuating that an independent Basutoland, under British protection, would be a vital barrier against the expansion of Boer influence. In his old age, Moshweshwe lost part of the control over his own, somewhat loosely knit political federation of Sotho-speaking people and a disastrous war with the Boers of the Orange Free State ensued in 1865. Retreating to their mountain fastness the Basotho literally starved as the Boer commandos drove off their cattle and harvested their crops. The Basotho were thus forced to sign the 'Peace of the Kaffir Corn'. (The very name of this treaty explains its purpose. It was made to keep the Boer commandos out of the sorghum fields on the east bank of the Caledon.) But the Boer victory under which the economic base of Basutoland, the relatively rich arable lands to the west and south of the Caledon river, was incorporated in the Orange Free State alarmed the British who in 1868 declared a Protectorate over Basutoland.

The purpose of the British was essentially strategic and, by and large, they had accepted Moshweshwe's insistent demand that Basutoland be ruled through him and his chiefs. But Moshweshwe was now dead and the British, whose primary concern in Lesotho's domestic policies was to avoid all expense, handed over the Basuto lock, stock and barrel, and without any pretence at consultation, to the administration of the Cape Colony. Simultaneously a hut tax of 10 sh. was introduced. Rule from the Cape between 1870–84 proved ultimately disastrous for Lesotho. The Cape Parliament insisted on applying to Basutoland a policy of disarmament and the Basotho, realising full well that without British protection this would leave them at the mercy of the Free State Boers, refused. The result was the 'Gun Wars' in which the Cape attempted unsuccessfully to enforce disarmament and a handing over of all weapons.

Meanwhile, these political and strategic moves were having enormous consequences on the economy of Basutoland. In the short run the establishment of the British Protectorate, internal peace and an end to Boer depravations led to a tremendous economic growth. New lands were brought under cultivation and iron ploughs were introduced in vast numbers. One major reason for this economic prosperity was that the early 1870s witnessed the opening up of the Kimberley diamond fields which in turn created a huge demand for food which Basotho and Boer stepped in to meet. In 1873 an estimated 100 000 bags of grain and 2 000 bales of wool were exported from Basutoland.[52] In the following years there was a considerable increase in the circulation of money and the establishment of trading stations. In 1878, Basutoland earned an estimated £400 000 from exports of grain and £75 000 from exports of wool. Much of this prosperity was smashed by the Gun Wars, but even as late as the early 1890s Basutoland was exporting vast quantities of foodstuffs to the Free State and the Transvaal.

Simultaneously, a considerable labour migration was set in motion.

> Labour migration is not new to the Basotho and is, in fact, nearly as old as their contact with Europeans. During the famines and the troubled times of the Free State Wars (intermittently from 1851 to 1868) numbers of men sought employment with the Europeans in Natal and the Cape for money to buy food. After the political settlement of 1868, work abroad became more regular, and considerable scope for employment was offered only 180 miles away by the opening of the Kimberley diamond mines. Thither men flocked in their thousands to work for money for guns, clothes and agricultural implements and for the ten shilling tax imposed in 1869. By 1875, out of a total population of 227 325, of which the number of able-bodied men was estimated at 20 000, 15 000 men were getting passes to work outside the territory for long or short periods. And by 1884 this number had doubled itself.[53]

This picture of an economy which was developing both as a source of peasant production and as a labour reserve is confirmed by de Kiewet.

> There is little doubt that in the closing years of the 1860s the Basotho began to pass from an economy that was largely pastoral to one that was more pronouncedly agricultural. . . . But it was chiefly the more violent causes that were undermining the pastoral economy of the natives. The tremendous

loss of cattle and land which was a result of the war with the farmers made a greater concentration on agriculture imperative. The other alternative which masses of natives adopted was to enter into the services of their victors. After 1869 Basutoland became the more or less permanent labour force of the Free State.[54]

The capacity of the agricultural resources of Basutoland's foothills and mountains to absorb this double strain of a labour reserve and an agricultural export began to be felt early on. The first to issue warnings were, naturally, the people of the country. At the annual *Pitsoes* (assemblies) there were constant references to overcrowding, to the return of Basotho people from all over southern Africa and a constant demand for more land for the people. The Colonial administration, too, gradually began to see the problem of overcrowding. The acting Resident Commissioner reporting in 1895 noted that

> The mountains, formerly common pasture, are being largely occupied and cultivated and contain practically no unalloted spheres . . . export of grain is taking place by the thousand bags to feed the mining camps, the Free State and some districts of the Colony . . . the magistrates must be sturdy men indeed, if their arms do not ache with the endless counting of money and sheep and the signing of receipts.[56]

However, ten years later, evidence of soil erosion prompted the following comments.

> At the sight of the deep ravines which traverse Basutoland in every direction and which continue to grow from year to year, progressively draining and desiccating the most fertile parts, one of our Christians remarked the other day: 'Naha e sa Tsofala', the land is ageing.[57]

Despite this tremendous exhaustion of Basutoland's natural resources, three other factors played a very important part in so raising the 'effort price' of Basotho participation in the product market. One was certainly a number of restrictions imposed by the Boer Republics to restrict free competition from Basutoland. Details of tariffs and other restrictions are not known but the *Annual Report of the Resident Commissioner* to London notes the deleterious effects of a tariff on Basuto grain entering Transvaal and estimated to cost £20 000.[58] And the same report five years later reported the closing of big consumer markets to Basutoland cereals. A second factor was the role of Cape and British officials in actively promoting labour migration. Records of that time[59] constantly cite the role of district administrators in advocating work at Kimberley, in railway construction and in the white mines. The trading stations here played a very important part in transforming discretionary requirements into necessities and acting as direct labour recruiting agents as has been the case until the 1950s. A third, though more intangible factor, was the lack of any profitable investment for the surplus generated from sale of produce and labour. Certainly a large part of this surplus in Basutoland has, historically, gone into education. The Basotho's educational effort is simply staggering. From the early 1870s teacher training institutes and trade schools were started, but given the total monopoly of trade and commerce by British and Boer it was impossible for this investment to yield returns.

In sum, while the evidence is scattered and the economic history of Lesotho in this period remains to be written, it does suggest the following. The present structure of labour migration did not emerge because the Basotho failed to respond to the demands for the modernisation of their country but precisely because they responded positively. The results of the conquest of the lands of Basotho people in the Free State did not reveal themselves immediately. But the long-run results were a gradual ecological debilitation of the country. By the time of the Boer War (1899–1902) the capacity of the agricultural economy to both achieve self-sufficiency and to provide for an export surplus had collapsed. Proletarianisation had reached the point of a *condition of subsistence* of the household economy in the mines, farms and railroads of South Africa. Specifically, the response of the Basotho to the opening up of the mining industry and the opportunities of wage employment is not conditioned by any surplus of labour in the traditional sector, but by the operation of a set of 'non-economic' factors which begin to distort the economy and bring about a long-term ecological decline.

However this is interpreted the function of Lesotho as a labour reserve both within the political economy of South Africa and in the international capitalist system was quite clear to current observers. Its role is indeed described in the *Annual Report of the Resident Commissioner* for the year 1898–9.

> Though for its size and population Basutoland produces a comparatively enormous amount of grain, it has an industry of great economic importance to South Africa, viz. the output of native labour. It supplies the sinews of agriculture in the Orange Free State, to a large extent it keeps going railway works, coal mining, the diamond mines at Jagersfontein and Kimberley, the gold mines of the Transvaal and furnishes in addition a large proportion of domestic services in surrounding districts... these facts are the best rejoinder to those who urge that Basutoland is a useless native reserve. To others, who urge higher education of the natives, it may be pointed out that to educate them above labour would be a great mistake. Primarily the native labour industry supplies a dominion want and secondly it tends to fertilize native territories with cash which is at once diffused for English goods.[60]

The structure of labour migration has continued relatively unaltered to this day. There is a certain tendency, within the social formation of migrant labour, for two groups to emerge. On the one hand, a more or less permanent proletariat which goes out to work at the mines and the farms, usually returning to the same place of work. This is particularly true of mine labour. On the other hand, a less proletarianised group of migrant workers who

Table 5.5. Per Cent of Miners Spending Specified Percentages of Working Life in Mines[61]

Working life in mines (Per cent)	Miners (Per cent)
0–10	17·6
11–20	14·8
21–30	11·0
31–40	12·6
41–50	16·9
51–60	12·6
61–70	10·4
71–80	4·1

regard wage earnings as a supplement to subsistence production and whose periods of migrations are both shorter and less constant. This tendency was noted as early as 1907 and has been confirmed by recent studies (see Table 5.5). McDowall, who used the table, comments

> From the above table it can be seen that there are two basic but diffused groups: a sizeable group, who spend less than 20 per cent of their working life in the mines, and another sizeable group who spend around 45 per cent in the mines.[61]

The bulk of this labour is recruited by the NRC (Mine Labour Organisations) on behalf of the South African Chamber of Mines. As many have noted, while the numbers of recruits varies from month to month, the numbers in employment are much more stable (see Tables 5.6 and 5.7).

To understand the nature of migrant labour as a social formation, Arrighi's point about the tradition of a subsistence wage is essential. The essential point is that mines wages – which in effect did not rise at all in real terms between 1890 and 1969 – have not

Table 5.6. Lesotho Citizens Recruited For South African Mines[62]

	1964	1965	1966	1967	1968
Monthly average	5 258	6 741	7 105	6 278	6 726
Yearly total	63 094	80 895	85 264	75 331	80 712

	1969	1970	1971	1972	1973
Monthly average	7 202	8 099	7 409	8 460	9 248
Yearly total	86 420	97 185	88 909	101 515	110 978

Table 5.7. Lesotho Citizens Employed in South African Mines By End Of Month Returns[62]

	1964	1965	1966	1967	1968
Monthly average	62 365	66 527	80 251	77 414	80 310

	1969	1970	1971	1972	1973
Monthly average	83 063	87 384	92 747	98 822	110 227

provided the household economy with the means of its sub-sistence. The result is that the economy of the migrant household – all, but a small elite of chiefs and the 'political class' – is depen-dent on migrant earnings and on cash crop/food crop production. Any scheme for 'development' which involves weakening the bonds between the migrants' earnings and the subsistence pro-duction of the family will meet with resistance.

The political consequences of this type of 'semi-pro-letarianisation' have been to dissipate the political and organisa-tional strength of what is, in effect, a part of the South African working class. The mining 'tradition' provided by the experience of worker consciousness and organisation – especially in the late forties and early fifties – provided a great part of the basic strength of the Basutoland Congress Party, however petit-bour-geois and reformist their programmes and policies. In the sixties this experience found expression within Lesotho in a burst of political activity that accompanied the movement towards de-colonisation. The state of emergency imposed in 1970 largely crushed political opposition in Lesotho and, when coupled with the pass laws that controlled the movement of 'foreign labour' from Lesotho to the Republic, helps to explain the seeming poli-tical passivity of the mineworkers in this period.

(b) Current perspectives

It may well be argued that the main thrust of this chapter – that backwardness or 'non-development' in Lesotho is not a result of a pristine traditionalism of the Basotho people but of the political violence waged against them at the crucial period of their economic development – is largely irrelevant. It tells little of con-structive value to development planners and to those who are 'concerned' with the economic development of Lesotho. I suspect that this argument is quite valid. But if the frame of reference is so redefined as to relate to the Basotho people as a whole, then reflections on their history and struggle do give rise to three very important considerations that are very burning and immediate.

1. There is at present an acute labour shortage in the South African mining industry which the Basotho mineworkers have seized on to better their situation and to achieve a better understanding of their role 'between' Lesotho and the

Republic. This labour shortage could and should be exploited by Lesotho, in conjunction with Mozambique, Malaŵi and Botswana who together comprise about 75 per cent of the black labour force in the mining industry, to secure pay and working conditions for their miners and taxation from the mining companies that would entail a real and substantial transfer of wealth from South Africa to Lesotho. At present, the social overhead costs of the reproduction of this labour power are borne largely by the women of Lesotho who scratch a living from parched and eroded soils. A substantial transfer of this labour surplus would have direct and immediate benefits.

2. A knowledge of the long and courageous battle of the Basotho people to assert their dignity and worth is in fact a resource and a political weapon of incomparable significance in the long-term battle for the liberation of southern Africa. Viewed in terms of the apologetic tradition in social science, the power and wealth of white South Africa appears immutable, the poverty and economic and military insignificance of Lesotho derisory. But in terms of the emerging political realities of southern Africa – especially since the coup in Portugal in April 1974 – the history of the struggle of the Basotho people and the very degree of their integration into the black working class of South Africa is a formidable weapon.

3. This view is strengthened when we demand of social science a broader historical perspective. In essence, the imposition of apartheid in the early 1950s was the response of white-settler South Africa to the growing strains and tensions that African nationalism had produced in South Africa and throughout the third world. Apartheid was the imposition of a form of fascist state by which the total direction of labour and the extension of the migrant labour system serves to suppress black worker consciousness. But, *vis-à-vis* such labour reserves as Lesotho that lie outside the political boundaries of the Republic this form of fascism is not possible. An uneasy form of 'neo-colonialism' is practised here by which the political elite is expected to control the forces that intense labour exploitation in South Africa generates. And in this lies one of the seeds of what will, in the last resort, destroy apartheid.

Notes

1. Samir Amin, *Accumulation on a World Scale: a critique of the theory of under-development*, Monthly Review Press, New York, 1974; and *Le Développement Inégal*, Maspero, Paris, 1973, pp. 287–91.
2. L. Barnes, *The New Boer War*, quoted in Jack Halpern, *South Africa's Hostages*, Penguin, Harmondsworth, 1965.
3. See L. B. Monyake, 'Lesotho – Land, Population and Food, The Problem of Growth in Limited Space', paper presented at the National Population Symposium, Maseru Stadium Hall, 11–13 June 1974 (duplicated).
4. For an analysis of 'vicious-circle' explanations, see T. Szentes, *The Political Economy of Underdevelopment*, Akadmicai, Budapest, 1971, chs. 2 and 3.
5. The term 'underdevelopment' is rhetorical and unscientific. I think it is justified only in terms of the specific analysis of dominant capitalism in Lesotho.
6. W. A. Lewis, *Economic Development with Unlimited Supplies of Labour*, Manchester School, May 1954.
7. P. P. Rey, 'Sur l'articulation des modes de production', in *Les Alliances de Classes*, Maspero, Paris, 1973.
8. Colin Bundy, 'The emergence and decline of a South African peasantry', *African Affairs*, lxxi, 285, Oct. 1972, pp. 369–89.
9. I am greatly indebted to Professor Archie Mafeje of the Institute of Social Studies, The Hague, and specifically to his paper, 'The fallacy of dual economies revisited', in *Dualism and Rural Development in East Africa*, Institute for Development Research, Copenhagen, 1973.
10. Despite the efforts of Althusser and Poulantzas, the basic continuity is clearly revealed in such works as E. Mandel, *The Formation of the Economic Thought of Karl Marx, 1843 to Capital*, Monthly Review Press, New York, 1971.
11. This remark is in no sense intended to denigrate the work of such Marxists as Gunder Frank, Samir Amin, Paul Sweezy, etc. The real point is why do such works strike a chord at the time? P. Baran's *The Political Economy of Growth*, Monthly Review Press, New York, 1957, took nearly ten years to gain such acceptance.
12. A. G. Frank, 'The sociology of development and the underdevelopment of sociology', in A. G. Frank, *Latin America: Underdevelopment or Revolution?* Monthly Review Press, New York, 1969; James Peck, 'The roots of rhetoric: the professional ideology of America's China watchers', in Edward Friedman and M. Selden, eds., *America's Asia: Dissenting Essays on Asian–American Relations*, Pantheon Books, New York, 1969, pp. 40–66; Lars Rudebeck, 'Political development: towards a coherent and theoretical formulation of the concept', *Scandinavian Political Studies*, 5, 1970, pp. 21–64; Henry Bernstein, 'Modernization theory and the sociological study of development', *Journal of Development Studies*, vii, 2, Jan. 1971, pp. 141–60; Maj Palmberg, 'Den funktionalistiska utvecklingsteorin' (The functionalist theory of development), in *Haften for Kritiska Studier*, 1–2, 1971; Jose F. Ocampo and Dale L. Johnson, 'The concept of political development', in J. D. Cockcroft,

A. G. Frank and D. L. Johnson, eds., *Dependence and Underdevelopment*: *Latin America's Political Economy*, Anchor Books, Garden City, New York, 1972.

13. P. Vilar, 'Marxist history, a history in the making: dialogue with Althusser', *New Left Review*, 80, July–Aug. 1973, pp. 65–106.
14. G. Arrighi, 'Labour supplies in historical perspective; a study of the proletarianization of the African peasantry in Rhodesia', *Journal of Development Studies*, vi, 3, April 1970, pp. 197–234.
15. *Ibid.*, p. 205.
16. *Ibid.*, p. 200.
17. *Ibid.*, p. 217.
18. S. Amin, 'Contemporary Migrations in West Africa', UN Africa Institute for Economic Development and Planning, Dakar, 1972.
19. S. Amin conceded that land may alter the picture but not for the manufacturing sector.
20. Amin, 'Contemporary Migrations in West Africa', p. 26.
21. Lesotho, *First Five-Year Plan 1970/71–1974/75*.
22. International Bank for Reconstruction and Development, *The Economy of Lesotho*, IBRD Report No. 331a–LSO, Washington.
23. Arie C. A. van der Wiel and Pieter J. T. Marres, *The Poverty Datum Line, Part I*, Lesotho, Aug. 1974.
24. L. B. Monyake, 'Lesotho – Land, Population and Food, The Problem of Growth in Limited Space'.
25. See the comparison in Lesotho, *Agricultural Statistics 1950, 1960 and 1965, 1970*, Bureau of Statistics, Maseru, Jan. 1973.
26. IBRD, *The Economy of Lesotho*.
27. W. J. A. Macartney, 'Case study: the Lesotho general election of 1970', *Government and Opposition*, viii, 4, Autumn 1973, pp. 407–31.
28. M. Ward, *Lesotho: Hard Labour for Life?* (duplicated).
29. IBRD, *The Economy of Lesotho*.
30. J. Jenness, *Lesotho Labour Migration: deferred pay and remittances through recruitment agency channels* (duplicated draft).
31. M. Ward, *Lesotho: Hard Labour for Life?*
32. M. McDowall, *Basotho Labour in South African Mines – An Empirical Study*, Oct. 1973 (duplicated).
33. For example, M. Ward, 'Independence for Lesotho?', *Journal of Modern African Studies*, v. 3, 1967, p. 359.
34. G. M. E. Leistner, 'Economic structure and growth', *Communications of the Africa Institute*, 5, 1966.
35. Percy Selwyn, 'The dual economy transcending national frontiers: the case of industrial development in Lesotho', *Communications of the Institute of Development Studies*, p. 105.
36. *Ibid.*, pp. 11–12.
37. F. Wilson, *Labour in the South African Gold Mines 1911–1969*, Cambridge University Press, 1972, Africa Studies Series No. 6.
38. Leistner, 'Economic structure and growth'.
39. J. C. Williams, 'Lesotho: economic implications of migrant labour', *South African Journal of Economics*, xxxix, 2, June 1971, pp. 149–78.

40. See for example, a useful analysis by G. Wellmer, 'Mission and Migrant Labour', *Ministry*, x, 1, 1970.

41. S. Wallman, *Take Out Hunger: Two Case Studies of Rural Development*, Athlone Press, London, 1969.

42. Williams, 'Lesotho: economic implications of migrant labour'.

43. Basutoland, *Annual Colonial Report 1901/1902*.

44a/b. *Report on the Financial and Economic Position of Basutoland* (The Pim Report), Jan. 1935: (a) Appendix VIII; (b) Appendix V.

45. Except for a small Xhosa-speaking minority in the Orange River Valley.

46. Richard F. Weisfelder, *Lesotho: An Unstable Irritant Within South Africa*, African Studies Association, Boston, 1970; 'Defining Political Purpose in Lesotho', paper delivered to the African Studies Association meeting, Los Angeles, Oct. 1968; and, 'The Basuto Monarchy: A Spent Force or a Dynamic Political Factor?, paper delivered to the 14th annual meeting of the African Studies Association, Denver, Nov. 1971.

47. Weisfelder, 'Defining Political Purpose in Lesotho'.

48. See B. M. Khaketla, *Lesotho 1970: An African Coup Under the Microscope*, University of California Press, Berkeley, 1972.

49. Lesotho, *First Five-Year Development Plan*, foreword.

50. *Ibid.*, pp. 21–2.

51. S. Montsi, Acting Director, Central Planning and Development Office, *Brief Review of Plan Implementation*, 10 June, 1974.

52. The Pim Report.

53. H. Ashton, *The Basotho*, OUP, London, 1952, p. 162.

54. C. W. de Kiewet, *History of South Africa, Social and Economic*, OUP, London, 1942.

55. Basutoland, *Report of the Acting Commissioner (Langden) to the Colonial Office*. No. 152.

56. Robert C. Germond, *Chronicles of Basutoland*, Morija Sesuto Book Depot, 1967, p. 321.

57. *Ibid.*, pp. 409–10.

58. Basutoland, *Report of the Resident Commissioner for 1887*, Colonial Report No. 31.

59. See the English translations of *Leselinvnana*, the Protestant newspaper for the period 1874–80.

60. Basutoland, *Annual Colonial Report 1898/1899*, No. 288.

61. McDowall, *Basotho Labour in South African Mines* Section 9.

62. J. Jenness, *Lesotho Labour Migration – Numbers Recruited for Mine Labour* (draft).

63. See Wilson, *Labour in the South African Gold Mines 1911–69*.

64. *Financial Mail* (Johannesburg) 13 Sept. 1974.

65. This paper was written in early 1974. Since then a considerable number of changes, particularly the increase in the black South African labour force, which now comprises over 50 per cent of the total, have made such a 'labour cartel' argument exceedingly problematic.

Part 3 Political Change and Participation

Africa's large number and wide range of political systems have made it a fruitful area for comparative analysis. Structural-functional theories of politics were developed to explain change and continuity in Africa and the continent has more recently become a fruitful field, as we have seen in the previous Part, for examining the nature of dependence and 'neocolonialism'. The first two chapters (6, 7) in this Part are case studies of domestic politics within the states of Sierra Leone and Malaŵi respectively. The third examines the continuing politics of nationalism in Southern Africa and the differential support extended to particular parties within the liberation movement by Zambia. The liberation movements on the continent retain their faith in mobilisation and socialisation despite the demise of such optimism in most independent states. Their demands for political change are still based on popular participation, whereas incumbent elites in post-independence Africa are more ambivalent about either change or participation, as the cases of Sierra Leone and Malaŵi reveal.

Cartwright (Ch. 6) evaluates the impact of leadership in Sierra Leone along the dimensions of legitimacy and style. He analyses the behaviour of the Margai brothers in both the 'residual' and the 'modern' sectors and presents a political history of this new state since independence. He emphasises their different attitudes towards the political economy of Sierra Leone as indicated by the debate over the 'Open Door' policy. The elder brother, Dr Milton Margai, had a 'conservative' rather than 'innovative' policy and a 'brokerage' rather than a 'creative' political style; he secured traditional support whereas Sir Albert Margai depended more on the modern sector. Cartwright suggests that both leaders were products of their time and neither was able to overcome his limited basis of support and encourage nation-building or development.

Hodder-Williams (Ch. 7) examines the utility of Easton's notion of support to explain the apparent stability of the politics of Malaŵi. He attempts to explain patterns of participation and support in Malaŵi compared with other African states. He suggests that Dr. Banda runs a 'classically Gaullist system of government' in which his control does not exlude other centres of potential political power. He argues that studies of African politics have ignored personalities and private motives. He also indicates that while a conceptual apparatus is necessary, analysts of African politics should not pre-judge their findings by importing inappropriate theories into the continent. Hodder-Williams is cautious about the tenuous nature of political support in Malaŵi.

The final chapter (8, by Anglin) in this Part focuses on the role of Malaŵi's Central African neighbour, Zambia, in political change in the region. Anglin's essay analyses the escalation of Zambia's commitment to the liberation movements as majority rule in its white-ruled neighbours continued to be delayed. Zambia's gradual disengagement from an inheritance of integration in Southern Africa has been matched by its growing support for guerrilla struggle, although, at least until recently, it has always advocated negotiation rather than violence and preferred 'moderate' to 'radical' parties. Anglin points to the centrality of regional conflict for Zambia's foreign and development policies and suggests that the constraints of its strategic and economic vulnerability have gradually been overcome. He examines the position adopted by President Kaunda towards the confrontation in southern Africa and indicates how Zambia's support has affected factional conflicts within and between the liberation movements. Its distribution of financial support, recognition, radio time and operational facilities has been controlled and conditional. Zambia, like other host states, has encouraged common fronts among the nationalist movements from each country, it has attempted to isolate the movements from Zambian society and it has imposed operational restrictions on the guerrillas in Zambia.

Anglin indicates that Zambia has taken considerable and calculated risks in its support of the liberation movements and that this policy has affected its national development and priorities;

external support has influenced internal politics as well as *vice versa*. He suggests that support for the liberation of southern Africa is generally compatible with the national interest and ideology of Zambia. Zambia has been particularly concerned about the possibility of 'radicalisation' in the region which would have profound implications for itself, Malawi and the continent as a whole. However, with the breakdown of regional 'détente' and the re-emergence of the factionalism that has often bedevilled the Zimbabwean nationalist movements, Dr Kaunda has adopted a more militant posture on the process of liberation in Zimbabwe than in the period examined by Anglin. His chapter remains important as an analysis of Zambia's changing policies and the dilemmas that produced them. The prospect of further radical regimes being established in southern Africa after protracted armed struggles is likely to affect the future of political change and participation not only in the region but throughout the African continent.

John Cartwright

6 The Limits to Leadership: Sierra Leone Under the Margais

This chapter attempts to provide a framework for analysing how far an individual leader of an African state can shape his polity, and how the interaction of various constraints limits his choice of actions.[1] I shall attempt this by examining a situation in which the effect of variables other than leadership has been reduced to a minimum; this situation comprises the successive periods as Prime Minister of Sierra Leone of Sir Milton and Sir Albert Margai, from 1951 to 1964, and 1964 to 1967 respectively.

Before examining the activities of these two men, however, we need to establish our framework for analysis. We may define the leader of a polity in structural terms as that individual occupying the political role which entails compliance from the broadest range of other office-holders in the political structures, while at the same time not himself expected to obey other specified individuals. However, when we talk of 'leadership', we are generally referring to how a person acts, rather than to the expectations that attach to the role he is filling. We therefore need a definition of 'leadership' which enables us to evaluate how well an individual fills the structural role of 'leader'. A satisfactory definition is Richard Neustadt's notion that leadership consists of getting others to do what the leader wants, for their own or for society's good rather than for his own.[2] Power thus inheres in the role of leader, whereas leadership is the measure of how effectively the person occupying the role uses this power.

The person occupying the role of head of government in an independent state interacts in a wide variety of ways with other persons and institutions. For purposes of this analysis, we need only indicate that the range of structural relationships may range from those in which the others involved are directly subordinate to the leader in a hierarchy, through those who share the common values of the society but work in autonomous institutions, through those who both work through autonomous institutions and lack any commitment to the society's common values (e.g. multinational corporations). These two variables of institutional autonomy and degree of commitment to common values will interact with the further variables of extent of resources and intensity of concern over questions at issue to establish the extent to which these other actors will act as constraints upon the leader.

We can take these institutional relationships as establishing a set of fixed constraints on the role of leader in any polity. The leader can change some of these relationships, (for example, by abolishing local governments, or nationalising a foreign company) but only by utilising resources which he already possesses. We need, therefore, to consider the resources which a leader possesses or can develop in his dealings with other factors, in order to develop the greatest margin of committed support over committed opposition, with his success in this being a measure of his leadership. His most basic task here is to establish his *legitimacy* as a leader; beyond this, his means of developing support can be analysed in terms of *policies*, and what for want of a better word I shall call his *style*.

The most fundamental resource for a leader when seeking to obtain active support for his objectives is legitimacy in the eyes of his putative supporters. Now in most polities there is a broad middle-ground between support and opposition, or at another level, between legitimacy and illegitimacy; many members of the polity will acquiesce in the exercise of power by persons occupying particular roles without necessarily accepting their right to exercise that power. But a leader needs more than this acquiescence; he needs persons who feel bound to him in such a way that they will comply with his wishes voluntarily. Legitimacy can be regarded as a necessary though insufficient condition for this support.

Legitimacy can be viewed along two dimensions, which can be combined to give us four 'ideal types' of relationship between leaders and other actors. One of these dimensions is the extent to which legitimacy adheres to the leader as an individual or to the leader as occupant of a specific role. The other is the extent to which acceptance of the leader is based upon expectation of some personal benefit or deprivation (e.g. patronage, liquidation) or upon more selfless considerations, which might be described broadly as 'acceptance-for-its-own-sake', or perhaps, using the term very loosely, 'spiritual' considerations. This gives us the following 'ideal types' of linkage between a leader and those subject to his authority:

| | | Commitment to leader is as: | |
		Individual	Institution
Nature of reward for supporters is:	Spiritual	(charismatic)	(rational-legal, theocratic)
	Material	('boss', caudillo)	(patrimonial)

Clearly no one of these 'ideal-type' relationships predominates for long in the relations between a leader and all the members of his polity. But at any given time, the ties between a leader and a given section of the polity will approximate one of these types, and will require the deployment of specific types of resources by the leader. The charismatic relationship will require a high degree of self-abnegation on the part of the leader, but no great deployment of material resources or adherence to established patterns of leadership behaviour. The 'boss' relationship will require little beyond a plentiful supply of whatever material resources the followers desire. (However, this is undoubtedly the most unstable of all the four types of leadership, lacking as it does any basis for commitment by the followers beyond a continuing stream of material payoffs.)[3] The rational-legal and the theocratic relationships, besides requiring a show of willingness by the leader to put the general good above his own, require him to adhere carefully to established conventions. The patrimonial relationship, while it can appear arbitrary and capricious in its treatment of individuals, also operates within a broad framework of established conventions, and additionally requires a considerable outlay of material rewards.[4] To some extent a leader can seek a middle ground between these conflicting demands for resources, or shift from one type of relationship to another, but the further he goes towards one type, the more difficult it becomes to change to another; the convention-breaking entailed in charismatic leadership, for example, will generate opposition to a ready acceptance of the leader's claims to rational-legal legitimacy, and similarly the distribution of largesse entailed by patrimonial leadership will work against subsequent claims to be endowed with a self-abnegating 'gift of grace'.

Beyond the broad underpinning for his position provided by legitimacy, the leader tries to establish support for himself through his policies and his manner of presenting them. We may diagrammatically represent the range of possible policies open to a leader, the decisions on who gets what, as a sea urchin, with varying degrees of change represented by spines running outward from a central point of 'things as they are'. The ideal-type 'conservative' is the leader who maintains the *status quo* in all his policies; we may contrast him with the policy 'innovator', the leader who makes a change in any policy in any possible direction. Different 'innovators' of course may make policy changes in opposed directions (for example, towards greater or lesser equality of income distribution) or on quite different planes (for example, in social welfare services or in foreign alliances), but all 'innovators' have in common the consideration that some members of their polity will gain and some will lose from their innovation. What the innovating leader needs to consider, then, is whether his margin of support in the polity will be improved or worsened by his changed policy.

To some extent a policy innovation will automatically attract or repel certain members of the polity, regardless of how the leader seeks to bring it about. But generally a good deal of the success of a policy depends upon the leader's *style*, the ways in which he goes about building support for his policies. Here again we can contrast two ideal types of style, the 'brokerage' and the 'creative'. The 'brokerage' style takes as given the constellation of overt interests in the polity, and tries to put together those combinations of interests that seem most likely to provide the leader with the support he needs. The 'creative' style, by contrast, seeks to bypass or override opposition from existing interests by calling into being new groupings, either through attracting new participants into the national political arena or by inducing some present participants to look at events in new ways.

The brokerage and creative styles of leadership are thus appropriate for diametrically opposed situations. The broker functions best where role expectations both for himself and for others are clearly established, where most potential interests are already articulated, where the range of policies sought by these interests is not too divergent, and where there is no widespread discontent over the existing balance of forces in the polity. The creative leader functions best where role expectations and the pattern of alignment are relatively fluid, and where he can call into being new alignments to provide him with support, either by appealing to hitherto passive members, or by 'up-grading the common interest' by making politically salient those areas in which there is the greatest potential for a consensus supporting him.

If we now narrow our focus for the study of leadership down to the African states, and specifically Sierra Leone, we can note certain features which establish further limits on what leaders can do. A dominating feature of African states is the existence of two quite distinct sectors in the polity, which Zolberg has termed 'modern' and 'residual'.[5] These sectors hold different perceptions of the role of leader, provide different bases of legitimacy, and support different political institutions. While the distinction between these two sectors is an analytical one cutting across a continuum of attitudes, and while Zolberg is right in stressing that individuals can operate successfully in both, still the fact of these broad differences forces African leaders to struggle with a divergence of expectations that leaders in more integrated societies are spared. In the performance of his role, and in establishing the legitimacy of that role, the African leader has often to decide which sector he will concentrate on, and by that concentration risk alienating persons in the other sector.

The nature of the choices an African leader has to make, and the extent of their mutual incompatibility, can be illustrated by two models portraying the expectations surrounding the role of leader held by members of the residual and the modern sector respectively. Such models, of course, are gross over-simplifications of reality; but at the same time they may help us to pin-point the areas of conflict that exist.

To the member of the 'residual' sector – say, an ordinary African farmer – the national leader is expected to behave as a traditional chief writ large. He is a 'father' to his people, using his powers for the good of all, and with restraint, and is unselfish and even-handed in his dealings with all his people. He works within the framework of established customs, not necessarily those laid down by an alien 'constitution' but those accepted by the ordinary people as appropriate to a chief. While he has to work within the national political structures established by the colonial power, he also needs to show respect for the traditional local institutions which have more significance for the ordinary person. At the same time, while the leader is expected to work within the conventions of behaviour laid down for the institution of chieftaincy, the occupants of other roles are expected to mute any opposition they may have to him.

To persons in the 'modern' sector – say, a secondary school graduate holding a government clerkship – expectations of what a leader should be are quite different. The leader must be capable of moving the society towards the new statuses and material amenities associated with an industrial society which the 'modern' youth regards as the supremely important goals. To do this, he must be prepared to break down the large number of established structures with a vested interest in the *status quo*, and to build up both new institutions and new bases of support. The means he uses toward this end are of no great concern, provided that he recognises the skills of the 'modern' sector as being of critical importance and providing the basis for a redistribution of privilege. Partly because the leader's role is as yet undefined, the 'modern' youth tends to accord legitimacy to the leader on a personal basis, or on the basis of the beliefs he espouses, rather than on the basis of an institutionally defined role.

Persons in these two sectors clearly will employ quite different criteria for legitimacy in a leader, as well as requiring from him quite different policies and styles. The problem for a leader is how to resolve these conflicting demands. For the balance of this chapter, I should like to focus on how two successive leaders of Sierra Leone tried in different ways to deal with three specific problem areas. First, how did each of the Margais try to establish or maintain his legitimacy? Which sector did each draw upon, and in what ways? Second, which of their significant policies could be considered as 'innovative' and which 'conservative', and how were these policies received in the two sectors? Third, how did each seek to build support for himself and for his policies? To what extent did each seek support among members of each of the two sectors, and through what intermediaries?

Two Leaders in Action

Before examining the two Margais' specific actions, a very brief sketch of the political environment in which they operated is necessary. Sierra Leone is a small (28 000 square miles (72 520 sq km), 2·1 million people), poor (estimated GDP in 1961 was £50–100 million) and socially backward (literacy rate of 7·7 per cent in 1963) country, economically dependent upon diamond and iron mining and with most of its population engaged in small-scale agriculture.[6] When the British began decolonisation in 1947 three loose blocs of articulate interests could be discerned.[7] The Creoles, settlers in the Colony (the peninsula around the capital city of Freetown), dominated the 'modern' sector through their near-universal literacy and their professionally and technically trained personnel. Their skills gave them the hope of dominating the national civil service once Africanisation began, as well as the Freetown municipal government and most non-political organisations. However, there were only 40 000 of them, a tiny minority once a universal franchise was attained.

The educated Protectorate men were far fewer than the Creoles, but possessed an important reserve of strength in that nearly all were members of the traditional ruling families of the Protectorate. They thus were less firmly committed to operating in the 'modern' sector than their Creole rivals, although their entry into occupations such as teaching, medicine and surveying generally took them away from their home chiefdoms, where alone their high status and participation in groups which could furnish significant resources for politics, such as the men's secret societies, could help them. The central arena was ideal for their skills, but they had to gain entry to it through the local ones.

The third bloc, less cohesive than the educated men, was the chiefs, the heads of the 200 and more local governments in Sierra Leone.[8] Although increasingly chiefs were coming to be chosen from the ranks of the educated, their base of support was still essentially in the 'residual' sector, even though they were subject to central government administrative control. Their strength lay not just in their command of the machinery of local government, but in their pervasive social role as judges, peace-makers, initiators and generally 'fathers' of their chiefdoms. While many individual chiefs fell considerably short of their peoples' expectations for the role, largely because of their tendency to use the office for personal enrichment, still the institution retained the support of most persons in the residual sector.

For a number of reasons, foremost among them the unwillingness of most Creole leaders to attempt to moderate Creole dislike of 'the aborigines', the Creoles became increasingly isolated in the period 1948–51, and an alliance of the Protectorate educated men and the chiefs emerged as the Sierra Leone People's Party (SLPP) in 1951. Dr (later Sir) Milton Margai, the oldest among the educated men and the one who had been most solicitous of the chiefs' interests during his years as a government doctor, emerged as leader of this 'party'. Its party activities were limited, however, to a handful of chiefs and party activists bestowing the party symbol on the most promising candidate at election time.

With the unofficial Legislative Council majority in 1951 came a share of Executive Council posts for the SLPP leaders, and slowly more power was handed to them. In 1954 the embryonic Cabinet took over from the Governor the power to depose Paramount Chiefs; in 1958 the last British officials left the Cabinet (though they continued to man most top civil service posts until after Independence); and in 1961 came Independence and control over external affairs and defence.

Up to Sir Milton's death in 1964, the SLPP maintained its base among the chiefs and others in the 'residual' sector, while the opposition shifted considerably. The Creoles, despite a disproportionate share of Cabinet posts and a predominant position in the senior civil service, generally remained aloof from the SLPP, although they did not oppose it until Albert Margai came to power. A number of younger educated up-country men, led by Albert Margai, broke away from the SLPP from 1958 to 1960, partly out of impatience over Sir Milton's unwillingness to curtail the chiefs' privileges and hasten the pace of change, but despite their success in drawing a new group of lower-status young men into political activity, and direct elections for the legislature from 1957 onward, they gained little support outside the towns. In 1960, when their People's National Party (PNP) was absorbed into a government coalition, a new party based on the lower-status young men from the north emerged. By this time northerners were becoming aware that their region was less prosperous and less socially developed than the Mende south, yet the coalition increased an apparent trend toward 'Mende dominance' within the government. The All Peoples' Congress (APC) attempted to transcend tribal and regional lines with a 'class' appeal against the privileged groups, but its initial leadership and the workings of the electoral system in the 1962 election[9] firmly established it as 'the Northern man's party' against the 'Mende' SLPP. After 1964, the APC's growth and ultimate triumph over the SLPP in 1967 consisted of adding further elements to its 'modernising' northern core, with considerable assistance from Sir Albert Margai's alienation of northerners, Creoles, and a good many of the more conservative members of the residual sector.

In evaluating the two leaders' performance, we need to remember two advantages enjoyed by Dr Milton Margai. First, his ten years' advantage in age over any other educated up-country men gave him a security denied his younger brother. Second, being the first Prime Minister and SLPP leader allowed him to shape expectations as to how these roles should be filled, leaving Albert Margai the more difficult task of altering established roles.

The basic values with which each leader sought to underpin his legitimacy differed sharply, with Dr Margai basing his legitimacy heavily upon his occupancy of the top position in a hierarchy of deference, whereas Albert sought his mandate on the egalitarian basis of popular consent. Both Dr Margai's hierarchical values and his leanings towards the 'residual' sector were clearly shown by his attitudes towards the chiefs and the young men. He backed the chiefs against 'trouble-makers' except in the most flagrant cases of oppression, consulted them on all major matters, and stressed publicly that people owed them obedience. Towards the 'youngmen' he was considerably less solicitous, even antagonistic; his remark that 'I am not going to build something up to see some young men destroy it'[10] epitomised his view that youthful impetuousness needed to be kept under firm control. He seems to have delayed Africanisation of the civil service at least in part because the young educated men's arrogance towards older but less educated men was antithetical to his view of proper behaviour among youth, and almost invariably he confined his dealings in local matters to the chiefs and elders, rather than consulting directly with the commoners. At the same time, he acted in a chief's role as 'father' to his people; a person in need could count on assistance from him, and on his up-country tours he always contrived to give back as much in gifts as he received.

This stress on the legitimacy of a hierarchy, and its obverse, the lack of concern with popular consent for his leadership, was fully compatible with the readiness in Sierra Leone's 'residual' sector to accord considerable deference on the basis of superior rank. In the 'modern' sector, however, there was less acceptance of this basis of legitimacy. Some more radical individuals wanted a less sharp differentiation of statuses; many Western-educated persons were quite happy to maintain wide differentiations of status, but they did not accept Dr Margai's criteria. In the 'modern' sector Dr Margai gained little legitimacy beyond what was inherent in the role of Prime Minister and a small increment from his professional status.

From his first entry into politics in 1948, Albert Margai had sought a very different basis for legitimacy, the basis of mass consent. He professed repeatedly to be the servant of all the people of Sierra Leone, and sought direct contact with all, both through mass political rallies and also after becoming Prime Minister, through a policy of allowing anyone to bring their problems directly to him. While to some extent this could be viewed as a different interpretation of the chief's role of 'father', the motivation for it seems to have been much more that these were voters from whom he must ultimately seek support. In crises also he sought to legitimate his actions by appeals to 'the people'; thus in 1964 when the Freetown Council's legality was impugned in a court ruling, his response was to dissolve the council and hold fresh elections to clear away the problem.[11]

The other side of this attitude was a lack of respect for hierarchical values. This was shown in numerous ways: by his challenge to his elder brother in 1957 for the leadership of the SLPP; by his willingness to permit young ministers and civil servants who were his supporters to insult and ridicule older persons[12]; and most seriously, by his forcing all chiefs into an active role in supporting the SLPP, even where this would lead them into severe conflict with their people. In the eyes of those firmly in the 'modern' sector, who had scant respect for the chiefs, such behaviour would not hurt his position, and his responsiveness to popular demands would enhance it; but in the eyes of the much greater number of persons in the 'residual' sector, Albert Margai's behaviour violated basic canons of conduct.

In most of the policies they pursued, the two leaders were in sharp contrast, with the elder Margai on the whole being extremely 'conservative', while his brother sought in several areas to be 'innovative'. However, Albert Margai's attempted innovations were hamstrung by the constraints developed out of his brother's conservatism, in several instances as unintended side effects. I shall focus here on two of the most significant policy areas for each of the two leaders: party organisation and foreign investment.

From its beginnings, the SLPP had been entwined with the chiefs to a degree unsurpassed by any other governing party in Africa.[13] With the advent of the popular franchise in 1957, the party had a chance to establish cadres of organisers independent of the chiefs, but Dr Margai showed no interest in such a move. Admittedly, there were difficulties; the growth first of the PNP and then of the APC required the SLPP to turn to the chiefs to suppress these opposition groups at the local level, and to develop party cadres would require either an 'ideological' appeal such as motivated the PDG in Guinea, or material payoffs on a scale not readily obtained under British supervision. But the chance was there, even if Dr Margai declined to take it.

Working through the chiefs left two problems. First, a party built on such locally-oriented individuals would have a hard time getting beyond an allocation of resources in accordance with each area's bargaining strength to a national outlook which might alleviate regional disparities. Regional imbalances would thus tend to remain unchanged or even worsen over time. Second, such a party could not develop the cohesive and ideologically committed leadership and cadres necessary to mobilise domestic resources for self-development. This meant that economic growth could only be promoted, if at all, through an 'Open Door' policy of relying on substantial foreign investment, even though this might lock the country into a permanent role as a peripheral raw-material exporter.[14] The only major innovative policy, giving most of a foreign corporation's diamond leases to licensed Sierra Leonean diggers, had been introduced over Dr Margai's objections, and in such a way as to ensure that the chiefs, through their control over licences, were among the main beneficiaries.[15]

When Albert Margai came to power, some of the fruits of Sir Milton's policies were already apparent. Strong opposition parties were entrenched in both the north and the Kono district, basing their appeal on both regional and anti-chief appeals. There had been little development since the 'Open Door' policy was announced, although expectations were growing. The SLPP as a party was still an aggregation of local notables, without any organisation of a type amenable to central control.

Albert's first step was to try to rebuild the SLPP into a more centralised organisation capable of re-allocating privileges from the chiefs and others in the residual sector to persons more firmly committed to the modern sector. Not surprisingly, this attempt encountered great resistance from the chiefs and other beneficiaries of the *status quo*. But Albert might have managed to bring about this change had it not been for the strength of the opposition in the north and Kono, which forced him back to relying on the chiefs as his main instrument for the containment of the opposition parties. A third factor, scarcity of material rewards for building a party machine independent of the chiefs, also limited his opportunities for innovation. In his efforts to overcome this shortage of funds, he entered into a number of 'development agreements' which turned out to be financial disasters for the country, and because of the suspicion of corruption that accompanied them, helped to alienate (*inter alia*) the still predominantly Creole civil service.[16]

In the area of policy, we can draw three conclusions. One is that some major 'decisions', such as the use of the chiefs as the SLPP's local personnel, and the 'Open Door' policy, were not decisions or choices in the sense of consciously considered selections from among alternative courses of action; rather, they developed as the lines of least resistance out of an existing situation, until by the time their consequences became apparent, the costs of changing policies were too high. Another is that Albert Margai's attempts to innovate were blocked not so much by direct resistance as by the indirect effects of his predecessor's policies. A third conclusion is that Albert Margai's innovations needed to be presented in special ways if they were to be accepted, and it is to this question of how he and his brother presented their policies that we will now turn.

Dr Milton Margai's was almost a pure 'brokerage' style. Those groups which had made their identities manifest – Creoles, educated up-country men, chiefs, tribal authorities, lorry drivers, Poro members, Christians, Muslims, and so on – were included in his calculations of how resources should be allocated; those which remained latent – small farmers, diamond diggers, northerners – were ignored. While this made for a less hazardous calculus than attempts to call latent groups into being, it had its own perils, most dramatically demonstrated in the development of ethno-regionalism as the dominant 'encompassing principle' for political alignments in Sierra Leone.[17] The political division which ensured Dr Margai's rise to leadership was that between Creoles and 'countrymen', a division which brought the SLPP into being in 1951 as 'the countryman's party', and which served as its rallying cry in the next (1957) election. But in encouraging this electorally advantageous alignment, Dr Margai legitimatised an ethno-regional basis for subsequent alignments, thus facilitating the establishment of opposition parties based on northern and Kono grievances.

More broadly, one could say that the 'brokerage' style encouraged a tendency to drift, to allow forces outside the political sphere to determine events while the political leaders merely reacted to these events. In such areas as economic development, where this approach meant that desire for imported manufactured products would be allowed to grow unchecked while the country sought to pay for these by exporting raw materials, such an approach was likely to increase Sierra Leone's dependence on the industrialised states.

While a 'creative' approach might have averted the problems built up by the 'brokerage' style's neglect, in Albert Margai's case it was vitiated by the side effects of his predecessor's approach. In essence, Sir Albert was trying to align all those wishing to hasten social change – the 'modernisers' – behind him, leaving his residual sector opponents the difficult task of organising themselves in opposition. Unfortunately for him, this alignment was overborne by the ethno-regional one. The Creoles, originally sympathetic, turned against him because of his apparent favouring of Mendes, his self-enrichment, and his attempts to cut away legal safeguards they saw as necessary to protect their position. Northerners' initial suspicions of one Mende succeeding another were heightened by what they interpreted as 'tribal' biases in appointing Mendes to key civil service posts, building airports near Sir Albert's homes in Mendeland, and using northern chiefs against their people to keep the 'Mende' SLPP in power. If Sir Albert had appeared less self-seeking, and had managed to remove the focus for opposition by bringing the APC into a coalition, he might have overcome northern hostility and achieved his 'modernising' alignment. But the fact that he had to keep using the chiefs for support because of the party structure bequeathed him by his brother, coupled with his need to acquire resources to support a patrimonial approach, made this 'creative' appeal impossible.

What tentative conclusions can we draw from the experiences of these two leaders regarding the scope for leadership? With respect to policies, we might suggest that conservative policies tend to safeguard the legitimacy of the leader, in that while they may not be liked they at least are understood and seen as falling within the proper parameters of the leader's role. Against this advantage is the hazard that independently of whatever the leader may do, some members of the polity may come to see his role as requiring policy innovations, though for a mass of indiv-iduals to organise for concerted action to bring about a policy innovation is a more difficult task than to resist such a change.

The innovator, by contrast, is trying to bring more support (or reduce the opposition) to his leadership. To the extent that the policy he seeks is widely desired, he may succeed, but he faces three quite severe hazards. First, he may miscalculate the balance of interests for and against his innovation; in particular, latent elements upon which he counts may fail to rise to his support. Second, the policy he proposes may not work; any innovation risks being worse than what preceded it. Third, the policy may have unforeseen side effects in quite a different field, which again may create more difficulties for the leader than the ones which originally led him to introduce his policy innovation. All in all, the policy innovator faces more clearly perceivable risks than does the conservative; yet unless the *status quo* is considered desirable, a situation rarely found in the Third World, a leader must consider some innovations.

With respect to style, in a situation where new interest are constantly developing out of a largely latent pool of possible elements, a 'brokerage' approach risks allowing poorly articulated discontents to build up to explosive proportions. On the other hand, it does give reasonable assurance that those elements which are articulate (for example, labour unions, civil servants, the military) receive resources in proportion to the strength of their demands, and while this is hardly just, it does help avert a breakdown of civil order. The 'creative' style may if skilfully used draw members of the polity away from dangerously divisive alignments such as regionalism and 'tribalism', and more positively, create a balance which will enable the leader to push toward an equitable and prospering society. On the other hand, the leader may find that the potential supporters he wishes to incorporate are not available to him, while his attempts to incorporate them lead to the loss of support elsewhere. More often the problem confronting the 'creative' leader is simply that manifest identities in the polity are so well established that more salient new ones cannot emerge. In such a situation the leader must revert to 'brokerage' politics, working within the existing framework whatever the costs.

Perhaps the most striking feature to appear from this study is the extent to which such courses are largely forced before their consequences are perceived. Such developments as the relationship of the chiefs to the governing party, with all its implications for subsequent regional conflict and for efforts at a 'creative' style, were largely settled on the basis that they were the only 'thinkable' course of action at the point where alternatives could have been pursued. If, for example, the SLPP leaders had organised party machinery before the 1957 election on a scale comparable with the CPP in Ghana, or even the Nigerian Action Group, the chances of regional discontent being allowed to grow, or of Albert Margai finding his own party an unusable instrument, would have been much less. Yet at the time when a choice could have been made, few people saw a choice as necessary.

What this points to as a conclusion is the need for an effective leader to be a far-sighted one. An ideal leader will try to find bases for legitimacy in both modern and residual sectors, will try innovative policies where he can be reasonably sure the gains will outweigh the losses, and will attempt to create new groupings in order to carry through his innovations. But above all he has to be able to foresee the range of implications of any course of action, to anticipate what will be the consequences if he does not make choices while the opportunity to choose is open to him.

Notes

1. The material for this study is drawn from J. Cartwright, *Political Leadership in Sierra Leone*, Croom Helm, London 1978.
2. Richard Neustadt, *Presidential Power*, Wiley, New York 1960 p. 46.
3. Max Weber seemed to regard these attachments for personal advantage as so unstable that they should not be regarded as a basis for legitimacy. See *The Theory of Social and Economic Organization*, trans. A. M. Henderson and Talcott Parsons, Free Press, Glencoe, Ill., 1974, p. 325.
4. Weber, from whom I have taken this type, does not make clear just where along the 'personal-institutional' continuum a patrimonial ruler rests. My own feeling is that any patrimonial ruler must operate within certain broad limits of expectation, no matter how arbitrary (and thus outside established rules) certain specific actions may appear. See *ibid.*, p. 347, for Weber's use of the term. 'Patrimonialism' as a concept is further analysed by Aristide Zolberg in *Creating Political Order: The Party-States of West Africa*, Rand-McNally, Chicago, 1966, pp. 141–5, and Guenther Roth, 'Personal rulership, patrimonialism and empire-building in the new states', *World Politics*, xx, 2, Jan. 1968, pp. 194–206.
5. Zolberg, *Creating Political Order*, pp. 131–4.
6. Population and literacy figures are taken from the 1963 *Population Census of Sierra Leone*, vol. I, Table 1 and vol. II, Table 12. The estimates of GDP are taken from Ralph Saylor, *The Economic System of Sierra Leone*, Duke University Press, Durham, N.C., p. 6. Saylor stresses that these estimates are based on a highly arbitrary figure for per capita private consumption. Diamonds and iron ore provided £20·6 million of a total of £25·2 million in exports in 1961. Seventy-seven per cent of the employed population worked in agriculture, and according to the *1965–66 Survey of Agriculture*, 38 per cent of these farmers sold no cash crops at all.
7. The material for this section is drawn, except where otherwise specified, from my *Politics in Sierra Leone*, University of Toronto Press, 1970.
8. These local governments, the chiefdoms, each headed by a Paramount Chief, were again largely shaped by the British. Their number had stabilised by the mid-1950s at just under 150.
9. Twelve of its sixteen seats in 1962 were won in the north (the other four being in the Western Area), and the fact that all but one of its successful candidates were northerners helped confirm its regional base. This in turn contributed to its inability to spread into Mende country.
10. Quoted in his obituary, Sierra Leone *Daily Mail*, 30 Apr. 1964.
11. He was badly shocked when the electorate failed to respond to his appeal for support for his new era; much of his suspicion of 'the Freetown people' seems to have stemmed from this election.
12. One particularly serious incident occurred when a Mende Minister slapped a northern Paramount Chief and was not even rebuked publicly by the Prime Minister.
13. Though the scale of the Emirates of Northern Nigeria was vastly different from the Sierra Leone chiefdoms, still the interrelationship between the Emirs

and the Northern Peoples Congress was quite similar to that of the chiefs and the SLPP. See Bill J. Dudley, *Parties and Politics in Northern Nigeria*, Cass, London, 1968, for a discussion of the Northern Nigerian situation.

14. It is only fair to note, however, that formulations of alternatives to reliance on foreign investment, such as Julius Nyerere's Arusha Declaration, did not gain wide currency until late in the 1960s, after the period under discussion.

15. For details of the diamond mining operations, see Laurens van der Laan, *The Sierra Leone Diamonds*, OUP, London, 1965, and for an analysis of the political effects on the Kono district, see Victor Minikin, 'Local Politics in Kono District, Sierra Leone', unpublished Ph.D. thesis, University of Birmingham, 1971.

16. For a slightly partisan post-mortem on several such deals, see *Broadcast Talk by the Honourable Prime Minister Dr Siaka Stevens*, 28 Mar. 1969, Government Printer, Freetown, 1969.

17. See Leo Kuper, 'Theories of race and race relations', *Comparative Studies in Society and History* 13, Jan. 1971, pp. 87–107.

Richard Hodder-Williams

7 'Support' in Eastern Africa: Some Observations from Malaŵi

I

The Ghanaian military coup of February 1966 was observed by Jack Goody. He noticed the 'immediate and visible' reaction of approval among many of the citizens of Accra, the Youth Leaguers even parading with hastily amended banners proclaiming that 'Nkrumah is NOT our Messiah', and began therefore to question the extent to which apparent support represented any real commitment to the authorities.[1] The ease with which apparent support could evaporate had been predicted by the Nigerian Chinua Achebe, whose novel *A Man of the People* appeared prophetically as civilian rule collapsed in Nigeria and Ghana.[2] His villagers, more cynical even than their leaders and apathetic into the bargain, had nothing directly to do with the overthrow of the politicians, but their public loyalties changed overnight, from expressed support for the corrupt yet powerful local member of Parliament to vilification of his practices.[3] In January 1971, President Obote of Uganda left for Singapore to the cheers of a flag-waving crowd; within days, the streets of Kampala were filled with palm-bearing citizens enthusing over Idi Amin's military usurpation of power. Wise after the event, one journalistic comment implied that in a country 'packed with corruption, torn by tribal dissension, held in check only by force', it required merely the President's absence from the country for the government to collapse and a new order be instituted.[4]

It is debatable, of course, whether these analyses do justice to the complexities of the relationships between governments and people. Beneath the outward expression of delight to be seen in Accra lay reserves of affection and approval for Nkrumah and many of his policies; doubtless some villagers in Nigeria, and elsewhere too, have been less fickle and cynical in their loyalties than Achebe's characters; and in Uganda also, those who waved flags and those who waved palms were not necessarily the same people; it has been argued further that the downfall of Obote was actually preceded by a growth in government support and a diminution of antagonisms.[5] Nevertheless, however future historians may ultimately interpret such events, two basic points remain. First, there is the fact, and it is a fact, that public manifestations of support are quickly replaced by public expressions of enthusiasm for the displacement of former authorities. There exists, then, a real problem in attempting to gauge the opinions of the public. Second, it is noticeable that the people, so often symbolically and undifferentiatedly capitalised, seem to play but a minor part in the confrontations through which systems of government and their incumbents are displaced. There thus exists a further problem, perhaps indeed one of prior importance, in discovering whose support is critical and whose unimportant.

This, in its turn, opens a whole Pandora's box of inquiry and argument, into which Africanists have thrown themselves with some zeal. At one level, it must be decided to what end support is supposed to be critical or unimportant. The notion of 'support', hitherto employed in a cavalierly commonsensical fashion, is deeply rooted in the systems analysis of David Easton,[6] and thus inevitably shares by association much of the criticism of his approach to the study of politics. Many of the assumptions embedded in systems analysis revolve around the idea of stability. Crudely oversimplifying, it might be said that some analysts hold that political systems have an in-built tendency to adapt to disruptive elements within and without the political process to ensure their survival. Others have objected to this view, not merely because some systems in reality fail to adapt – a possibility in fact widely considered by Easton – but because systems analysts advance, if only implicitly, the normative belief that stability is desirable and ideologies or structures or policies which assist this state are therefore also desirable. In Easton's most massive treatment of the concept, *A Systems Analysis of Political Life*,[6] its centrality to the problem of stability, or instability, recurs almost from page to page. 'Where the input of support falls below a minimum', he writes in one summarising passage, 'the persistence of any kind of system will be endangered. A system will finally succumb unless it adopts measures to cope with the stress'.[7] However, he is not wholly unmindful that there is more in heaven and earth than the continuation, perhaps ossification, of a political system. For it may do more than merely survive; it can also be 'a means through which the resources and energies of society are mobilized and oriented to the pursuit of goals'.[8]

Those who object to the essentially conservative image of systems analysis have concerned themselves far more with the 'pursuit of goals', with the consequences of political action, with the distribution of wealth and status and opportunities, with the progress the new states make towards some goal these analysts hold up as desirable and proper. Openly and unashamedly normative in outlook, this approach nevertheless requires 'support' from the citizenry for the social and economic changes necessary for the transformation which they desire.[9] One can hardly have the second type of support without the first. The energies of a society cannot be harnessed over a lengthy period of time, especially if much change in behaviour and attitude is sought, without some set of institutions persisting through which binding decisions may be taken for the whole people.

However the question about the purpose of support may be answered, there is a further difficulty inherent in the high level of abstraction with which Easton formulates the concept. For him, any continuing political system requires some cohesion or sense of political community, a stable set of rules and structures through which authoritative decisions may be made, and a relatively stable set of authorities operating the structures. These three analytically separable requirements are all objects to which individuals within the state can relate with more or less enthusiasm and the net extent of that enthusiasm, whether expressed openly by positive action or covertly by approving attitudes, represents the level of support to the individual political system. This much may be admitted. But to put such a formulation into operation presents acute problems. Any calculation of the level of support will have to recognise that the actions of some members of the political system are potentially more significant for its survival, or for the implementation of particular goals, than others, and the intensity of feeling, and therefore readiness to act, will differ from one person to another. This recapitulates, in a slightly different form, the earlier query about whose support is critical and whose unimportant. Easton hides away in a footnote a crucial passage: 'All that needs to be remembered is that when I speak of the members of a system, unless the context indicates otherwise, I shall be referring to only that segment that research would indicate to be politically relevant at the given time and place.'[10] Here is the rub. The politically relevant people whose support a political system needs differ from country to country and from historical epoch to historical epoch as well as from the vantage point of the observer.

To be aware of gradations of relevance suggests that some conceptual refinement is needed, if the concept of support is ever to be anything more than a summary variable into which all manner of potentially influential factors can be combined. A crude but suggestive development is to conceive of members of a political system as being either politically relevant, or politically marginal, or politically peripheral. The politically relevant would include those whose actions are related in a direct manner with the object of study, such as cabinet or party executive members and senior advisers in the administration for the formulation of policy, the coercive powers for the regime's survival, or the cultivators themselves for agricultural transformation. The politically marginal are those whose actions have a more indirect effect; they may create the political climate with which the national elite operates, provide the support needed for individuals' continuance in power, and cooperate in the implementation of policies. In the short term such groups can be ignored but in the medium term their political impact can be considerable. The politically peripheral would describe those whose behaviour, while probably related in devious ways to the object of our study, is essentially irrelevant. Thus, it could be argued that the civilian crises with which this chapter began involved only a few politically relevant groups, mainly within the coercive powers; the manifestations of open support came from groups who were politically marginal; the peasantry in the rural areas remained politically peripheral. If, however, the focus of the study concentrated on, say, the transformation of Tanzanian society and that country's policy of socialism and self-reliance, the peasantry would become politically relevant and the support they give to the nation's institutions would be critical for the success of the government's policies. Successful continuation in power as well as successful social engineering requires support; but that support is provided by different classes or groups or individuals to differing degrees. While this conceptual scheme may be of *some* assistance, it clearly leaves unresolved any estimation of the precise relevance of various groups, and the degree of their interconnectedness.

Introducing a rough and ready set of categories like politically relevant, politically marginal, and politically peripheral is important, although clearly imprecise and open to the definitional problem inevitably associated with all relativistic concepts. What it does do, however, is emphasise a point not fully covered in Easton's analysis as well as incorporating one of the new growth industries in African studies. There are different levels of political community; that is, the geographical unit delineating the rules and structures for decision-making with which the individual most strongly identifies and with which he is most intimately involved may well differ. Whether one is talking in a historical context about diffuse focus, local focus, and national focus,[11] or in a more contemporary context about arenas,[12] the vast bulk of modern research into political behaviour at the parochial level suggests that national politics are mediated to the village level, and thus frequently distorted, by intermediate institutions and personalities. Patron-client networks are the commonest arrangements for such mediation.[13] Some societies, admittedly, fail to produce readily definable patrons or clients,[14] but the precise nature of an individual's perception and identification with the political process, the heart of any study of support, is only discoverable within a picture of African politics which acknowledges some degree of differential focus.

Another simple tripartite division may be apposite then. Villagers are linked to the political system through their local leaders, traditional authorities or party officials as the case may be; these local dignitaries rely for their position as members of the local elite on fulfilling the demands made on them by villagers, but they also rely for their resources to meet these demands largely on a third category, the national elite. Individual members of the national elite – and it is crucial to conceive of the national elite, however much it may share certain values, as being divided at least into potentially rival factions – can base their power on close relations with local dignitaries, and thus indirectly draw on popular support, or more directly, and more problematically, with the populace, thus affecting the options open to the local dignitaries. There is normally a two-way process of communication, peasant dissatisfaction filtering through local dignitaries to their patrons at the centre, and government policies working their way down through local officials to the village. The latter path is more likely to produce action since the resources available to the national authorities, both developmental and coercive, are greater than those exercisable by unorganised peasants; consequently, the intermediaries prefer to keep in with their powerful patrons and, provided they can obtain some resources to distribute in their locality, they can meet (or exclude) sufficient local requirements to ensure their own survival. By conceiving political interactions in this way, it becomes possible to see that the policies of a popular government may be frustrated because peasant support is articulated through their relations with local officials and these officials are unpopular. The distance of the national leadership from the village, both physically and psychologically, may be more significant than the generally high regard felt for them in abstract. Similarly, participation in an election, far from being a stabilising force as is normally assumed,[15] may well be a destabilising force and represent a lack of support for the national authorities if voting is decided by allegiance to local dignitaries who are out of sympathy with the national leadership. Thus, the context of a particular action is almost as important for its interpretation as the action itself.

Apart from distinguishing between the purposes of support and differentiating between the relative importance to be assigned to the cooperation of different groups within the state, it is necessary finally to examine briefly the status of support as an explanatory tool. Easton's observation, already quoted, that too low a level of support will result in a political system succumbing, is hardly adequate. Such a presentation, for all the sophistications which may surround it in the text, leads to a hopelessly mechanistic, and disappointingly common, view of African politics. The scenario, in caricature form, runs something like this: independent governments, lacking financial and manpower resources while beset with a revolution of rising expectations and competition for scarce resources often manifesting itself in tribalistic conflicts, increasingly need the coercive powers to control dissidents and encourage agricultural change; without the skills or experience to convert overloaded demands into acceptable policies, a rapid erosion of support for the governmental system as well as the government itself takes place in a context of cumulative inequality, growing authoritarianism, and unprincipled self-interest until some other body, usually the Army, enters the stage as a *deus ex machina* to start again – in equally unpromising circumstances.[16] Such a scenario undoubtedly has appeal. As an *ex post facto* explanation, it serves well enough at first sight as a general summary of, say, Nigeria's disintegration, where irreconcilable demands and widely mistrusted political structures produced an output of decisions and coercion which failed to temper demands and weakened support, which in turn exacerbated conditions . . . until the political system succumbed. But political systems do not just succumb. Men and women overthrow authorities and regimes. Eastonian analysis may help to highlight the preconditions for a government's overthrow; it may even suggest some of the precipitants; but it provides no explanation, let alone any necessary correlations, why a particular group of individuals at a particular moment in time should step in and overthrow the existing pattern of relationships by which the authoritative allocation of values for the country is made. Stability, in colloquial and largely in Eastonian terms, really refers to the persistence of one set of rules for deciding how disputes should be settled and decisions made for a country; it is in this sense that the term is used in this chapter.[17]

Depersonalising politics is an inevitable consequence of a high level of generality. There is a danger that theory becomes so beset with exceptions as to be hardly applicable at all or so general as to be obvious or tautological. Furthermore, the tendency to underplay the importance of institutional frameworks and overstress the role of political culture, itself a consequence of the flight from the study of discrete and observable events, encourages the mechanistic view of the processes of change. In the study of new states, the fragility of institutions in the sense of their rapid metamorphoses should not hide the twin truth that most political activity continues unchanged and that those in command of the armed forces or the party, if it is not moribund, and those who form the nation's Cabinet or Party Executive are in incomparably more influential positions than those who are not. Similarly, while the peasantry may be critical for the production of an agricultural surplus or the creation of *ujamaa* socialism, the new monopoly of sophisticated weaponry and communications at the call of the government makes any nationwide challenge to the regime from the countryside highly unlikely. This general point is not applicable to colonial situations, of which pre-revolutionary Burundi may be thought of as one, since the communicators between peasantry and government do not get absorbed into the national structure of politics but remain among the peasantry to articulate their disparate grievances and coordinate their otherwise diffuse actions. The significance of each sector of society thus depends to a great extent not only on the focus of the analyst and on its relationship with other sectors (a reciprocal relationship, since people in institutionally critical positions require the support of particular subordinate groups), but also upon its organisational strength and position within the formal institutions of the nation.

The concept of support, at first sight an attractive and useful notion, involves on a closer acquaintance a whole range of further analyses and investigations if it is to be of any empirical use. In the brief study which follows, this gloss on the concept of support and the relevance of the doubts I have about its applicability at anything but a very high level of generality, are illustrated essentially in the context of Malaŵi's history since its independence in 1964. The choice of Malaŵi arose in part because there was such a paucity of detailed studies on the country, and in part because it provides an example – or counter-example if the conventional wisdom about the inherent instability of modern Africa is accepted – of a decade of stability (and thus poses some questions raised at the outset in Goody's analysis of Ghana).

One final observation is necessary. This chapter was originally presented as a paper to foster discussion at a conference and is in some senses an academic exercise. To concentrate on examining the nature and form of support in Malaŵi is not to express the view that this is one of the more intrinsically important tasks for an academic to perform; nor am I in any way implying that institutional or regime stability in Malaŵi is a good thing. In fact, my own fundamental interests lie in the realms of policy-making and mass politicisation and mobilisation. Nevertheless, it is precisely because of this preference that I have undertaken the exercise of attempting to operationalise a general concept like support. Without denying the general usefulness of such concepts, I hope that more academics will concern themselves with detailed studies on the sort of topics suggested in this paper.

II

When Malaŵi became independent in July 1964, there at least appeared to be clear evidence of widespread support for the regime. Like Tanzania, it gained independence without the distractions of rival nationalist parties. The Malaŵi Congress Party displayed a remarkable control in 1961 when a turnout of over 90 per cent in the twenty lower roll constituencies produced a landslide victory for the party, all opponents losing their deposits. As Lucy Mair suggests, 'the election provided, not an opportunity to test the support for alternative views, but an occasion for a demonstration of solidarity'.[18] Towards the end of 1963, the party organised a country-wide registration campaign, and in less than two months 1 871 170 individuals had registered, although rough calculations had shown that the maximum to be expected was only 1 500 000! On 15 March 1964, approximately 100 000 people gathered near Thyolo to hear Dr Banda announce the party's candidates for the fifty-three seats up for election; no other candidates were even nominated.[19] And the country swept to independence, apparently more united, more mobilised, more active than any other in Eastern Africa.

Such outward unity, however, did not necessarily mean that once the colonial presence had been removed, national commitment and elite unity would survive. To give an example from another African state, Tanzania, the clean sweeps of the Tanganyika African National Union (TANU) in the pre-independence elections in fact obscured the lack of politicisation in many parts of the country, and the decay of the national party demanded the personal attention of Nyerere to revitalise it. The election of 1965 was intended, and to some extent perceived, as an event to develop and consolidate a national awareness, or, rather, an awareness of the nation, since the issues with which the electorate became involved related in only a peripheral way to national priorities.[20] Nor has TANU lacked intra-elite conflicts. There has, in fact, been a constant dialogue over the nature of the party and the form of socialism to be espoused; the progression from Nyerere's '*Ujamaa*: the basis of African Socialism' through the Arusha Declaration to the Party Guidelines (Mwongozo) of 1971 are closely related to the continuing debate within the Party.[21] The optimism among most observers following the 1965 election derived largely from the evidence it gave of a wider participation and more national consciousness among Tanzanian citizens, which was thought to assist in the establishment of a stable governmental system and in the development of more transformational social policies.

But awareness of the national context within which the Tanzanian election of 1965 took place did not prevent local issues and demands from dominating the attention of political activists. The socialist commitment inherent in the Arusha formulations demanded support from the mass of the peasantry which the local focus of the election failed to develop. Thus the 1970 election, which permitted participation, nevertheless continued to prevent a consciousness of the 'realities of imperialism and the full severity of the development challenge' and the local focus for demands was 'irrational if measured against the priorities articulated in the national planning exercise'.[22] Support has thus not been generated for the major social changes desired by Tanzania's leadership; the electoral system encouraged a kind of campaign that made ideology a secondary consideration and the tradition remained that saw politics as a means of solving individual and local problems through the provision of grass-roots support for a successful intermediary.[23] Not only have a very high proportion of the peasants who have entered into new *ujamaa* villages done so from instrumental reasons, even many of the leaders, whether as candicates or local party officials in the villages, have managed to evade the socialist behaviour associated with the ideology.

Tanzania, therefore, remains facing two problems. As is to be expected, 'government stability is for many purposes coterminous with ruling-class stability'[24]; peasant support, which may be adequately generated for the production of an increasing agricultural surplus, has yet to be harnessed to the ideological goals associated with Tanzania's leaders.

In Malaŵi, too, the tendency to identify to some extent with the state but to think 'parochially' may also be discerned, although the consequences are rather different. The politicisation and commitment of the 1950s struggle against the Central African Federation did create a bond which united many of the peasantry and assisted in building a consciously united elite (the prisons of Southern Rhodesia being a powerful influence), but there have been no symbolic national elections in which the mass of the people could get involved and no obvious cultural or historical basis on which national sentiment would naturally continue.[25] The intra-elite conflict of 1964 is but one indication of the comparatively fragile unity to be associated with nationalist movements. The removal of the colonial bogey withdraws the binding force and allows regional, ideological, and personal frictions freer rein.

Nevertheless, three factors of recurring significance assist in creating some set of factors with which the individual Malaŵian can identify on a national level. In the first place, a very high proportion of adult males, probably as many as 60 per cent, have at one stage or another in their lives left Malaŵi to work elsewhere, in the mines on the Witwatersrand and the Zambian Copperbelt or on the tobacco farms of Southern Rhodesia. There they were identified indiscriminately as 'Nyasas' and, latterly, as 'Malaŵians'. Just as some sort of Kikuyu unity was created by outsiders failing to differentiate among the Kikuyu, just as Africans in Nairobi lump the Baluhyia or the Wahindi together regardless of clan or linguistic differences, so southern Africans have helped to consolidate a sense of Malaŵianess among the migrant workers of the country. The elite too was held together to some extent by another dimension of Malaŵi's connection with Southern Africa, for it was well aware that Malaŵi was the 'odd man out' in black Africa, a pariah at the OAU, and this enhanced the solidarity among themselves.

In the second place, the Malaŵi Congress Party remains the only legal party, visible and vocal if not particularly constructive, a symbol of past unity and present promise. Like TANU, its tentacles are by no means all-embracing[26]; like TANU, its local officials are local leaders first and Party ideologues second[27]; admittedly its activities, especially the sporadic campaigns to increase membership – which sometimes involve allowing only those with party cards access to markets or buses – can create hostility and resentment instead of commitment, for zealots not infrequently fail to draw the line between advocacy and force. But there is no denying its ubiquitous presence, nor the enthusiasms, often overflowing into downright fixing, with which the individuals compete for local office. In the lower ranks of the Party there are many elections and a regular turnover of personnel. The politically marginal are therefore harnessed to the system, symbols of a national unity and spokesmen for local interests and prejudices. And these, as we shall see, are often listened to.

The third factor is Dr Banda himself. Attachment to national institutions, largely perceived as imported devices in any case, is much weaker than attachment to individuals. In Banda's case, a determined and eminently successful attempt by the young nationalists in the 1950s to create a human symbol round which anti-colonial feelings could unite has carried over in its consequences into the post-independence years. And Banda has capitalised on this. A conscious effort to ensure the continuation of strong, personal links between himself and 'his people' has encouraged him, not altogether unwillingly, to adapt certain trappings of traditional leaders and to reiterate publicly the importance of this bond. Frequent tours through the rural areas and a shrewd awareness of the parochial demands of the delegates to the party's annual conventions go some way to cementing the link between those with parochial focus and the Head of State.[28]

A failure to differentiate between a supportive attitude to Malaŵi and support for Banda confuses two of the objects of support to which Easton draws attention, the political community and the authorities. It is by no means an uncommon practice. People unfortunately do not perceive the world around them as tidily as some political analysts would like. Not only may support for the political community be so linked with the national leader as to be virtually synonymous, the regime at the national level may be as intimately linked. The perceived distinction is probably between local political structures and their authorities on the one hand and the national institutions and personel on the other. Nevertheless, there is no denying the fact that stability and development are seriously impeded if sizable groups do not accept the boundaries of the state and act out this preference by attempts to create a new state. Here the widely held sense of Malaŵianess helps, for few Malaŵians act as though they believed that Malaŵi was not the appropriate geographical unit within which decisions ought to be taken. The Chipembere 'invasion' of

1965, whose repercussions still deeply affect Malaŵi today and the Mangoche area especially, and that of Chisiza in 1967 were not aimed at secession or otherwise altering the geographical boundaries of the state but at replacing existing authorities through force rather than through the institutional procedures. While Uganda has been faced with border problems in the north and a secessionist movement in the south-west, and Kenya with recurring troubles among the Somalis of the Northern Frontier District, Malaŵi has been mercifully free of movements challenging the very definition of the state. Counter examples are hard to find. Banda's public utterances suggesting that parts of Zambia and Tanzania properly belong to Malaŵi are bargaining counters rather than genuinely irredentist claims,[29] and the Jehovah's Witnesses' exemplifications of 'nomadic self-determination', especially that of 1972, were really the natural responses to discrimination rather than conscious rejection of the Malaŵian state.

The passive acceptance of the nation's borders and even some feeling of common nationality are not necessarily sufficient to prevent major differences based upon ideological cleavages, ethnic inequalities, or class competition from manifesting themselves in violent form. Such differences may be exaggerated by a view of politics which sees government merely as an institution from which to garner advantages. This extractive view of politics, exemplified classically in the politics of Nigeria's Eastern region,[30] is common throughout Eastern Africa too. It is found in the motives of Tanzanian voters,[31] in the preoccupations of Kenyan activists,[32] among notables and the rank and file in Uganda.[33] In countries of minimal resources, to be on the losing side is not just a pity, as in the rich countries of the world, but a disaster. Truly, 'the Wrath of the Lord is as a roaring Lion, but his Love is as the dew on the grass'. Politics is therefore an activity of considerable importance and prestige, an appreciation which imparts to the institutions most visible to the political actor a high standing. These institutions are to be manipulated and their incumbents invested in, with the result that the power inhering in specific positions is used to the full. The apparent disintegration of the political process, in fact the working out of local norms on imported institutions, is thus often a sign of its very real vitality.

What different classes *actually* expect out of politics and how they react to thwarted expectations remains a very unresearched area. Hyden's study of Bukoba is particularly disappointing in this respect, although it illuminates much else.[34] The evidence collected for Uganda by Leys and Oberschall[35] is more suggestive. The extractive view of politics is pervasive, yet, 'while stated desires are generally high, both desires and expectations operate within a framework of realistic calculation' and 'despite the high volume of personal dissatisfaction . . . Ugandans are aware and appreciative of improvements since independence'.[36] Notions of relative deprivation become apposite and the unevenness of development which has become so obvious to many outside observers may have its major impact not on the peasantry but on the intellectuals. Their political models are drawn essentially from theoretical considerations, although practices often contrast with their public attitudes. It is probably dangerous to extend our own egalitarian attitudes and sympathy for the underprivileged into an unchallenged acceptance of egalitarian expectations among Africans, peasants or leaders. In many societies the 'premise of inequality' survives; in all, the unequal vagaries of nature are part of life and 'a tradition which accepts inequality as natural' – a phrase used of Tanzania recently[37] – is unlikely to cavil at a certain amount of inequality. After all, the logical corollary of an extractive view of politics is differential rewards. One does not want to take this argument too far; the 'Wabenzi' tribe grew from ordinary men's disapproval of flaunted privilege and the taunt against Obote – 'here comes the Common Man in his Common Car' – has its seeds in popular disquiet. As Achebe noted, once one takes 'enough for the owner to see', one has overstepped the limits of propriety.[38]

Nevertheless, there is a fundamental problem about what is, and what is not, tolerated. At one level, leaders' tolerance for dissident views may be low, and certainly the rapidity with which laws have been introduced throughout Eastern Africa abridging what would normally be thought of as fundamental rights supports this. Harsh preventive detention laws are freely used; information from Amnesty International suggested that in the middle of 1973, while only half-a-dozen were detained without trial in Kenya, the numbers in other countries were quite high, 60 or so on the Tanzanian mainland, the same number on Zanzibar,

1 500 in Malaŵi (compared with about 350 before the Jehovah's Witnesses troubles), more than 80 in Zambia.[39] Intolerance of opposition may be an insufficient explanation of these figures. They *may* signify that in all East African countries there are a number of people, presumably of political relevance, whose refusal to accept and support the existing regime rules leads national leaders to remove them from political activity. At another level, dissidents in the villages may not be tolerated. This, of course, is one theme constantly reiterated in discussions of traditional practices, often extended into justifications for one-party states. Willi Abraham, for instance, writes that

> to go against the consensus of the people even in expression of opinion, let alone action, was a piece of rashness looked upon with scant favour. The time to express one's eccentricity was in the period of deliberation. To persist in one's individual opinion, when this deviated from the public opinion deliberately arrived at and publicised, was a piece of malice.[40]

Hyden's findings in Bukoba provide some evidence to support such a view; Ingle's research in a very different part of Tanzania is also partially supportive, when he argues that 'the legitimacy of force in developmental efforts may have from the earliest independence been accepted to a greater degree by the people than their leaders'.[41] The use of force may be accepted because there is no alternative and the experience of colonial days taught that little joy followed active expressions of opposition to a government; but, as some of Tanzania's problems about setting up *ujamaa* villages indicate, it does not bring willing cooperation.

Both the extractive view of politics to be found among the peasantry and local dignitaries and the transformational outlook of national leaders emphasise the potential capabilities of the political process. 'An important task for a new government', it has been written, is

> to create confidence in, and respect for the institutions of government as such so that they become legitimate in the eyes of the populace who begin to distinguish between the permanent institutions and the transient members of those institutions.[42]

A decade is a short time in which to create such a distinction, but few East African countries have made much attempt to weaken the philosophy, inherited perhaps from the colonial experience, that government is above all a source of power to be used. In such à society, and in an internal economy dominated by government, it goes without saying that those in the institutionalised positions of authority are invested with immense powers.

Nevertheless, they still require support from the other two tiers of the polity. From the vantage-point of stability analysis, agricultural resources must be produced to meet internal consumption demands and provide a surplus for foreign exchange purposes. Local dignitaries, whose satisfactory relationships with the peasantry are necessary for extracting these outputs and preserving a placid and harmonious countryside, must be satisfied and rewarded. The less the use of the coercive powers, the more energies can be turned to other matters, whether private gain or beneficent leadership, for the exercise of naked power incurs many costs. From the developmentalist's viewpoint, these requirements are more urgent. The Malaŵi Government has survived and extracted a considerable response from the peasantry in terms of increased production and economic reorganisation. It has done this by encouraging local political competition, thus involving the peasantry and engaging the energies of many men and women whose aspirations outreach their skills.[43] These activities have seemed worthwhile to the participants, and the regime has thus been supported, because resources have been widely allocated and local demands, usually conservative, traditional, and essentially 'petty capitalistic' have been listened to. The advantage of this system is that the national leadership has a moderately free hand to delineate the major lines of foreign, economic and social policy.

It has been said that 'it is through elections that members of a polity have the opportunity to express their acceptance of the decisions of party or elite, and to endorse the formal structure of the political system, as a viable method for making acceptable decisions'.[44] This may be so for a country where inter-party competition and regular elections form the major channels through which the majority of the citizenry perceive their political efficacy. And certainly the Tanzanian elections were designed not only to increase the sense of nationhood, as has already been pointed out, but also to permit the people some say in their choice of rulers. Yet the openness of national elections is limited by the desire, perhaps even the need, of the elite leadership to control the limits within which dissent on policy matters may take place. And the significance of parliamentary elections is reduced when there is no clear alternative to the personnel already described as the government and policy is in any case formulated and articulated in a body only indirectly affected by electoral results. Once more the supportive function of political practices is closely related to the arena in which they take place. Local elections satisfy a number of requirements, but they do not directly legitimise either the government or its policies.

National elections in Eastern Africa, it needs stressing, are seldom about policy issues or alternative governments. They provide a fine example of that extractive view of politics to which I have already alluded. There is no question of denying the government its mandate, though certain individual members, mainly junior, may be removed; what is at issue is the personnel to act as the linkmen between people and government, to intercede on behalf of the villages at the level where important decisions affecting its livelihood are made. In Uganda, for example, politics before Amin was dominated by intra-elite conflict and Obote's energies were expended on creating a coalition among rival factions within the elite in such a way that the period from 1962 to 1969 was concerned almost exclusively with the elitist problem of creating a Parliamentary majority to ensure Obote's political survival. The Common Man was largely immaterial; indeed, it has been argued that 'talk about the Common Man was more often than not cynical in the extreme',[45] and the run up to the 1971 elections, themselves organised to strengthen Obote's leadership position and national unity rather than any socialist commitment of the leadership or class consciousness among the peasantry, was noticeable for the way in which local luminaries used the occasion to advance their own, and their clients', instrumental demands.[46] The Common Man's Charter, carefully eschewing anything like Tanzania's leadership code, was 'addressed primarily to a small urban elite and nascent proletariat'.[47] While Uganda may be an extreme case, the experience of Kenya, Tanzania, and Zambia where the mass of the population has participated confirms the essential point that the choice at elections revolves around personalities and their, often local, qualities. National elections are thus largely concerned with legitimising the power of elites. The chief result of the 1969 Kenyan Primaries was to protect and sustain the process of 'elite consolidation' which had been in progress since Independence.[48] And Saul feared that Tanzanian elections might have an anaesthetising consequence where the privileged became freed from popular pressure; from one perspective, the election confirms an elite in power, while from another it selects patrons or delegates to act as inter-mediaries, but in either case there is no challenge to existing power relationships.

Malaŵi's experience emphasises much of this. Because there was little popular participation, the exercise was manifestly designed as a process of intra-elite recruitment and reinforcement combined with an opportunity for local dignitaries to compete for office. Banda clearly wanted some competition. He spent much time haranguing Parliament in March 1971 to stress that any constituency for which only one name emerged would be looked at with suspicion. He wanted at least three, but preferably five, names to be forwarded to him. In the end nearly 5 000 delegates, varying from 79 to 369 in the District Conferences, produced over 200 names for the 60 constituencies. The delegates were drawn from a large number of organisations, from the Party itself naturally enough, from its active Women's and Youth Sections, and included District Councillors, town councillors where possible, as well as chiefs and sub-chiefs. The element of control appeared in the way that Banda could, and did, refuse to accept the most popular nominee and to this extent the election may have been somewhat counter-productive.[49] Yet this formalistic presentation almost certainly underplays the openness of the system. The large number of delegates were themselves elected and in a small country with active village politics each delegate, representing only about 500 adults, is conscious of local preferences. Nor are Banda's interventions necessarily a product of his own preference. MPs who become very unpopular in their constituencies are summarily removed. While too much deviation from government policy is not allowed, the primary role of the MP as a channel of communication between the periphery and the centre is widely accepted, and very similar to the Tanzanian experience.[50] Their actions and Banda's public definition of their duties testify both to the extractive view of politics permeating the country (the Budget debate, for example, is normally a succession of speeches applauding the minister's excellence and calling for preferential treatment for the member's constituency) and to the essential role of intermediary between the peasantry and the policy-making elite.

Although Banda runs a classically Gaullist system of government in that he makes the most crucial decisions himself and then appeals over the heads of the intermediaries for personal support, he does not ignore the intermediaries. He allows them many of the trappings of power, while denying them the reality. In this, the party conference plays a central role, for Banda is careful to listen to local demands over Asian penetration into rural markets, or modern sartorial fashions offending local susceptibilities, or increasing power to traditional authorities, or the non-cooperation of religious sects like the Jehovah's Witnesses. It is possible, then, to envisage a political system like Malaŵi's surviving peaceably on a minimal amount of participation at the national level, provided that the local leaders, one of the politically marginal groups, are themselves involved in the competition for office, enjoy the fruits of success, and receive support from the peasantry. Too much participation could be unhealthy, since it may represent not contentment with the authorities but disaffection from them[51]; what is required will be a satisfactory working relationship between local elites and the ordinary villagers. Local elites do have standing, authority and resources to distribute, if only symbolic ones in some cases, so that an active political life can operate in a rural area with very little direct relationships with the national arena. This is similar to Bienen's analysis of Kenyan politics, where he too emphasises the differential focus of peasantry and elite.[52] In Malaŵi, the local elites are caught up in politics and have access, if not to the decision-making positions which control the nation's economic and foreign policy, at least to a forum which responds in some degree to locally felt demands, in any case the most salient to villagers.

Saliency is central to any study of the relationship between government and people. It is governmental action, or inaction, which provides the raw material from which supportive attitudes are reinforced or weakened. Banda's policy of dialogue with South Africa between 1964 and 1973, which to outsiders may seem so potentially divisive an issue, is seen differently once its salience is analysed. Extractive politics, parochial focus, the universal unconcern for foreign policy issues, elite links with South Africa, all combine to reduce the policy of dialogue in internal politics to comparative insignificance. There are other factors which prevent dialogue being a major source of internal friction. The relationship between villagers and notables is a reciprocal one. The villagers will, for those issues which lie outside their personal understanding, experience, or concern, follow the cue leadership of notables they trust, but the notables themselves need the support of the villagers to consolidate and prolong their status as notables. Ideologies and foreign policy are not the subjects, in Malaŵi as elsewhere, by which to generate popular support. The position is well expressed in a study of Ugandan politics:

> The factors which effectively motivated voters in 1970 were mainly those involving local issues and grievances, cleavages of kinship, tribe and religion, and long-standing disputes or factional squabbles within the UPC itself . . . candidates . . . made certain that local issues were dealt with and local cleavages manipulated.[53]

In some situations this mutual dependence is skewed so that a leader of standing in a community, because of his established and personalised ascendancy, can foster and encourage views on policy issues outside the ken of local leaders and villagers. Banda's position in Malaŵi, however much the concept of charisma has been overworked, certainly has many attributes of the charismatic, and it is surely true to argue that 'as in most African states, the political system is highly personalised, foreign policy in particular being regarded as the special preserve of the Head of the State'.[54] Nearly all groups accept the President's cue leadership in matters of foreign policy – as indeed they do on most economic and social policies – but this is due as much to structural factors as to political culture.

There is the simple point that Banda is Life President of the party and of the country, the constitutions of which give him enormous power of appointment and dismissal as well as residual sources of strength in the countryside through such active bodies as the Young Pioneers and the Youth League. A leader cannot be removed nor policies altered if there is no rival around to which men of importance and power can rally. The events of 1964, in which much of the younger and articulate leadership of the party was removed, therefore remain of crucial significance. Most of the major populist figures of the nationalist movement fled the country; Banda's hold over patronage ensured that it was difficult to establish a power base other than through the President's good will; a conscious policy of courting the essentially conservative forces of the peasantry and local notables together with the continual emphasis on the party watchwords of Unity, Loyalty and Obedience effectively by-passed the new generation of potential political leaders. A policy of Africanisation which provided sufficient outlets to absorb most of the skilled Malaŵians without actually removing the expatriate presence from the sensitive ministries, educational establishments, or the coercive powers, completes Banda's consolidation of power. But politics do not stand still. And in recent years the process of Africanisation has brought an increasing number of Malaŵians into the critical positions, into a few of the critical ministries as Permanent Secretaries, as commanders of the Army and police, and even of the Special Branch itself.[55] Structural factors cannot be ignored.

Once again we return to the nuts and bolts of politics, to institutions and their incumbents, to differentiation and its consequences, and move away from mechanistic analyses of political decay and system fragility. In Malaŵi there are distinct political arenas which absorb the energies of different groups of people and, broadly speaking, at the local and intermediate levels there are sufficient opportunities for participation and discussion to prevent a groundswell of popular discontent bursting out into non-cooperation or violence.[56] At the national level, the unity of the elite, once the 1964 crisis was past, was fostered in part by the expanding bureaucracy and parastatal organisations providing jobs for the aspiring educated and in part by shared experiences and values deriving from colonial days. Structural factors militated against intra-elite conflict, as did Banda's superiority in argument and control of detail, and no issue arose round which a rival could, if permitted, attempt to rally opposition to the country's leadership or institutions. The issue of dialogue stirred neither the elite nor the peasantry; the issue of class formation did not appeal to an elite which profited from it nor to local notables who could feed off rich patrons. Above all, the institutions satisfied those who participated in them and the government's demands on the peasantry were balanced by rewards, both practical and symbolic. The comparatively even tenor of Malaŵi's political life owes much to the absence of rivals to the Malaŵi Congress Party (MCP) in 1964 round which opposition to the governmental system could coalesce and Banda's shrewd combination of participation and control within an essentially pragmatic philosophy appropriate to local demands, though not to an egalitarian socialism.

This chapter, as I have said, is something of an academic exercise. It has failed to describe the components of support in Eastern Africa for reasons more connected with theoretical problems than research deficiencies. Put bluntly, the difficulty lies in the sheer improbability of ever putting the concept into operation. Although the refinements made here to Easton's concept, refinements implicit on occasions in his analysis, are neither startling nor inventive, they highlight the enormous complexity of any operation designed to calculate the level of support, let alone the political consequences of the level discerned. There are, to start with, problems of terminology. Stability seems related not so much to a political system as to the political regime; to collapse or to succumb denies outside agencies, particularly human initiative; in short, the disconcerting lack of interest in the precise processes which are presumed to link attitudes or dispositions to relevant political action is symptomatic of the refusal to accept the crucial, if not primary, importance of named individuals and their specific relationships and beliefs.

The first observation which arises from this chapter, then, questions the use of support as an analytical tool at all. 'Regime changes', the *sine qua non* of lack of support, become virtually analogous to the lack of support, and the critical level of support is thus only discovered after an inadequate level has already manifested itself. If support is to have explicative value, then there must be consideration of the various dimensions of the concept to which I have drawn attention, the need to specify the observer's focus, to differentiate between degrees of political relevance, and to articulate the inter-relationships between various groups within society. The categories which have been used in this paper are gross simplifications, for there is much differentiation within the tripartite division of political forces, peasantry, local notables, national elite, as well as disagreement over the relevance of different classes. All this emphasises the subjectivity and the complexity of the concept itself.

There is a very genuine and concrete problem about theorising on African politics. Gavin Kitching, for instance, found that the propositions his research on Tanzania was generating were:

> either specific propositions which were of use comparatively only in the rather negative sense that they could be used to refute broad generalisations, or they were so general and flaccid that they were applicable to Tanzania (or even tropical Africa) only because they applied almost everywhere.[57]

There is much truth in this. Nevertheless, even this small study has stressed at the very least some of the questions which ought to be asked before any understanding of the political process in Eastern Africa can be complete. The answers may well differ from country to country, but to expect otherwise is to join the still large band of African commentators who persist in believing that the vast and disparate continent, presumably for some undisclosed reason of geography, practices a single, unique brand of politics. It also neglects the variable process of class formation. Above all, however, it ignores personalities. Men and women overthrow regimes and galvanise people into action. To overcome the too mechanistic models of breakdowns, we need detailed knowledge of the relationships between named individuals in institutionalised positions of authority and power, Army officers (for they are surely uniquely 'relevant'), and Cabinet Ministers, who precisely because of their formal positions, are in a far more significant position to change governments than most other individuals. My second observation, thus, draws attention to the need, not to ignore studies of political culture or peasant mobilisation (which are central to questions of social transformation and the style of politics), but to value more highly some African variation of Kremlinology and to reinstate private motives as significant forces in political developments.

There is, however, a third matter, probably of even greater significance. It derives essentially from the implicit assumption in this chapter that Dr Banda *is* widely supported, that the political structures satisfy popular demands, that there is indeed a close causal connection between a high level of support and political stability or economic development. There have, in fact, been plenty of occasions in the last decade when the government of Malaŵi has been faced with opposition outside the constitutional channels.[58] How much, then, of the tranquillity associated with Malaŵi is genuine, and how much merely a facade, a shrewd calculation of advantage in a society which dislikes deviants and in a polity which deals harshly with dissidents?

Where Malaŵi has changed in the last few years is in the increase of Malawians in positions of political relevance, in nominal, if not actual, control of the armed forces and of the police, in positions within the party or cabinet or Civil Service from which to mount or assist an attempt at reversing Banda's life tenure of office. There are more Malaŵians in politically marginal positions, in the Civil Service, in business, in parastatal bodies, in the sprawling surrounds of Blantyre, who might lend their encouragement, their brains, or their muscle power to an aspiring usurper. It is they who create the pre-conditions, publicise the grievances, articulate the doubts and disappointments, on which coups are based. But we do not know much about their cohesion, their bases of power, their private ambitions, or ideological beliefs. Nor do we know much about the coercive powers, about their leaderships, about the strength of allegiance among lower ranks to their President or their commanders. Once again, knowledge about named individuals in specific positions is required. More to my particular point, the stability of the Malaŵian political system since 1964 may be due not to any high level of support from among the mass of Malaŵians but to structural factors which denied access to the high command posts to Malaŵians. Similarly, the growth of the Malaŵian economy since independence in both the 'subistence' and 'modern' sectors may be due to factors quite unrelated to increased support among the state's members. A recession before 1964 and the minimal amount of development investment expended there in the days of the Central African Federation probably meant that *some* improvement was inevitable. The provision of improved marketing and transport facilities, made available as a result of increased overseas grants, strengthened this tendency as did the instrumental values of most Malaŵian farmers. If the problem of anticipated reactions is introduced and notice is also taken of the possibility that compliance with governmental initiative is merely a response to expected governmental punishment for non-cooperation rather than an expression of individual commitment, the evidence of increased productivity tells us precisely nothing about support.

My final observation is therefore directed against a practice, more common I suspect outside the United Kingdom, of predicating research on the reification of a theoretical concept. It would be absurd to deny the crucial place of theory in the organisation of a complex and diffuse amount of data, but there is a real danger that those who wish to study support or elites or poliarchies will, because they are looking for them, discover them. This is a criticism properly levelled at this chapter for it was consciously predicated on the assumption that stability was directly related to a high level of support.[59] It was possible to find plausible explanations for a high level of support and thus, or so it appeared, the existence of that support was established. The argument fails because of the initial assumption that stability depends upon support in a general way, rather than on the support of specific people within an observable political structure. While my intuitive appreciation of the Malaŵian situation convinced me that the Malaŵi of 1974 differed markedly from the Ghana of 1966, I would not be altogether surprised to read in a year or two's time: 'The situation in contemporary Malaŵi (Ghana) illustrates the ease with which apparent support can evaporate . . .'.[60]

Notes

1. See Jack Goody, 'Consensus and dissent in Ghana', *Political Science Quarterly*, lxxxiii, 3, Sept. 1968, pp. 337–52.
2. Chinua Achebe, *A Man of the People*, Heinemann, London, 1966.
3. *Ibid.*, pp. 161–2, 166.
4. *Daily Telegraph*, London, 26 Jan. 1971.
5. M. Twaddle, 'The Amin coup', *Journal of Commonwealth Political Studies*, x, 2, July 1972, pp. 99–112.
6. David Easton, *A Systems Analysis of Political Life*, Wiley, New York, 1965.
7. *Ibid.*, p. 220.
8. *Ibid.*, p. 153.
9. A fine example of this genre is J. S. Saul, 'The nature of Tanzania's political system: issues raised by the 1965 and 1970 elections', *Journal of Commonwealth Political Studies*, x, 2, July 1972, pp. 113–29 and x, 3, Nov. 1972, pp. 198–221.

11. J. Lonsdale, 'Some origins of nationalism in East Africa', *Journal of African History*, ix, 1, Jan. 1968, pp. 119–46.

12. F. G. Bailey, *Politics and Social Change: Orissa in 1959*, University of California Press, Berkeley, 1963, pp. 219–34.

13. See, for instance: R. Sandbrook, 'Patrons, clients and factions: new dimensions of conflict analysis in Africa', *Canadian Journal of Political Science*, v, 1, Mar. 1972, pp. 104–19; and R. Lemarchand, 'Political clientelism and ethnicity in tropical Africa: competing solidarities in nation-building', *American Political Science Review*, lxvi, 1, Mar. 1972, pp. 63–90.

14. G. Kitching, 'Local political studies in Tanzania', *African Affairs*, lxxi, 284, July 1972, p. 287.

15. A. J. Milnor, *Elections and Political Stability*, Little Brown, Boston, 1969.

16. See, for instance: J. O'Connell, 'The inevitability of instability'. *Journal of Modern African Studies*, v, 2, Sept. 1967, pp. 181–92; and I. Wallerstein, 'The range of choice: constraints on the policies of governments of contemporary African independent states', in M. Lofchie, ed., *The State of the Nations: Constraint on Development in Independent Africa*, University of California Press, 1971, pp. 19–33, esp. 33: 'As long as the state machinery remains fragile and the state's revenue so uncertain, there will be a chronic gap between promise and reality, and *hence* chronic instability'. (My italics.)

17. Leon Hurwitz, 'Contemporary approaches to political stability', *Comparative Politics*, v, 4, Apr. 1973, pp. 449–63.

18. L. P. Mair, *The Nyasaland Elections of 1961*, Athlone Press, London, 1962, p. 81.

19. H. R. Rowland, 'Nyasaland general elections, 1964', *Journal of Local Administration Overseas*, iii, 4, Oct. 1964, pp. 230–1, 238–40.

20. L. Cliffe, ed., *One Party Democracy*, East African Publishing House, Nairobi, 1967, pp. 239, 241, 276, emphasises the national dimension; J. S. Saul, 'The nature of Tanzania's political system', p. 202 questions this.

21. J. K. Nyerere, *Freedom and Unity*, O.U.P. Dar es Salaam, 1966, pp. 161–71; J. K. Nyerere, *Freedom and Socialism*, O.U.P., Dar es Salaam, 1968, pp. 231–51; 'The TANU guidelines', *Mbioni*, vi, 8, Aug. 1971, pp. 4–17. On internal dissension see H. Beinen, *Tanzania: Party Transformation and Economic Development*, 2nd edn., Princeton University Press, 1970, pp. 203–58; L. Cliffe and J. S. Saul, eds., *Socialism in Tanzania*, vol. 2, East African Publishing House, Nairobi, 1970, pp. 304–58; C. Mulei, 'The predicament of the left in Tanzania', *East Africa Journal*, ix, 8, Aug. 1972, pp. 29–34; and W. Tordoff and A. A. Mazrui, 'The left and the super-left in Tanzania', *Journal of Modern African Studies*, x, 3, Oct. 1972, pp. 427, 466.

22. Saul, 'The nature of Tanzania's political system', p. 202.

23. C. Hyden and C. T. Leys, 'Elections and politics in single-party systems: the case of Kenya and Tanzania', *British Journal of Political Science*, ii, 4, Oct. 1972, pp. 413, 416; cf. also, 'Whether (the candidate) is a socialist or not is a secondary matter. It is not his ideological orientation but the confidence he enjoys among the people that matters' (pp. 412–13).

24. Saul, 'The nature of Tanzania's political system', p. 204.

25. The 1971 elections publicly only involved the local district dignitaries; unlike Tanzania, or Zambia, the electorate at large was not allowed to choose between the two candidates (or three in Zambia) which the Party proffered as a result of the District Conferences. Nor was the Kenyan system of replacing the District conferences by a popular primary instituted. The Empire of Maravi, it might be added, covered an area and involved peoples significantly different from what is incorporated into Malawi today.
26. This is the major theme in Beinen, *Tanzania: Party Transformation* . . . .
27. See, for example, D. Brokensha, 'Handeni revisited', *African Affairs*, lxx, 279, Apr. 1971, pp. 159–68.
28. For an elaboration of this argument, see R. Hodder-Williams, 'Dr Banda's Malawi', *Journal of Commonwealth and Comparative Politics*, xii, 1, Mar. 1974, pp. 105–7.
29. See J. Mayall, 'The Malawi–Tanzania boundary dispute', *Journal of Modern African Studies*, xi, 4, Dec. 1973, pp. 618–19.
30. M. Vickers, 'Competition and control in modern Nigeria: origins of the war with Biafra', *International Journal*, xxv, 4, Oct. 1970, pp. 603–33.
31. Cliffe, ed., *One-Party Democracy, passim;* Hyden and Leys, 'Elections and politics in single-party systems', pp. 415–16.
32. C. Gertzel, *The Politics of Independent Kenya*, Heinemann, London, 1970, *passim.*
33. I. Gershenberg, 'Slouching towards socialism: Obote's Uganda', *African Studies Review*, xv, 1, Apr. 1972, p. 86, quotes approvingly O. Sembene, *God's Bits of Wood*, Doubleday, New York, 1970, p. 277: 'To us, their mandate is simply a license to profiteer'. See also G. Glentworth and I. R. Hancock, 'Obote and Amin: change and continuity in modern Uganda politics', *African Affairs*, lxxii, 288, July 1973, pp. 253, 254: 'The frame of reference may be described as follows: government exists to benefit those who are in control . . . The goal is the enrichment of this group . . . Amin represents not an aberration within Uganda's recent history but an extension of existing tendencies of Uganda politics . . . What has been done has been to convert a dominant theme into an exclusive preoccupation'.
34. G. Hyden, *TANU Yajenga Nchi: Political Development in Rural Tanzania*, Uniskol, Lund 1968.
35. C. T. Leys, *Politicians and Policies*, East African Publishing House, Nairobi, 1967; and A. R. Oberschall, 'Rising expectations and political turmoil', *Journal of Development Studies*, vi, 1, Oct. 1969, pp. 5–22.
36. Oberschall, 'Rising expectations', pp. 16, 13.
37. Hyden and Leys, 'Elections and politics in single-party systems', p. 416.
38. It may not be coincidental that in those countries where a commitment to socialism was public, Tanzania and to a lesser extent Uganda, the anti-elitist feelings were more publicly expressed. Kenya and Malawi, and Zambia too, exemplify systems of cumulative inequality without many popular expressions of resentment.
39. Private Communication, 7 Aug. 1973. The situation in Uganda was beyond Amnesty International's ability to monitor. Other personal sources would alter some of these figures, lowering Malawi's 1973 total while increasing its

average for early years, increasing mainland Tanzania's, and noticing that 1973 was the best year for some time in Kenya.

40. W. E. Abraham, *The Mind of Africa*, Weidenfeld and Nicolson, London, 1969, pp. 75–6.

41. C. R. Ingle, 'Compulsion and Rural Development in Tanzania', *Canadian Journal of African Studies*, iv, 1, Jan. 1970, p. 99.

42. Y. P. Ghai and J. P. W. B. McAuslan, *Public Law and Political Change in Kenya*, O.U.P., Nairobi, 1970, p. 506.

43. The Party rules call for many meetings at the lowest level. One consequence of this, given the essentially parochial focus of most members at that level, is an obsession with deviants and scapegoats, of which the witch-hunt against the Jehovah's Witnesses and some of the more inexplicable deportations may be some indication.

44. Milnor, *Elections and Political Stability*, p. 1.

45. S. D. Ryan, 'Economic nationalism and socialism in Uganda', *Journal of Commonwealth Political Studies*, xi, 2, July 1973, p. 152.

46. D. L. Cohen and J. Parson, 'The Uganda Peoples Congress branch and constituency elections of 1970', *Journal of Commonwealth Political Studies*, xi, 1, Mar. 1973, pp. 46–66.

47. Gerschenberg, 'Slouching towards socialism', p. 93.

48. Hyden and Leys, 'Elections and politics in single-party systems', p. 405.

49. In five constituencies all five nominees were ignored. Candidates were shuffled from constituency to constituency and changes made because the conferences, perhaps too representative of local opinion, selected too few women and graduates. One minister was not nominated, but Banda used his powers to reappoint him all the same, though he was later dismissed in somewhat unsalubrious circumstances.

50. See R. F. Hopkins, 'The role of the MP in Tanzania', *American Political Science Review*, lxiv, 2, Sept. 1970, pp. 754–771. Malawian MPs, however, seem less ready to challenge the bourgeois style and economic practices of their leaders from a populist perspective.

51. W. H. Morris-Jones, 'In defence of apathy', *Political Studies*, ii, 1, Mar. 1954, pp. 25–37. Cf. also L. Cliffe, ed., *One-Party Democracy*, p. 280, where, despite a basic emphasis on the virtues of participation, a certain indifference in the 1965 Election in Bukoba was deemed to be healthy. Seeing that it was Bukoba's tendency to return independents against official TANU candidates which precipitated the establishment of the Presidential Commission on the One-Party State, this seems questionable. Later troubles in Bukoba confirm this.

52. H. Bienen, *Kenya: the Politics of Participation and Control*, Princeton University Press, 1974.

53. Cohen and Parson, 'Branch and constituency elections', p. 58.

54. J. Mayall, 'Malawi's foreign policy', *World Today*, xxvi, 10, Oct. 1970, p. 435.

55. See R. Hodder-Williams, 'Malawi's decade under Dr Banda: the revival of politics', *The Round Table*, 252, July 1973, pp. 463–70.

56. There are plenty of separate instances of disquiet with government policy, normally based upon land grievances, but no general or coordinated unrest.

57. Kitching, 'Local political studies in Tanzania', p. 283.

58. See Hodder-Williams, 'Dr Banda's Malawi', pp. 107–10.

59. Or a high level of coercion or a balance between the two. Although several hundred Malawians are normally in detention at any one time, the openness of participation at the local level suggests that the coercive forces' chief influence may be their potential. Since this chapter was written there has been much greater recourse to detentions, imprisonment, and even straightforward killing.

60. Goody, 'Consensus and dissent in Ghana', p. 351.

Douglas G. Anglin

8   Zambia and Southern African Liberation Movements: 1964–1974*

Zambia and Southern Africa

Zambia is the most strategically positioned and dangerously exposed host state engaged in the liberation struggle in Southern Africa. Not only is she the only landlocked country fully committed to the cause, until 1974 she was surrounded on three sides by target regimes. This gave her borders with Southern Africa that were far longer than those of any other state – more than 1 600 miles in all. Moreover, she abutted four of the five major theatres of guerrilla activity: Tete province, the Zambezi valley, Caprivi and Eastern Angola; no other host state has been involved on more than one front. A further complicating factor is Zambia's unique copper wealth. While this has been a major source of strength, it has also meant that her vital lines of communication and industrial installations have provided inviting targets for retaliatory action by hostile neighbours.[1]

Although Southern Africa has constituted the central focus of Zambian foreign policy, direct support for liberation movements has formed only one element in a broader strategy. The key to this has been Zambia's determination to develop her economic, political and military capabilities as rapidly as possible in order to provide the requisite freedom of action for an effective role as a host state. Accordingly, there have been sustained efforts to disengage from the South, to strengthen and diversify the country's economic infrastructure, and to foster national unity, most recently through the enactment of a one-party participatory democracy. An incidental purpose has been to ease the fears of

---

*This chapter does not analyse developments since 1974, when circumstances and Zambia's response were in some respects very different.

the minority communities in Southern Africa by providing a clear example of peace and prosperity under African majority rule. 'We hope that by forming a good government', a UNIP spokesman explained in early 1964, 'we will influence these countries to realise that what is possible here is possible there.'[2]

In addition to embarking upon a radical internal restructuring of the country, Zambia turned to diplomacy. Although the possibility of direct contact with Southern African regimes was never ruled out, repeated rebuffs taught the President to be sceptical of this approach. Instead, he sought to mobilise international support for the confrontation with Southern Africa. Here, the attitude of the Western powers was seen as crucial. For this reason, a major effort was directed to persuading and pressuring them, directly and through the UN and OAU as well as through non-governmental channels, to intervene decisively in favour of justice in Southern Africa. However, as faith in the power of reason diminished, the complementary policy of supporting armed struggle assumed enhanced importance. Nevertheless, it remains only one instrument, admittedly a vital one, in a coordinated Zambian strategy designed to effect a political transformation in Southern Africa. The individual liberation movements, and especially their leaders, are regarded as means to this end, and not ends in themselves. As Vice-President Simon Kapwepwe indicated in 1968, guerrilla warfare is not 'the only means of solving the Rhodesian problem'.[3]

There are compelling reasons for Zambia's outspoken support for the liberation struggle in Southern Africa. Morally, the case for self-determination and racial equality is unanswerable. Ideologically, the government is committed to Nkrumah's dictum that independence is 'meaningless unless it is linked up with the total liberation of Africa'.[4] An element of 'kith and kin' sentiment is also present in the understandable concern expressed for the fate of 'our brothers'. A further motive for Zambia's policy is her concern to project a pan-Africanist image; accordingly, she is keenly sensitive to any suggestion that she is not responding as positively as she might to OAU initiatives. However, there are even more fundamental explanations solidly rooted in Zambia's domestic and international interests. The political transformation of Southern Africa is the ultimate answer to the country's dependence on the minority regimes to the south. Moreover, the perpetuation of racial conflict there threatens not only to inflame the whole subcontinent but to engulf Zambia as well. At stake are her economic prosperity, her fragile experiment in non-racialism, her political stability, her internal and external security, and perhaps even her independence. In connection with the latter, government spokesmen have been outspoken in articulating their grave suspicions concerning the ultimate aims of South Africa's 'outward looking' foreign policy.

At the same time, the liberation struggle in Southern Africa confronted the government and people of Zambia with a series of moral and political dilemmas concerning the means by which their commitment to 'the total liberation of Africa'[5] should be translated into concrete measures of support. To begin with, there were doubts concerning the legitimacy of a resort to violence and of Zambian government involvement in it. There was also uncertainty concerning the extent to which a host state should concern itself in the domestic affairs of liberation movements. Finally, the government has had to face up to the implications for its internal and external security of offering hospitality to freedom fighters.

The delicate position of a host state deeply committed to the cause of liberation is rarely fully appreciated either by 'microphone revolutionaries' who can safely indulge in ringing calls for sacrifice from the security of their distant capitals, or by the freedom fighters themselves who understandably press for open-ended undertakings of support and a complete free hand to pursue their goals. How Zambia has sought to reconcile her revolutionary idealism with the realities of her exposed position on the front line of freedom in Africa is the subject of this chapter.

1. Liberation Support

According to a government spokesman, 'Zambia's policy since Independence has consistently remained one of rendering every possible assistance to the liberation movement in Southern Africa within the framework of the decisions of the OAU'.[6] Yet, what did 'rendering every possible assistance' mean in practice? The spectrum of options available to Zambian authorities to express their solidarity with Southern African liberation movements ranged from simple moral encouragement to overt military intervention. It is scarcely surprising that the employment of Zambian armed forces directly in a liberation role has never been seriously contemplated, except possibly in the form of aerial retaliation against Southern African capitals in the event of bombing attacks on Zambian towns.[7] Yet, at one time, even the granting of moral support posed a problem.

Acceptance of the legitimacy of armed struggle was a particularly painful personal decision for President Kenneth Kaunda. As a Gandhian pacifist by nature and conviction, he was long firmly committed to the resolution of conflict by non-violent means. During Zambia's struggle for independence, he had consistently urged moderation upon his more militant followers, and had largely succeeded in confining their agitation to peaceful channels.[8] Moreover, initially he had even opposed the creation of a Zambian army, except for purely ceremonial purposes. As late as 1961, he had resisted the despatch of army cadets to Britain. Yet, under the ineluctable pressure of events in Southern Africa, the President gradually reconciled himself to the necessity of armed resistance to minority oppression.[9] In April 1964, he was offering ZAPU (see Table 8.1) 'every possible moral and material aid short of military aid'; and in December he declared before the United Nations: 'I do not call for violence'.[10] Even his insistent demands that the British overthrow the rebel regime in Rhodesia by force were attempts to pre-empt large-scale racial violence. The turning point in Dr Kaunda's outlook came in late April 1966 following Prime Minister Wilson's announcement of the proposed 'talks about talks' with Ian Smith, and the Sinoia massacre two days later when seven ZANU freedom fighters were killed by Rhodesian security forces.[11] Thereafter, all ambiguity in his attitude to the instrumental use of violence fell away, though he continued to regard it as a necessary evil. The authoritative Lusaka Manifesto of 1969 accurately reflected his thinking:

We have always preferred ... to achieve [the objective of liberation] without physical violence. We would prefer to negotiate rather than destroy, to talk rather than kill. We do not advocate violence; we advocate an end to the violence against human dignity which is now being perpetrated by the

Table 8.1 The Principal Southern African Liberation Movements in Zambia: 1964–1974

Angola
FNLA:	National Liberation Front of Angola
MPLA:	Popular Movement for the Liberation of Angola
UNITA:	National Union for the Complete Liberation of Angola

Mozambique
COREMO:	Mozambique Revolutionary Committee
FRELIMO:	Mozambique Liberation Front

Namibia
SWANU:	South West Africa National Union
SWAPO:	South West African People's Organisation

Rhodesia
ZANU:	Zimbabwe African National Union
ZAPU:	Zimbabwe African People's Union
FROLIZI:	Front for the Liberation of Zimbabwe
ANC:	African National Council

South Africa
ANCSA:	African National Congress of South Africa
PAC:	Pan-Africanist Congress of South Africa
UMSA:	Unity Movement of South Africa

oppressors of Africa. If peaceful progress to emancipation were possible, ... we would urge our brothers in the resistance movements to use peaceful methods of struggle.... But while peaceful progress is blocked ... we have no choice but to give to the peoples of those territories all the support of which we are capable in their struggle against their oppressors.[12]

Hence, the vigorous espousal of the liberation cause in rhetoric and in resolution at the United Nations and elsewhere.

Yet it is one thing to approve of freedom fighting and quite another to sanction Zambian involvement with it. Decision-makers in Lusaka have naturally been concerned to avoid providing the minority regimes with legal pretexts for engaging in hot pursuit or pre-emptive strikes. Accordingly, every effort has been made to minimize the extent of direct Zambian assistance.[13] This has had the paradoxical consequence of lending credence to contradictory accusations: first, that Zambia has not been as supportive of freedom movements as she might have been and, secondly, that she has been far more deeply implicated in 'terrorism' than has actually been the case.

(a) Recognition

A necessary preliminary to the provision of administrative or operational assistance to liberation movements is some measure of recognition (see Table 8.2). Initially, this was a party function, but since Independence it has become a government responsibility. During the period under review, recognition has, in practice, taken three forms: official designation (as with ZAPU, FRELIMO, MPLA, ANCSA, SWAPO and later the ANC in Rhodesia), de facto acceptance (ZANU, FNLA at times, FROLIZI briefly, COREMO until 1974, and UMSA), and passive toleration (UNITA). The PAC of South Africa enjoyed second category status until August 1968, when it was banned and its leaders expelled.[14] The previous year, the entry permit of the UNITA leader had also been withdrawn. However, his party continued to maintain an unofficial, though on occasion highly visible, presence in Lusaka. Following the Portuguese coup, it was gradually restored to grace. Similarly, FNLA, which had long been inactive in Zambia, was once again accorded de facto recognition. On the other hand, SWANU appears to have lapsed permanently into oblivion and, with it, any status it may once have possessed. Opposition groups from independent African states have no standing, formally or informally, in Zambia. Those that did operate there during colonial times, such as the Basutoland Congress Party and the Bechuanaland People's Party, were required to disband once their countries had attained Independence.

Several criteria have governed decisions on recognition. Perhaps the most important has been OAU policy. Zambia has followed the OAU lead in all cases except with respect to ZANU, FNLA and, since 1968, PAC. On the other hand, COREMO, the Unity Movement, FROLIZI and UNITA, none of which had, at least until the 1970s, any official standing with the OAU Liberation Committee, have been accorded varying degrees of recognition. Where there were divided movements, the decisive consideration has been the government's judgement as to which faction commanded majority support at home. In the case of Rhodesia, President Kaunda early asserted that, 'Africa must do as was done

Table 8.2 Recognition, organisation, and operations

Country/ Liberation movement	Found-ing Date	Formal recognition by:		Lusaka office		Guerrilla operations			
		Zambia	OAU	Opened	Status	Launched Front	Date	Zambia fronts Front	Date
Angola									
MPLA	1956	1965	Nov. 1964	1965–1968–74	regional headquarters	Luanda	4 Feb. 1961	Moxico	18 Mar. 1966
FNLA	1957	(1975)	Aug. 1963	1962–66, 1974–76	sub-office	north	15 Mar. 1966	Lunda	May 1968
UNITA	1966	(1975)	Jan. 1975	1966–67 1968–76	headquarters sub-office	Moxico	1 Mar. 1966	Moxico	1 Mar. 1966
Mozambique									
FRELIMO	1962	1965	1964	1964–75	regional	Cabo Delgado	25 Sept. 1964	Tete	8 Mar. 1968
COREMO	1965	—	—	1965–74	headquarters	Tete	24 Oct. 1965	Tete	24 Oct. 1965
Rhodesia									
ZAPU	1961	1964–75	1964	1963–75	headquarters	Zambezi	13 Aug. 1967	Zambezi	13 Aug. 1967
ZANU	1963	—	1964	1963–75	headquarters	Zambezi	29 Apr. 1966	Zambezi	29 Apr. 1966
FROLIZI	1971	—	—	1971–75	headquarters	Zambezi	1971	Zambezi	1971
ANC	1971	Dec. 1974	Jan. 1975	1975	external hdqrs	Northeast	1975	—	—
South Africa									
ANC	1912	1965	1964	1964–	regional	—	—	(Zambezi)	(13 Aug. 1967)
PAC	1959	—	1964	1964–	regional	—	—	(Tete)	(June 1968)
UMSA	1943	—	—	1967–	regional	—	—	—	—
Namibia									
SWAPO	1959	1965	1964	1965–	headquarters	Caprivi	26 Aug. 1966	Caprivi	26 Aug. 1966
SWANU	1959	—	1964–65	—	—	—	—	—	—

in Zambia and support the majority – and clearly ZAPU com-
mands the majority'.[15] Quality of leadership, personal friendships
and demonstrated operational effectiveness, all of which might be
thought to have favoured ZANU over ZAPU and, to a lesser
extent, PAC over ANC (though not FNLA over MPLA), proved
less significant. Dar es Salaam, on the other hand, assessed these
conflicting considerations differently and, hence, backed ZANU
rather than ZAPU, and welcomed the PAC leaders deported from
Zambia. This is one issue on which Presidents Kaunda and
Nyerere agreed to differ. One incidental consequence of this has
been to make it more difficult for them to wield a credible threat
to withhold (or withdraw) recognition as a means of imposing
unity on warring liberation groups.

(b) Administrative and financial assistance

Recognition, whether formal or *de facto*, entitled 'foreign nationalist parties' to the administrative facilities of the African Liberation
Centre established in 1965 on the outskirts of Lusaka, to the use of
Zambian travel documents, and to various other minor material
perquisites including the inclusion of the names of six leaders on
the State House protocol list. Six of the eight Southern African
liberation movements long recognised by the OAU, as well as
three splinter groups, have had representation in Zambia. Nearly
half have, at one time or another, had their external headquarters
in Lusaka. The only significant group not currently located there
is the banned South African PAC.

Apart from equipping and maintaining the Centre and making
available certain other services in kind, Zambia provides only
limited and essentially *ad hoc* financial assistance to liberation
movements on a bilateral basis. She prefers, on principle, to have
all administrative and operational support funnelled through the
OAU Liberation Committee's Special Fund. In 1963, UNIP had
been one of the Committee's earliest beneficiaries[16] and, since
then, Zambia has been among its most loyal contributors.
Although her assessment amounts to only a modest percentage of
the total budget, the record of most OAU members, at least until
recently, in supporting the liberation struggle with anything more
than ringing rhetoric and resounding resolutions has been so
deplorable that Zambia's contribution has in some years consti-

tuted more than a quarter of the funds actually received. In fact, in 1969, she was one of only five member states not in arrears in her payments.[17]

(c) Radio propaganda

One sphere in which a distinction has usually existed between the privileges accorded movements which were officially recognised and those which were not, is external broadcasting. Before Independence, Dr Kaunda denied any intention of allowing radio facilities to be used to broadcast propaganda to Rhodesia.[18] The Unilateral Declaration of Independence changed that. Within a few days of the declaration, and in advance of an OAU request on the subject,[19] ZAPU was granted the use of Radio Zambia to mobilise its supporters across the Zambezi.

The consequences were disappointing. Initially, the programmes were hastily produced, poorly conceived, frequently crude, and generally of a low quality. It was not simply that the language employed was inevitably pretty uncompromising. ZAPU leaders were desperate men who had been publicly ridiculed and accused of betrayal by President Kaunda (and others) for being 'stupid idiots' in doing nothing to resist Smith.[20] The more frustrated they felt, the more virulent their vernacular appeals became.

The broadcasts proved partially counterproductive. The response from the Zimbabwean masses appears to have been minimal. The Smith regime, on the other hand, reacted strongly, skilfully exploiting nationalist excesses to embarrass the British Government to whom both sides looked for salvation. In two widely-distributed pamphlets entitled 'Britain's Part in the Incitement of Murder, Arson, Sabotage and Destruction in Rhodesia' and 'Murder by Radio',[21] the Rhodesian rebels catalogued in extravagant terms the sorry tale of alleged British complicity in the ZAPU broadcasts. There was no substance to the charges. Nevertheless, Salisbury's formidable propaganda offensive was undoubtedly damaging. Whether for this or other reasons, in 1966, political broadcasts to Zimbabwe were curtailed. Thereafter, ZAPU broadcasters were confined to reading the news in Shona and Sindebele three times daily (until March 1971, when the announcer was restricted, along with other party leaders) and producing news commentaries on world affairs (until July 1972 when the person concerned was ordered deported).[22]

The fading of the voice of Zimbabwe did not end political broadcasts to Southern Africa. In January 1971, MPLA instituted a daily 45-minute programme, 'Angola Combatente', which quickly acquired a wide audience. Then in May 1973, Zambia formally inaugurated its new External Service – 'the war of words channel' – with the aid of powerful new Chinese transmitters. FRELIMO, ZAPU/ZANU, MPLA, ANC and SWAPO were each allocated an hour a day. As a result, Radio Zambia blanketed the sub-continent for more than forty hours a week in twenty-two languages, with the liberation movements accepting responsibility for almost all the content.[23] This constituted assistance on a massive scale, and undoubtedly had a significant impact on African opinion throughout Southern Africa.

(d) Operational Facilities

The really delicate issue for Zambia is the provision of operational assistance to freedom fighters, as this could have serious implications for the country's internal and external security. Basically, the liberation movements have sought four concessions from host states: transit rights, transit camps, training camps, and finally operational bases. Granting freedom of transit was the easiest for the government to rationalise; there seemed nothing improper in permitting Southern Africans to return home, with their arms, to carry on the struggle inside their own countries. Certainly, there has been no attempt to deny that freedom fighters are crossing Zambia, with official approval, on their way south. 'Zambia', one Minister explained, 'is doing no more than giving these people from abroad the right of way into the country they are fighting for'.[24]

Yet, in practice, the problem proved more complicated than this. It was not always feasible to insist on uninterrupted passage of cadres through to the battle zones, particularly during periods of comparative inactivity or where, as in the case of Rhodesia until recently, no liberated area existed. Accordingly, the need for transit camps arose. Eventually, it was concluded that these too could be safely sanctioned, provided the length of stay of the visitors was limited to a few days, or a week at the most.[25]

However, even these less stringent regulations proved difficult to enforce. While instances have occurred of individual freedom fighters being jailed for lingering too long, in many cases there appeared to be no alternative to further extensions in the period of grace.

Nevertheless, the government has continued to insist that all freedom fighters, apart from designated party officials and certain transport personnel, are merely in transit, and are to be treated as such. For this reason, they acquire no rights to residence or to freedom of movement; nor are they entitled to pursue their normal activities. In particular, they are forbidden to engage in military training. On this, the government has been adamant, despite numerous accusations to the contrary.[26] 'We have no training camps in Zambia', President Kaunda declared categorically, 'none whatsoever'.[27] So confident was the government of its innocence in this regard that it publicly invited the South African Government and anyone else to undertake a tour of inspection. 'We are ready to take them to every inch of Zambia', the Foreign Minister promised. One South African journalist accepted the challenge, but failed to confirm his suspicions.[28] Admittedly, a certain amount of informal training may be carried on clandestinely, but it is unlikely to be militarily significant. Certainly, there has been nothing comparable to the major training centres in Tanzania and Algeria. Nor is it easy to understand why these would be necessary in view of the availability of superior facilities elsewhere. Yet, despite this, critics have continued to confuse training camps, which were not authorised, at least until recently, with transit camps which are.

Zambia has been equally insistent that she has allowed on her soil neither operational bases from which attacks can be launched against neighbouring countries, nor privileged sanctuaries to which freedom fighters can return. 'It has always been the policy of my Government', President Kaunda asserted, 'not to allow "freedom fighters" or any other type of military or para-military unit to operate from Zambia against or within neighbouring territories. . . . Zambia cannot and does not tolerate the use of its soil as a base for military or para-military operations. . . .'[29]

The principle of a liberation struggle waged inside the target territory rather than by raiding parties from staging points outside is sound revolutionary theory, but it has not always been

consistent with OAU rhetoric – to which Zambia claims to sub-
scribe – on the responsibilities of host countries. As a result, an
inevitable element of ambiguity has crept into her public pronouncements. When, at the 1972 OAU Summit Conference, King
Hassan called on all border states to 'accept military bases' and,
with them, 'all the inconveniences, such as the right of pursuit and
reprisals . . . even if they are bombed day and night by the enemy',
as happened to Morocco during the Algerian war, President
Kaunda felt constrained to respond somewhat equivocally that
the decisions taken on the basis of the King's 'reported statement'
would be implemented in the 'spirit of Rabat'.[30] The Rabat conference also concluded that 'the proposed Combat Posts within
Member States' were 'unnecessary at present'.[31] This was no doubt
a welcome relief to the Zambian Government which was anxious
to avoid a public commitment to a policy so obviously calculated
to provoke reprisals – at least until the country was in a better
position to defend itself. Nevertheless, it is only realistic to assume
that some two-way freedom fighter traffic across Zambia's borders
has occurred that the authorities have either been unaware of, or
unable to control, despite attempts to keep it within reasonable
limits.

2. Controls

From the outset, the Zambian Government was determined to
ensure that it exercised adequate control over freedom fighter
interactions with each other, with the Zambian population, and
even with the Southern African regimes. The activities of liberation movements within Zambia caused understandable concern
with the implications for internal and external security of the
presence in the country of even modest numbers of armed and
not always fully disciplined cadres. Although the units involved
were in no way comparable, quantitatively or qualitatively, with
the Palestine liberation armies in Jordan and Lebanon, in relation
to Zambia's small and already over-extended defence forces, they
represented a serious potential threat. As for guerrilla operations
in the field, economic as well as security considerations dictated
the need for constraints.

The ultimate weapon at the disposal of the government was the power to bestow or withdraw recognition, and with it the privilege of operating in Zambia. However, this was a blunt instrument that could only be wielded in exceptional circumstances, especially as there was always a risk of incurring OAU displeasure. In any case, the government was anxious not to take sides in quarrels between or within exile parties. Accordingly, it sought as far as possible not to promote its own ideological line or to influence the course of the constant internecine struggles for power. Such restraint was never easy, and occasionally proved impossible.

The one 'domestic' issue that the government considered was its legitimate concern was disunity within the ranks of the liberation movements. This manifested itself in two forms: the failure of rival parties to form common fronts, and intraparty conflict.

(a) Common fronts

Zambia has been less doctrinaire than many OAU members in her approach to the thorny problem of unity among national libera-tion movements. The reason for this is rooted in her own nationalist experience: UNIP was itself a breakaway party. There was less inclination, therefore, to condemn secession in all circumstances; a surgical action was not always dysfunctional. On the other hand, Zambian leaders recognised the utility of their own tactical coalition with the opposition ANC during the tran-sitional period 1962 to 1964 and, in the much more difficult struggle Zimbabweans faced, unity was considered even more essential; Algeria, ˙not Zambia, was the appropriate model.[32] Besides, Zambia had every interest in avoiding chaos on her borders. There was, therefore, a predisposition in Lusaka to favour the single-party system of Tanzania (and subsequently Mozambique) as it appeared to offer greater prospect of an orderly transfer of power in Rhodesia and Angola than the multitude of parties with which Zaire embarked on indepen-dence.

Zambian involvement, through UNIP, the government and the OAU, in efforts to reconcile divided liberation groups dated back before Independence (Table 8.3). Not surprisingly, the earliest and most intimate contacts were with ZAPU and ZANU. Many of their leaders were friends and colleagues of Zambian leaders

Table 8.3 Zambian Efforts to Promote Unity Among Southern African Liberation Movements: 1964–1974

| Dates | Place | Initiative | Good offices | Liberation movements | | | Comments |
				Zimbabwean	Angolan	Mozambique	
1964							
Jan.–Feb.	Lusaka	UNIP	Kaunda, Sipalo	ZAPU/ZANU			
Aug. 14	Lusaka	OAU	Malawi, Tanzania	ZAPU/ZANU			Zambia hosted meeting
1965							
Mar.	Lusaka	Zambia	Kapwepwe (Foreign Minister)			all but FRELIMO	COREMO formed June 1965
July 20–22, Aug. 27–29	Nairobi	OAU	Ethiopia, Kenya, Malawi, Tanzania, Uganda, Zambia	ZAPU/ZANU			Subcommittee: Kenya, Tanzania, Zambia
Oct.	Accra	OAU	Ghana, Sierra Leone, Tanzania, Zambia	ZAPU/ZANU			
Oct.	Lusaka	Savimbi	Kaunda		FNLA/MPLA		Meeting never held
1966							
Feb.	Dar es Salaam	OAU	Tanzania, Zambia plus 3	ZAPU/ZANU			Reconciliation Committee (of five) Appointed March 1966
Sept.	Lusaka	OAU Kaunda	Kaunda, Nyerere Kaunda	ZAPU/ZANU	FNLA/UNITA		
1968							
		OAU	Congo(B), Egypt, Ghana, Zaire, Zambia		FNLA/MPLA		Committee of Five, appointed Sept. 1967
		OAU	Kenya, Tanzania, Zambia	ZAPU/ZANU			Appointed Sept. 1968

Date	Place	Convener	Participants	Zimbabwe movements	Angola movements	Outcome
1972						
Sept. 9	Dar es Salaam	OAU	Congo(B), Tanzania, Zaire, Zambia		FNLA/MPLA	Appointed June 1971
Dec. 13	Kinshasa	OAU	Congo(B), Tanzania, Zaire, Zambia		FNLA/MPLA	Kinshasa Agreement
1973						
Mar. 14–17	Lusaka	OAU	Cameroon, Ghana, Kenya, Tanzania, Zambia	ZAPU/ZANU		Agreement on Political Council and Joint Military Command
May 31–June 1	Kitwe	Mulungushi Club	Kaunda, Mobutu, Nyerere		FNLA/MPLA	
Oct. 27–29	Mwanza	Mulungushi Club	Kaunda, Mobutu, Nyerere		FNLA/MPLA	
1974						
May 7–9	Dar es Salaam	OAU	Congo(B), Tanzania, Zaire, Zambia		FNLA/MPLA	
May 25–26	Lusaka	Kaunda	Kaunda, Mobutu, (Nyerere)		FNLA/MPLA/ UNITA	
July 27–28	Bukavu	OAU	Kaunda, Mobutu, Ngouabi, Nyerere		FNLA/MPLA factions	Bukavu Agreement
Aug. 12–21	Lusaka	OAU	Congo(B), Somalia, Tanzania, Zaire, Zambia (observers)		MPLA factions	MPLA Congress
Sept. 1–3	Brazzaville	OAU	Kaunda, Mobutu, Ngouabi, Nyerere		MPLA factions	Brazzaville Agreement
Nov. 7–10	Lusaka	Kaunda	Kaunda, Nyerere, Seretse Khama	ANC/ZAPU/ ZANU		
Dec. 4–7	Lusaka	Kaunda	Kaunda, Nyerere, Seretse Khama	ANC/ZAPU/ ZANU/ FROLIZI		Zimbabwe Declaration of Unity

from school and university days or during the struggle against the Federation. There was not the same history of personal collaboration with nationalists from Angola, Mozambique and other territories; besides, a language barrier frequently intervened.

In April 1964, after months of agonising appraisal, UNIP formally declared its support for Joshua Nkomo and ZAPU rather than Ndabaningi Sithole and ZANU.[33] Although the timing of the announcement – three days after Nkomo's restriction – may not have been entirely coincidental, the decision was based principally on evidence supplied by UNIP branches throughout Rhodesia that ZAPU was overwhelmingly the majority party.[34] This was a political judgement that Zambians felt uniquely qualified to make, and explains their consistent support of ZAPU ever since, despite the strong pro-ZANU sentiment in other African states including Tanzania. Nevertheless, in practice, the Zambian attitude has been more evenhanded than this firm commitment suggests, partly no doubt because ZANU managed to establish close personal and political relations with an influential minority in the Cabinet. In any case, the government and the party have never ceased to seek unity.

Efforts to heal the breach began shortly after the split in August 1963, with both Kaunda and Sipalo, UNIP's Secretary for Pan-African Affairs, attempting to bring the two sides together.[35] Then, the following August, Lusaka hosted an OAU meeting at which the Tanzanian and Malawian Foreign Ministers offered their good offices to bring about a 'united front'. As both ministers were ZANU sympathisers, the presence of Zambian spokesmen in the wings helped to restore the balance – and, incidentally, reinforce ZAPU intransigence.[36] A year later (1965), the depressing routine was repeated in Nairobi where a Special OAU Commission of six 'neighbouring' states headed by Zambia, and subsequently a sub-committee of three including Zambia, again failed to record any progress towards a 'common front'.[37] A similar fate befell the efforts of the Reconciliation Committee established at the OAU Summit Conference in Accra in October 1965.[38] Thereafter, OAU pressure on the warring factions slackened, partly because of a sense of utter frustration but mainly because of UDI. Although in March 1966 Presidents Kaunda and Nyerere were asked to mediate the dispute,[39] and informal conciliation attempts continued, the general feeling was that the two liberation movements should be allowed to demonstrate their relative military capabilities inside Rhodesia.

When the long-promised masterplans[40] failed to unfold, disillusionment deepened. Dr Kaunda had already given vent to his feelings in a remarkable outburst three days after UDI, when he bitterly denounced the leaders of both parties as 'chicken-in-the-basket' freedom fighters who, through their high-living, arrogance and inactivity, had betrayed Zambia as well as their own people. 'The only reason why I have tolerated the presence of these idiots', he said, 'is that I respect the four million Africans and Europeans ... in Zimbabwe.'[41] Eighteen months later, he reverted to the same theme in more measured tones. 'The situation calls for real unity', he declared. 'I don't want to be harsh here, but everyone concerned with the welfare [of ZAPU and ZANU] is getting very much upset by the inability of the nationalists even in their divided form to be effective in the situation in Rhodesia.'[42] Concerted action, therefore, was essential. ZAPU redeemed its reputation temporarily when, jointly with the South African ANC, it launched its incursion into the Wankie area in July 1967, shortly before the Kinshasa OAU Summit. Nevertheless, disquiet at the continuing disunity among Zimbabwean freedom fighters, and frustration at the apparent helplessness of the African states to do anything about it, persisted. The OAU continued to go through the annual ritual of appealing to ZAPU and ZANU to close ranks. In September 1968, Zambia, Kenya and Tanzania were again asked to use their good offices to effect a 'united front',[43] but the results were invariably and predictably nil. In fairness, however, it must be admitted that political and ideological divisions within the OAU as well as Soviet opposition were contributing factors in the Organization's inability to impose unity.

In 1971, a new approach was attempted. By then, ZAPU was so rent by internal strife as to be organisationally immobilised, whereas ZANU had successfully restructured itself operationally (and ideologically). The Zambian Government took advantage of this altered power relationship to encourage those elements within both movements which favoured the formation of a new organisation embracing the existing parties but not necessarily under the same leadership. President Kaunda made it abundantly clear that ZAPU and ZANU had 'got to choose between coming together or forfeiting Zambia's readiness to accommodate them'.[44] Out of this confusion, FROLIZI emerged in October 1971. Zambia eagerly promoted its claims to OAU recognition but, before this could be formally accorded, the most promising effort to date to reincarnate a united Zimbabwean nationalist movement lost momentum. Instead of one party, there were now three, each more tribal than ever. In the circumstances, FROLIZI withered and, in June 1973, effectively disintegrated. Its most notable achievement was to compel ZAPU and ZANU to talk seriously about unity.

Faced with the threat by angry OAU members of withdrawal of recognition (and, for ZAPU, a possible switch in Soviet policy), the two factions issued a 'declaration of intent' to unite. Then, in March 1972, they signed the Mbeya agreement establishing a Joint Mlitary Command.[45] From the first, it proved a dead letter. A year later, five African foreign ministers meeting in Lusaka managed to extract a new agreement,[46] but only after Zambia had reportedly threatened ZANU – now the stronger partner militarily – with expulsion. Nevertheless, after two attempts to set up the Joint Military Command, even the façade of unity was quietly abandoned.

The Portuguese military coup in April 1974, and the subsequent promises of early independence for Mozambique and Angola, compelled all actors in the Southern African drama radically to re-write their Rhodesian scenarios. Dr Kaunda was among the first to recognise the dramatic new possibilities which the collapse of the Portuguese empire opened up. Despite the obvious political risks involved, he responded positively to overtures from South Africa's Prime Minister Vorster, and thus secured the release of Joshua Nkomo, Ndabaningi Sithole and other Zimbabwean leaders who had been under restriction or detention in Rhodesia for more than a decade. Then, at historic meetings in Lusaka in early November and early December, the Zambian President, with the full support of the Presidents of Tanzania and Botswana, finally secured the firm agreement of ZAPU and ZANU (as well as of the FROLIZI rump) to 'unite' under the banner of Bishop Muzorewa's African National Council which, as the sole legal nationalist organisation in Rhodesia, all undertook to recognise as the 'unifying force of the people of

Zimbabwe'.[47] It was a remarkable, though shortlived, achievement. Bitter memories of past antagonisms and intensified jockeying for power as well as the best efforts of the Smith regime eventually undermined the fragile unity so painfully constructed.

The Zambian Government has been far less deeply embroiled in Portuguese African emigré politics. Its one excursion in the Mozambique field was not an entirely happy experience. In March 1965, Foreign Minister Kapwepwe convened a conference in Lusaka to forge a united nationalist movement out of the array of splinter groups scattered through neighbouring countries. From this, COREMO emerged[48] but, as FRELIMO boycotted the meeting, the unintended consequence was to polarise divisions. The continued hospitality Lusaka extended to COREMO also cast a minor shadow over Zambian-FRELIMO relations that took several years to fade. In June 1974, however, on the eve of FRELIMO's takeover in Mozambique, Zambia pressed COREMO to dissolve itself and join the ruling party. When it declined to do so, and in fact joined with other groups to form the National Coalition Party, Lusaka finally expelled its leaders.

In October 1965, President Kaunda, at the suggestion of Dr Jonas Savimbi, tried unsuccessfully to bring the MPLA and FNLA leaders together in Lusaka. A year later, however, he managed to arrange a meeting between Holden Roberto (FNLA) and Savimbi, who had now emerged as leader of UNITA.[49] Unfortunately, nothing came of this initiative and, on the two occasions when further meetings were organised, Holden failed to attend.

Attempts to reconcile MPLA and FNLA were complicated by conflicts between their principal patrons – the two Congos – as well as by the impact of international ideological forces. The Committee of Five on Angola, which the OAU established in September 1967 and of which Zambia was a member, found itself unable even to meet until the following June.[50] However, with the improvement in relations between Zaire and her neighbours and the refusal to recognise FNLA as a government-in-exile in June 1971, the OAU designated the foreign ministers of four member-states, including Zambia, to assist in the task of reconciliation.[51] A year later, the two parties were finally brought together. The ensuing negotiations eventually resulted in the Kinshasa Agreement of December 1972 which provided for joint political and military institutions. Unhappily, it was never implemented.

During the next two years, Presidents Kaunda, Mobutu and Nyerere at their periodic meetings as members of the informal 'Mulungushi Club' of central African heads of state, strove valiantly to resurrect something from the wreckage of the Kinshasa accord. The task assumed even greater urgency when, following the Portuguese coup, it became evident that Angola could have her independence virtually for the asking. This served as an incentive for a further series of conciliation initiatives culminating in another illusory agreement at the Bukavu summit meeting in July 1974. By this time, the problem had been greatly complicated by the internal divisions renting MPLA. In the end, the most that could be attained, even when confronted with an impending constitutional conference on independence with the Portuguese in January 1975, was agreement on a 'common political platform' hammered out largely as a result of the diplomatic skill of Dr Jonas Savimbi, the UNITA leader.[52] This modest success was greatly welcomed in Lusaka. Unfortunately, it too proved short-lived.

Although Zambia was, during this period, a firm supporter of MPLA's claim to represent the Angolan people, her overriding concern has not been ideology but the promotion of nationalist unity both to strengthen the hand of the freedom fighters in their struggle with the Portuguese and to ensure an orderly transition to majority rule. Zambians hoped to avoid a repetition of the Zaire situation along their western border or astride their vital rail outlet to the Atlantic.

(b) Interparty and intraparty conflict

Freedom fighters in Zambia, in common with exile groups everywhere and throughout history, have inevitably suffered from feelings of insecurity, anxiety and frustration. These have frequently found expression in maladaptive behaviour. This has been apparent not only in the characteristic reluctance to collaborate with rivals, but also typically in the marked propensity to indulge in bitter conflict both within and between parties.[53] Understandable as this is in the circumstances, the Zambian Government nevertheless could not afford to tolerate these periodic violent releases of tension. Its concern here has not simply been with preserving law and order. Equally important have been the consequences of internal strife for the military effectiveness of the movements. PAC, ZAPU and MPLA, in varying degrees, have in this way all been seriously weakened as fighting organizations.

In Zambian experience, the Zimbabweans have been the most frequent offenders. Armed clashes between ZAPU and ZANU supporters were particularly prevalent during the first year after the split. The following year, UNIP recognition of ZAPU signalled a fresh outbreak of fighting. This compelled the government to issue a 'stern warning' that it was 'not prepared to allow Northern Rhodesia to be a fighting ground between members of political parties of other countries', and that it would not hesitate to close down party offices or deport those responsible. Government recognition 'did not entitle members of ZAPU to eliminate their rivals by methods which disturb the peace of the country'.[54] Nevertheless, interparty violence remained a recurring feature of the Zambian scene.

More serious, however, has been the succession of volcanic eruptions within liberation movements. The first victim was the Pan-Africanist Congress of South Africa. It had long suffered from personal and ideological rifts. In August 1968, it was banned and forty-five of its members deported to Tanzania for illegal entry, 'contravening regulations' governing nationalist organisations, and 'indulging in detentions and counter-detentions within their party'.[55] There were also allegations of plots to assassinate Zambian ministers.[56] Consequently, the government decided to take no chances.

The internecine strife that has riven ZAPU was pursued at times with a passion befitting a religious crusade. Its roots lay in a combination of personality feuds, power struggles, ideological, strategic and generational differences, tribal rivalries and accusations of spying; but above all it was a reflection of the years of tension, isolation, deprivation and disappointment that the leaders had endured. The event that first compelled direct Zambian intervention was an armed assault in April 1970 on a ZAPU hostel in a Lusaka suburb where Shona supporters of the Chikerema faction apparently attempted to eliminate three Ndebele members of the party's war council. In the ensuing gun battle, three persons were wounded, one of whom is alleged to have died later.[57] A Presidential ultimatum, demanding that the warring groups either patch up their differences or face expulsion, succeeded in restoring some semblance of unity, but only temporarily.

The following March, the Chikerema wing succeeded in kidnapping over twenty of its opponents at gunpoint.[58] This time, government patience was exhausted. In a major security operation, it rounded up the cadres of both groups, placed them under restriction in a remote bush camp, and impounded their arms and property. When, after several months, no progress had been made in effecting a reconciliation and, in addition, the rebels were displaying increasing defiance of the government, the President detained the more prominent among them, including the thirty-nine so-called 'militants'. Shortly afterwards, nearly 120 lower echelon supporters, some of them suspected spies or deserters, were (after consultation with the OAU) deported to Rhodesia where most of them were promptly arrested and three have since been sentenced to death.[59] Even this drastic action failed to instil a sense of sobre realism into the ZAPU leadership. In October 1971, the party formally split on the issue of FROLIZI, with the Chikerema faction joining the new movement and the rest remaining aloof. The only beneficiary of this tragic upheaval has been the Smith regime; from 1970 to 1972 ZAPU was for all practical purposes militarily incapacitated.[60]

MPLA has also experienced internal dissension. By early 1973, the split in party ranks inside Angola had reached Zambia, with armed clashes flaring up in transit camps.[61] Although the fighting appears not to have posed a serious security problem, it did adversely affect military operations against the Portuguese. This was deeply distressing to the Zambian Government, especially as it had accorded more unqualified support to MPLA than to any other liberation movement.

Despite inspired reports alleging Zambian complicity in various plots to topple MPLA President Agostinho Neto in favour of Vice-President Daniel Chipenda, leader of the 'Eastern Revolt', Lusaka did not in fact take sides in the dispute, other than to provide Chipenda and Neto with police protection.[62] At the same time, it struggled desperately to head off a final rupture. Apart from hosting MPLA's first congress near Lusaka in August 1974 (which unfortunately failed to forge party unity but instead ended in Dr Neto walking out), President Kaunda has been personally deeply involved in the extended Zambian efforts to reconcile the warring factions. In addition, he participated along with the presidents of Congo(B), Tanzania and Zaire in two major meetings of the OAU conciliation commission at Bukavu in July and Brazzaville in September. The latter encounter appeared to have resolved the conflict with Chipenda accepting Neto's leadership, but three months later the rift re-emerged, resulting in Chipenda's expulsion from MPLA.

(c) *Isolation*

The Zambian Government has sought to isolate foreign nationalist parties from close contact with Zambian society and especially from members of their own communities resident in Zambia. This is consistent with the Zambian conception of freedom fighters as essentially transit visitors who were entitled to a corridor through the country, but not into it. The principal motive for this policy, however, has been the desire to minimise the risk of direct or indirect alien involvement in domestic politics.

In implementing this approach, the first requirement was adequate supervision of liberation movement activities. This has been the responsibility of a small secretariat within the office of the President.[63] In addition, UNIP acts as a watchdog. Since 1971, there has also been a sub-office of the OAU Liberation Committee in Lusaka.[64] When this was first mooted, there appears to have been some concern felt in Zambia that it might undermine the government's authority. These fears have since been dispelled; the director is a Zambian, appointed by Zambia and fully acquainted with government policy.

In January 1965, the government issued a directive 'curtailing the activities of foreign African nationalist movements in Zambia'.[65] The resemblance of this to earlier instructions governing embassy operations in Zambia was not entirely coincidental, as initially the government regarded the offices of recognised liberation organisations as having quasi-diplomatic status. Under these regulations, liberation movements were required to close their branches outside Lusaka, to confine their activities to the capital, and not to travel beyond 10 miles from the centre of the city without government permission. In addition, they were forbidden to campaign for funds, and the number of resident officers allowed was limited to six designated officials.

The Lusaka Liberation Centre, where the administrative offices of liberation movements are located, was until 1972 in the care of the President's Personal Representative, the idiosyncratic Mukuka Nkoloso, also known for his exploits as the self-styled Director-General of the National Academy of Science, Space and Astronautical Research. The shepherding of the various organisations into a single compound under government supervision has not always been regarded by the freedom fighters as an unmitigated blessing. The Zimbabwean parties, in particular, have resisted centralisation, and have managed to retain the offices they had acquired before Independence. In all other cases, the government's wishes have prevailed.

Table 8.4 Southern African Communities in Zambia[67]

| | | Total populations (1 Sept. 1969) | |
| | Refugees | | |
Alien Africans	(1 Jan. 1970)	By citizenship	By birth
Angolans	8 192	8 405	28 919
Mozambicans	3 124	4 338	8 699
Rhodesians	—	34 549	57 781
South Africans	284	1 490	4 246
Namibians	838	398	756
Total	12 438	49 180	100 401

The injunction on direct interactions with southern African communities within Zambia was to ensure that the liberation movements did not develop the kinds of domestic political bases that gave Palestine liberation organisations an almost unchallengeable leverage with the governments of Lebanon and Jordan. In the case of Zimbabweans and Angolans, the local communities were substantial (Table 8.4). Accordingly, firm steps were taken to insulate as far as possible the refugee camps from contact with freedom fighters by moving them well away from the borders. In addition, party political activities were curtailed. Occasional meetings have, however, been allowed to commemorate important anniversaries, and these have sometimes been addressed by ministers or top UNIP officials.[66]

(d) Operational restrictions

The calculation of the risks incurred in Zambia's commitment to the liberation of Southern Africa is most critical in the case of the operational activities of cadres, whether in transit through Zambia or in action in the field. Figure 8.1 represents an attempt to

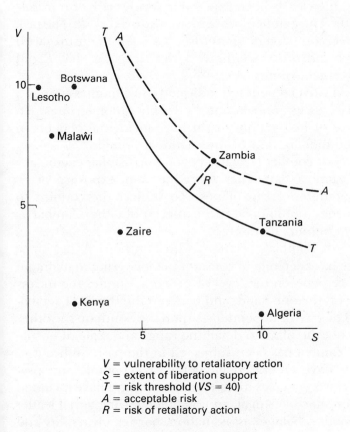

V = vulnerability to retaliatory action
S = extent of liberation support
T = risk threshold (VS = 40)
A = acceptable risk
R = risk of retaliatory action

Figure 8.1. Risk Threshold in Southern Africa

conceptualise the problem on the basis of relative indices of host state support for liberation activities (S) and vulnerability to economic and military retaliation (V). These are quantified on a purely judgemental basis and can only be regarded as suggestive, not empirically tested. It is also assumed that the risk of retaliation is a function of V and S, and that a risk threshold (T), beyond which the threat of retaliation may be actualised, exists. Here, T is arbitrarily set at 40, that is,

$$T = VS = 40$$

On this basis, Tanzania is judged to have struck a rational balance between vulnerability and support, whereas Zambia (alone among African states) has clearly been exposed to serious risk of reprisals from the South. The extent of this risk is measured by R. The task of Zambian decision-makers, therefore, has been to ensure, with respect to each individual southern African regime, that R did not exceed acceptable limits (A).

The Zambian Government has indicated its willingness to pay a substantial price as its contribution to the liberation struggle. In fact, a measure of martyrdom might have incidental benefits in assisting in the mobilization of international opinion. Nevertheless, if the level of conflict escalates beyond occasional exemplary punishment, Zambia has either to reduce her exposure or to strengthen her defence capabilities. To subject the country to crippling damage would not be in the interest of either Zambia or of the freedom fighters themselves.

The history of Zambia's relations with Southern Africa since Independence has been one of constant manoeuvring to maintain a viable balance between the level of provocation and the means of deterrence on the one hand, and between the threat of retaliation from and degree of dependence upon the South on the other hand. This is not the place to detail the range and scale of hostile acts to which Zambia has been subjected in the past. Suffice it to say that these have embraced elements of economic and psychological warfare as well as military measures, and have included blockades, economic blackmail, rumour-mongering, aerial leaflet raids, subversion, sabotage, assassination, border incursions and bombings.

Precautions taken to control the logistical operations of liberation movements inside Zambia have centred on the supervision of arms shipments in transit and on the avoidance of concentrations of men and material that might invite pre-emptive strikes. In the case of transit camps, these have deliberately been kept small, mobile and scattered. The arms traffic issue was more serious as it confronted the government with a policy dilemma: whether to pretend it did not exist or whether to attempt to regulate its flow, thereby according it a measure of legitimacy. There was no third alternative; whatever the government's real wishes in the matter, there was no way it could hope to eliminate gun-running completely.

Initially, Zambian authorities were tempted simply to tolerate the 'illegal' activities of the liberation movements, but this quickly led to abuses and a rash of arrests.[68] Moreover, as the scale of operations increased, the government became alarmed. Efforts were then made to suppress the traffic completely. Shortly before UDI, President Kaunda declared

> While it should be understood and very clearly too that we in Zambia support the struggle against colonialism in Africa, I believe it is my duty to warn participants in that struggle that the use of our country as a transit route for the transport of arms must cease. In the interest of Zambia and its people, we cannot tolerate the presence of unsupervised arms in the country. It is highly dangerous and, therefore, I would wish it to be clearly understood that from now on it is Government policy that this traffic should be stopped. I have given fair warning to organizations who indulge in this activity of Government's policy and . . . they will contravene this at their own peril . . . no country whatsoever anywhere in the world can allow free traffic of arms within its country.[69]

Predictably, this approach proved ineffective.

UDI, in 'legalising' resistance to the Rhodesian rebel regime, led to some relaxation of Zambia's stringent arms regulations. Nevertheless, the problems persisted. In the end, therefore, the government appears to have reluctantly concluded that it had no alternative but to assume much more direct responsibility for the control and transit of arms through its territory to ensure that they were neither diverted nor stock-piled. Even so, it would be surprising if the liberation movements always cooperated fully with the authorities in adhering strictly to established procedures. If the number of court cases is any indication, a certain amount of unauthorised smuggling continued.[70]

Limitation on the operational freedom of action of liberation movements within Zambia requires no justification. What may be surprising is the extent to which Lusaka has felt constrained to influence the conduct of guerrilla operations beyond its borders.

It has not been a question of Zambia directing the military campaigns of the liberation organisations, but rather of advising them what she would prefer that they *not* do. Three factors have entered into Zambian thinking: humanitarianism, economic interest, and military security.

Zambian spokesmen have repeatedly made it clear that they strongly disapprove of the indiscriminate killing of Europeans in Rhodesia – on humanitarian as well as pragmatic grounds. In chiding the Zimbabwean parties for their inactivity, President Kaunda added, 'I don't mean they should go cutting people's heads off. They could be very effective indeed ... by weakening [the rebel regime] in many fields which touch the purse'.[71] On an earlier occasion, in criticising ZAPU broadcasts, he argued that, 'It is stupid to shout from the comforts of Zambia, "We are going to kill all white men". How does that help?'[72] Similarly, following the death of a Rhodesian farmer, and accusations by Salisbury, a government spokesman asserted that 'Zambia does not support killing by anyone. Murder is condemned no matter whether this is perpetrated by rebels or freedom fighters.'[73] In other words, terrorism as such is rejected.

Pending the reorientation of her economy and, in particular, completion in 1975 of the railway to Dar es Salaam, Zambia had a vital economic interest in preventing freedom fighters from disrupting her residual lines of communication through and sources of supply in Southern Africa. This meant insistence on no interference with the rail routes to Beira and Lobito,[74] with Kariba electricity and (until 1972) with Wankie coal. When, on Christmas Eve 1966 and later in March 1967, UNITA forces blew up sections of the Benguela Railway, Lusaka retaliated by refusing to renew Dr Savimbi's residence permit.[75]

Security has been the major concern compelling Zambia to urge operational restraints on liberation movements. In an attempt to avoid offering excessive or unnecessary provocation, she argued that military operations must be initiated from within Southern Africa, preferably well away from the border, and that cadres should not seek sanctuary in Zambia, thus risking violations of Zambian territory by Southern African forces in 'hot pursuit'. Nor have liberation movements been authorised to airlift supplies into liberated areas. These conditions appear to have been reasonably well respected but, as even Ian Smith has admitted, there are definite limits to the extent to which Lusaka can enforce its writ throughout its vast and generally remote and scantily populated border area, let alone beyond them.

3. Conclusions

The first conclusion to which this chapter points is that there has been a steady evolution over time in the Zambian Government's commitment to the cause of Southern African liberation. British failures to act decisively in Rhodesia immediately after UDI, and again six months later following Labour's election victory, mark significant stages along the way, but even more crucial have been the massive economic disengagement from the South and the build-up of defence capabilities. The inevitable caution that characterised the early Independence era has given way to a new confidence and bolder policies. In terms of Fig 8.1 as vulnerability (V) diminished, liberation support (S) increased correspondingly without the risk of retaliation (R) exceeding acceptable limits (A).

Nevertheless, vital Zambian national interests, which ultimately the liberation movements also share, have dictated the imposition of some constraints. This poses two questions: to what extent have these been unreasonable, and have they prejudiced the success of the liberation struggles?

Zambian guidelines on the behaviour of liberation movements can be summarised in the following principles:

1. The priority task of freedom movements is to liberate their homelands; anything that detracts from that purpose should be discouraged and anything that contributes to it merits support.
2. Liberation movements must not interfere in the domestic affairs of the host country, or add to its internal security problems.
3. Liberation movements must avoid actions that harm the host country substantially more than the target country.
4. The level and character of military activities in both the host country and the target country must not be such as to provoke retaliation against the host country on a scale that exceeds acceptable limits.

None of these restrictions is inherently unreasonable. In fact, the last two in particular imply substantial sacrifices on the part of the host country. In practice, Zambia has generally accorded the liberation movements all the assistance that could reasonably be expected in the circumstances. Moreover, as Zambian capabilities have increased, so has the measure of support. Nevertheless, Zambian policies have necessarily involved an element of restriction, however justifiable. What effect has this had on the course of the liberation struggles?

There is no easy answer to this question, but a few comments may be pertinent. In the first place, a major constraint on the effectiveness of liberation forces has been the endemic disunity between and within the movements. The empirical evidence suggests that *the greater the degree of unity in a national liberation movement, the greater its success in the field.* It is difficult to see any way in which Zambian restrictions have contributed to this fragmentation. On the contrary, major resources of time, energy and emotion were expended to try to bridge the divisions within the nationalist movements.

A second handicap affecting the liberation movements has been a shortage of trained manpower, modern equipment and supplies. Again, it is possible to formulate a proposition which has some empirical support, namely, that *progress towards the end is proportional to the availability of the means.* Here, too, these deficiencies cannot be attributed to Zambian actions. Nothing could have been achieved in training camps in Zambia that could not have been done, certainly more safely and probably more efficiently in a number of countries farther from the front line. Similarly, the supply situation has depended on external, not Zambian, sources. Finally, Zambian restrictions, though sometimes irritating, did not seriously impede FRELIMO's progress. There is no good reason, therefore, to suspect that they were significant factors in the more limited successes of guerrilla forces elsewhere.

The physical hardships and psychological strains that are the inevitable lot of freedom fighters are sufficiently daunting to deter all but the most dedicated among them. It is understandable, therefore, that they should resent and resist any constraints at all on their freedom of action. Nevertheless, Southern African liberation movements have been fortunate that the most strategically positioned host state in independent Africa has proved so willing and able to be both sympathetic and sacrificial in its support.

Notes

1. See D. G. Anglin, 'The politics of transit routes in landlocked Southern Africa', in Z. Cervenka ed., *Landlocked Countries of Africa*, Scandinavian Institute of African Studies, Uppsala, 1973, pp. 104–11, 129.
2. Aaron Milner, UNIP Deputy Secretary-General, *Star* (Johannesburg), 8 Jan. 1964, p. 17.
3. Zambia Information Service (ZIS), *Press Release* No. 1488/68, 21 Aug. 1968, p. 1.
4. *Axioms of Kwame Nkrumah*, Nelson, London, 1967, p. 52.
5. Preamble, Constitution of Zambia, 1973.
6. ZIS, *Press Release* No. 1518/68, 24 Aug. 1968, p. 1.
7. *Sunday Times of Zambia*, 17 Sept. 1972, p. 1.
8. Fergus Macpherson, *Kenneth Kaunda of Zambia: The Times and the Man*, O.U.P., Lusaka, 1974, pp. 308–10, 314; *Black Government*, United Society for Christian Literature, Lusaka 1960, pp. 99–102; Kenneth D. Kaunda, *Zambia Shall Be Free*, Heinemann, London, 1962, *passim*; Ali Mazrui, *The Anglo-African Commonwealth*, Pergamon Press, Oxford, 1967, pp. 14–17.
9. 'Rhodesia and the World', in B. V. Mtshali, *Rhodesia: Background to Conflict*, Hawthorn Books, New York 1967, pp. 6–7.
10. *The Times* (London), 20 Apr. 1964, 12; UN General Assembly, 4 Dec. 1964, A/PV. 1291, p. 2.
11. Robert C. Good, *UDI: The International Politics of the Rhodesian Rebellion*, Princeton University Press, 1973, p. 235.
12. *Manifesto on Southern Africa*, Government Printer, Lusaka 1969, pp. 3–4. The liberation movements were profoundly disturbed by the Lusaka Manifesto which they interpreted as 'abandoning the struggle'. Nathan Shamuyarira, 'The Lusaka Manifesto on Southern Africa', *African Review*, i, 1, Mar. 1971, p. 77.
13. ZIS, *Press Release* No. 1724/67, 27 Aug. 1967, p. 1.
14. *Ibid.*, No. 1518/68, 24 Aug. 1968, p. 1.
15. 4 Aug. 1965, *Africa Research Bulletin: Political Social and Cultural Series*, 1965, p. 353.
16. UNIP received $238 000 prior to the January 1964 general elections.
17. *Minutes of the Fifteenth Session of the Coordinating Committee for the Liberation of Africa*, Dakar, July 1969, cited in B. V. Mtshali, 'Zambia's Foreign Policy: The Dilemmas of a New State, 1964–1970', Ph.D. thesis, New York University, 1972, pp. 286–8.
18. *Confidential News Report* (Salisbury), 14 Jan. 1964, p. 5.
19. ECM/Res. 13 (VI), 5 Dec. 1965, para. (5).

20. ZIS, *Background* No. 47/65, p. 4, 14 Nov. 1965. In fact the nationalist reaction to UDI, while less than the promised uprising, was far from negligible.

21. *Activities of the Zambian Broadcasting Corporation: Britain's Part in the Incitement of Murder, Arson, Sabotage and Destruction in Rhodesia*, Government Printer, Salisbury, Feb. 1966; and *Murder by Radio*, Ministry of Information, Immigration and Tourism, Salisbury, July 1966; see also Kenneth Young, *Rhodesia and Independence*, Dent, London 1969, pp. 352–3.

22. Saul Ndhlovu, *Times of Zambia*, 15 Aug. 1972, p. 1.

23. *Programmes* (Lusaka: ZBS, Sept. 1973).

24. Mainza Chona, Minister without Portfolio, ZIS, *Press Release*, No. 681/68, 15 Apr. 1968, p. 1. When, in 1968, Kaunda was asked if 'these guerrillas pass through Zambia on their way down to Rhodesia and South Africa', he replied: 'Certainly. Going and coming back to their own country, they pass through Zambia.' *US News and World Report*, 2 Dec. 1968, p. 65.

25. *Economist*, 10 May 1969, pp. 31–2.

26. For example, S. L. Muller, cited in Colin Legum and John Drysdale, *Africa Contemporary Record: 1968–69*, Africa Research Ltd., London 1969, p. 249; *France-Soir* (Paris) 20 June 1970, p. 8; 'Secret bases in Zambia', *To the Point* (Johannesburg, ii, 3, (Feb. 1973), pp. 25–9.

27. ZIS, *Background* No. 31/67, 22 Oct. 1967, pp. 7, 9; see also, *Times of Zambia*, 25 Oct. 1967, p. 1; Zambia *Nat. Ass. Deb.*, 17 Oct. 1967, col. 34.

28. ZIS, *Press Release* No. 2114/67, 7 Oct. 1967, p. 1; *Times of Zambia*, 12 Apr. 1968, 1; *Zambia News* (Ndola), 27 Oct. 1968, p. 1.

29. ZIS, *Background*, No. 25/71, 22 Mar. 1971, p. 3.

30. *Sunday Times of Zambia*, 18 June 1972, p. 2; *Times of Zambia*, 22 June 1972, p. 7.

31. *Organisation of African Unity Special 9th Summit*, OAU, Addis Ababa, Sept. 1972, p. 39.

32. *The Guardian* (London), 30 May 1967, p. 8.

33. *The Times*, 20 April 1964, p. 12.

34. *Central African Mail* (Ndola), 12 June 1964, p. 12.

35. Op. cit., 26 Mar. 1964, p. 1; *Africa 1964* (London), No. 5, 6 Mar. 1964, p. 3.

36. 'Visit of Foreign Ministers', press statement, Lusaka, 15 Aug. 1964; *Central African Mail*, 21 Aug. 1964, p. 12.

37. Immanuel Wallerstein, *Africa: The Politics of Unity*, Pall Mall, London, 1968, pp. 166–7.

38. *Rhodesia Herald*, 22 Oct. 1965, p. 1.

39. *Daily Graphic* (Accra), 4 Mar. 1966, p. 19; *Africa Research Bulletin*, 1966, p. 483.

40. See ZANU's 'Call to all Africans of Zimbabwe' (June 1963), in N. Sithole, *African Nationalism*, 2nd edn, OUP, London, 1968, pp. 41–2.

41. ZIS, *Background*, No. 47/65, 14 Nov. 1965, pp. 4–5. A general strike centred on Bulawayo was quickly crushed, Nov. 22–23; Good, *UDI: The International Politics . . .* , pp. 82–3.

42. *The Guardian* (London), 30 May 1967, p. 8; *Zambia Mail* (Lusaka), 29 Apr. 1966, p. 12.

43. OAU resolution CM/Res. 153 (XI), para. 12.
44. *Zambia Daily Mail,* 17 Aug. 1971, p. 7.
45. *Africa Contemporary Record, 1972–73,* C41.
46. *The Times,* 19 Mar. 1973, p. 4.
47. Lusaka agreement, 7 Dec. 1974.
48. Wallerstein, *Africa: The Politics of Unity,* p. 165.
49. Christian P. Potholm and Richard Dale eds., *Southern Africa in Perspective,* Free Press, New York 1972, p. 197.
50. *Africa Confidential* (London), 1967, No. 21, 20 Oct. 1967, p. 8; OAU resolutions, CM/Res. 137 (X), para. 10 and CM/Res. 151 (XI), preamble; *Africa Contemporary Record: 1971–72,* C20.
51. *Africa Research Bulletin,* 1971, p. 2128.
52. *Daily News* (Dar es Salaam), 21 Dec. 1974, p. 1.
53. For a sympathetic and insightful discussion of the 'perceptual and behavioural problems of exile politics', see John Marcum's analysis in Potholm and Dale, *Southern Africa in Perspective,* pp. 270–2. He identifies 'four types of dysfunctional behaviour' as normal psychological impediments of exile: 'personal aggression, regression, apathy, and compulsive repetition'.
54. Information Department, Northern Rhodesia Government, *Press Release,* No. 695, 12 May 1964, 1; *Central African Mail,* 20 Mar. 1964, p. 6.
55. ZIS, *Press Release* No. 1518/68, 24 Aug. 1968, p. 1, and No. 1536/68, 28 Aug. 1968, p. 1.
56. *Africa Confidential,* 1968, No. 18, 6 Sept. 1968, p. 5.
57. *Zambia Mail,* 25 Apr. 1970, p. 1; *Observer,* 26 Apr. 1970, p. 5; AFP *Africa* No. 1676, 15 May 1970, p. 23. The Minister of Home Affairs insisted that the victim had died from a dog bite, not gun wounds.
58. *The Times,* 15 Mar. 1971, p. 6; *The Observer* (London), 28 Mar. 1971.
59. *Government Gazette* (Lusaka), vii, 76, 24 June 1971, p. 569; John Hatch, 'Zambia under stress', *Venture,* xxiii, 9, Oct. 1971, pp. 10–11; *Africa Research Bulletin,* 1971, pp. 2295–6.
60. 'It is a historical fact that in 1970 James Chikerema and George Nyandoro suffered the temptation to seize the party, weaken the leadership of Comrade President Nkomo and use the army to impose not only their dominance but also their tribe which they mistakenly believed they represented. This adventure was finally crushed on 21 August 1971 in the bushes of Zambia. They branched off to form the abortive FROLIZI. ZAPU survived purified and invigorated.' Publicity Bureau of ZAPU-Patriotic Front, 'ZAPU: Its Origins and Direction', World Conference against Apartheid, Racism and Colonialiasm in Southern Africa, Lisbon, 16–19 June 1976, p. 8. In June 1971, the OAU Secretary-General reported that the crisis within ZAPU was 'so serious that it could affect for a long time the liberation struggle' in Rhodesia: *Africa Research Bulletin,* 1971, 2124. By 1974, ZAPU guerrilla operations had resumed on a modest scale.
61. For text of MPLA Note of 3 June 1973 to the Zambian Government, see *Africa Contemporary Record, 1973–74,* C74–75; see also *Sunday Times of Zambia,* 4 Aug. 1974, pp. 1, 4.

62. Ruth Weiss, 'Factionalism delays Angolan independence', *Montreal Gazette*, 14 Sept. 1974, p. 8; ZIS *Background* No. 18/76, pp. 13–15. The ready acceptance of the belief in a Zambian commitment to Chipenda appears to have been due to the fact that he resided in Lusaka, that his faction was militarily more active than Neto's forces – at least along Zambia's western border – and that he happened to accompany Kaunda to Bukavu in the same way that Neto, Andrade and Holden Roberto came with their patrons, Nyerere, Ngouabi and Mobutu.

63. *Government Gazette* iii, 19, 3 Mar. 1967, p. 158; ZIS, *Background* No. 35/68, 10 May 1968, p. 2.

64. *Zambia Daily Mail*, 29 June 1971, p. 4, and 16 Oct. 1971, p. 5.

65. Radio Zambia, 29 Jan. 1965; *Africa Research Bulletin*, 1965, p. 229.

66. For example, *Times of Zambia*, 5 Feb. 1972, p. 7; *Zimbabwe News: Official Organ of ZANU* (Lusaka), vii, 9, Sept. 1973, pp. 6–7.

67. UNHRC, *Report on Current Operations, 1970*. Annex II/A(i), and *Zambia Census, 1969*. The refugee population appears to have been included in the census returns.

68. *Central African Mail*, 13 Mar. 1964, p. 1; *Times of Zambia*, 10 Sept. 1965, p. 1.

69. ZIS, *Background* No. 35/65, 9 Sept. 1965, pp. 1, 4, 5; see also *Background* No. 47/65, 16 Nov. 1965, p. 4. Kaunda also announced that, three weeks earlier, the Portuguese had lifted their ban on Zambian arms in transit through Mozambique, following assurances that they would not be diverted to FRELIMO.

70. For example, *Times of Zambia*, 30 Apr. 1966, p. 6; 11 Nov. 1967, p. 1; and 14 Aug. 1970, p. 1; *Zambia Mail*, Magazine, 30 Dec. 1966, p. 6.

71. *Guardian*, 30 May 1967, p. 8.

72. ZIS, *Background* No. 47/65, 14 Nov. 1965, p. 5.

73. ZIS, *Press Release* No. 1080/66, 14 June 1966, p. 1; *Observer*, 22 May 1966, p. 2.

74. *Africa Diary*, 1970, p. 4932; *Daily Times* (Lagos), 31 Dec. 1971, p. 13; *Daily Telegraph* (London), 17 Jan. 1973. It has been argued that FLNA rather than UNITA was responsible. C. K. Ebinger, 'External intervention in internal war', *Orbis*, xx, 3, Fall 1976, p. 682.

75. *Economist*, 30 May 1970, p. 4; David M. Abshire and Michael A. Samuels, eds., *Portuguese Africa: A Handbook*, Praeger, New York, 1969, p. 397.

Part 4 Aid to Africa: Interdependence or Dependence?

The aid relationship between Africa and the rich states cannot be dissociated from the overall structures of dependence which exist between them. Aid was initially extended at the time of independence to accelerate the pace of growth and modernisation. Although aid has now a relatively long history, the economic development of recipient countries has continued to lag, and the gap between the rich and poor nations to widen. The result has been two-fold: on the one hand, increasing political pressures for more generous aid programmes, and on the other hand, the emergence of a much more critical body of scholarly writings that tends to identify aid as a new form of imperialism, or, at best, as being unable to effect the necessary changes in economic structures and relationships. Out of the resulting controversy, at least a refreshing emphasis has emerged on the importance of indigeneously determined national priorities and of self-reliant development strategies. The two chapters (9, 10) that comprise this Part fall into neither extreme category. They are critical, informed and original contributions to the debate over aid; both scholars are particularly concerned with Canada's own assistance strategy.

Helleiner (Ch. 9) examines the aid relationship from the perspective of the recipient, a perspective which Okuda laments as little known. Helleiner presents a critique of the dependence approach, arguing that a reduction of external relations does not necessarily lead to domestic development or equality. Rather, quoting the Tanzanian case, he argues that what is important is to establish, and implement, a general development strategy. He presents data on the evolving nature of the aid flow to Africa and suggests that while most African *countries* are in absolute terms not very aid-dependent, many African *governments* are more so. This dependence of regimes affects their bargaining position with donors and serves to reinforce dependence rather than lead to a more rational definition of national or group interests. Helleiner indicates how the issues of type and terms of aid get intertwined with politics within the recipient's bureaucracy and he analyses the debate over the desirability and costs of technical assistance. He asserts that the bargaining power of the aid-receiving government or department rests largely upon its capacity to say 'no' and to regulate its own requests. Helleiner recognises that even this definition of independence is beyond the physical and psychological capacity of many African regimes because they inherited, and continue to accept, dependence on the rich states and donors. His critical evaluation of aid from an African perspective may also be compared with Okuda's assessment of Canadian aid from the viewpoint of the donor.

Okuda (Ch. 10), like Helleiner, touches on possible criteria for evaluating aid from the position of both donor and recipient. Moreover, although these two authors are economists, they both deal with non-economic as well as economic criteria. Okuda examines the concentration of Canadian aid in specific countries and sectors and concludes that there has been growing sophistication in meeting the needs of the African nations. He also suggests that in general Canadian aid is considered to be quite appropriate, responsive and flexible by recipients although as the Canadian International Development Agency (CIDA) grows, its apparent acceptability may decrease. The different perspectives adopted by Helleiner and Okuda lead to rather different conclusions, reflective of distinctions between donor and recipient criteria and interests. Further, aid cannot be separated from the general pattern of relations between Africa and the rich states such as Canada. The overall structure of inherited dependence serves to limit the prospects of African states or regimes declining aid. It also means that Canadian assistance cannot be evaluated without reference to other Canadian interests in Africa.' The flow of Canadian and other aid to Africa may lead to inequalities as well as to development, as reflected in the chapters in the final section.

Note

1. On these see: the recent contributions by Robert O. Matthews, 'Canada and Anglophone Africa', and L. Sabourin, 'Canada and Francophone Africa', in Peyton V. Lyon and Tareq Y. Ismael, eds., *Canada and the Third World*, Macmillan, Toronto, 1976, pp. 60–161; and S. Langdon, 'Canada's role in Africa', in N. Hillmer and G. Stevenson, eds., *Foremost Nation: Canadian Foreign Policy and a Changing World*, McClelland and Stewart, Toronto, 1977, 178–201.

Gerald K. Helleiner

9 Aid and Dependence in Africa: Issues for Recipients

1. Introduction

So much has been written in the last decade or so on aid and development – their interrelationships, their measurement, their objectives, optimal policies, etc. – that one may at first despair of saying anything new on the subject. Yet, in looking over the field and considering the welter of views, frequently mutually contradictory, which have already been expressed, one cannot but be struck by the disproportionate share of the discussion which has been accounted for by analysis from the developed countries. In the introduction to a recent best-seller describing American history from the viewpoint of the North American Indian the point is made that the history of the white man's westward expansion across the continent had previously always been presented from the perspective of a man looking westward.[1] In the same spirit, it is necessary to consider the question of aid and development from the perspective of the man looking 'north-ward'. More than enough analyses have already been presented from a 'southward'-looking perspective by apologists for the present international system, consultants to aid agencies, liberal reformers and radicals in the 'north'.

Adoption of the perspective of the aid recipient rather than the donor immediately demonstrates the assumptions and values implicit in much of the aid literature's terminology. The concept of 'leverage', for example, even where applied with reference to the effort to generate more 'suitable' developmental policies rather than to the protection or pursuit of the donor's obvious self-interest,[2] can be seen to incorporate the judgement that the donor government or agency knows better than the recipient one what is in the best interests of the recipient government or country. (See section 4 (p. 236) for an account of the donor's interest in 'levering for development'.) As this is so unlikely on *a priori* grounds to be true, since so many of the donor's domestic policies are themselves economically irrational and since donors obviously *do* have interests of their own to pursue in the conduct of their foreign policy, aid recipients understandably resist attempts to 'lever' them.

All 'performance' criteria for donor selectivity among countries, about which much has been written, are also obviously donor-oriented. Economists' suggestions seem, in any case, rarely to have carried much weight in actual intercountry aid allocation decisions. There is no more reason to expect many donors to adopt measures of social progress, as Seers suggests,[3] or such absurd criteria as Harberger's project evaluation capacity,[4] as their intercountry allocative criteria than there was for them so to adopt measures of 'self-help' fifteen years ago.

'Absorptive capacity' is another value-loaded term in the aid lexicon. From the perspective of the recipient it can carry no meaning: further resources will certainly be welcomed and employed if they are provided in valuable and usable form. The capacity to absorb resources when the per capita income is $150 per year must be considerable! To those who employ the term one must ask: 'capacity to absorb what?' and 'for what purposes?' There may indeed be a limit to the capacity of a potential recipient in further project loans if it has no further manpower to undertake 'project preparations' and cannot acquire it. There are also many countries where further resources would probably be consumed rather than invested at low rates of return. But further untied grants will assuredly be absorbed.

This chapter attempts to survey the major issues surrounding the questions of foreign aid dependence in Africa. It is particularly concerned with the viewpoint of the aid recipient. Before considering some of the issues associated with aid from the perspective of the receiving country, it seems sensible to set the stage with some general observations on aid and dependence, and some data showing the dimensions of the flow of official development assistance to Africa in recent years.

2. Dependence and Aid

No state without an economy basically oriented to production for national needs, without a high level of technological capacity, or without the capacity for generating nationally at least the bulk of the investible surplus and educated-skilled manpower necessary for rapid and sustained growth has the economic base for fully meaningful independence. Without them, a state remains dependent on other more economically powerful states or on large economic interest groups based in such states.[5]

According to most current definitions of 'dependence', the politically independent African states are still 'dependent'; and for the vast majority of them, it is difficult to see how they can be otherwise for many decades to come. This 'dependence' is the product of their small size and extreme poverty, and their very limited power in international markets and institutions. Indeed one may well wonder whether the word 'dependence' *adds* anything to one's understanding of the Third World's essential dilemma of poverty and powerlessness. If 'dependence' is defined as a state in which developmental experience is substantially affected by developments in the metropoles of the international (capitalist) economy, then it is little more than a synonym for 'underdevelopment' (which may or may not be 'developing'). Calling upon African countries to reduce their 'dependence' amounts, then, to advising them to give up their poverty and/or powerlessness! Yet there may be more to the issue than this.

Breaking 'dependent' relationships with the international system which exploits them is recommended by many analysts of the left. The trouble is that this recommendation, when proffered to governments of a reactionary character, is both unlikely to be accepted and unlikely to alter the exploitative character of their own regimes. The control of the government or the state must therefore be, and is, a fundamental issue in the orthodoxy of 'dependence' analysis. The 'development of underdevelopment' is seen, in this analysis, to proceed with a certain inevitability unless and until state power becomes vested in an 'independent' class (or group?)[6] Once a 'progressive' or 'independent' government is *in* power, however, advice with respect to the *breaking* of international ties appears no longer so appropriate. What the 'dependence' analysts really must mean to recommend, then, is a radical change of government. Their militancy on the question of 'dependence' is therefore another instance, of which there are already more than enough in the development literature, of the fallacy of misplaced concreteness.

Once a suitable class or group attains power, the policy question, as far as the 'dependence' issue is concerned, would seem to become that of how best to achieve self-reliance, independence, and development for the country over which they exercise it. But 'the country' may not be the most useful concept in the analysis of dependency relationships.[7] It is a familiar enough proposition in the aid literature that the interests of the government may not be coincident with those of the nation. It may therefore make sense to seek relationships among individuals or groups or classes, each presumably with their own interests to pursue, in order to understand the meaning and purpose of the 'policy' which eventually materialises from their interactions. Even the concept of 'the government' may be too aggregative for the purposes of such analysis, for it may well be that the interests of the Principal Secretary of the Ministry of Finance, for example, may not coincide with those of the Ministry of Foreign Affairs. Development assistance, at this level of analysis, can be seen as merely another instrument through which the political struggles within African nations manifest themselves.

However such analysis is conducted, it would appear that the domestic impact of 'dependent' relationships is not perceived by radical analysts as so pernicious following the assumption of power by an 'independent' class, group or government. Carefully controlled relationships with the international capitalist system can then, apparently, be permitted when they are in the social interest (or in the interests of those now in possession of power). What would, on the face of it, appear to be 'dependent relationships' may therefore continue or even be intensified so long as there is an 'independent' government in power which is pursuing a long-run objective of self-reliant development. Thus Cuba's return to sugar (the campaign for 10 million tonnes) – the pursuit of orthodox comparative advantage with rare determination (to say nothing of the degree of market concentration of its exports) – is apparently not a reflection of a 'dependent' state. In the context of development assistance, it appears that the same size of loan for the same type of project at the same terms may be offered to two countries at the same time, yet be interpreted as a skilled use of foreign assistance for the development of a self-reliant economy in one case and characterised as another indication of dependency in the other. Perhaps the essence of the matter is whether the government (or country) in question itself has (or seeks) *control* over its external relationships. (A problem remains when a government or country *has* control but chooses not to employ it.[8]) To a considerable extent, the degree of 'dependence' does seem to rest in the eye of the beholder and, in particular, his assessment of the relevant Third World governments.

Clearly there *are* feedback effects and interrelationships between 'open-ness' to economic relationships with the West and the political complexion of these Third World governments. But by now it should be evident that 'before the revolution', relationships with the West are not the *crux* of the radicals' problem; and after it, they still are not. (Those anticipating different relationships among *socialist* states of differing power should consult the literature on Soviet–East European economic relationships, and the history of barter deals between the socialist states and the less developed countries. It is not obvious that the same general rules of international economic relationships do not apply to those among socialist governments as to those among capitalist ones.)

Since autarky or even very greatly diminished reliance on economic relationships with the rest of the world – trade, borrowing of capital, skill and technology, etc. – is at present out of the question for small and poor African states, the potential for overcoming their 'dependence' lies very largely in their *own* 'attitudes of mind' (to borrow a phrase from the Nyerere of an earlier period). When radical analysts prescribe greater 'inward orientation' for the Third World, the natural reaction of the bourgeois economist is horror at the prospect of losing the gains from trade. This horror is usually expressed with even greater vigour since reactions to such prescriptions are typically (and understandably) solicited from economists specialising in the field of *international* economics, a group which naturally enough places particularly great emphasis upon external economic relationships. Yet is not some of the apparent total disagreement unrelated to policy disagreements? 'Turning inward' or 'reducing dependence' *need* not mean diminishing external relationships so much as consciously *employing* them as one of several instruments for the pursuit of a truly *independent strategy*. (It is worth noting that Tanzania's dependence upon exports and upon foreign financing for its development programme is just as great today as it was before the Arusha Declaration. Yet most observers consider its 'dependence' to be lower.)

The paramount necessity, at least for the present, is for the establishment of clear general developmental objectives into which specific policies are to fit. Export strategy, the composition of the import bill, the acceptance of development assistance, the use of private foreign capital, skill and technology, are all then viewed as instrumental to the 'inner-directed' development effort. Thus official development assistance which comprises the pursuit of the stipulated objectives will be rejected; indeed the development programme will be erected, if possible, in such a way as to minimise the disruption which might be caused by the failure of foreign sources of finance to materialise. (This is easier said than done.) Similarly, export development is viewed 'functionally' with reference to the objectives: thus Cuba can return as a matter of strategy to enormous reliance on sugar exports, its traditional export, while remaining invulnerable to radical attack, because of the context in which this return takes place. Supporters of increased equity in distribution, new and more appropriate technologies, and radical alternatives in the Third World[9] *must* consider the detailed policies which should be pursued with respect to external trade and sources of capital in those countries already in a position to experiment in these directions.

'Traditional' development analysis *has* overemphasised the export sector and the role of foreign capital in the development process at the expense of other ingredients; and advice *has* too frequently consisted of blind advocacy of maximum export expansion and the maximum pursuit of foreign official and private capital without adequate attention to the other elements of strategy, and without a framework within which such advocacy might make sense and be placed into appropriate perspective.

It is unlikely that adoption of a functional approach to trade strategy, such as is being suggested, is likely to affect fundamentally the level or structure of African nations' exports to the industrial world in the next few decades, whatever the development objectives they set for themselves. An individual African government typically has very little influence upon the world economy. It cannot hope to alter the rules of the international commercial game or the terms of the bargains offered it on world markets. It will gain from exporting activities whatever it can. Its major influence, rather, derives from its power to affect the manner in which the international market makes an impact upon the economy over which it has some control[10]; and even that may be limited by the weak administrative base available for control. Yet the adoption of a functional approach to external economic relations may well have profound implications for the planned structure of imports and the use of foreign capital.

Within the context of an international system in which the industrial powers are dominant and vigorously pursue their own self-interest against much weaker Third World states (as well as each other), each individual African government has an 'interest' to pursue in its relations with the various industrial powers, which differs from the interests of each of those powers. That African interest may be pursued wisely, poorly, or not at all. The explanations for the latter phenomenon may lie in the will of the governments concerned or in their present limited capacity to do otherwise; the 'will' may itself be the product of subversion or the influence, direct or indirect, of foreign powers, public or private. Among the most obvious instruments of such foreign influence is capital assistance, not only for development but for military and political purposes as well. Official development assistance is also the *easiest* area within which independent governments may demonstrate their power, even if it is only a veto power, with respect to more powerful foreign states.

Benefits *can* be realised by decision makers, governments, etc., in the less developed countries in consequence of their economic relationships with the rest of the world. They can be larger or smaller depending upon the sophistication and skill with which their objectives are pursued; and they can, of course, be distributed in various ways to classes, groups, or areas within the nations over which they exercise control. It is quite possible for the effects of their acquisition of these benefits either for the nation as a whole or, much more likely, for components thereof, to be negative. From the perspective of these decision makers the object is, through care and control, to extract the maximum from those with whom they deal internationally, regardless of their intentions as to domestic distribution.

3. The Dimensions of Aid to Africa

On a per capita basis, Africa has received much more aid than South Asia, slightly more than Latin America, considerably more than the Middle East and Europe, but less than the Far East (see Table 9.1). As a share of imports and of GNP, official development assistance looms larger in most tropical African countries than in the rest of the Third World.

Table **9.1** Development Assistance 1969–71 Annual Averages[11]

	Per capita net official receipts ($)
Africa, total	5·50
North of Sahara	5·52
South of Sahara	5·34
Middle East, total	3·34
South Asia, total	2·06
Far East, total	5·92
Latin America and West Indies	5·18
North, Central and Indies	6·38
South	4·35
Europe	3·24
Total	4·27

The total money value of official bilateral and multilateral development assistance to Africa has changed little over the 1960s. In the light of the steady price inflation during this period for all components of the aid flow except food (which was not at that time of great importance in development assistance to Africa), the real value of official development assistance must have declined by about 15 per cent.[12] At the same time, since population has been growing in Africa at an annual rate of about 2·5 per cent, the money value of per capita development assistance must have deteriorated by about another 30 per cent. Towards the end of the decade the terms of official financial transfers to Africa were hardening as well. Between 1965 and 1970 the grant element in aid to Africa fell from 67 to 61 per cent.[13] The per capita value of development assistance to Africa at the end of the decade must have been less than two-thirds of that in the relatively palmy early 1960s!

There are no direct estimates of the costs of aid-tying to Africa but there is no reason to believe that they are any lower there than elsewhere in the Third World. Particularly galling in skill-scarce Africa is the 'high opportunity cost of the government staff time required to manipulate commercial trade channels and procedures in order to satisfy tied-aid requirements – staff time that, from an economic point of view, would be far better spent evaluating projects more closely and administering their substantive aspects more intensively'.[14] A discount of 20 per cent[15] can therefore safely be applied to the estimate of per capita grant element in aid to Africa which one can derive from OECD data,[16] reducing the per capita figure to about $3·65 in 1971. This is bound to be an upper limit.

One striking characteristic of aid to Africa, about which more later, is the high share (roughly half) of technical assistance in the total. For the present, suffice it to say that assigning a recipient's value to technical assistance is particularly difficult; some of it amounts merely to internal income redistribution within the developed economies and it may even carry a negative value to the recipient. Most of it comes in 'tied' form. It is necessary also to consider some of the more subtle costs of foreign aid – especially, the transfer of inappropriate (because they employ too much capital and too many imports) technologies and tastes.[17]

While Africa is more 'aid dependent' than most other parts of the Third World, its absolute level of dependence is still small. All things considered, it is difficult to see how the value of aid to the recipient could amount to more than about 3 per cent, on average, of African GNP; in the more advanced of the African countries it is rather less. Moreover, as has been seen, it has been falling; as African per capita income continues to rise and real aid levels to fall, this degree of dependence on aid will fall further. 'Dependence' may also have been reduced in consequence of the significant shift in the composition of donors. The contributions of the major bilateral donors (France, the US, UK, Belgium) have declined in importance relative to those of a number of smaller donors and multilateral sources.

If all aid ceased tomorrow, the effects upon African countries would obviously not be catastrophic. Yet while most African *countries* are in absolute terms not very aid-dependent, many African *governments* are. Assuming that the typical African government budget amounts to about 15 per cent of GNP, official foreign assistance can be seen to average about 20 per cent of it. Since the cost of basic administration accounts for a fairly high proportion of African governmental expenditures, aid's relative impact upon the state's 'marginal' development programmes may be considerably greater still. Even self-reliant Tanzania's post-Arusha development plan budgeted for 40 per cent of its development programme to be financed through aid, and has actually so far financed slightly more than that proportion (and these figures exclude the Tanzania–Zambia railways).[18] Thus while the total dimensions of potential aid to African *countries* cannot justify the devotion of inordinate proportions of the scarce time of skilled government manpower to the subject of its acquisition, the interests of the African *governments* frequently do.[19]

4. Aid Recipient Policies

What, then, are the policy options available to a government (or decision maker inside or outside government) with respect to development assistance? At the extremes there are the obvious possibilities of:

1. rejecting all official development assistance, so-called, and paying one's way for whatever one seeks in the world economy; this does not necessarily imply autarky with respect to external trade and investment although in practice that may be how it turns out;
2. accepting all offers of official development assistance and actively pursuing more, in considerable disregard of the detailed terms or the wider implications of 'aid' proffered.

The first extreme is sometimes recommended as the only appropriate response to the undesirable features of existing aid and associated relationships. While Third World aid recipients must not, and are unlikely to, harbour any illusions about the primary motivations of aid donors (which are, of course, multi-dimensional) neither must they be totally bemused by them. Advocacy of aid refusal on the ground that its donors' motivations are counter-developmental[20] implies that the recipients are unwilling or unable to control and manipulate it so as to promote their own interests. This seems an unnecessarily pessimistic and condescending view of the capacities of recipient governments, agencies, and individuals, even in Africa which must be at the low end of the 'capacity spectrum'.[21] The perceptions which lead observers to this recommendation, which would eliminate virtually all aid flows, should lead them instead to a more positive recommendation – for *automaticity* in the aid relationship (such as is implicit in the proposal that world liquidity requirements be fed by direct allocations of special drawing rights in the International Monetary Fund (IMF) to the less developed countries).

What about the more narrowly economic case for reducing 'dependence' – on the grounds that aid hinders autonomous development? The apparently 'reasonable' proposition that some extra resources are better than no extra resources (like the traditional tenet of international trade theory that some trade is better than no trade) can perhaps be married to the aid opponents' proposition that increased dependence upon foreign resources can throttle the development of skill, institutions of savings mobilisation, suitable technologies, equitable distribution, self-confidence and self-reliance, through a longer term Hirschman-esque approach. If one stands far enough back from the action, it may indeed be true, as Hirschman provocatively suggests, that 'In order to maximise growth the developing countries could need an appropriate alternation of contact and insulation, of open-ness to the trade and capital of the developed countries, to be followed by a period of nationalism and withdrawnness.'[22] Perhaps one *ought* to abandon the search for optimality, as he suggests, and focus upon sensible *sequences* and the notion of 'alternation and oscillation'.[23] But the reflections of the historian do not cut much ice with the African policymaker unless they can readily be translated into policy advice; and, in this case, this is not easy to do. Which African countries are now ready for a spell of 'withdrawnness'? How much? For how long? Neither Hirschman nor any of the rest of us have ready answers for such questions.

No doubt these considerations explain why Africa has no representative (like the Burma of the last decade) of the former extreme strategy. It does, however, have several countries which seem to have approached the latter option.

There are several African countries (among them, Rwanda, Burundi, Niger, Upper Volta, Somalia and even such countries as Malaŵi and Tunisia) with quite extraordinary degrees of aid dependence. The overall scene may, however, be changing. Self-conscious pursuit of independent national (or group or class) interest *has* recently expanded in independent Africa. French influence in Africa remains considerable but it is not what it was. Apart from Guinea which long ago left the fold there have been rumblings, reflecting discontent, in many other Francophone countries, including the Congo, Malagasy, Cameroun, Niger and Mauritania. The Yaounde associates, long vocal about their failure to realise larger trade gains in the EEC, are now strengthened by the accession of other Anglophone African states to the Lomé convention. At the same time, Zaire has turned far more aggressively nationalistic in recent years. The experience of the civil war and the rapid expansion of oil revenues have created a new climate of self-confidence and independence in Nigeria, which is bound to be reflected in its approach to foreign aid as well as other foreign policy questions. Tanzania's widely praised policy of 'self reliance' has created a different and far more hardheaded approach to foreign aid than before – an approach which is of greater significance than any such purely statistical 'successes' as shifts in the proportion of the development budget financed from overseas.

Apart from these changes, the accumulation of experience and the development of an indigenous expertise has led to an increased sophistication in the recipients' approach to foreign aid donors. The cutbacks in aggregate aid totals may also have played a role: they have made it difficult for African governments to maintain 'relaxed' postures of dependence and forced them to devise development strategies based more firmly upon their own efforts.

In the study of development assistance, as in that of foreign investment and external trade, the major research question to be asked today is *not* so much whether it is, on balance, beneficial or harmful to the country concerned, although that question continues to be the subject of endless debate. Rather, one must ask, in the context of a *theory of bargaining*, and from the perspective of the recipient government, what is the best means of extracting the most gains at the least cost from the other parties to the bargains – the foreign aid agency, investor, or purchaser. (As has been noted, considerable attention has already been devoted to the analysis of this question from the standpoint of the donor.) It is useful to know the range of possible outcomes within which the bargain must be struck, and for that purpose the proponents of the extreme cases for and against aid may shed some interesting light; but the practical questions of bargaining strategy between the extremes must remain the key questions. There is a whole host of Third World policy questions to be explored in the 'real world' of unchanged donor practices and continuing aid (and trade) relationships.

A useful basis for such an approach is the perspective offered by Bailey on the villagers' view of his specialised (or single-interest) relationships with outsiders.[24] Aid recipients, like Bailey's villagers, do not view their single-interest relationships with aid donors with ethical displeasure. 'Such relationships, being with outsiders, are not *im*moral so much as *a*moral: when one is dealing with an instrument, standards of what is just and unjust do not apply: one wants only to use the instrument most effectively.'[25] The aid donors are like the 'men in bush shirts and trousers ... who come on bicycles and in jeeps, but never on their feet. These are the people to be outwitted, these are the people whose apparent gifts are by definition the bait for some hidden trap.' Whatever the objectives or ideological positions of African governments, Finance Ministries, or particular civil servants (and these need not have much to do with 'development') they all may be presumed to seek to employ development assistance as one of a number of instruments in their pursuit. (Similarly coldblooded assessments of donor motivation have been frequent. Recipients, on the other hand, are usually presumed to be 'passive' actors in the relationship, simply grateful for what they can get and concerned to acquire more.) From the aid recipients' point of view, 'partnership' in development or 'gratitude' for 'assistance' have little to do with the realities of the aid relationship unless as sometimes useful smokescreens. The aid recipient is unlikely to expect to receive anything for nothing; the point is to make the most of his bargaining position and, at all events, to come out absolutely ahead.

In White's terms, the recipient governments or government departments ally themselves with external donors for the pursuit of their own domestic interests against other domestic (and foreign) actors. At times, the former departments are themselves largely staffed by expatriates in which case the whole relationship begins to look more than usually 'conspiratorial'. Neither the external environment nor the domestic scene are sufficiently homogeneous for simpleminded dependence theories to be very helpful for an understanding of what is actually taking place. It may be doubtful whether aid can play any greater role in the maintenance of a government's political power or in the strengthening of particular classes, groups or departments, in the country, than it can in the promotion of economic development. In neither case does it usually contribute a necessary or crucial input. In the usual overall scheme of things, aid simply is not that important. On the other hand, as has been seen, it can be of considerably greater relative significance to governments than its limited dimensions in the perspective of the total economy might at first suggest.

What the aid relationship *is* actually being employed for in the recipient country may be virtually impossible to ferret out:

> the more effectively *any* external group *seems* to be operating, the more opaque the nature of what it is 'really' doing will be, and the more likely it will be that its operations will work to the disadvantage of groups that it never even sees. ... The alien social scientist who tries to prescribe forms of action upon these relationships – or the aid agency which tries to take them into account in its efforts to ensure that aid promotes 'development' – is like a blindfolded man with his leg chained to the door post and one hand tied behind his back, in a totally unfamiliar room in which someone whom he cannot see and does not know keeps on moving the furniture round ...[26]

So much for aid models, dependence models or any other attempts to offer crude simplifications of complex socio-economic realities!

When viewed 'from below', the favourite topic for debate within the developed countries – which countries to assist – becomes the policy question of what it is necessary to do in order to acquire more official development assistance assuming, for the moment, that more is considered to be better than less. (There is also, again, the analogous question of from whom to accept assistance.) The answer depends upon the stated or apparent motivation of the donors. Whether it is a matter of political alignment, treatment of foreign investors, 'commitment to development' or 'self-help' according to the lights of various potential donors, or efficiency in the administrative arm of the government which carries responsibility for aid negotiations, there are obvious costs in terms of forgone opportunities accruing from actions initiated for the purposes of earning more development assistance, which must be set off against the potential benefits. In some instances, of course, the aid rewards arise from actions which would have been undertaken regardless of the aid calculation, in which case the recipient government or Ministry derives a pure gain (quasi-rent) from the resulting assistance. Where the donors' criteria are at variance with one another (as, for instance, with respect to political alignments), gains may be realisable through a very visible ambivalence and uncertainty.

The greater the variety of potential aid donors, the greater are the freedom and flexibility of potential aid recipients in the formulation of their overall political and economic development strategy in the sense that aid costs from the selection of any one can safely be neglected. (A wide distribution of donors has the further advantage of offering insurance against cutbacks motivated by balance of payments or other *economic* factors, which are unlikely to be perfectly correlated one with another in the donor nations.) Correspondingly, the greater the variety of donor citeria for acceptability of aid projects the better for the recipient countries. Thus the creation of consortia and consultative groups, in which the activities of the donor governments are coordinated, may be a mixed blessing for the recipient country. So eventually may be the development of a powerful multilateral aid institution in replacement of a variety of bilateral ones, although this is seen by many 'liberals' as preferable to the present system of aid distribution. (Against the disadvantages of aid consortia and multilateral cooperation for the aid recipient must be placed at least two advantages: 1. Gains in terms of reduced costs of tying; and 2. The reduced administrative costs of dealing with a variety of donors one by one.)

Whether programme and sector assistance to the recipient are truly preferable to project assistance, as most economists are inclined to believe, depends upon the terms upon which these alternative forms of assistance are made available. Programme assistance is certainly preferable on purely economic grounds, all other things being equal. But if qualification for programme assistance requires detailed involvement and influence on the part of the donor in the entire development strategy and macro-policy of the recipient, it may be preferable to do without it.[27] If small donors like the Scandinavian countries or Canada, with fewer possibilities and therefore aspirations for leverage, were to move in the direction of more programme assistance this would probably be an unmixed blessing.

The disadvantages of the projects approach can to some extent be offset by the fungibility of funds.[28] Aid not available for one purpose may actually finance another since the recipient can endlessly reshuffle his total budget. Those expenditures of which aid donors most disapprove can be domestically financed. The donors' projects approach may thus have little impact upon the total project composition of a recipient's development programme, although it still constitutes an enormous nuisance to hard-pressed African budget officials. On the other hand, in the African context, costs of projects are likely to incorporate rather less welcome 'technical assistance' content (some of which is not only welcome but essential) than elsewhere; while it may distort the technology and/or inflate the cost of particular projects, 'forced' technical assistance seems nevertheless less likely to be prejudicial to the overall national interest as seen by the recipient government in this form than in overall policy matters.

In a most revealing analysis of how aid donors can be expected to behave in the pursuit of their own versions of what is economically best for a recipient country, an economist who has served on both ends of the aid relationship in Africa has analysed the relative merits of project and programme aid in the achievement of policy 'leverage'. The crux of the leverage question, forgetting for the moment its obvious political possibilities, is the nature of the technical advice offered in conjunction with the capital assistance.

Directing its aid toward a specific project or programme often places a donor in a position to affect nearly every aspect of it. If the donor insists on getting into the picture at the earliest stages of planning a project . . . it may be able to rewrite the terms of reference for the feasibility study which constitutes the main planning input. The donor may also influence the selection of the consultant to execute the study (a decision which is often of critical importance in defining the final shape of the project), and it may influence the study while it is underway and exercise the deciding voice in such matters as size, location, capital and foreign exchange *versus* labour and local-cost intensity, type of processes and equipment to be used, conditions of procurement, identity of the executing agency and its relationship with other public and private entities, qualifications of the participating personnel, timing and phasing of the investment amounts, sources and terms of financial contributions, and pricing of the goods or services to be produced. . . .

. . . when the donor's goal is to influence the macro-economic policies of the borrower government, encompassing the monetary and fiscal fields, exchange-rate management, trade regulation, price control, investment stimulation, employment policy, etc. . . . a programme loan, preferably much larger than the amount required to finance any typical individual project (so that the borrower will consider it worth its while to sacrifice some independence in national policies) . . . is, on the face of it, a superior mechanism for extracting commitments to particular macro-policies. Nevertheless, where the magnitude of specific project aid from a single donor or co-ordinated group of donors is so large as to finance a significant share of the total investment programme and/or capital import bill, the donor, or group of donors, has a strong bargaining position from which to insist . . . that there should be a general aid agreement committing the borrower to certain macroeconomic policies, self-help efforts and targets.[29]

The author of this passage scrupulously refrains from comment as to whether the recipient government or the donor's technical 'experts' are most likely to 'know what is best' for the country concerned. From the perspective of the recipient governments the question is, of course, ridiculous. From that of particular departments of government or particular officials, among whom agreement is incomplete, it may be less so. The views of foreign aid donors, missions, and 'experts' can be effective instruments for the pursuit of the objectives of Planning or other Ministries within recipient countries' polities. If only the motive and biases of the foreign contributions were beyond suspicion! As it is, there may be more political mileage in some African countries in *opposing* foreign advice – whatever its nature – than in employing it as a supportive instrument.

As has been seen, technical assistance makes up a very high proportion of the official development assistance to independent African states – roughly half of the value received in terms of grant-equivalents. The loan of 'human capital' throws up some particularly difficult problems for the analyst and policymaker in Africa. There does seem by now to be quite general agreement that:

> technical assistance has been ... probably the least efficient segment of all foreign aid; ... Africa, which has enjoyed roughly half the technical assistance furnished to the Third World since 1960, seems to have done less well with it than anybody else.[30]

The measurement of the real value of technical assistance is exceedingly difficult. The value of this form of 'aid' is conventionally taken as its cost; this procedure, which involves problems enough when it is employed for commodity 'aid', can be quite misleading in the case of technical assistance in view of the impossibility of accounting for quality differentials. Small tropical African states are at the bottom end of most international civil servants' and technical assistance personnel preference lists; while there are many exceptions, they consequently tend to receive assistance in the form either of extremely young and inexperienced individuals or of rejects from more desirable postings. The recipient governments frequently do not possess the

technical expertise to assess independently the value of the technical assistance they are offered or indeed that which they have
already received. (The situation is analogous to that in
technology markets, wherein weak states seek to purchase
information the value of which cannot be assessed without the
possession of that, and other, information.) A common recommendation from foreign advisers and technicians, particularly
those not so productive themselves, is for the expansion of technical assistance; advisory missions frequently advise further more
detailed, and more expensive, advice.

Discussion of 'free' technical assistance sometimes proceeds as if
it were totally costless to the recipient. This is only very rarely so.
In most cases there are substantial direct local costs associated
with technical assistance personnel. Most obvious are the costs of
housing, transport, office space and furniture, and secretarial
services – some of which can no doubt be set against tourist
expenditures which would not otherwise have been made. Less
obvious is the opportunity cost of the time of the skilled and
dedicated personnel 'on the ground' as they train and listen to, or
read the outpourings of the frequently less experienced and/or
less able, recently imported, short-term 'experts'.

Reliance on skilled expatriate expertise, even in the best of
circumstances, can throw off detrimental effects for autonomous
development. The insidious logic of technical assistance produces
the paradoxical result that where it is most useful it is also
most likely to block longer-term progress. When a department,
research station, school or Ministry find an expatriate employee
who is effective, there is every reason for the relevant local
decision-maker, who may himself have been placed in authority
prior to his having acquired much skill or self-confidence, to
retain the services of the expatriate for as long as possible; the
success of his own career may even be or become dependent upon
him. As younger and usually better-trained Africans emerge from
the educational system, they find their promotion and prospects
for real participation blocked by skilled expatriates upon whom
the established administration is dependent. The expatriates may
be able to protect the older African generation by concealing its
deficiencies from the younger. Established civil servants and other
decision-makers may quite sensibly prefer a continuous succession of contract foreigners to the promotion of local manpower

even when the talents of the two groups are equal. But they are, of course, frequently not equal; the young African graduate is likely to lack experience and judgement which can only be acquired through practice. The tragedy is that he may not be given the opportunity to practice because of the fact that he has not already had some practice. Thus a succession of expatriates learn more and more about developmental decision-making while the Africans below them in the hierarchy become progressively more alienated and discontented. The experience and collective 'memory' which is accumulated during the process of development is thus appropriated by foreigners who subsequently leave the country carrying these invaluable assets with them. The alienated Africans tend to move to those sectors in which they have the freedom to perform and to learn without blocks to their progress. Thus the strongest African sectors may well be those in which were found the weakest and the least numerous expatriates. Some of these tendencies might have been averted had adequate in-service training and staff development programmes been put in place in the 1960s.

Between allowing oneself to be swamped by foreign teachers and advisers and excluding them altogether through total reliance on indigenous manpower there is a difficult path to tread. Overreaction to the incompetences and excesses of expatriate personnel can be as counter-productive as over-reliance upon them. What a particular government *can* do is a function of its existing skill base and the objectives it has set for itself. Well-formulated plans, which are infrequently actually encountered in Africa, can allow for a varying volume and character of expatriate manpower over time. One must sympathise, however, with the exasperation of those who question 'technical assistance which recommends technical assistance for planning technical assistance'.[31] The object of the importing country must, of course, be to identify that degree of reliance upon foreign skills which is acceptable and the specific imports it desires, and to pursue *only* these. Only after that is done, can one grapple with the questions of sourcing and financing.

Aid which assists in the financing and/or recruitment of skills already identified by the purchaser can be extremely useful, but there will always exist some risk, particularly where the 'helpful' intermediary is providing the financing, that the world search for the skill in question is improperly deflected. Aid donors are likely to seek to persuade weak African governments that their needs for imported skills are great, and that they are best met by those (typically from the donor country) recommended and financed by the donor in question. 'Disinterested' academics from donor countries, who have interests of their own to pursue, are likely to generate the same type of advice. The point of these remarks is not totally to discredit such attempts at persuasion or advice for they are usually, in the essence, sound enough; rather, it is to highlight the inherent biases which they are likely to exhibit. Recipient governments should be aware, as they formulate their own independent approaches to technical assistance requirements, that they will be advised to import more than they require and that the process of recruitment to meet their needs is not one which simply seeks the best talent for the minimum cost.

Since the cost of imported human capital is already very high and is certain to grow at a rapid rate – roughly the rate at which per capita income grows in the developed world[32] – import substitution in this field and, if possible, the development of less skill-intensive and import-intensive technologies, not only in the productive sectors but in the social ones as well, are matters of very high priority.

5. Conclusions

This discussion has by no means exhausted the subject of strategies and policies available to African governments and decision-makers in their pursuit of their own objectives through the use of the difficult aid relationship. Indeed it is no more than a beginning. The totality of relationships with foreign powers can be quite complex. One cannot assess any one aspect of the aid relationship in isolation from the complete picture. Thus, for example, the toleration and even renewal of a technical assistance scheme which has clearly gone wrong may reflect the African government's calculation that 'exposure' could harm longer-term commercial relationships and/or the prospects for larger amounts of aid in other more important sectors. Again, technical assistance may actively be sought by particular departments not so much because of a technical 'need' for it as from a calculation that such personnel may speak credibly on their behalf in the donor councils.

Above all else, the bargaining power of the aid-receiving government or department rests upon its capacity to say 'no' and to regulate its own requests. Official development assistance – whether it is project or programme aid, technical assistance or food – must be assessed, wherever possible, on a case by case basis, on the basis not only of its economic but also its political value to the recipient or the interests the recipient represents. All forms of 'aid' *can* be useful. But there are at present *none* which *necessarily* are. Nor are there signs that the international community is moving towards the automatic redistribution mechanisms which might unequivocally be described as 'useful' aid.

Whether African governments or departments are sophisticated and capable enough to be able to conduct such evaluations and self-regulation effectively must be a matter of judgement. There are reasons for believing that by now the overwhelming majority of them are. Whether they are also primarily *interested* in the development of their countries may be a matter of greater dispute. No doubt it will depend on the individual cases and on what one means by 'development'.

Notes

I am grateful for comments on an earlier draft from Douglas Anglin, Jonathan Barker, John Loxley, Frank Mitchell and David Nowlan, none of whom is to be held responsible in any way for the views here expressed. This paper was originally prepared for publication in 1972. I have made no attempt to bring the references or the discussion up to date, except for the repair or removal of certain obvious statistical or factual anomalies which would otherwise have remained.

1. Dee Brown, *Bury My Heart at Wounded Knee*, Bantam, New York, 1971, p. xii.
2. 'Any argument that suggests that aid should be provided or withheld in accordance with an explicit valuation of the users is an argument for leverage.... Bullying, to give the practice a plainer name, has unpredictable results ...': John White, 'Who uses aid ... for what?' *Institute of Development Studies Bulletin*, University of Sussex, iv, 2/3, June 1972, p. 24.
3. Dudley Seers, 'What types of government should be refused what types of aid?', *Institute of Development Studies Bulletin*, University of Sussex, iv, 2/3, June 1972, pp. 6–15.

4. Arnold C. Harberger, 'Issues concerning capital assistance to less developed countries', *Economic Development and Cultural Change*, xx, 4, July 1972, pp. 631–40.

5. Reginald H. Green, 'Stages in economic development: changes in the structure of production, demand and international trade', *Yale University Economic Growth Center Paper*, No. 125, Institute of Banking Studies, Bank of Sudan, p. 60. Green is among the very few who have attempted to operationalise the concept of 'dependence' through quantification. See Green, 'Stages in economic development', 64A; and 'The economy of Cameroon Federal Republic', in P. Robson and D. A. Lury, eds., *The Economics of Africa*, Allen and Unwin, London, 1969, p. 251.

6. Andre Gunder Frank, *Capitalism and underdevelopment in Latin America*, Monthly Review Press, New York and London, 1967. See also, Robert Rhodes, ed., *Imperialism and Underdevelopment*, Monthly Review Press, New York and London, 1970.

7. On this approach, I have been much influenced by John White, 'Who uses aid . . . for what?' and 'The poor country's view of a wicked world' (mimeo., Nov. 1971).

8. How one deals with an independent government which freely (without influence) calculates that its interests coincide with those of an industrial power and acts accordingly is an interesting question.

9. For instance: Mahbub ul Haq, 'Developing country alternatives', in H. Hughes, ed., *Prospects for Partnership, Industrialization and Trade Policies in the 1970s*, Johns Hopkins, Baltimore, 1973, pp. 128–37; and Frances Stewart, 'Trade and technology', in P. Streeten, ed., *Trade Strategies for Development*, Macmillan, London, 1974, pp. 231–63.

10. John White goes even further: 'Developing countries do not have foreign policies in the conventional sense. They have policies for manipulating the way in which the external environment encroaches upon the domestic'. See White, 'The poor country's view of a wicked world', p. 3.

11. OECD, *Development Assistance, 1972, Review*, OECD, Paris, 1972, pp. 238–9.

12. The OECD applies a price index, based on 1960 as 100, to official development assistance. In 1970, this index stood at 125·1: OECD *Development Assistance, 1971 Review*, OECD, Paris, 1972, p. 148. When applied to the roughly 8 per cent growth in the aid total this gives roughly a little less than 15 per cent reduction. Prices rose further in 1971.

13. World Bank, International Development Association, *Annual Report 1972*, World Bank, Washington, 1973, p. 87.

14. Clive S. Gray, 'Tied versus local-cost foreign aid in the light of aid objectives', *Eastern Africa Economic Review*, iii, 2, Dec. 1971, p. 8.

15. Jagdish N. Bhagwati, *Amount and Sharing of Aid*, Overseas Development Council, London, 1970, pp. 13–18.

16. Since there are no data on the grant element in aid to Africa, I have employed the figure for the whole Third World.

17. Streeten also suggests deducting those 'aid' payments which were designated for the compensation of settlers from the donor country, the payments of

pensions to ex-colonial civil servants, etc., although it may be difficult to establish how many of these obligations were tied directly to aid: Paul Streeten, 'Aid to Africa'. Paper presented to the Fifth Joint Economic Commission for Africa/Organisation of African Unity Meeting on Trade and Development, Geneva, August 1970, pp. 38–9.

18. United Republic of Tanzania, *The Annual Plan for 1972/73*, Government Printer, Dar es Salaam, 1972.

19. The official data of the 'aid tables' do not provide a complete picture of the actual assistance which developed countries provide, on balance, to the less developed countries. It makes very little sense to discuss the effects of official development assistance upon Africa without at the same time considering the effects of the 'donor' governments' other external economic policies, since changes in 'aid' totals can be simultaneously offset by alterations in official commercial policies. Unfortunately this is not easy to do in a quantitative fashion. Some general comments are all that are at present possible.

    African states which still engage mainly in primary rather than manufactured product exports are not as hampered by the protectionist trade policies of the developed world as are those states elsewhere which are embarking upon export-oriented industrialisation. Moreover, most African states even enjoy preferential entry to the markets of the EEC, although the 'value' of this entry is, to a large extent, extracted from other Third World states. Despite difficulties with the negotiation of an international cocoa agreement, continuing protectionist policies in the field of agriculture, and some residual revenue duties levied upon their exports, Africa probably loses less from the commercial policies of the developed world than either Asia or Latin America. On the other hand, relationships with foreign investors may be less fruitful in Africa than elsewhere in the light of the host states' usual small size, weak bargaining strength, and inadequate planning and advisory capacity. The 'least developed' countries are typically unable to manage foreign firms in such a way as effectively to maximise the host country's own returns from their participation there. Whether the behaviour and earnings of private corporations can be attributed to official policies of developed country governments, in the same way that trade barriers can, may be subject to argument.

20. 'Poor countries should accept aid only from governments and organisations which will not attempt to influence their priorities' and not from 'those whose primary aim is to prevent revolution': T. J. Byres, 'From what types of government should poor countries accept what types of aid?', *Institute of Development Studies Bulletin*, University of Sussex, iv, 2/3, June 1972, pp. 17–18.

21. This raises the interesting question as to whether independent African states should accept aid from South Africa. The logic of this argument would offer an answer of 'yes' provided that control over the aid was complete; thus a recipient might insist upon terms, unlike Malawi, such that only totally untied grants would be acceptable and that no South Africans would be permitted access. Whether South Africa would agree to such terms is another matter.

22. Albert O. Hirchschman, *A Bias for Hope*, Yale University Press, New Haven, 1971, p. 25.
23. *Ibid.*, p. 26.
24. F. G. Bailey, 'The peasant view of the bad life', Afras/IDS Joint Reprint Series No. 7, University of Sussex; as quoted in White, 'Who uses aid . . . for what?'
25. This and subsequent quotations from Bailey are taken from White, 'Who uses aid . . . for what?
26. *Ibid.*, p. 6.
27. Albert O. Hirschman and Richard M. Bird, 'Foreign aid – a critique and a proposal', *Princeton University Essays on International Finance*, No. 69, International Finance Section, Princeton University, 1968; I. G. Patel, 'The aid relationship', in Barbara Ward, Lenore d'Anjou and J. D. Runnalls, eds., *The Widening Gap*, Columbia University Press, New York, 1971, pp. 295–311; Teresa Hayter, *Aid as Imperialism*, Penguin, Harmondsworth, 1971; and White, 'Who uses aid . . . for what?
28. H. W. Singer, 'External aid: for plans or projects?', *Economic Journal*, lxxv, 299, Sept. 1965, pp. 539–45.
29. Gray, 'Tied versus local-cost foreign aid in the light of aid objectives', pp. 14–5. For an expression of how the World Bank sees its role in Africa in this respect, see Andrew M. Kamarck, 'Assessing economic performance', in Sayre P. Schatz, ed., *South of the Sahara: Development in African Economies*, Macmillan for Temple University Press, London, 1972, pp. 259–75.
30. Philip M. Allen, 'The technical assistance industry in Africa: a case for nationalization', *International Development Review*, 3, 1970, p. 8.
31. This phrase was employed by the local representative of a United Nations agency in Kenya while considering some of the limitations of technical assistance.
32. Between 1963 and 1970 the price index for technical assistance provided by DAC members increased by 57 per cent, an increase unaccompanied by any detectable improvement in its productivity. OECD, *Development Assistance, 1971 Review*, pp. 148–50.

Kenji Okuda

10   Canadian Government Aid: A Critical Assessment

This chapter seeks to assess bilateral Canadian aid to Africa. More specifically, it will concentrate upon the activities of the Canadian International Development Agency (CIDA), the foreign assistance arm of the Canadian Government.[8] Section 2 will discuss possible criteria with which to evaluate the Canadian assistance effort. Section 3 will deal with CIDA operations and apply the criteria to these activities, and section 4 will examine Canadian aid from the perspective of the African nations.

1. The CIDA and its Activities

Canada's involvement in foreign aid and development assistance can be traced back to the Colombo meetings of 1950. It was not until a decade later, however, with the move from colonial to independent status in Africa, that Canadian assistance to African nations began. The initial efforts were on a very small scale and concentrated upon the provision of technical assistance and educational and training facilities within Canada. The growth of bilateral allocations to Africa has been rapid, particularly since the mid-1960s, and totalled over $257 million in 1973–74.[1] In 1972–73, the last year for which detailed data are available, Canada was assisting thirty-five of the forty-two independent nations of Africa.[2] The nations of Africa which received no Canadian aid were the Union of South Africa, the United Arab Republic, Libya, Liberia, the Sudan, Somalia and Gambia.[3]

The allocation to African nations for 1973–74 amounted to over 37 per cent of total bilateral commitments for that year and almost 30 per cent of total official Canadian development aid.[4] Although assistance to Africa bulks large in the Canadian programme,

Canada has provided less than 10 per cent of all bilateral aid received by African nations.[5]

The population of the African countries to which Canada provides assistance is estimated at 255·5 million (mid-1970).[6] Canadian bilateral commitments in 1973–74, therefore, amounted to about a dollar a head. Gross National Product at market prices of these same African countries is estimated at over $25 billion for 1970.[7] Canadian aid in 1973–74 amounted to less than 1 per cent of total GNP. This provides a sobering perspective for any analysis of the possible impact of Canadian aid upon the development efforts of African nations.

2. Criteria and Evaluation

To assess aid performance it is essential to establish relevant criteria. There has been considerable discussion in the literature about the overall impact of aid itself as well as possible yardsticks for measuring aid effectiveness. Some have argued that aid is no more than a new form of colonialism and designed to benefit the donor rather than the recipient nations.[9] Studies have been published indicating a negative impact of aid upon economic growth and well-being.[10] Others have presented arguments contending that aid, by adding to the resources available to a developing country, has had a positive impact upon development.[11] Quantitative studies which support this contention have also been published.[12] Without going into the arguments on this question, this chapter takes as its basic premise the position taken by the latter group, that aid can have a positive impact upon the development effort.

A variety of possible criteria upon which to allocate foreign aid have been advanced. It is possible to utilise the same criteria to assess the effectiveness of aid. One argument which has been advanced is that aid should be tied to performance. Nations which demonstrate their ability to direct their resources into development efforts most successfully and presumably achieve high growth rates, should receive priority claim on assistance funds. The gains from aid expenditures would be higher than if aid were allocated on some alternative basis. There are a number of difficulties present with this criterion. It would be difficult to agree upon performance criteria. Some have suggested changes in the marginal savings rate as a measure. Others have argued for the rate of GNP growth, others for per capita income growth rates. All of these do not take account of matters of more recent concern, for example the distribution of the gains from economic growth. Another criticism is that the performance criterion discriminates against the poorest countries, nations which are so poor and lacking in economic and social overheads that growth itself depends upon the availability of substantial volumes of external assistance. Another difficulty with the performance criterion is the availability and accuracy of the data used to determine aid allocation.

The assessment of Canadian aid, a fraction of total aid, on such a basis becomes even more difficult. To the extent that aid itself has a positive impact upon whatever quantitative variables are used to measure effective development, it is the sum of total aid rather than the Canadian contribution which would be related to the 'successful' allocation of aid.

Another criterion might be the quantitative impact of aid upon the growth rate. Apart from the difficulty of measuring the impact or even agreement on whether aid has a positive effect upon growth, the relatively small role of Canadian aid as noted earlier makes such an assessment virtually impossible. If, to take the most favourable case, aid is all in the form of capital goods, and a low incremental capital output ratio of two is assumed, Canadian aid to Africa in 1973–74 would increase African GNP by $125 million. This amount is less than 0·5 per cent of the GNP of the nations receiving the aid. Given the degree of accuracy of African GNP estimates, such small effects would be virtually impossible to isolate. Put in per capita terms, the impact of aid as calculated above would be around 50 cents.

A somewhat broader and less quantitative criterion would be the recipient nation's commitment to development and its willingness to pursue policies which support economic growth and well-being. Here, further problems arise. First, there is less than total agreement upon the goals, let alone the policies which are necessary to achieve the goals. Quite clearly, even within a set of national policies, some may be considered to have positive, others negative, effects upon the achievement of development goals. How, then, can one assess the overall impact of such policies and use such assessment for aid allocation and assessment purposes?

Another alternative is to rely upon the goals and targets of the developing nations themselves. In other words, has Canadian assistance to Africa effectively helped the African nations to meet their development targets? This approach, however, presents another set of difficulties. An examination of published plans indicates that there are a number of targets included. These range from numbers of children to be accommodated in the primary, secondary and post-secondary educational facilities to miles of roads to be constructed during the plan period. Given the variety of targets, the achievement of any one or even a group of such targets may have little impact upon the development process itself. For example, the Third Five Year Plan for Uganda includes the establishment of external broadcasting facilities as one of its targets. There can be considerable argument as to whether foreign aid provided for the purchase and installation of such facilities has much relationship to economic welfare and the growth potential of the nation. The plan targets as set forth in published documents are the result of economic, political and social pressures within a nation. Clearly, not all of the announced goals or activities of any plan document would be considered significantly related to development by neutral observers.

Another possible criterion is the objective(s) of the donor nation. Has aid as implemented met the objective(s) of the donor government? Canada's objectives for aid have undergone considerable change over the past decade. Increasingly, attention has been given to the concepts of partnership and socio-economic development. Most recently, special attention has been given the least developed twenty-five nations as identified by the United Nations.

Partnership in international development assistance efforts requires a greater awareness and knowledge of conditions in and the needs of the developing countries as determined by them. As the President of CIDA expressed it, 'we are more and more aware of the pressing requirement that developing countries participate in designing and preparing the projects to be realised in their land'.[13] Partnership, however, is not very relevant as a criterion for aid assessment. Donor and recipient can agree with full participation on both sides to undertake projects which may have little impact upon the development effort. Again, as an example, agreement to assist in the development of a short-wave broadcasting facility can hardly be considered an effective use of limited foreign assistance funds.

The need to utilise criteria other than economic has been a matter of considerable attention: 'Our international development strategy, we hope, will redirect our future actions away from a development concept which leaves social value trailing after economic concerns.'[14] These will presumably involve greater attention to '... the needs of populations'.[15] Thus, 'we will see to it that our program responds more and more to priorities defined by the people with whom we cooperate. This assumes that we can really listen to the needs and know the efforts of the developing countries by diversifying our ways of consultation ...'[16]

Again, a number of difficulties arise in attempting to apply such criteria. First, it is unclear what is meant by social values as contrasted with economic concerns. Social improvement in the form of increased educational opportunities, improved health facilities, and intensified rural development efforts are a normal feature of development plans and receive considerable resources, both internal and external, in most developing nations. Moreover, rapid expansion of these services depends critically upon economic growth and the expansion of total output with the attendant expansion of resources available internally to government. When it comes to 'priorities determined by the people with whom we cooperate', it is far from clear just which people are referred to. Is it the villager eking a subsistence living from the soil? If so, how are his needs being expressed and through what agency? It is far too optimistic to assume that governments with which Canadian bilateral aid must deal necessarily reflect the aspirations and desires of the mass of the population.

Of the twenty-five least developed nations identified by the United Nations, sixteen are African.[17] Whether Canada provides or does not provide aid to them can hardly be used to assess Canadian aid to Africa. Thus, the announced targets of CIDA are not very helpful in formulating assessment criteria.

The assessment of Canadian aid to Africa is forced to fall back upon judgements of the extent to which Canadian aid has aided the economic and social development of the recipient nations. A detailed examination of specific projects and programmes and their impact upon development is beyond the capacity of the paper. Rather, comments will be made upon some of the types of projects and programmes undertaken. Some of the difficulties and pitfalls faced by donor nations will be examined.

3. Application of Criterion

Canada has provided four kinds of aid to Africa. These are project, technical assistance, programme, and food aid. Project aid covers agreements to fund, in whole or in part, specified activities which normally carry a significant physical capital component. The provision of locomotives and freight cars to the East African Railways, and the water supply improvement and expansion scheme in Ghana are two recent examples. Project assistance will often incorporate technical assistance, the provision of experts to improve the efficiency of railway operations or the training of well drillers as a component of the water supply improvement programme. Strictly, technical assistance activities involve the provision of specialists to meet the needs of the developing nations and the provision of training facilities in Canada and outside of the recipient nations to nationals of that country. Much of Canada's earlier efforts were in the form of technical assistance, particularly in education.

Programme aid covers the provision of funds which can be utilised by the recipient nation to import raw materials, machinery, and other items which it needs for the maintenance and growth of its economy. Programme aid to Africa has been rather limited, the main recipients being Nigeria, Algeria and the Ivory Coast. No specific project or activity, therefore, is covered by this form of assistance.[18] Finally, food aid is provided to meet emergency conditions such as drought or other natural disasters as well as to augment limited domestic supplies on a longer-term basis.

Roughly one-quarter of Canada's assistance to Africa consists of technical assistance. The largest part of the balance is in the form of project assistance and covers activities ranging from forestry, geological and land surveys to industrial development projects.

Canada's assistance terms are among the most generous provided by donors. Most technical assistance is on a grant basis as is food aid. Programme and project aid are given either in the form of grants or loans depending upon an assessment of the recipient economy and its capacity to finance external debt. Loan terms are also generous, normally a repayment term of 50 years, a 10-year grace period, and at zero interest. Under the Organisation for Economic Cooperation and Development (OECD) definition, the grant element in Canada's assistance is over 90 per cent and, for many of the African nations, 100 per cent.

Canadian aid has a substantial tied component. CIDA must, overall, ensure that at least 80 per cent of its bilateral assistance funds are spent on Canadian goods and services.[19] The latter include technical assistance and training facilities within Canada. Under these guidelines, it is possible to undertake projects in Africa where Canadian content is less than 80 per cent and, in exceptional cases, much less. This overcomes, at least to a limited extent, the very serious problem, particularly among the poorest nations, of their inability to undertake even highly worthwhile and productive activities because of limited local resources.

Canadian assistance is, for understandable reasons, limited to areas and activities in which there is Canadian competence. Thus, technical assistance activities are undertaken only in areas where there is demonstrated Canadian expertise. Given the wide variety of needs for specialised skills, in the African countries and considerable breadth in Canada's capabilities, this does not appear to be a particularly limiting factor. In project assistance, Canada's capabilities are perhaps somewhat more limited although this is not likely again to be a restrictive factor in utilising the limited resources made available for assistance purposes. CIDA has, both for purpose of effective management and to utilise available Canadian resources most effectively, attempted to concentrate efforts within a limited number of fields. These are education, natural resources, transport, agriculture, fisheries, electric power and telecommunications.

Returning for a moment to the expressed interest of CIDA in promoting social development, the areas of Canadian specialisa-tion are not clearly related to such social development. Education is a broad section, but the bulk of the efforts in this area have been devoted to secondary and post-secondary activities. Given the limited numbers who require these types of education, the welfare of the larger part of the population in the developing countries is not likely to be significantly affected. Natural resources, transport, and fisheries, again, are not areas in which the social impact is likely to be of major magnitude. In the field of power, rural electrification appears to be one possible mass benefit facet, although the criticisms of uneven and limited benefits have been levelled even in countries which have undertaken rural electrification schemes. Telecommunications again are likely to benefit the middle and upper income urban dwellers. It appears, then, that social benefits and a more equitable distribution of economic gains, in so far as they can be directly affected through foreign assistance, are difficult to realise given Canada's particular skills and competence.

We turn next to (1) the allocation of aid to the several nations and (2) the reasons for such allocation. Table 10.1 gives the amounts disbursed under Canadian assistance to the nations of Africa in 1972.

The funds disbursed in 1972 varied from a low of $1000 to Sierra Leone to a high of $15·2 million to Botswana. Given the significant differences in population size among the African nations, per capita aid disbursements give a better indication of inter-country variations. Canadian aid per capita ranged from a low of 1 or 2 cents to a high of $24·82 for Botswana. The last figure reflects the substantial mineral development programme which Canada along with other donors and the International Bank for Reconstruction and Development (The World Bank) are financing. Indicating the special circumstances of Botswana is the fact that the next highest per capita disbursement is $2·67 for Tunisia. Again, this last amount is over 50 per cent larger than the disbursement in Niger ($1·76) which is third on a per capita basis.

CIDA has stated that although assistance is given to a large number of African nations, its efforts are concentrated on selected countries. These have been identified for Commonwealth Africa as Ghana, Nigeria, Zambia, Botswana, Lesotho, Swaziland and the three East African nations, Kenya, Tanzania and Uganda.[21] After earlier identifying Tunisia, Senegal and Cameroon as countries of concentration in Francophone Africa, the whole of French-speaking Africa was subsequently designated a concentration area.[22]

Within the Commonwealth Africa concentration group, disbursements per capita in 1972 ranged from 9 cents to $24·82.

Table 10.1. Canadian Aid Disbursements – 1972[20]

Country	Population mid-1970 (millions)	Aid ($) millions)	Aid ($) Per capita	Technical assistance ($ millions)	%	Other ($ millions)	%
Anglophone							
Botswana	0·611	15·166	24·82	0·079	0·52	15·085	99·46
Ghana	8·640	4·060	0·47	2·092	51·52	1·968	48·47
Kenya	11·250	2·344	0·21	2·255	96·20	0·089	3·80
Lesotho	0·923	0·082	0·09	0·082	100·00	—	—
Malawi	4·440	0·410	0·09	0·044	10·73	0·366	89·27
Mauritius	0·836	0·029	0·03	0·028	96·55	0·001	3·45
Nigeria	55·070	11·979	0·22	1·917	16·00	10·062	84·00
Rhodesia	5·310	0·096	0·02	0·096	100·00	—	—
Sierra Leone	2·555	0·001	0·00	0·001	100·00	—	—
Swaziland	0·423	0·060	0·14	0·060	100·0c	—	—
Tanzania	13·270	6·119	0·46	3·143	51·36	2·976	48·64
Uganda	9·814	1·762	0·18	1·232	69·92	0·530	30·08
Zambia	4·136	1·702	0·41	1·052	61·81	0·650	38·19
East African Community	(34·330)*	4·322	0·12	0·985	22·79	3·337	77·21
Total	117·278	$48·132	$0·41	$13·066	27·15	$35·064	72·85
Francophone							
Algeria	14·330	4·825	0·34	1·092	22·63	3·733	77·37
Burundi	3·544	0·223	0·06	0·222	99·55	0·001	0·45
Cameroon	5·836	4·551	0·78	2·151	47·26	2·400	52·74
Central Africa	1·552	0·245	0·16	0·237	96·73	0·008	3·27
Chad	3·596	0·257	0·07	0·244	94·94	0·013	5·06
Congo Republic	0·899	0·114	0·13	0·109	95·61	0·005	4·39
Dahomey	2·708	2·250	0·83	0·335	14·89	1·915	85·11
Gabon	0·310	0·374	1·21	0·373	99·73	0·001	0·27
Guinea	3·980	0·014	0·00	0·014	100·00	—	—
Ivory Coast	4·941	6·517	1·32	1·580	24·24	4·937	75·76
Malagasy Republic	7·310	0·613	0·08	0·565	92·17	0·048	7·83
Mali	5·018	0·762	0·15	0·228	29·92	0·534	70·08
Mauritania	1·170	0·584	0·50	0·159	27·23	0·425	72·77
Morocco	15·495	4·282	0·28	1·012	23·63	3·270	76·31
Niger	4·020	7·085	1·76	1·022	14·42	6·063	85·58
Rwanda	3·596	1·821	0·51	0·882	48·43	0·939	51·57
Senegal	3·870	5·564	1·44	1·733	31·15	3·831	68·85
Togo	1·956	2·200	1·12	0·411	18·68	1·789	81·32
Tunisia	5·075	13·557	2·67	1·806	13·32	11·751	86·68
Upper Volta	5·384	0·975	0·18	0·316	32·41	0·659	67·59
Zaire	18·800	1·065	0·06	0·573	54·80	0·492	46·20
Total	113·390	$57·878	$0·51	$15·064	26·02	$42·814	73·98
Other							
Ethiopia	24·625	0·237	0·152	0·085	100·0		
Other and Unallocated		1·152	0·77'5	0·377			

* Not included in total for Africa.

Again, excluding Botswana, the range was from 9 cents to 47 cents (see Table 10.1). Thus, significant variations exist even within the group. For Francophone Africa, the range is even wider, from a low of 6 cents per capita to a high of $2·67. Whatever the reasons for designating the whole of French-speaking Africa as an area of concentration, there are considerable differences in the amounts of assistance provided the several countries. It would appear more appropriate to designate specific nations within the group upon which assistance efforts will be concentrated.

Given the limited amount of resources available, concentration is desirable, if only to assure that sufficient assistance goes to a few countries to affect appreciably their development efforts. These countries are selected on the basis of the following criteria:

1. The economic needs of a country, and Canada's ability to help meet those needs.
2. The importance which Canada attaches to helping that country's performance.
3. Its past performance in using developing aid effectively, and its prospects for doing so.
4. The extent to which Canadian assistance can have a perceptible impact or 'beneficial leverage' on that country's development.
5. The level and types of aid that are available from other donors – the consideration that Canada should help some of these countries which other donors tend to overlook.[23]

The most important criterion is reported to be the first, that of need. It is difficult to understand, however, how one determines or assesses the relative intensity of need since it appears a reasonable assumption that virtually all of the African nations 'need' additional resources to stimulate and facilitate the development process. Following this criterion, however, one would expect that aid to Nigeria will be reduced since the rapid rise in the price of oil reduces Nigeria's need for assistance relative to other African countries.

The second consideration, the importance which Canada attaches to helping that country's performance, is again a very nebulous concept. This would appear to justify aid to any country since the very provision of aid reflects the decision to provide it. And who determines whether it is of importance to Canada? The third criterion, past performance, may be measurable and thus more objective and easier to apply. However, since earlier aid has been primarily in the form of technical assistance, past performance becomes more a judgement of the efficiency of organisation and governmental structure than of development performance itself.

The fourth criterion, that of 'beneficial leverage', should apply to all development assistance. Clearly Canada is not deliberately trying to provide aid which does not have a perceptible impact upon the country's development. If the perceptibility of impact is a quantitative measure, then a substantial allocation to a specific country would generate the desired effect. This becomes a justification for concentrating aid, not a criterion by which countries are selected for concentration. The last criterion, total aid provision, can be quantified and serve as a policy guide. However, Canada's ability to 'balance' out total aid allocations is quite limited given the fact that Canada has provided less than 10 per cent of total bilateral aid to Africa.

One consideration cited in the foreign policy review is not explicitly included in the criteria, the availability of well-prepared and potentially productive projects and programmes.[24] While it is true that the availability of such proposals can be affected by the provision of technical assistance, project proposals can and are generated by a variety of sources, including assistance provided by other bilateral and multilateral agencies, as well as the recipient country technicians themselves. Also, the variety and scope of proposals submitted for Candian assistance are affected by Canada's willingness as seen by the African nations to give sympathetic and expeditious consideration to the requests.

The relative allocations to the several African nations, and particularly to countries of concentration, appear to reflect past foreign aid development and domestic political pressures, and possibly the preference of senior CIDA officials. It would be possible to establish a 'rational' or objective allocation basis.[25] Whether an allocation using more objective criteria would be of greater benefit to African development than present practices is far from clear.

Of perhaps greater importance than the countries and area of concentration for purposes of assessment are the kinds of activities financed by Canadian assistance. An assessment is concerned with the effectiveness and impact of the specific projects which have been financed. Capital projects may be assessed by comparing project proposals, costs and anticipated results with actual developments. Thus, a multi-purpose project such as a dam for power and irrigation can be studied to determine whether the anticipated benefits have, in fact, been achieved. Difficulties arise when, as is often the case, results differ from anticipations and projections. A further set of questions can be raised concerning the project itself as to whether it was the lowest cost or most effective means of achieving the desired results. Thus, judgement is inevitably involved whether one assesses the project in terms of results as compared with anticipated benefits or the broader question of whether the project was the most productive use of assistance resources.

The assessment task is complicated by the wide variety of activities covered by Canadian assistance efforts. In the area of technical assistance, the efforts are directed toward institution building, training and education. The provision of secondary school teachers, for example, meets a need for trained personnel to cover requirements until indigenous teachers have been trained in sufficient numbers to staff the school system. Canada has attempted to put more effort into the development of teacher training, vocational, and professional education as teacher supply problems have eased. In all these efforts, however, reasonably objective assessment is difficult if not impossible. Much depends upon the personalities and capabilities of the assistance personnel as well as the calibre of the indigenous staff which in turn reflects government priorities, capabilities and social preferences.

Canada has provided considerable assistance in the form of surveys and mapping activities. These quite clearly have added to the stock of knowledge about national resources. This is an essential component of national development activities, but the immediate or even long-term impact may be quite limited. Geological surveys which do not uncover potentially exploitable natural resources add to the stock of information but will not generate further development efforts. However, to the extent that these provide a training ground, the longer-term benefits are the increased capability of the recipient nation to continue such efforts on their own, hardly a quantifiable benefit.

There has been criticism of a rural development project which Canada has been assisting. It is clear that with the predominant portion of Africans still living on the land, rural development is a critical component of any economic expansion effort. Such a project involves technical assistance ranging from agricultural extension to community development, the provision of capital based upon the needs and requirements as assessed by technical advisers and their counterparts, and the development of local organisations capable of carrying on the programme. Such projects clearly take time to establish and implement. It is also difficult to demonstrate the benefits of the effort, particularly in the earlier years of the project. Furthermore, project design, organisational structure, and the manpower assigned, both advisers and their counterparts, may lead to difficulties and possible failure. It is by no means an easy matter to determine whether a project should be terminated because of the circumstances and problems faced. And critics will find it easy to attack such efforts because of the many intangible considerations which go into the total effort.

It is necessary, also, to recognise Canada's capabilities in the foreign assistance field. Although there has been considerable attention lately to improving the lot of the smallest and the landless farmers, Canada's expertise and experience in dealing with this problem area is clearly limited. Thus, in assessing Uganda's agricultural potential, Canada concentrated its efforts on an examination of the potential for medium-size farm development. From such studies could come both technical assistance and project proposals which would lead to further Canadian involvement. This type of involvement in which Canada's assistance can be offered at critical points in an evolving sector development effort could lead to country concentration as further assistance activities are identified. Such evolutionary concentration appears to have greater justification than the present situation where a variety of relatively unrelated activities are assisted in countries of concentration.

Over the past decade, with the expansion of Canadian aid to Africa, there has been growing sophistication in meeting the needs of the African nations. While errors and failures have undoubtedly occurred, these are inevitable in the complex process of development. As Canadian experience and expertise grows, however, the likelihood of similar mistakes is reduced.[26] There appears to be greater emphasis on evolutionary integrated programme and project development, for example in the area of rural development, than on specific relatively isolated projects, a number of which make up the country's assistance effort. Finally, the expansion of field staff has improved the ability of Canada to perceive and assess the needs of the developing nations. Here, however, it appears desirable to improve analysis and assessment capabilities in Ottawa by the development of an effective policy planning and review staff which can concentrate on research and policy questions without being unduly involved in the day-to-day activities of the aid agency.

4. The Perspective of Recipient Nations

Although material on the recipient nations' perspectives of the aid process is extremely limited, an effort will be made to present some observations based on limited personal experience. In the search for material, an observer is struck by the fact that the writings in this area are rarely by direct participants in the aid process.[27] The process of donor–recipient relationships is not one which can be neatly diagrammed or described. The donor nation, in this instance Canada, indicates its interest in providing assistance to a developing nation. The government bureaucracy in the developing nation is made aware of this interest in a variety of ways. Some are informed through the local press, others may be contacted by Canadian aid officials indicating interest in assisting sectors for which they are responsible, and still others by the government agency which negotiates with aid donors.

Possible project and technical assistance requests are discussed informally within the ministries directly involved, then with the planning and finance agencies within the government and often with representatives of the donor government. If and when agreement is reached within the government of the developing country that foreign assistance will be actively sought, a more formal request will be submitted, and, if the potential donor indicates that the project will be assisted, a formal agreement must be negotiated and signed. This whole process is often lengthy and time-consuming. Two to three years from initial discussions of a project or programme proposal to a formal aid agreement is not uncommon. Delays and difficulties in reaching agreement may occur on both sides. There may be disagreements between ministries in the developing country on the priority of the project proposals, inter-ministerial battles in terms of jurisdiction over the project and disagreements on the proposed terms of the formal agreement. The donor government may find proposals get 'lost' in their own internal assessment procedures and bureaucracy. There may be disagreements among aid agency personnel on the importance to be given a particular proposal. It is sometimes rather surprising that despite all these difficulties, agreements do get signed and aid funds do flow.

From the point of view of the Africans nations, Canadian aid performance can be assessed by comparing it with that of other donor nations. The concern here is not of quantitative magnitude, although most African nations would undoubtedly like to receive more aid from most donors including Canada.[28]

One common problem in aid donor–recipient relationships is the way in which actual projects and programmes to be assisted are determined. Although some government agency, often the planning ministry, is given formal responsibility for determining priorities as among project proposals, some donors work directly with specific operating ministries, agree to proposals, and then submit them to the central coordinating or 'clearing' agency for *pro forma* approval. The central agency often has little choice but to approve the project regardless of the assessment of its relative importance. Canadian aid officials appear to have been quite sensitive to these hazards and have attempted to ensure that the recipient government's internal coordination mechanism was not by-passed or treated as an unnecessary intrusion.

Another matter of concern to developing countries is the ability to programme foreign assistance for more than one year at a time. Planning and programming efforts are simplified if at least the minimum level of foreign assistance for two to three years ahead can be anticipated. Canada has been among the leaders in this area since it uses the present levels of aid as the minimum allocation for the next few years with the understanding that additional funds can be made available provided agreement is reached on mutually acceptable projects and activities.

Canada has also demonstrated considerably greater speed of response and flexibility as compared with most other donors. The delays in response to aid requests for particular projects are often frustrating. As with manuscripts submitted for publication, it is not considered desirable to submit a particular aid request to more than one donor at a time. Delays in response, particularly if the potential donor decides not to support the proposal, can generate further delays in an already time-consuming process. In general, requests to Canada have involved less lag than similar requests to other donors. A part of this is undoubtedly due to the smaller size of Canada's aid effort and may be lost as the size of the aid programme and personnel numbers grow.

A source of considerable concern to developing nations is the tying of aid. The 80 per cent 'Canadian content' requirement has been applied very flexibly so that a number of projects in Africa receive considerable local currency support. While Canada's requirements may not be a significant constraint, other donor countries do provide aid on less restrictive terms in Africa. Thus, a further easing of the content requirement could increase the perceived benefits from the point of view of the recipient nations.

In general, Canada's performance as seen by the African nations compares very favourably with that of other donors. It is critical, therefore, that Canada's perception of the development process, particularly the recent emphasis on the social aspects of development, does not lead to major differences concerning policies and programmes with the developing countries themselves.

5. Conclusion

An assessment of Canada's foreign aid activities is extremely difficult. None of the generally recognised criteria can be used effectively in determining the effectiveness of one nation's aid programme which is intermingled with other donor efforts. The efforts to concentrate Canadian activities in particular sectors and a selected group of African nations have great merit, but the actual pattern of aid disbursements indicates that the policy goals take time to achieve. Canada's aid efforts appear to be more flexible and responsive to the wishes of the developing nations than the programmes of other donors. There is considerable danger that this quality may be lost as the size of the Canadian programme increases unless special efforts are made to retain the flexibility and speed of response which has been a notable feature of Canada's efforts in Africa.

Notes

1. CIDA *Annual Aid Review 1973*, CIDA, Ottawa 1974, p. 15. The figure cited is the total of aid commitments entered into in the fiscal year 1973–74. There has been a major increase of over $100 million in new commitments to Francophone Africa compared with the previous year.
2. For a list of the countries which received Canadian aid disbursements in 1972–73, see Table 10.1.
3. The assistance as disbursed to Rhodesia is minimal and probably reflects financial support for black Rhodesian students in training outside the country.
4. CIDA, *Annual Aid Review 1973*, p. 15.
5. The 10 per cent refers to Canadian aid disbursed. With the rapid growth of commitments, disbursements will increase in the years ahead and undoubtedly rise considerably over the 10 per cent ratio.
6. IBRD, *World Bank Atlas 1972*, IBRD, Washington, 1972.
7. *Ibid.*, p. 5.
8. CIDA was established in 1968 to take over foreign aid responsibilities previously handled by the Exernal Aid Office.
9. For an example of this position, see A. G. Frank, 'The development of underdevelopment', *Monthly Review*, xviii, 4, Sept. 1967, pp. 17–31.
10. Among the studies which fall into this category are K. B. Griffin and J. L. Enos, 'Foreign assistance objectives and consequences', *Economic Development and Cultural Change*, xviii, 3, April 1970, pp. 318–27.
11. See, for example, *Report of the Commission on International Development: Partners in Development*, L. B. Pearson (Chairman), Praeger, New York, 1970.
12. H. B. Chenery and N. G. Carter, 'Foreign assistance and development performance, 1960–1970', *American Economic Review*, lxiii, 2, May 1973, pp. 459–68.
13. P. Gerin-Lajoie, President CIDA, 'Statement Before the Standing Committee of the House of Commons on External Affairs and National Defense', 24 May 1973, Queen's Printer, Ottawa, 1973, p. 8.
14. *Ibid.*, p. 8.
15. *Ibid.*, p. 2.
16. *Ibid.*, p. 10.
17. The African nations are Botswana, Burundi, Chad, Dahomey, Ethiopia, Guinea, Lesotho, Mali, Malaŵi, Niger, Rwanda, Somalia, Sudan, Tanzania, Uganda, and Upper Volta.
18. The distinction between programme and project aid is often blurred. Thus, aid which was given an industrial development company in Uganda to finance new investment was utilised to purchase supplies needed by a hotel subsidiary, certainly not the original intent of the loan.

19. Canada allocates over 20 per cent of its aid to multi-national institutions such as the IDA, the regional development banks, and UNDP. While some of this allocation is tied, the larger part is freely usable. Thus, the overall tying requirement is considerably less than 80 per cent.

20. Canada, *1972 Report to OECD Development Advisory Committee.*

21. CIDA *Annual Aid Reviews,* particularly 1970–71, p. 14.

22. CIDA *Annual Aid Review 1971–1972,* p. 29.

23. CIDA *Annual Aid Review 1970–1971,* p. 14.

24. Canada Department of External Affairs, *International Development – Foreign Policy for Canadians,* Queen's Printer, Ottawa, 1970, pp. 18–19.

25. For one such effort, see Dan Usher, *The Level of Aid,* 1969.

26. The rapid expansion of CIDA personnel as well as the associated shifts in responsibilities have, in turn, created a problem of 'collective memory'. Mistakes made in the past may be repeated simply because those who were acquainted with the mistakes have either been transferred elsewhere, moved upward or left the agency.

27. The comments of Edward Martin, Chairman of the Development Advisory Committee, seem particularly appropriate at this point. There is danger that in listening to the academic and journalistic commentaries on aid, we are ignoring what is really happening in the development assistance arena. 'The only tie (of the observers) really lies in the integrity and wisdom of the individual participants, not always easy for the operators to be sure about.': E. M. Martin, *Development Cooperation: Efforts and Policies of the Members of the Development Assistance Committee,* OECD, Paris, 1973.

28. The term 'most donors' is used deliberately. In the past Japanese 'aid' has been offered on terms which many developing nations considered unduly onerous with relatively short repayment periods and close to market rates of interest.

Part 5   Africa and International Politics

Africa, symbolised by the Organisation of African Unity (OAU), is both the largest and biggest regional organisation in world politics; it is also the least important in world trade. In this concluding Part, four scholars analyse the international relations of Africa, both its continental politics and its relations with European and global organisations. Africa has a much longer and more distinguished history of involvement in international politics than is indicated by the recent celebration of the first decade of the OAU. Its recapture of international status and influence has been advanced by its ability to act as a vote-wielding coalition over issues such as Southern Africa, the Middle East, association with Europe, and the redistribution of global resources. Nevertheless, there is a continuing tension among African states over the definition and direction of African unity, so that the maintenance of a continental consensus is expensive, involving frequent consultations and conferences.[1] These four final chapters examine patterns of cooperation and conflict among African states and between continental and other international organisations.

The chapter by Johns (Ch. 11) presents and explains data on diplomatic exchange within Africa. He draws attention to the problems and limitations of this mode of analysis but nevertheless indicates its utility in describing the growth of diplomatic reciprocity among African states. A small group of states appear as the most active in diplomatic relations, especially Egypt, Nigeria and Zaire; that these are emerging as the 'great powers' of Africa appears from other indicators as well. Johns also analyses exchange at the regional level, pointing to the regionalisation of continental politics. While the author recognises the characteristic dependence of the continent as a whole he suggests that there are growing inequalities within Africa as well; he foresees a hierarchy of diplomatic power within the African international system, a concern repeated in the examination of support for international organisations by Clark in Chapter 13.

Mayall (Ch. 12) presents a comprehensive analysis of one aspect of Africa's organisational politics – its association with the European Economic Community (EEC). EurAfrican ties have been characterised as being both neo-colonial and developmental. Mayall reviews African criticisms of neo-colonialism and collaboration with Europe and analyses the precarious nature of the continent's united stance towards Europe because of the diversity of its interests and associations. He reviews the intent and impact of the Yaoundé Conventions and explains how the asymmetry of Africa and Europe led to an abandonment of 'reciprocity'. He notes that 'radical' African states have been reincorporated in the revised and enlarged EurAfrican arrangement and that neither they nor all of the critics of dependence believe any more that the Lomé Convention will prevent development: he asserts that it is simply not true that African states have no power to reorientate their economies. The new Convention, Mayall argues, will not retard national policies, and may even advance Africa's interests and growth. The EEC Association is one of several institutions examined in the following chapter.

The penultimate chapter (Ch. 13) in this collection is by Clark on the support given to international organisations by African states. This original contribution complements those by Johns on diplomatic exchange and by Shaw (Ch. 14) on the mixed actor system. Clark presents a typology of non-state actors, and proceeds to analyse African support in terms of financial contributions, provisions of personnel, participation in conferences, and 'general' political support. He uses a range of indicators of such support, from financial flows to summit attendance and judgemental opinions. He then ranks overall commitment to intergovernmental institutions and analyses the bases of competition for support among those organisations. Clark suggests that 'subregional' institutions are generally more successful in achieving support than continental or global organisations and he indicates that more research needs to be done on the complementarity or incompatibility of this ever-growing range of organisations. He concludes that despite the rhetoric of pan-Africanism and Third

World cooperation, such inclusive organisations have been less successful in achieving support from among members than have sub-regional, multi-purpose organisations composed of a select group of states with similar colonial backgrounds.

The final chapter (14) by Shaw has two themes, the second of which examines issues already raised in Clark's essay – the rich inheritance of diplomacy in Africa and the development of a continental mixed-actor system. This analysis of continuities and discontinuities in Africa points to the exchange of diplomats between African states in the pre-, as well as post-, colonial period and the continuing problems posed by the choice between confrontation and collaboration with extra-continental powers, a concern running throughout this collection of essays. Shaw suggests that the pattern of African international relations in pre-colonial times was essentially one of intergovernmental regional subsystems; the colonial period was one of transnational imperial subsystems; while the trend in post-colonial Africa is towards a comprehensive continental subsystem. The era of nationalism in Africa has been superseded by a mixed-actor system which includes a variety of non-state organisations.

Shaw concludes by presenting one possible scenario of future international relations of Africa in which global, continental and internal inequalities are inter-related and produce new hierarchies. Africa's developing *realpolitik* will likely be determined by the ambivalent role of its emerging 'middle powers' who are simultaneously subordinate and superordinate in global and continental relations. He thus supports the findings of Johns on the emergence of stratification in Africa. This final set of essays indicates the problems and opportunities posed by the diversity of states and actors in Africa in the achievement of unity and development. Like the other four sections it is generally pessimistic about the prospects for an early end to dependence and underdevelopment on the continent.

Note

1. See Leon Gordenker, 'The OAU and the UN: can they live together?', in Ali A. Mazrui and Hasu H. Patel, eds., *Africa in World Affairs: the next thirty years*, Third Press, New York, 1973, p. 105. See also Berhanykun Andemicael, *The*

OAU and the UN: relations between the Organization of African Unity and the United Nations, Africana, New York, 1976; and Zdenek Cervenka, *The Unfinished Quest for Unity: Africa and the OAU*, Friedmann, London, 1977.

David H. Johns

11   Diplomatic Exchange and Inter-State Inequality in Africa: An Empirical Analysis

1. Introduction

This chapter examines diplomatic exchange, that is, the establishment of diplomatic missions, within Africa by African states
for a ten-year period. The data on which the discussion is based
were published annually from 1966 to 1975. Thus, given delays in
recording and publishing the data, the time span coincides more
or less with the first decade of the Organisation of African Unity
(OAU). The focus is not upon diplomatic exchange between
individual states themselves. Rather it is upon each state's activity
within the OAU system and as compared with other OAU states.
Which states receive the most diplomatic missions, which ones
establish the most, and which states exchange missions on a
reciprocal basis the most? What sort of pattern emerges over the
ten-year period? Do some states establish or receive a disproportionately large number of missions? In other words, does
the configuration of diplomatic exchange, especially for the data
published in 1975, suggest that certain states now dominate or at
least have the potential for dominating African international
relations? Has there developed in Africa, as within the international system generally, a form of stratification or hierarchy in
diplomatic exchange?

Since the analysis of diplomatic exchange is a relatively new
focus for students of African international relations, perhaps a
few introductory comments to point out the relevance of
diplomatic exchange and to summarise trends within Africa are in
order.[1] Clearly the establishment or retention or closing of
missions is at least one indication of states' foreign policy orien-
tations. It reflects deliberate action or inaction or reaction of the
states and, in any event, is a specific and tangible measure of

foreign policy behaviour. Thus diplomatic exchange may be used in an assessment of relationships between particular states or, as in this paper, among the OAU states more generally at any point in time or over time.

There are numerous instances in which *coups d'état*, civil wars or secessionist threats within a state have affected diplomatic exchange. On occasion this has led to the closing of diplomatic missions and/or non-recognition – two relatively strong methods of registering political disapproval and demonstrating foreign policy decisions. This occurred in Ghana following the 1966 overthrow of President Kwame Nkrumah. Both Egypt and Mali closed their missions in Accra, while Zambia, which refused to recognise the new regime, asked Ghana to close its mission in Lusaka. Nigeria responded to Tanzania's – and later Gabon's, the Ivory Coast's and Zambia's – decision to recognise breakaway Biafra by terminating diplomatic exchange. The opposite sort of phenomenon may occur as well. This was Uganda's experience after the coup which ousted President A. Milton Obote. Both the number of missions established in Kampala and the number of Ugandan missions elsewhere in the continent increased.

There are other examples – perhaps less frequent – in which policy changes have affected diplomatic exchange. For instance, both Egypt and Ghana opened missions in Malaŵi shortly after the latter's independence, only to close them when Malaŵi began to move towards diplomatic exchange with South Africa. Likewise, the establishment of a Libyan mission in Uganda following the 1971 coup reflected, at least as much as the coup itself, Uganda's changed diplomatic and military orientation with respect to Israel.

For the most part, however, diplomatic exchange is not directly affected by these domestic and/or international conflicts. On the contrary, it proceeds more or less routinely. Diplomatic missions are closed only as a last resort and instances of such action are exceptions rather than typical behaviour within the African international system. Other time-tested techniques, such as the recall of envoys for consultation or the lowering of the level of the mission or the rank of the chief diplomat, are used. This was the pattern which Libya and Morocco followed between July 1971 and January 1975 when, rather than an exchange of ambassadors, the states had chargés d'affaires accredited to each other's governments. The reason for this cooling-off period was Libya's precipitous and premature recognition of the 1971 abortive coup in Morocco – an action which the Moroccan government did not view favourably.

Because most African states are relatively weak and have limited power, diplomatic exchange may be especially important. It may be one major – perhaps the only – source of leverage in African international relations. Therefore it may be used in a deliberate effort to compensate for other and obvious political, military or economic weaknesses. Concern with diplomatic exchange as an instrument of power was perhaps more pronounced in the first years of independence. Each government had to decide as a matter of policy how many and which missions to establish. Some states, especially the ones more readily identified with a radical or militant stance in pan-Africanism, were more active and their decisions often were made on ideological grounds or perhaps for personal reasons. The decisions set a tone and indicated a pattern. Even if, as was occasionally the case, the decisions were rather arbitrary and reflected only accident, chance or whim, they were regarded as important policy decisions.

Yet sooner or later all states, including the more active and more radical, had to review and re-evaluate the importance and relevance of missions. No doubt a panoply of different domestic, regional, continental and even international (that is, outside of Africa) factors were taken into account, but decisions tended to become increasingly pragmatic. They reflected a more careful evaluation of interests and of limited resources. Attention was given to establishing missions in contiguous states and in states within the same region in order to support more positive and cooperative efforts for development. Additionally, some consideration was given to establishing missions in states outside the region, states which commanded more importance in the continent. Simultaneously, decisions tended less and less to take into account how the governments came into power or their political, economic and social ideologies. Stated differently, rather than using diplomatic exchange as an instrument of power, a new emphasis was placed upon it as an instrument for administrative and economic cooperation – more as a functional than as a political instrument.

Given this change in emphasis, the number of embassies established within a state came to reflect to a greater extent the evaluations of other states as to which states were more important for the realisation of their respective interests. It is therefore possible, as in this chapter, to look at diplomatic exchange with a view to examining certain perceived and/or actual power relationships among the states. That is, the number of missions established within a state is one measure of the relative importance attributed to that state. Likewise, the number of missions which a state establishes is one indication of its perceptions and abilities regarding diplomatic activity. A third index, in addition to the number of missions received and established, is reciprocity. It designates the states that attract more missions because of their relative visibility or power and, at the same time, initiate more activity such that their reciprocal exchanges reinforce their diplomatic relationships. In sum, these various means of tabulating diplomatic exchange denote certain inequities and inequalities, real or imagined, within the African international system.

2. Diplomatic Exchange Examined

The data on which the study is based are shown in Tables 11.1, 11.2 and 11.3.

These figures were obtained from lists of diplomatic accreditations within each of the forty-one OAU member states. (The former Portuguese territories are not included, for their independence dates were too close to the end of the time period to allow for their inclusion in the published data.) It must be stressed that the data and figures do not include special ties and other arrangements which several states have entered into, such as a pooling of diplomats or the appointment of cabinet ministers with responsibilities for regional cooperation, unless there was formal diplomatic exchange as well. Nor do the data and figures take into account the number of diplomats per mission or their particular qualities, expertise and on-the-job performance. The data considered in this paper are quantitative measurements only.

Table 11.1 shows the number of missions established within each state at a given time. Such a determination was based upon

Table 11.1 Number of African Missions Established Within Each African State: 1966–75*²

	'66	'67	'68	'69	'70	'71	'72	'73	'74	'75
Algeria	5	8	7	7	14	14	14	16	17	19
Benin	2	2	3	3	3	3	3	3	3	3
Botswana	0	0	0	1	1	1	1	2	2	2
Burundi	1	2	2	2	2	2	2	2	2	2
Cameroun	7	7	7	9	9	7	7	6	6	6
CAR	2	2	2	2	2	2	2	5	5	6
Chad	3	2	2	2	5	5	4	4	4	5
Congo(B)	1	1	1	1	2	3	3	4	4	8
Egypt	14	14	22	23	23	23	23	23	23	25
Eq. Guinea			0	2	2	2	3	3	3	0
Ethiopia	1	11	12	12	12	12	12	22	22	22
Gabon	0	0	0	0	0	0	0	5	4	4
Gambia	0	0	0	0	0	0	0	3	3	3
Ghana	14	13	13	15	15	15	14	14	14	14
Guinea	3	1	1	1	1	1	1	5	5	5
Ivory Coast	8	8	8	7	7	13	13	14	14	15
Kenya	4	7	7	8	10	12	12	12	13	13
Lesotho	0	0	0	0	0	0	0	0	0	0
Liberia	13	12	12	12	12	12	12	10	10	10
Libya	4	4	3	3	3	4	3	8	9	12
Malagasy	0	0	0	0	0	0	0	0	0	0
Malaŵi	0	2	0	0	0	1	1	1	1	1
Mali	3	1	1	1	1	1	1	1	1	1
Mauritania	0	0	2	2	3	3	4	2	2	2
Mauritius			0	1	1	1	1	1	2	2
Morocco	6	8	8	8	8	8	8	7	7	12
Niger	0	0	0	0	0	2	2	3	3	3
Nigeria	19	18	18	18	16	14	14	18	20	24
Rwanda	0	0	0	1	1	1	1	2	3	3
Senegal	9	13	13	13	13	13	13	13	12	12
Sierra Leone	5	5	5	5	5	5	5	7	7	7
Somalia	3	3	3	3	3	3	3	3	3	4
Sudan	4	4	4	4	10	10	10	10	11	11
Swaziland			0	0	0	0	0	0	0	0
Tanzania	10	11	9	9	9	9	9	9	9	9
Togo	4	4	4	4	1	2	2	3	2	3
Tunisia	9	9	10	10	◆	10	10	10	11	10
Uganda	5	4	4	4	1	4	4	8	9	9
Upper Volta	0	1	0	1	1	1	1	3	1	1
Zaire	9	5	12	12	13	12	12	22	22	24
Zambia	2	1	4	3	3	3	3	2	7	8
Totals:	170	184	199	209	228	234	233	286	296	320

* Dates are those of published data rather than number of missions established within state in given year.

Table 11.2 Number of African Missions Established by Each African State: 1966–75*[3]

	'66	'67	'68	'69	'70	'71	'72	'73	'74	'75
Algeria	7	8	8	8	9	10	10	11	12	12
Benin	5	2	3	3	3	2	2	2	2	2
Botswana	0	0	1	1	1	1	1	1	1	1
Burundi	0	2	4	4	4	4	4	6	6	6
Cameroun	6	6	6	7	8	7	7	9	9	8
CAR	1	1	2	2	4	5	5	8	10	11
Chad	4	4	4	4	5	4	4	6	6	7
Congo(B)	3	2	3	3	3	2	2	5	5	5
Egypt	15	17	19	20	20	21	21	25	24	25
Eq. Guinea			0	0	0	0	0	3	3	3
Ethiopia	8	9	10	10	10	11	11	11	11	11
Gabon	0	0	0	1	1	2	2	3	3	8
Gambia	0	1	1	1	1	1	1	2	2	2
Ghana	14	16	15	17	18	17	18	15	16	15
Guinea	6	7	7	7	7	7	7	8	7	8
Ivory Coast	5	5	7	7	7	7	7	8	8	9
Kenya	0	0	0	1	1	1	1	4	5	6
Lesotho	0	0	0	1	1	1	1	1	1	1
Liberia	10	11	10	10	10	9	9	11	11	11
Libya	6	6	6	6	7	8	8	8	8	10
Malagasy	0	0	0	1	2	3	3	3	2	2
Malawi	0	2	2	2	2	2	2	2	3	3
Mali	7	8	6	7	7	6	6	4	3	4
Mauritania	2	3	4	4	5	5	5	6	6	7
Mauritius			0	0	0	0	0	0	0	0
Morocco	9	9	9	9	10	10	9	9	9	9
Niger	3	4	4	4	5	5	5	6	6	7
Nigeria	14	14	13	12	15	15	15	22	22	23
Rwanda	1	0	0	0	0	0	0	3	5	6
Senegal	9	7	9	9	9	9	9	10	10	10
Sierra Leone	4	3	4	4	4	4	4	7	7	7
Somalia	2	3	3	3	5	5	5	5	6	10
Sudan	10	10	10	10	11	11	10	11	12	13
Swaziland			0	0	0	0	0	0	1	1
Tanzania	0	1	3	3	3	3	3	4	6	6
Togo	2	2	2	2	2	2	2	2	2	3
Tunisia	7	7	7	6	6	7	7	9	8	8
Uganda	0	0	1	2	2	2	2	4	5	5
Upper Volta	3	3	3	3	3	3	3	3	3	3
Zaire	5	7	8	9	11	14	14	20	21	23
Zambia	2	3	5	6	6	8	8	9	9	9
Totals:	170	184	199	209	228	234	233	286	296	320

* Dates are those of published data rather than number of missions established within state in given year.

Table 11.3 Number of African States With Which Each State Had Reciprocity in Missions: 1966–75*[4]

	'66	'67	'68	'69	'70	'71	'72	'73	'74	'75
Algeria	3	6	6	6	8	9	9	10	11	11
Benin	2	0	0	0	0	0	0	1	1	1
Botswana	0	0	0	1	1	1	1	1	1	1
Burundi	0	0	2	2	2	2	2	2	2	2
Cameroun	4	4	4	4	4	4	4	5	5	5
CAR	1	1	1	1	2	2	2	4	5	6
Chad	2	1	1	1	3	3	3	4	4	5
Congo(B)	1	0	0	0	1	1	1	3	3	5
Egypt	10	10	17	19	19	19	19	20	21	22
Eq. Guinea		0	0	0	0	1	1	1	0
Ethiopia	1	6	7	7	7	8	8	11	11	11
Gabon	0	0	0	0	0	0	0	1	1	3
Gambia	0	0	0	0	0	0	0	2	2	2
Ghana	9	10	10	12	13	12	11	11	12	12
Guinea	2	1	1	1	1	1	1	5	5	5
Ivory Coast	3	4	4	3	4	7	7	7	7	8
Kenya	0	0	0	1	1	1	1	4	5	6
Lesotho	0	0	0	0	0	0	0	0	0	0
Liberia	8	7	7	7	7	7	7	8	9	9
Libya	3	3	3	3	3	4	3	6	7	9
Malagasy	0	0	0	0	0	0	0	0	0	0
Malawi	0	0	0	0	0	0	0	0	1	1
Mali	2	0	0	0	0	0	0	0	0	0
Mauritania	0	0	2	2	2	2	2	2	2	2
Mauritius		0	0	0	0	0	0	0	0
Morocco	6	7	7	7	7	7	6	7	7	8
Niger	0	0	0	0	0	1	1	2	2	2
Nigeria	11	10	10	8	10	9	9	15	18	19
Rwanda	0	0	0	0	0	0	0	1	2	2
Senegal	7	7	9	9	9	9	9	10	10	10
Sierra Leone	4	3	4	4	4	4	4	6	6	6
Somalia	1	2	2	2	3	3	3	3	3	4
Sudan	4	4	4	4	7	7	6	8	10	10
Swaziland		0	0	0	0	0	0	0	0
Tanzania	0	0	2	2	2	2	2	2	4	4
Togo	2	2	2	2	2	1	1	2	1	2
Tunisia	6	6	7	6	6	7	7	7	7	7
Uganda	0	0	1	2	2	2	2	3	4	4
Upper Volta	0	0	0	1	1	1	1	1	1	1
Zaire	2	2	6	6	8	9	9	19	20	22
Zambia	0	0	3	3	3	3	3	2	7	7
Totals:	94	96	122	126	142	148	144	194	216	232

* Dates are those of published data rather than number of missions established within state in given year.

the number of states with diplomats resident in the host country and hence assumed to have established a diplomatic mission there. Table 11.2, based upon a reconstruction of the lists of diplomatic accreditations, indicates the number of missions which each state had established at a given time. Table 11.3, based upon a state-by-state analysis from the data used for Tables 11.1 and 11.2, lists the number of states with which each state had a reciprocal exchange in missions at a given time.

In constructing the tables no distinction was made as to the level (embassy, high commission, consulate-general, legation or mission) of the exchanges; nor was any differentiation made with respect to the rank (ambassador, high commissioner, chargé d'affaires, or minister) of the diplomat in charge of the mission. In those instances in which the lists showed the highest diplomatic post vacant, the exchange was counted on the assumption that the vacancy was temporary and that the mission itself was still open. In those instances where no address was given for the accredited diplomat or mission, the state was not included on the assumption that the diplomat lived outside the country and hence no mission had been established. The several instances, then, in which a state followed a policy of having one man accredited simultaneously to several states but had separate missions in each were not included except for the 'home base' of the diplomat.

This type of data is subject to error at both the initial reporting stage and in the publication of the lists. Moreover, it is liable to considerable and varying delays, for foreign offices may make information available irregularly and, in any event, do not gear it to meet external publication deadlines. Therefore the aggregate data for a given state and for the OAU are more reliable. Also trends over periods of time greater than any two consecutive years are more likely to be significant. Finally, it need be added, data published in recent years are deemed more accurate as both diplomatic and reporting procedures regarding the establishment of missions have developed and improved.

3. Analysis of the Data

The data summarised in the tables are more or less self-explanatory. With one exception – in the data published in 1972, there was an annual increase in the number of missions established. There was a sharper rise towards the end of the decade, with a steep rise, in number of missions and percentage-wise, in the data published in 1973 and another relatively large rise in the data published in 1975. Reciprocity in diplomatic exchange followed a more or less identical pattern of growth, but with a significant rise in the data published in 1968 and 1970, and an even sharper increase for the data published in 1973.

At the outset of the decade there were 170 missions. Thus, the average state received missions from, and had established them in, about four other OAU states. Diplomatic exchange represented 10 per cent of the possible total. (It was slightly higher, given the fact that three states were not yet independent in 1966.) Of the 170 missions, 94 involved reciprocity. Hence, because there were 47 pairings, the average state had reciprocity with only one other OAU state. By the end of the decade there were 320 missions. Now the average state received missions from, and had established them in, about eight other states. Diplomatic exchange represented about 20 per cent of the possible total. Of these 320 missions, 232 involved reciprocity – a substantially larger percentage of the total number of missions. The average state therefore had reciprocity with almost three other states.

Throughout the period, there was a disparity between the states. Several of them accounted for a disproportionately large share of the diplomatic exchanges. The following fourteen states according to the data published in 1975 hosted ten or more missions: Egypt (25); Nigeria and Zaire (24); Ethiopia (22); Algeria (19); the Ivory Coast (15); Ghana (14); Kenya (13); Libya, Morocco and Senegal (12); Sudan (11); and Liberia and Tunisia (10). Four of these – Egypt, Ghana, Liberia and Nigeria – hosted ten or more throughout the decade. Of these four states Egypt showed a substantial increase in the interim with virtually all of the increase occurring in the data published in 1968. Nigeria showed a decline and then a relatively rapid growth beginning in 1973. Ghana became relatively less attractive while Liberia became absolutely less attractive. Substantial increases also occurred in the data published for Algeria in 1970, for Ethiopia in 1967 and again in 1973 and for Zaire in 1968 and again in 1973. Libya and Morocco hosted ten or more missions only in 1975.

The following twelve states according to the data published in 1975 had established ten or more missions: Egypt (25); Nigeria and Zaire (23); Ghana (15); Sudan (13); Algeria (12); the Central African Republic, Ethiopia and Liberia (11); and Libya, Senegal and Somalia (10). All except the Central African Republic and Somalia also hosted ten or more missions. The Ivory Coast, Kenya, Morocco and Tunisia, four other states which hosted ten or more missions, were not as active in establishing missions. Four of the ten – Egypt, Ghana, Nigeria and Sudan – had ten or more missions throughout the period. Over the interim the Central African Republic, Egypt, Nigeria, Somalia and Zaire showed considerable growth in activity. Sharp increases in activity in consecutive years were less common. Both Nigeria and Zaire did show substantial increases in the data published in 1973 and Somalia a large percentage jump for the data published in 1975. Ghana, Liberia and Senegal all became relatively less active.

The following eight states according to the data published in 1975 had reciprocity with ten or more states: Egypt and Zaire (21); Nigeria (19); Ghana (12); Algeria and Ethiopia (11); and Senegal and Sudan (10). Liberia and Libya, the other states which hosted and had established ten or more missions, did not have reciprocity with that number of states. Only Egypt had reciprocity with ten or more states throughout the decade. Nigeria had reciprocity with more than ten at the outset, but dropped below ten in several instances. Zaire showed the most remarkable increase in the decade. Algeria, Egypt, Ethiopia and Nigeria also showed considerable increases. Much of the increase for Egypt was reported in the data published in 1968, for Nigeria and Zaire in 1973. Of these eight states, clearly Egypt, Zaire and Nigeria – in that order – were the most active states diplomatically. Ethiopia and Algeria – especially in hosting missions – and Ghana – especially in the number of missions established – were also considerably more active. Senegal and Sudan were also active but to a perceptibly lesser extent than the other six states.

It need be noted, too, that there were many states which were inactive as late as the end of the decade and often throughout the ten years. Four states – Equatorial Guinea, Lesotho, Malagasy Republic and Swaziland – hosted no missions in the data published at the end of the decade. Another three (Malaŵi, Mali and Upper Volta), although each had had more than one mission at its capital city in the interim, hosted only one state in the data published in 1975. Four other states (Botswana, Burundi, Mauritania and Mauritius) had but two missions; five states (Benin, Gambia, Niger, Rwanda and Togo) only three; and two (Gabon and Somalia) only four. Accordingly, almost one-half of the OAU member states hosted missions from one-tenth or less of the other states. Likewise, one state (Mauritius) had established no missions; another three (Botswana, Lesotho and Swaziland) had only one; yet another three (Benin, Gambia and the Malagasy Republic) had but two; four (Equatorial Guinea, Malaŵi, Togo and Upper Volta) had only three; and one (Mali) had four. Taken together, then, about one-third of the OAU member states had missions in one-tenth or less of the other states. Such inactivity was obviously reflected in reciprocity totals; 20 states had reciprocity with one-tenth or less of the other states. These 20, virtually one-half of the OAU, had reciprocity with only half again as many states as Egypt or Zaire alone.

4. Diplomatic Exchange Within Regions

Diplomatic exchange was examined from a regional perspective as well. The same method was followed to determine which states were most active and which were least active. Also it was possible to compare diplomatic exchange within regions with that within Africa more generally. Which states were active both within the OAU system and within their respective regions? Which states were active only in one of these? Was there a pattern of actual or potential diplomatic dominance within regions? Table 11.4 shows diplomatic exchange among groups of states within each of the five regions delineated by the United Nations Economic Commission for Africa. It summarises the data for 1975 only.

Within the north African region itself there was considerable activity. No state dominated diplomatic exchange in the data published in 1975. Egypt, the most active in the OAU system; Algeria, one of the more active; and Libya, a relatively active state, had reciprocity with all of the states in the region. Sudan, also active in the OAU system, was the least active in its own region.

Diplomatic exchange within the west African region had evolved into a somewhat different pattern. Nigeria, among the most active, and Ghana, among the more active in the OAU system, were also more active in the region – much more so than

Table 11.4 Diplomatic Exchange Among African States Within UNECA Regions: 1975*[5]

	Recd	Sent	Recp		Recd	Sent	Recp
North Africa				**Central Africa**			
Algeria	5	5	5	Cameroun	3	2	2
Egypt	5	5	5	CAR	5	5	5
Libya	5	5	5	Chad	2	3	2
Morocco	4	5	4	Congo (B)	4	3	3
Sudan	4	3	3	Eq. Guinea	0	1	0
Tunisia	4	4	4	Gabon	4	4	3
				Zaire	5	5	5
West Africa							
Benin	3	1	1	**Eastern Africa**			
Gambia	3	2	2	Burundi	0	4	0
Ghana	9	8	7	Ethiopia	8	2	2
Guinea	3	3	3	Kenya	5	3	3
Ivory Coast	6	4	3	Malagasy	0	1	0
Liberia	5	6	5	Malawi	1	3	1
Mali	1	1	0	Mauritius	1	0	0
Mauritania	1	2	1	Rwanda	2	4	1
Niger	1	4	1	Somalia	2	5	2
Nigeria	9	10	9	Tanzania	4	2	1
Senegal	5	5	4	Uganda	3	2	1
Sierra Leone	6	5	5	Zambia	4	4	3
Togo	2	2	2	**Southern Africa**			
Upper Volta	1	2	1	Botswana	0	0	0
				Lesotho	0	0	0
				Swaziland	0	0	0

* Data for 1975 refer to publication date rather than number of missions established in given year.

most other states in the region. Senegal, the other regional state which was among the active states within the continental system, was slightly less active within West Africa than Liberia, one of the relatively active states, and Sierra Leone, a state not too active in the OAU system. Among the relatively inactive states five received and/or had established no more than one mission. Several states showed some imbalance in number of missions hosted or established. Niger had established three more missions than it hosted while Benin and the Ivory Coast each hosted two more than they had established within the region.

Within the central African region, Zaire, one of the most active within the OAU system, was no more active than the Central African Republic, a relatively active state. Apart from Equatorial

Guinea, which was virtually isolated within the region – as well as from the rest of Africa – the remaining states were more or less equal in activity. None of the seven central African states displayed any marked imbalance in number of missions hosted and established.

The pattern was more disparate for the eastern African states. Ethiopia, one of the more active within the OAU system, hosted more missions from regional states than any other state. Yet four states – Burundi, Rwanda, Somalia and Zambia – had established more missions than Ethiopia. Kenya and Zambia, which had reciprocity with three other regional states, were most active in this category. A majority of the states had an imbalance in number of missions hosted or established. Burundi had established four but hosted none. Somalia had established five and it hosted only two. Ethiopia hosted six more missions from regional states than it had established throughout the region.

Within the southern African region, quite clearly, there was no diplomatic exchange. The very limited activity which Botswana, Lesotho and Swaziland had within the OAU system, took place entirely with states outside the region.

5. Conclusions

By the end of the decade, then, diplomatic exchange within Africa had evolved to the point where several states were disproportionately active. Perhaps this was true throughout, but it was more pronounced and involved some different states in the data published in 1975. Only eight states – about one-fifth of the OAU membership – had reciprocal diplomatic exchange with one-quarter or more of the OAU member states. Clearly a pattern had emerged which suggested a significant stratification and hierarchy within the OAU system. The states which were dominant were, for the most part, among the most active states within their particular regions. In the regions, however, the disparity among the active states was not pronounced and a larger proportion of the states were more or less equally involved. In the sub-Saharan regions there were some states which were inactive, without any substantial involvement even within their respective regions.

No doubt factors such as relative size in population, Gross National Product, and armed forces contributed to the disparity within the continent and within regions. In fact, six of the eight most populous states – all except Morocco and Tanzania – were states which by the end of the decade had reciprocity with ten or more other states. Ghana and Senegal, ranked eleventh and twenty-second, respectively, were not included. Similarly, six of the eight states with the largest GNPs – all except Libya and Morocco – were also among the eight disproportionately active states. Ethiopia and Senegal, ranked ninth and eighteenth, respectively, were not included. Finally, again six of the eight states with the largest armed forces – all except Morocco and Tunisia – were among the eight disproportionately active states. Ghana and Senegal, ranked eleventh and nineteenth, were not included. In other words, on the surface these factors of size seem quite significant.[7] Clearly, however, there were other determining factors.

Egypt, Zaire and Nigeria, as suggested, were the most diplomatically active. They not only attracted a considerable number of missions but they also had established a large number. Further, they were set apart from the rest of the states in reciprocity. The three were involved in more than one-half of the reciprocal pairings. Egypt's role requires little explanation. It was perhaps the only state which played a significant role outside the African international system, fulfilling Nasser's vision of Egypt at the centre of three circles – the Arab world, the Muslim world and the African world. Recognition of Egypt's role followed the 1964 OAU and non-aligned meetings and more or less coincided with the 1967 confrontation with Israel. The involvement of both Zaire and Nigeria was more obvious by the end of the decade. It reflected their movement away from a preoccupation with domestic concerns. In effect, Nigeria – no longer encumbered with its civil war – was reasserting the role in pan-African politics which it had staked out earlier. Zaire, too, was now claiming a presence in African international politics. At the outset the OAU had been preoccupied with the crises in the former Belgian Congo. Now Zaire involved itself actively.

Algeria, Ethiopia and Ghana also had important diplomatic leverage within the African subordinate state system. Ethiopia's role was determined for her by her involvement with the OAU itself, primarily because its headquarters were situated in Addis Ababa. Its large imbalance between the number of missions established within and the number established by the state – the largest among OAU member states and the largest within its region – was indicative of this. Ghana's role reflected her high level of involvement earlier in the decade – a level, in relative terms, which the post-Nkrumah regimes did not maintain. Algeria's involvement, one which grew more pronounced towards the end of the decade, is less easily explained. This is also true of Sudan and Senegal. Sudan's size was important as was its location – at the periphery of north and sub-Saharan Africa and contiguous with more states than any other state. Senegal's activity, split almost evenly between the region and states outside the region, is perhaps least explicable.

Further research is necessary regarding the question of inter-state inequality in Africa. Yet the evidence presented here with respect to diplomatic exchange indicates the potential, if not the actuality, of a hierarchy of diplomatic power within the African international system. A diplomatic stratification – for whatever reasons and with its obvious and other uncertain implications – has emerged. It is clear that the African system remains subordinate to the international system generally. But, at the same time it has, just like the international system, its own strengths and weaknesses and, more to the point, its own inequities and inequalities.

Notes

1. For earlier analysis of diplomatic exchange see, for activity with non-African states, Patrick J. McGowan, 'The pattern of African diplomacy: a quantitative comparison', *Journal of Asian and African Studies*, iv, 3, July 1969, pp. 202–21; and, for activity within the continent, David H. Johns, 'The "normalization" of intra-African diplomatic activity', *Journal of Modern African Studies*, x, 4, Dec. 1972, pp. 597–610.
2. Figures based upon data in *Europa Year Book, 1966–1975*, vol. II (London, Europa Publications Ltd., 1966–75).
3. *Ibid.*
4. *Ibid.*
5. *Ibid.*
6. Based on data published in T. N. Dupey and W. Blanchard, eds, *The Almanac of World Military Power*, 2nd edn, R. R. Bowker, New York, 1972.

7. Such factors of size are discussed and analysed more thoroughly in David H. Johns, 'Diplomatic activity, power, and integration in Africa', *Sage International Yearbook of Foreign Policy 3*, Sage Publications, Beverly Hills, 1975, pp. 85–105.

James Mayall

12   The Implications For Africa of the Enlarged European Economic Community

What are the implications for Africa of the enlargement of the European Economic Community (EEC)? Any answer to this question requires a prior assumption, that for historical, cultural and economic reasons 'Africa's relations with those who are more powerful than she is are likely to remain profoundly ambivalent'.[1] Such an assumption is necessary because the question is not merely, or even primarily, empirical. The negotiations, which were initiated in August 1973 and brought to a successful conclusion with the signature of the Lomé Agreement in February 1975, resurrected at the outset one of the most problematic questions in African diplomacy: what was to be the *appropriate* relationship between independent Africa and a European Community which included all the former imperial powers? In other words within Africa the implications of the enlargement of the European Community were not viewed merely as a matter of calculation, of deciding, on the basis of past experience, whether African states were likely to obtain a better deal in relation with the industrial powers within the context of an Association Agreement or outside it: they also involved the political and diplomatic ideology of the African states.

The relationship between what is known about EEC/African relations in the past and what is desired, both singly and collectively, by African states for the future raises several normative questions. This is clear from the two words, exploitation and partnership, which occur regularly in debate about the subject, as it is from the fact that the issue which proved most contentious in the run-up to the negotiations (that is to say whether or not any future agreement should be based on the concept of reciprocity[2]) is generally accepted as being of largely symbolic significance. The inter-African dispute over reciprocity (not to mention the inter-

European and United States–EEC dispute on the same issue) was important, however, because it focused attention on the most persistent criticism of the Association Agreements – the contention that they represent a form of neo-colonial control by Europe over African states. The difficulty of deciding whether, and to what extent, this charge is valid is compounded by the fact that the concept is used in two different, although overlapping, senses by those who accept the principles (though not necessarily the practice) of an open world economy and by Marxists. It would be tempting to discard the concept of neo-colonialism altogether on the grounds that it is too emotive to be useful in any systematic analysis, were it not for the fact that, like unity, the meaning of which is also contested, it is deeply embedded in African diplomatic thought.[3]

But if the question of neo-colonialism cannot be avoided, it does not follow that it can necessarily be answered in any final or substantive way. Instead what this chapter will attempt to illustrate is the relationship between some of the ideological issues raised in the diplomatic debate over Association, both within Africa and in the wider context of the international economic system, and the technical issues raised by the negotiations themselves. The argument falls into three main sections. The first section discusses the place of neo-colonialism in African political ideology. The second section then considers the record of the first two Yaoundé Conventions and the way in which experience and 'objective' analysis have reinforced or undermined earlier African attitudes towards Association. Finally, a third section considers both the practical and ideological implications of the dispute over reciprocity for African solidarity on the one hand and the international economic system on the other.

It will be apparent from this organisation that the argument is broadly conceived within the existing structure of Eur-African relations, and that, as a consequence, while it may have something to say about the liberal interpretation of neo-colonialism, it will, for the most part, bypass the structuralist or neo-Marxist interpretation of the Association Agreements. Since, at first sight, it is the Marxist rather than the liberal intellectual tradition which provides the source for African pronouncements on neo-colonialism, it is necessary, therefore, to make a second preliminary assumption. This is that the majority of African states, whatever their internal, social and political arrangements, have no practical alternative to seeking some form of accommodation with the European Communities, and that this is not just a consequence of their dependence (real as this is) but also of their own political and economic objectives. The accuracy of this assumption is, I believe, evidenced by the fact that such states as Guinea, and even Nigeria, both originally opposed to participation, were willing to participate once it became clear on the African side that the negotiations could be handled under the auspices of the Organisation of African Unity (OAU). Still it will not necessarily prove universally acceptable, and I have tried, therefore, in a brief final section, to safeguard the argument against a possible charge of irrelevance from the structuralist viewpoint.

1. Neo-colonialism in African Political Ideology

In the period immediately after Independence African statesmen not surprisingly tended to regard foreign policy as the 'continuation of the independence struggle by other means'. At the same time the division of Africa into rival blocs, which contested, among other things, the formula under which the common objective of African unity was to be pursued, provided fertile soil for an ideological dispute about the reality of the independence that had been achieved. For if, as most African politicians maintained, Europe was responsible for the 'Balkanisation' of the African continent, and its exploitation during the nineteenth century, how could an independence settlement be regarded as legitimate which broke up the French colonial federations, confirmed the cultural and economic division between French- and English-speaking states and left the vertical system of economic integration between France and her former colonies virtually unscathed? Here surely was a case where political independence masked the continuing reality of neo-colonial control.

This was, of course, primarily a 'radical' English-speaking African attitude. But it was never (and herein lay its strength) exclusively radical or exclusively confined to Commonwealth Africa. The terms under which the majority of Francophone states were originally associated with the EEC were negotiated directly by the French as part of the price of their own signature of the Treaty of Rome. Guinea broke with the system in 1958; since then President Sékou-Touré has always regarded the Association Agreements as a form of collective neo-colonialism, reinforcing the indirect control which France continues, in his view, to exercise in her former territories. On the more technical question of the legitimacy of the agreements in international law, it was Nigeria, under the far from radical government of Tafewa Balewa, which led the long, and inconclusive, struggle to have them declared illegal under the General Agreement on Tariffs and Trade (GATT).

But in this early period it was Kwame Nkrumah who relied most consistently (and coherently) on the theory of neo-colonialism in his bid for pan-African leadership.[4]

> Neo-colonialism is based on the principle of breaking up former large united colonial territories into a number of small, non-viable states which are incapable of independent development and must rely on the former imperial power for defence and even internal security. Their economic and financial systems are linked, as in colonial days, with those of the former colonial power.[5]

To break out of this system was, in his view, essentially a matter of politics not of economics.

> Non-alignment . . . is based on co-operation with all states, whether they be capitalist, socialist, or have a mixed economy. Such a policy, therefore, involves foreign investment from capitalist countries, but it must be invested in accordance with a national plan drawn up by the government of the non-aligned state with its own interest in mind. The issue is not what returns the foreign investor receives on his investment. He may, in fact, do better for himself if he invests in a non-aligned country than if he invests in a neo-colonial one. The question is one of power.[6]

In these passages we find the juxtaposition of three of the most persistent ideas in African political ideology.

1. European states deliberately divided Africa in their own interests. Further they continued the process in the independence settlement.

2. This has left many African states with the appearance but not the reality of independence. They are, therefore, constantly threatened by neo-colonial manipulation and control.

3. It is not necessary, however, to accept this state of dependence. So long as it is recognised that neo-colonialism represents imperialism at its most dangerous, a policy of non-alignment will allow African states to control their own development and break out of the vicious circle.[7]

There is one further crucial link in this ideological chain. Taken together, these ideas are generally held to require – and indeed to justify – the idea of African unity itself.[8]

In Nkrumah's thought – as the title of his book suggests – these ideas were built into a Marxist-Leninist interpretation of history and society. The fact that he was never a very consistent Marxist-Leninist matters less here than the fact that the ideas he used were (and still are), in a populist sense, common currency among African politicians. Nkrumah's strength in Africa between 1957–63 lay in his ability to appeal over the heads of other African leaders to the African masses, in a political vocabulary which the leaders themselves also employed. His weakness in this context lay in the fact that the African masses, in the Leninist sense, did not exist, and that more particularly there were a number of formal steps open to African statesmen which allowed them to recover the ideological initiative. Thus, for example, Nigeria abrogated its defence agreement with Britain in 1962. The Francophone states by contrast maintained their bilateral defence treaties with France, but renegotiated, this time on their own behalf, the Association Agreement with the EEC[9] and generally allied themselves with the Gaullist foreign policy, itself somewhat non-aligned, at least towards the United States. In 1962, President Nyerere, in a speech to the Afro-Asian People's Solidarity Organisation (AAPSO) which anticipated the positively anti-Marxist interpretation of Third-World exploitation advanced by Colonel Gaddafi ten years later, warned African states of the dangers of a second scramble for Africa, this time between the two great Communist powers.

The process of inter-African reconciliation, which led to the establishment of the OAU in 1963, falls outside the scope of this paper. But two specific aspects of this settlement have a direct bearing on the argument. First, the OAU Charter refers directly to both neo-colonialism and non-alignment. The preamble recalls the determination of African states 'to safeguard and consolidate the hard-won independence as well as the sovereignty and territorial integrity of our states, and to resist neo-colonialism in all its forms', while Article III.7 commits them to 'a policy of non-alignment with regard to all *blocs*'.[10] Secondly, part of the price of unity was the avoidance of any discussion of African relations with the EEC, let alone any debate about the legitimacy of the Association Agreement in the context of the OAU's resistance to neo-colonialism. Thus, although Article II.2(b) binds the member states to coordinate and harmonise their economic, transport and communications policies, until recently relatively little has been achieved in this respect. Partly, no doubt, this failure reflected the prior existence of the Economic Commission for Africa (ECA), which despite the resources at its command has not made any great impact either; partly it reflected the continuing, if uncomfortable, truth of President Senghor's observation that African economies 'are more competitive than complementary', and that therefore 'Africa cannot do without the other continents except at the price of increasing its relative backwardness'[11]; and partly it reflected the recognition that one could not, at the same time, acknowledge 'sovereignty, territorial integrity and independence' of African states (Article II.1(c)) and question the legitimacy of an international agreement covering the relations of one group of OAU member states with the EEC.

When the Yaoundé Convention was renegotiated in 1969 there was, therefore, no attempt to reopen the wider ideological debate. Admittedly there was still a doubt as to whether the Convention would inhibit economic cooperation among African states themselves. But little heat was generated on this issue, particularly since at the insistence of the Associates themselves, a new Article (13) was added to the agreement to allow them to form free trade areas or customs unions, or conclude economic cooperation agreements with other African states. The EEC, it seemed, was now accepted in Africa, if not positively liked. The Nigerian Agreement of 1966, the East African Association Agreement of 1969, and the agreements between the EEC and the states of the Arab Maghrib, all suggested that pragmatism had triumphed.

But like other disputes in inter-African relations the dispute over Association had been avoided, in the interests of unity, but not resolved. Moreover the entry into the EEC of Britain, Denmark and Ireland at the beginning of 1972 on the one side and the termination of the second Yaoundé agreement in 1974 on the other confronted the great majority of African states with the need to make a practical decision about their relations with Western Europe in a context within which it was virtually impossible to avoid resurrecting the broader ideological dispute also. For, if the EEC had been accepted in Africa, it was certainly not popular in the United Nations Conference on Trade and Development (UNCTAD), where Association has always represented an obstacle to the solidarity of developing countries generally. Moreover, British entry made the choice between a global and a regional trade and development strategy almost unavoidable: for unless Commonwealth African states reached an accommodation with the European Community, from 1975 onwards they would find themselves in a less favourable position in the British market than the existing Associates. At the same time, despite the agreement between individual states and the EEC, Commonwealth countries in general were suspicious of the institutional structure which surrounded the Association Agreement, regarding it as the formalisation of European neo-colonialism. Ironically this structure was created precisely to satisfy Associate demands that their sovereignty, equality and independence should be respected. From a pan-African ideological perspective the implications of European unity were contradictory. On the one side there was the possibly harmful impact of a successful European Community on what Ali Mazrui has called the 'intrinsic value of African unity as a moral achievement'[12]; on the other, the possibility that the enlargement of the EEC could provide African states with their first real opportunity since 1963 to demonstrate their solidarity in negotiations with a group of major industrial powers. In the event it was the latter possibility, of using the negotiations in an instrumental sense to create a new dimension of inter-African cooperation, which triumphed.

Two problems were involved: first, it was necessary to establish, within the context of inter-African diplomacy, that any united African position resulted from an African diplomatic initiative and was not merely a defensive or subservient response to a European initiative; secondly, it was necessary to demonstrate that by seeking a common deal for African states in their relations with Europe, inter-African cooperation could be promoted and consequently the threat of collective neo-colonialism reduced.

After a period when the various groups appeared to be staking out their positions a common front on both these issues rather surprisingly emerged from a series of inter-African meetings during 1973. Moreover it survived eighteen months of negotiations. Throughout this period the African states, together with those from the Caribbean and Pacific who also took part, were represented by a single spokesman. While there were often differences among the nine member states of the EEC, the ACP countries succeeded in containing their own divisions to an extent unprecedented in general economic negotiations between rich and poor states.[13]

If we ask how this unity was achieved, it is clear that it was largely the result of a progressive hardening of African attitudes, at least on the ideological plane. Although President Senghor, as the current Chairman of the Organisation Continentale de l'Afrique et de Madagascar (OCAM), declared himself in principle in favour of an agreement which would eventually help to transcend the barrier between French- and English-speaking states, the initial reaction of the Associates to the prospect of enlargement had been one of suspicion. When, in Protocol 22 to the Brussels Treaty, the EEC offered prospective Commonwealth Associates a choice between participation in the same convention as the existing Associates, a more limited form of convention of the Arusha variety or a simple trade agreement, the Associates not surprisingly were insistent that they should not suffer merely to overcome Commonwealth distrust of the formal apparatus of the Yaoundé Convention. As M. Bembello, Foreign Minister of Niger, put it at the Association Council Meeting in October 1972, 'we must endeavour to achieve a stronger, closer association and not resign ourselves to its being diluted and weakened in a wider scheme of things'.[14] At the other extreme Nigeria was initially opposed to any form of special agreement with the EEC[15] and was reported to have actively sabotaged attempts by the Commonwealth Secretariat to concert a common African approach to the negotiations.[16]

But after a year of diplomatic activity, the positions of the various African states changed fairly dramatically. The tenth OAU summit meeting, in May 1973, produced an Economic

Charter which contained eight guiding principles for negotiations with the EEC and other industrial powers.[17] This Charter effectively undercut the earlier Francophone position; and indeed Mr Ekangaki, the then Secretary-General of the OAU, later interpreted it as requiring that 'there should be no precondition and negotiation should not have as a basis any of the existing arrangements with specific groups or individual states within Africa'.[18] On the basis of an OAU response to the EEC, Nigeria, and the other non-Associates, were, for their part, able to overcome their earlier reluctance for a collective negotiation with the Community. But it was clear that the change in their position depended on the tacit agreement by the majority that what was being sought was not merely an updated version of Yaoundé II. General Gowon told the Lagos meeting of OAU trade and economic ministers in July 1973:

> It will not be enough to seek merely to perpetuate the *status quo* under new labels; or to insist on being doctrinaire in our approach, or to reform existing agreements in the context of past associations alone; or to emphasize existing advantages and privileges against long-term historical necessities.[19]

If, as the Commonwealth African states evidently believed, the Associates had hitherto been all too subservient in negotiating with the EEC, here was a line of reasoning which promised a genuinely independent African approach to the negotiations. It was an indication of how far the existing Associates had been put on the defensive that Francophone criticisms of the majority position at Lagos, as at the Brussels meeting in August, were confined to the muted, but perfectly correct, observation that some of the major issues at dispute, particularly the concept of reciprocity, had not in fact been resolved.[20]

On the issue of inter-African cooperation the problems have always been more practical than ideological, as the chequered history of the various sub-regional economic groupings in Africa testifies.[21] But the alleged threat of EEC neo-colonialism (seeking to extend European control through a new form of divide and rule policy) also introduces an ideological dimension to this side of the discussion. Since this is one of the points on which, in the past, the Associates themselves have criticised the Community, it was perhaps natural that the OAU Economic Charter should have stipulated that 'any agreement made with the EEC should not adversely affect intra-African co-operation'. President Nyerere put the same point more dramatically in his opening address to the Second Conference of OAU trade ministers, held in Dar es Salaam at the end of September 1973:

> You will have to take enormous care . . . to ensure that, wittingly or unwittingly you do not allow yourselves to be divided. For both the opportunities and the efforts towards such an end will not be lacking. . . . Africa has only one choice: to stand together and move forward in unity or else forever to remain a hostage in the industrial countries.[22]

As before, there were signs that some of the Francophone states were doubtful as to whether the unity achieved would survive the actual process of negotiation.[23] But they evidently neither felt strong enough, nor were probably willing, to challenge the majority position. Moreover, even if it proved to be a facade, the new economic radicalism was helpful in overcoming some old difficulties within the OAU. Despite long estrangement from both France and the EEC, Guinea was represented at the Lagos conference in July. On that occasion General Lanfane Diane prefaced a resolution calling for the creation of an African Common Market – a revival of one of Nkrumah's favourite projects – with the suggestion that this should be an essential counterpart, if not precondition, to any agreement with the EEC. Guinea was not represented at the August Eur-African meeting in Brussels, but did attend the subsequent meeting in October. By that time, however, the OAU Secretariat had been instructed to draw up proposals for the creation of free trade within Africa for consideration by a conference of African trade ministers in Algiers in May 1974.[24] M Ceyda Keyta, the Guinean representative at the Brussels talks, observed that there was at last an opportunity of putting European African relations on a new footing 'dépourvue de tout esprit néo-colonialiste.'[25]

If it is correct, as this account implies, that unity was achieved as the result of an apparent radicalisation of African attitudes towards the EEC, *why* did the existing Associates in particular, and the weaker African states in general, endorse the majority position? In the past their position had generally been of the 'bird in hand worth two in the bush' variety. Nor is it obvious that their external circumstances had changed radically over the past two years. Conceivably one reason could be that they had merely reserved their position, and that, while outwardly concurring in the ACP alliance, substantial conflicts of interest might emerge during the implementation of the Lomé Convention. Possible but unlikely: at several points the new agreements were addressed specifically to the needs of the poorest states. A more plausible answer, perhaps, was that these states had been promised a financial guarantee by one or more of the stronger states in return for a change of stance in the negotiations. Diplomacy of this kind is certainly not impossible in Africa. In a parallel situation Colonel Gaddafi claimed to have underwritten the reversal of policy towards Israel by a number of African states.[26] But although the Nigerian Government had hinted that it would be prepared to accept some responsibility for dealing with the special problems of the weaker African states,[27] and although the Nigerian delegation played a leading role throughout the negotiations,[28] no concrete proposals appear to have been made. Moreover, Nigeria's actual and potential economic power has seldom been viewed with unambiguous enthusiasm by her neighbours.

Two further explanations are, perhaps, even more plausible. First, the Associates were themselves increasingly restive about the possibility of securing their interests merely on the basis of the mixture-as-before (i.e., an updated Yaoundé Agreement). Secondly, it became increasingly clear that their major bargaining weapon within the negotiations – the concept of reciprocity – was now opposed not only by the majority of African states but by the majority of member states of the EEC also. It is to these questions, therefore, that we must now turn.

2. The Yaoundé Conventions – An Assessment

Any analysis of the two Yaoundé Conventions (1964–69 and 1969–74) must start with the simple observation that on neither occasion did agreement result from a direct confrontation of coherent and unified African and European interests. What was involved therefore was not a straightforward accommodation between the two sides but a multiple set of compromises, between the EEC and the Associates, between the African states, and, most importantly, between the six member states of the Community.[29] Even though what follows must be qualified to take account of the various interests of the states affected, two broad questions may be useful in setting the framework for the next stage in the argument. First, what are the interests of the Associates and how far were they met by the two Agreements? Secondly, what were the EEC's own interests in the Convention?

Critics of the Association agreement often assumed that no 'real' interests were served by them. Yet certainly, until the early 1970s the eighteen Associates made no secret of their commitment to the maintenance of the Yaoundé framework for their aid and trade relations with the Community. For its part, the European Commission argued that the enlargement negotiations provided 'a unique opportunity for the Community and a great number of developing countries to make a real joint effort to organise their cooperation within a common framework adapted to a new situation'.[30] How should we account for the apparent strength of this commitment on both sides? So far as the existing Associates are concerned, the Yaoundé Convention had two essential features. Within the legal framework of a free trade area (or rather eighteen free trade areas) it provided them with either duty-free access to EEC markets for their exports, or preferential access, and it provided them also with a source of multilateral aid through the European Development Fund (EDF), which was not available to non-Associates. In addition, and in the context of the argument that the agreement is neo-colonial, perhaps more important, it established a mechanism for multilateralising the Associates' post-colonial economic relations. After 1945, successive French Governments encouraged the production of tropical foodstuffs and cotton in their dependencies and virtually prohibited imports into metropolitan France from third countries. The result was that the Francophone and world markets were 'cut adrift, prices rose ... and by the mid-1950s most French colonies were uncompetitive by world market standards'.[31] It was largely this situation which led the French Government to insist on the inclusion of Part IV of the Rome Treaty as part of the price for its signature. Since 1958, the Associates, for their part, had been anxious that the agreement should cushion their gradual reincorporation into the world market, an outcome which they might or might not have desired as a means of reducing their dependence on France, but on which, in any case, the other five member states of the EEC insisted.

Let us now take in turn the three areas – trade, aid, and economic diversification – in which Associate interests are concentrated. In all three areas the conclusions are ambiguous. As regards trade, the commission reported that between 1958 and 1971 Associate exports

> rose from $896 m. to $1 638 m. after reaching a ceiling of $1 863 m. in 1970. For the period under consideration this trend represents a growth trend of 6·2 per cent a year, i.e., lower than that of the exports by all developing countries to the EEC (7·7 per cent) during the same period. However, if oil exports are excluded the average annual rate of expansion (6·2 per cent) is seen to be higher than that of exports of all developing countries to the EEC (5·5 per cent).[32]

As the commission admitted, however, the extent to which these modestly successful trading results should be attributed to the free trade system was doubtful. For not only was 'full-scale liberalization of trade . . . a relatively recent event but over two-thirds of Associate exports were concentrated in primary commodities on which the Common External Tariff (CET) stipulates a zero duty whatever the country of origin'.[33] Also the duty-free access provided for manufactured goods was of a higher potential than real value for countries which have not yet developed an export capacity to produce and export such goods on a large scale. The trading pattern for manufactures, moreover, was similar to that for exports generally, i.e., while the exports of manufactures by the Associates increased by over 200 per cent, moving from third to the second most important category of their exports to the EEC between 1959 and 1969, the exports of manufactures from other developing countries to the Community increased by over 400 per cent in the same period.[34]

It is, therefore, the continued dependence of the Associated states on the export of a narrow range of primary products[35] which presents them with their most acute problem, namely, how to improve the stability and increase the rate of growth of their export earnings. In this respect the Yaoundé Convention cannot claim very great success; for as the *Deniau Memorandum* showed, even when reasonable price stability has been achieved, the volumes imported into the EEC are often themselves subject to unpredictable fluctuation.[36] Yet unless the problem of stability can be solved there must be very restricted opportunities for economic diversification and hence for the development of new export industries.[37] Attempts to solve this problem by the EEC have so far been half-hearted and subject to most of the structural limitations found in other commodity stabilisation schemes,[38] while with the ambiguous exception of the oil-exporting countries (ambiguous because their relationship to the industrial world at the present time so obviously represents a special case) primary producers have so far found it difficult to combine to improve their position by a display of market power.

If neo-colonialism is interpreted as a situation in which the former colonial territories will largely continue to act as 'hewers of wood and drawers of water' for the industrial powers, it is difficult to avoid the conclusion that, at least in so far as trade is concerned, they are caught in a system of no escape. In this context the practical question for the eighteen states was whether they would be any *worse off* in a looser all-African arrangement (which might have corresponding political benefits) than within the existing EurAfrican structure.

The benefits to the eighteen states from the EDF were similarly open-ended. On the one hand it represented a very important source of external public finance – often over 30 per cent – particularly for the poorer states.[39] Since EDF aid is multilateral in character and provided predominantly in the form of grants it also met two of the conditions of foreign aid which are generally demanded by developing countries but less often satisfied. On the other hand the shift in Yaoundé II away from export subsidies and towards the tying of aid funds to 'directly productive investments', mainly in the industrial and tourist sectors, while theoretically desirable for economic diversification (and hence economic independence) also left the poorest Associates even more exposed to competition from relatively stronger economies in Africa and elsewhere in the Third World. Moreover, although the fund was increased by 25 per cent to $900 m. in 1969, no provision was made for the time lag between the ending of the old Convention and the start of the new one, while according to one commission official, inflation meanwhile reduced the real increase in the fund to a point where it barely covered the 'rise in the cost of operations undertaken by the Community'.[40]

Little wonder that the Associates were worried about any further dilution of their external resources due to the enlargement of the Community to incorporate Commonwealth and other African states. It may be that if an aid administration can be evolved which involves the African states themselves at all stages, as they have requested, this will also give rise to an allocation system which will be accepted as both fair and economically sensible. This would seem a desirable reform, whatever happens.[41] But even to raise the possibility is to beg the question: to judge by past allocations no general criterion of need appears to have been devised within the existing Community. Thus although there is a rough correspondence between aid receipts and size of population, there appears to be no relationship between aid and income per capita. Some relatively well-off countries, e.g., Gabon, have received little EDF money while others, e.g. Senegal and Ivory Coast, have received relatively large amounts.[42] It is too early yet to assess to what extent the new EDF will overcome these problems. Certainly the figure finally agreed upon, 550 m. units of account (1 UA=$2.40), was less than half of the ACP requests, although since Nigeria was not to be a beneficiary of the fund, the new figure does represent an advance on its predecessor.[43] The agreement also contains other improvements, notably a reserve of 10 per cent of the fund to be devoted to projects designed to promote regional cooperation in Africa itself.[44]

It is an ironical answer to the charge of neo-colonialism that it is in the field of economic diversification that the Association Agreements have been most effective. This holds for both vertical diversification (the encouragement of structural transformation) and for horizontal diversification (the geographical transformation of trade and investment patterns). On the first count, the preferential system contributed, as we have seen, to a fairly dramatic increase in the export of processed goods which now rival raw materials as the largest element in Associated export trade, while since 1969 the link between the EDF and agricultural export subsidies has been broken. Secondly, as regards trade, note that the Commission rested its defence of the Yaoundé Convention on the ground that the member states who in the past had no special relations with Associated states have increased their imports from those countries at a very much higher rate than the other member states, as the annual growth rate figures demonstrate: 10·7 per cent for the Netherlands, 11·2 per cent for Germany, and 12·6 per cent for Italy as compared with 3·1 per cent for France and 6·8 per cent for the Belgio-Luxembourg Economic Union.[45]

Although any non-revolutionary change in a country's trade pattern is by definition a drawn-out affair, it is true that these figures conceal the extent to which French influence still pervades what was formally the French Empire. Thus, not only are French exports and imports still very much larger in absolute terms than those of any other member state,[46] but France provides a relatively small amount – about 5 per cent – of its aid to the Associates through the EDF, whereas for other member states bilateral and mutilateral aid are much more closely balanced.[47]

There are two consequences of this asymmetry which are relevant here. First, it has been argued that French bilateral aid (at an annual average rate of about $600 m.) has maintained the existing structure of the economic relationship between the Associates and Europe and has thus had the indirect effect of slowing down the process of economic reforms.[48] Secondly, although the position has improved as a result of changes introduced into contracting procedures in 1969, France continues to gain more than her strictly fair share of the contracts gained from the fund.[49] There was thus a sense in which continued diversification through the mechanism of a Yaoundé-type Convention was in the interest of France (for economic reasons) but less obviously in the interest of the other five member states of the EEC, which have traditional interests elsewhere in the Third World.

This brings us to the second question raised at the beginning of this section, namely, the EEC's interest in the continuation of a Yaoundé-type Agreement. From the start, Germany, the Netherlands and to a lesser extent Italy were critical of the Association idea. They have also used their influence both to lessen the impact of the Association on their own traditional suppliers of tropical produce and, so far as possible, to reconcile the agreement with broader international rules and pressures. Thus, under the original Part IV of the Rome Treaty, Germany negotiated a special tariff-free quota for bananas, and Italy and Benelux similar quotas for coffee, with the purpose of guaranteeing traditional links with other non-Associated African and Latin American states. These quotas were not continued under Yaoundé I but the CET was reduced for coffee, cocoa and several other tropical products, thereby reducing the margin of preference enjoyed by the Associated states. Despite opposition from the Associates themselves this process was continued under Yaoundé II.[50] Moreover, at the insistence of the Dutch, who favoured the complete generalisation of preferences in line with UNCTAD demands, a way was left open for the subsequent introduction of the Generalised Scheme of Preferences (GSP). Such a scheme was eventually introduced in 1970, and although its terms for non-Associates were less favourable than those for Associates, it nevertheless had the necessary effect of reducing still further the margin of preference for Associates.

If support for the Yaoundé Convention within the European Community has always been uncertain it was greatly weakened by the enlargement of the Community. Indeed, the Associates now found themselves outnumbered on two fronts: not only was the convention unpopular in Africa, but it had little to offer the three new members of the Community which, on the basis of their own economic interests and history, were more likely to align themselves with the 'globalists' (Germany and Netherlands) than with the 'regionalists' (France and Benelux). True, the existence of the convention provided a coherent framework within which a common development policy might be developed; but while this was a point to which, for obvious reasons, the Commission attached importance, it was inherently unlikely that the privileged position of the Associates – residual as it was – could survive in any new agreement for the simple reason that the balance of economic and political power had shifted on both sides.

A growing awareness that the basis of their support within the Community was shrinking clearly led several Francophone states to reassess their interests and to search for allies elsewhere in Africa. This was evident from both the near disintegration of OCAM, an organisation which in the past has often provided a coherent core in the otherwise disparate group of Associate states,[51] and from the pressures throughout French-speaking

Africa for the renegotiation of the bilateral treaties which since
1960 have governed French relations with her former colonies.
In the context of negotiations with the EEC, however, it was
their abandonment of the principle of reciprocity which most
dramatically illustrated their predicament.

3. Reciprocity in Eur-African Relations

In the debate over reverse preferences, the practical and ideological implications of the enlargement of the European Community were welded together. In the past, reciprocity had been
accepted by the Associates as the only available weapon to insure
the *extension* of the Yaoundé Agreement for the future.[52] Thus in
1969 it was the African states which insisted on the maintenance of
reciprocity as the basis of Yaoundé II,[53] while at the outset of the
ACP/EEC negotiations they pointed out that to abandon the idea
of privileged access to their own markets was to deny themselves a
potential weapon (i.e., the extension of Most Favoured Nation
(MFN) treatment) in future negotiations with third countries, e.g.,
the United States. Nevertheless the concept of reciprocity was also
defended, particularly by Léopold Senghor, as the only way in
which the inevitable asymmetry of the Eur-African relationship[54]
could be reconciled with sovereign independence and human
dignity.[55] On this line of reasoning the political nature of any
Eur-African agreement is accepted as legitimate, the attempt to
obtain unreciprocated benefits from the industrial powers, on the
contrary, is seen as a device for perpetuating a neo-colonial
mentality, if not also neo-colonial control.

Among the Associables, on the other hand, both sets of
arguments were viewed differently. Unlike France, Britain
enjoyed few formal preferences in the markets of her African
colonies. As a result, when Commonwealth African states were
forced to establish a system of reverse preferences as part of the
price of agreement with the EEC, as in the abortive Nigerian
agreement and the Arusha Convention, they had to be instituted
afresh, a fact which focused attention on the lost revenue which, in
the African context, is an unwelcome but inevitable consequence
of reciprocity. Moreover, since the geographical distribution of
Commonwealth African trade was less concentrated than was the

case with Francophone Africa, the establishment of new preferences merely to protect an already established share of the market
(i.e., to prevent trade deflection) obviously appeared a less
acceptable proposition than it did for those states for which an
extension of preference would merely have widened the acces-
sibility of export markets (i.e. trade creation).

Ideologically, also, the Commonwealth African position rejected the concept of reciprocity. In seeking an accommodation with
the Community they aimed in other words at a *redistribution*
agreement. Intellectually this position derives from a characteristic blend of economic liberalism and social democracy.[56] Its
main characteristics are, on the one hand, the divorce of politics
from economics, and on the other, the establishment of *a
mechanism* which will ensure special treatment for developing
countries according to criteria of distributive justice and need. In
his address to the Dar es Salaam meeting of trade ministers,
quoted earlier (p. 294), President Nyerere defined African objectives in the negotiations with the EEC as follows:

> to obtain for ourselves that which rightfully belongs to us,
> remunerative trading arrangements in a dynamic context,
> through a scientifically worked out built-in mechanism within
> the framework of international trade exchange, and full
> reparations of past neglect imposed on us by colonialism.[57]

Here was a challenge with a vengeance to all the existing conventions governing international trade. By the prior acceptance
of reciprocity as the basis for negotiations, the Associates had
previously proclaimed that their special relationship with the
Community was not only in accordance with international law but
also represented a contractual relationship binding on the two
sides. Article 1 of the GATT establishes the MFN principle, i.e.,
non-discrimination, as the basic rule of international commerce.
But once it is accepted that there is nothing sacrosanct about the
territorial basis of the existing state system, then some provision
must be made to cover the circumstances under which MFN may
be legitimately breached. The EEC agreement with the Associates
had been justified under Article 24 of the GATT, which allows for
exceptions to the MFN rule in cases of custom unions and free
trade areas.

The non-Associates accepted the desirability of a contractual agreement but wished to reject Article 24 as a proper guide to relations between developed and underdeveloped countries. Having first appointed a Committee of Experts to report on this question[58] it was finally agreed in July 1974 to proceed on the basis of non-reciprocity.[59] But while this eased the problem of reconciliation between Associate states, it could not, of itself, solve the underlying problem: how to achieve a contractually binding agreement on the basis of non-reciprocity. It was for this reason, no doubt, that some of the existing Associates for some time continued to indicate that they intended to exercise their tariff autonomy by continuing to grant preferences to the EEC whatever happened. Meanwhile the then OAU Secretary-General, Mr Ekangaki, attempted to bridge the two positions. At the Lagos trade ministers' meeting he suggested that

> The contractual notion of the cooperation agreement shall be construed to be the acceptance of preferential tariffs from Europe, against the assurance of the provision of our raw materials and other goods to Europe at remunerative prices. The contractual notion shall not necessarily imply reciprocation of preferential tariffs.[60]

The formal abandonment of the reciprocity principle as the basis of the new agreement, however, reflected two other sets of considerations. First, it became clear that its abandonment was likely to be decided over the heads of African statesmen as part of a deal between the United States and the EEC. The doctrinal opposition to trade preferences in the United States goes very deep in American political thinking and indeed dictated their attitude to international commercial relations between all states until 1967. Even then, the US administration's conversion to the idea, proposed at the first UNCTAD, for a general preference scheme covering the exports of manufacturers from developing countries, was more apparent than real. In his speech at Punta del Este, President Johnson indicated that there was a good economic case for providing a stimulus to the manufactured exports of developing countries. It was, he implied, a collective responsibility of the industrial states and the success of the scheme would depend on there being no discrimination between all industrial states on the one side and all developing states on the other. In other words the principle of universality was to be maintained. The scheme depended on the phasing out of existing preferential arrangements in general and in particular of the reciprocal arrangements favouring the EEC in the markets of its Associates.

When this proved to be an unobtainable condition, the US administration and Congress retreated on their commitment. Moreover, the American position hardened as they faced up first to a continuing trade deficit, secondly, to the implications of the EEC enlargement and finally, to ramifications of the energy crisis. In his trade message to Congress in April 1973, President Nixon proposed that the Generalised Trade Preferences (GTP) should be extended to developing countries. But although he maintained the commitment in principle he went on to say that,

on the basis of international fair play we would take into account the actions of other preference granting countries, and we would not grant preferences to countries which discriminate against our products in favour of goods from other industrialized nations unless these countries agree to end such discrimination.[61]

There was, of course, a practical side to all this. The Americans were probably more concerned with the impact on their own interests of the EEC's special arrangements with non-member European states, and with Mediterranean and Near Eastern states than they were with the renewal or even extension of the Yaoundé Convention. For not only was the level of trade between the EEC and African states very small in absolute terms but since the Clay Committee reported in 1963 there had been a tendency in Washington to regard sub-Saharan Africa as a European responsibility. Trade with the Mediterranean and North African states, on the other hand, was not only much more significant in itself but was more heavily concentrated in commodities, such as oil and citrus products, in which the United States was an interested party, either as a potential consumer or as a competitive exporter, or both.

On the European side there is little doubt that, following the enlargement of the Community, the abandonment of the reciprocity provisions was offered by the commission in response to repeated requests by American officials who urged that a gesture was needed from Europe to offset the rising tide of protectionism in the United States and to convince the American administration of the EEC's good faith in future trade negotiations.[62] For the EEC this was after all a relatively painless gesture to make. Indeed, all that appeared to be necessary was a clarification, not a change at all. Thus the *Deniau Memorandum* published in April 1973 concluded that the future Association agreement, as in the past, should conform with GATT. But the memorandum also observed:

> That the acceptance by the Associated states of the mutual free trade area principle does not entail any obligation from them to grant preferences to the Community. They retained complete tariff autonomy in their relations with third countries and complete freedom to negotiate such matters.[63]

The degree of tariff autonomy which has been exercised in fact, as distinct from in law, is no doubt open to dispute but the Yaoundé agreement did explicitly refer to the possibility of discrimination, even against the EEC, in the context of economic cooperation among the Associates themselves or with other African states. And at least three Associates, Zaire, Rwanda, and Togo, extended to third countries concessions offered to the EEC.

By emphasising that there was no link between the EDF and reverse preferences, the commission also demonstrated their desire to be flexible and to reconcile, in any way consistent with GATT, any differences in attitude to the problems of so-called reverse preferences.

In a speech on 5 April 1973, Sir Christopher Soames added one further undertaking: that the Community did not seek to 'extend its policy of association and preferential trade agreements beyond the limits which history and close geographical links have made necessary'.[64] Here the rationale of these agreements was seen as the need to protect traditional suppliers from the adverse effects which the CET and the Common Agricultural Policy (CAP) would otherwise have on their exports. This, in the EEC view, was an immediate political problem on which the neo-classical theory, allegedly underlying US foreign economic policy, was understandably silent.

But it is one thing to base any future agreement on the principle of non-reciprocity; it is another to turn this essentially negative principle to advantage. After all, non-reciprocity was already

enshrined under Chapter 3 of the GATT as the principle governing participation by developing countries in trade negotiations
with industrial states. Experience of the Kennedy Round did not
suggest that it is a particularly effective mechanism.[65] There is no
doubt therefore that the second reason why the Associates
endorsed the majority position on reciprocity was that they sensed
the possibility of strengthening their bargaining position in areas
in which they were already dissatisfied with the working of the
Yaoundé Convention and where there were opportunities for
united African action. One such area was commodity price stabilisation, another improving the market for those commodities,
e.g., various kinds of vegetable fats and oil seeds which were
denied duty-free access because they compete with products
covered by the CAP.

The final outcome of the negotiations suggests that this
assessment was broadly correct: two factors seem to have been of
particular importance in enabling the ACP states to secure
significant concessions without the offer of formal reciprocity.
First, not only was the group of states much larger than in the
previous Association negotiation, but the ACP position was
strongly influenced by the economically most influential state,
Nigeria, which has consistently shown itself intent upon extracting maximum trade and aid concessions from the EEC.[66] The
points at which Nigeria's economic weight told in negotiations are
difficult to isolate: since its oil exports are now more than double
its traditional exports of ground nuts and cocoa there is a sense in
which Nigeria needs the EEC less than do the majority of African
states. For these latter states their small size alone militates against
an industrialisation strategy based on the development of domestic markets so that they need all the aid and all the trade
preferences for both traditional and new exports that they can
get. Conversely, 'the combination of varied resources and a large
domestic market should enable Nigeria to derive full advantage,
in due course, from duty-free access to the European market for
manufactured goods'.[67] Certainly the Nigerians among others
pressed strongly for a new kind of industrial cooperation between
developed and developing countries, i.e. joint projects which go
beyond import substitution and raw material processing.[68]
Secondly, it seems clear that, against the background of the
energy crisis and shortages of other raw materials, the EEC was

more sensitive than in the past to the need to protect future supplies. The scheme, first proposed in the *Deniau Memorandum* to stabilise the export earnings of a number of ACP staple exports, was not only included in the final convention, but extended to include commodities, e.g. iron ore to which the ACP states attached importance.[69] Indeed the EEC seems to have been more accommodating than in the past in responding to African pressure even where the domestic interests of its own member states were directly involved.

Thus some ACP agriculture exports – citrus fruit, tobacco and beef – which were previously excluded from the free access provisions of the Yaoundé Convention were liberalised in the course of the negotiations. At the outset this trade was worth $567 m., some 12·2 per cent of the total ACP sales in EEC market; by the time the convention was signed this figure had been reduced to 1·5 per cent.[70] On the African side there was clearly an awareness that the psychological milieu of the negotiations had shifted to their advantage. It was symptomatic of this new 'equality of bargaining power' that final agreement should have been held up while the ACP sugar producers extracted some further price concessions from the British government. By agreeing to make the new agreement dependent on a successful conclusion to the sugar talks the non-sugar producers in fact gave a very practical demonstration of ACP solidarity.

One broad conclusion seems to follow from the argument advanced in this chapter. It is that from both the ideological and economic point of view enlargement of the European Community has stimulated inter-African cooperation. Numerous conflicts of interest, of course, persist, particularly in the field of export competition for primary products. But since British entry to the Community meant that Commonwealth preferences would be abolished after 1975 there was, practically, little alternative but to attempt to resolve these conflicts within the context of a single agreement, or at least a related series of agreements.

There is an element of irony in the final outcome in the negotiations which led to the Yaoundé Convention. Inequality was compensated for, and honour satisfied, by the retention of formal reciprocity; by contrast the Lomé Convention was preceded by the abandonment of formal reciprocity but also by some fairly tough and fairly equal bargaining. Whether this new 'real' reciprocity will secure the interests of the ACP states better than the old variety will presumably become clear during the lifetime of the present agreement.

In this context, it is, perhaps, unfortunate that in the debate about trade and economic relations between rich and poor states, attention has been almost exclusively focused on a particular (and vulnerable) manifestation of the reciprocity principle, that is, the question of reverse preferences, at the expense of the underlying idea.

The case for reciprocity, however defined, is that is gives substance to the most important legal fiction in international society, namely the sovereign equality of states. A one-sided contract is by definition a one-sided affair. In practice, states have no alternative but to accept the hierarchical order of power. On the basis of reciprocity they can at least stay in business. And if some of the bargains they strike are inherently unequal, the acceptance of obligations as well as of rights is at least the first step in the direction of a relationship based on mutual advantage and respect.

4. Association and the Left

There is one obvious objection to the line of argument advanced in this paper. It comes in two forms. In its liberal version it is argued that the maintenance of a Yaoundé-type agreement will perpetuate the existing structure of trade and hence dependence between Africa and Europe and prevent the development of genuinely national and/or regional policies. As we have seen this was the original Nigerian position and it was eventually adopted by the OAU as the basis for future negotiations with the Community. The statistical evidence is equivocal. Nor is it clear that, despite its novel features, the Lomé Convention does *in fact* make a fundamental break with the past. But to refute the criticism, at least in principle, one only needs to refer to the three sets of conditions under which the Associated states could have been released from their obligations. First, they were allowed to retain or introduce import quotas when these were deemed necessary for development reasons or to meet balance of payments difficulties. Secondly, they could retain or introduce customs duties or charges having equivalent effect to the tariffs reduced under the free trade area formula when it was necessary to meet development needs or when these were intended to contribute to their budgets; and, thirdly, they were allowed to discriminate against the EEC when this resulted from a decision to form a regional customs union or free trade area.

The neo-Marxist version of the argument rejects this defence, rightly, one suspects, as superficial. On this view, what matters is not the nature of the agreement but the structure of the relationship. The present situation is characterised by the exploitation of the masses in the periphery (poor) states, in alliance with the centre (elites) in the periphery states.[71] The interest of the indigenous elites, it is maintained, will prevent any changes in structure of the relationship or any redeployment of resources in the interests of the masses of the population (the periphery in periphery states). Africa will continue to be a dependency of Europe because there is no politically coherent social force capable of changing things.

While this may seem a more formidable objection it ignores several important factors. First, it is essentially an *end state* analysis, that is, it tells us very little about how states in transitional stages of economic radicalism either are likely to behave *vis-à-vis* the outside world or should in fact behave. Thus, for example, Johan Galtung, in a highly critical study of the European Community written from a new left perspective includes the following in a list of reforms he considers necessary to transform the Eur-African relationship from one of exploitation to equity:

> higher prices for raw materials probably as a result of concerted action; much more import of goods genuinely manufactured in the poor countries; much more free transfer of technology of all kinds and a strengthening of horizontal trade amongst poor countries, regionally as well as universally.[72]

It is a programme which would be widely endorsed by most supporters of developing countries, as it would, one imagines, by most of the Associate states. But, apart from the proposal for concerted action by the primary producers, it is difficult to see how it might be achieved outside the context of an agreement with the Community, which Galtung considers undesirable on other grounds.[73] The same kind of point can be made about the far more penetrating analysis of north–south trade by Professor Arghiri Emmanuel. While Professor Emmanuel brilliantly argues the economic case for holding that the exports of developing countries are cheap because these societies are poor, while manufactured imports from the industrial world are expensive because industrial societies are rich, and hence is able to give a very precise meaning to the idea of exploitation, his practical proposals are confined to a cautious advocacy of cartel arrangements for raw materials and a government controlled export tax.[74] There is, in his analysis, no alternative for the developing countries other than to deal on the best terms they can obtain, with the industrial world. And if solidarity can indeed be achieved by negotiating *en bloc* with the European Community it is difficult to see the force of the theoretical argument against it.

Secondly, to the extent that the centre-periphery model is valid it holds for most, if not for all African states whether they are associated or not. But, thirdly, in view of the pressures in most African states for economically nationalistic policies, whether of the local capitalist (Nigeria) or socialist (Tanzania) varieties, it is doubtful whether it is valid. (Isolation is a theoretical alternative, although not one that Galtung advocates or Emmanuel thinks practicable, at least in the short run. But apart from any philosophical objections, there are strong grounds for doubting whether any African regime has either the unquestioned legitimacy, or the necessary coercive power, to enforce such a policy for long, even if it were desired.) As Dharam Ghai has recently argued, despite the surprising persistence of capitalism in Africa and the undoubted strength of expatriate capitalist influence on the African economy, it is simply not true that African states have no power to reorientate their economies, as witness the recent moves towards nationalisation in Zambia and eastern Africa.[75]

Finally it is worth noticing that at least three of the states, ostensibly committed to radical mobilisation of their populations, Congo, Somalia, and Tanzania, have reconciled their policies with Association, including its contractual basis, even before the ACP negotiations. In many respects, indeed, such countries are in much the same kind of position as those Eastern European countries which, despite a Socialist economic and social system, are deeply committed to expanding economic relations with the capitalist West. The point to note here, therefore, is that Socialist states generally, not least China, have always insisted on basing their commercial relations with all other states, including developing states, on the principle of mutual advantage. While this is invariably interpreted in bilateral rather than multilateral terms, it quite clearly reflects the principle, if not always the practice, of reciprocity.

Notes

1. Ali Mazrui, *Towards a Pax Africana*, Weidenfeld and Nicolson, London, 1967, p. 96.
2. For a discussion of contested ideas in African diplomatic thought see James Mayall, 'African unity and the OAU: the place for a political myth in African diplomacy', in G. W. Keeton and G. Schwarzenberger, eds., *Year Book of World Affairs 1973*, Stevens, London, 1973, pp. 110–33.
3. *Ibid.*, pp. 127, 132.
4. See K. Nkrumah, *Neo-Colonialism: The Last Stage of Imperialism*, International Publishers, London, 1965.
5. *Ibid.*, p. xiii.
6. *Ibid.*, p. x.
7. 'Neo-colonialism is also the worst form of imperialism. For those who practice it, it means power without responsibility and for those who suffer from it, it means exploitation without redress.': *Ibid.*, p. xi.
8. For Nkrumah's argument on this point see in particular his *Africa Must Unite*, Heinemann, London, 1963.
9. The first Yaoundé Convention was negotiated during 1962, signed in 1963, but as a result of de Gaulle's veto on British entry into EEC, not ratified until 1964. For the first text see D. C. Watt, James Mayall and Cornelia Navari, eds., *Documents on International Affairs, 1963*, RIIA, London, 1972, pp. 404–34.
10. For the full text see *ibid.*, pp. 436–50.
11. Quoted in Nicholas Hutton, 'Sources of strain in the Eur-African association', *International Relations*, May 1973, pp. 288–94.
12. Mazrui, *Towards a Pax Africana*, p. 88.
13. The negotiations occupied eleven months of working days, which included 183 joint EEC/ACP sessions and 493 ACP sessions: *West Africa*, London, 10 Feb. 1975, p. 153.
14. Quoted in Hutton, 'Sources of strain in the Eur-African association', p. 290.
15. *Le Monde*, 18–19 Feb. 1973.
16. *West Africa*, 7 May 1973.
17. The Heads of State set out the following guiding principles in the Charter: (1) non-reciprocity for trade and tariff concessions given by the EEC; (2)

extension on a non-discriminatory basis towards third countries of the provision on the 'right of establishment'; (3) revision of rules of origin to
facilitate the industrial development of Africa; (4) revision of the provisions
concerning the movements of payments and capital to take account of the
objective of monetary independence in African countries; (5) the dis-
association of EEC financial and technical aid from any form of relationship
with the EEC; (6) free and assured access to EEC markets for all African
products including processed and semi-processed agricultural products
whether or not they are subject to the common agricultural policies of the
EEC; (7) the guaranteeing to African countries of stable, equitable and
remunerative prices in EEC markets for their main products; and (8) any
agreement made with the EEC should not adversely affect intra-African
cooperation.

18. *West Africa*, 16 July 1973.
19. *Ibid.*
20. For example, the Senegalese Finance Minister told reporters that while
    Senegal now accepted non-reciprocity as regards trade preferences, the
    question of reciprocity in other fields remained open for negotiation: *Le
    Monde*, 27 July 1973.
21. Within Africa the basic problem here concerns the politics of income redis-
    tribution among states, all of which are poor, but not equally poor. Still,
    even here, the practical problems may have an ideological source as when
    one member of the group assumes a different strategy from the others: *cf.* A.
    Mazrui, 'Tanzania versus East Africa: a case of unwitting federal sabotage',
    in his *On Heroes and Uhuru-Worship*, Longman, London, 1967, pp. 73–95. In
    external relations it arises from the competitive nature of most African
    export industries, for example as between Nigeria and Senegal over the
    export of groundnuts or between the African and Malagasy Coffee Pro-
    ducers Organisation (Ivory Coast, Cameroon, Madagascar, Central African
    Republic, Togo) and the Commonwealth producers (Kenya, Tanzania, and
    Uganda): *cf.* Hutton, 'Sources of strain in the Eur-African association', p. 294.
22. *Financial Times*, London, 2 Oct. 1973.
23. In Brussels, President Diori of Niger doubted the reality of the unity that
    had been achieved. 'If now one wishes to say that there had been a common
    front, I wonder what it means. Is it demographic weight that one wants to
    throw on the scale? All the nineteen together are not even equivalent to
    Nigeria. Who would then have the decisive say? That is the problem.': *West
    Africa*, 1 Oct. 1973.
24. *Financial Times*, 4 Oct. 1973.
25. *Le Monde*, 24 Oct. 1973.
26. In an interview with Eric Rouleau of *Le Monde*, Colonel Gaddafi claimed that
    'Libya in two years has succeeded in isolating Israel from Africa; seventeen
    countries of the Dark Continent have broken relations with the Jewish state
    thanks to our efforts. We have reduced the Zionist state to the level of
    Taiwan.': *The Times*, London, 25 Oct. 1973.
27. Thus, General Gowon in his opening speech to the trade ministers' meeting
    in Lagos pledged that Nigeria would be prepared to make the necessary

sacrifices to fulfil her duties and obligations to Africa. He continued, 'We shall be the last to call on our brothers to commit economic suicide in the face of unknown realities.': *West Africa*, 16 July 1973.

28. It was, for example, General Gowon's letter to the EEC, written in his capacity as OAU Chairman, which was decisive in persuading the Community to accept a negotiation with the OAU, a formula which made it possible for Ethiopia, Liberia, Equatorial Guinea, Guinea-Bissau and Sudan to participate: *West Africa*, 10 Feb. 1975, p. 151. For a discussion of Nigeria's foreign economic policy towards her neighbours see Jean Herskovitz, 'Nigeria: Africa's new power', *Foreign Affairs*, liii, 2, Jan. 1975, pp. 314–33.

29. For a detailed analysis for these negotiations see I. W. Zartman, *The Politics of Trade Negotiations between African and the European Economic Community*, Princeton University Press, 1971.

30. 'Memorandum of the Commission to the Council on the Future Relations between the Community, the present AASM States and the countries in Africa, the Caribbean, the Indian and Pacific Oceans referred to in protocol no. 22 to the act of accession', *Bulletin of the European Communities*, Supplement 1/73 Luxembourg, 1973, p. 6 (hereafter referred to as the *Deniau Memorandum*).

31. G. and V. Curzon, 'Neo-colonialism and the European Economic Community', in Keeton and Schwarzenberger, eds., *The Yearbook of World Affairs, 1971*, p. 120.

32. *Deniau Memorandum*, p. 10.

33. The CET stipulates a zero duty for calcium phosphate, gum arabic, ores, crude oil, rubber, rawhides and skins, wood, cotton, sisal, copper, tin, cobalt, tea, seeds and oleaginous fruits.

34. There seems to be no professional agreement about the impact of the Yaoundé Convention on the Associates' export trade. Thus, while G. and V. Curzon ('Neo-colonialism and the EEC', p. 136) conclude that 'free access is having a noticeable effect on trade and production patterns in the AASM area by encouraging investments in manufactures rather than in extractive or in agriculture sectors', Timothy Curtin points out that while the share of manufactures in total Associate exports to the EEC increased from 22 per cent to 33 per cent in 1959–69, the less developed countries as a whole also increased their share of manufactures in total exports to the EEC, by 9 per cent to 15 per cent, a greater proportional increase of their total exports: T. Curtin, 'Towards Eur-Africa? Africa's relations with the enlarged EEC', *Moorgate and Wall Street*, Spring 1973, p. 66.

35. Even where Associates have diversified away from dependence on a single export crop or industry, they remain heavily dependent on a few primary exports. For example, the Ivory Coast on coffee, timber and coca, Togo on coffee, cocoa and phosphorus.

36. *Deniau Memorandum*, p. 11.

37. The main constraint here is the very small size of the domestic markets in Associate Africa, less than 70 m. people for all eighteen countries with an average GNP of \$110 per head. This latter figure, however, conceals a fairly wide spread from Gabon with \$5·50 per head and Ivory Coast with \$3·04 to

Rwanda with $45 and Upper Volta with $50 per head. This spread, which is wider than that for Commonwealth Africa, is itself a source of tension among the Associates. See Curtin, 'Towards Eur-Africa?' Tables IV and V, pp. 81–2.

38. Although Article 20 of Yaoundé II provides for grants in aid where a drop in world market prices would otherwise result in 'difficulties of a special and exceptional nature', and Article 21 provides for advances to the stabilisation funds of the Associate states, the *Deniau Memorandum* admits that 'past experience of the practical working of these two articles shows that they are incapable of providing a general and lasting solution to the problem of the instability of export earnings'.

39. *Ibid.*, p. 21.

40. Jacques Ferrandi, 'Africa and the EEC', *Standard Bank Review*, June 1973, pp. 2–8.

41. To be fair, the Commission's own views on this point go a long way to meet African criticisms. See *Deniau Memorandum*, pp. 91–134.

42. Curtin, 'Towards Eur-Africa?', p. 74.

43. While the EDF has roughly trebled in size, the population likely to benefit has roughly doubled.

44. *West Africa*, 17 Feb. 1975.

45. *Deniau Memorandum*, p. 11.

46. In 1971 for example French imports from the Associate states were $705 m. against Germany's $282 m., Italy's $203 m., and the Netherland's $120 m. In the same year French exports to the Associate states were $941 m. compared with Germany's $182 m., Benelux' $158 m., Netherlands' $87 m., and Italy's $133 m.

47. G. and V. Curzon, 'Neo-colonialism and the EEC', pp. 132–3.

48. *Ibid.*, p. 136.

49. Thus, under EDF I, France, together with West Germany, provided 34·4 per cent of the funds and gained 45·7 per cent of the contracts awarded (West Germany 4·9 per cent). Under EDF II France and Germany provided 33·75 per cent and France gained 39 per cent and Germany 22·9 per cent of the contracts awarded. Both sets of figures, however, probably underestimated French gains since many of the contracts awarded to Associate firms (29·2 per cent under EDF I and 17 per cent under EDF II) were to African subsidiaries of French firms. See *European Development Fund: Access to Contracts*, European Communities Commission, Brussels, 1970.

50. For example, CET on coffee was reduced from 9·6 to 7 per cent; on cocoa from 5·4 to 4 per cent, and on palm oil from 9 to 6 per cent.

51. In 1973, Cameroon, Chad and Madagascar all withdrew from the Organisation.

52. On the typology of agreements resulting from negotiations see Fred Ikle, *How Nations Negotiate*, Praeger, New York, 1967. In this chapter I have adopted the use made of Ikle's typology by Nicholas Hutton in the *Salience of Linkage in International Relations* (unpublished manuscript).

53. Although exports from the five to the Associates were low in absolute terms (see note 42 above) Yaoundé I did result in a degree of geographical

diversification. The *Deniau Memorandum* noted that 'exports from Member States having special relations with the Associated African States and Madagascar (AASM) only increased at a low annual rate (5·1 per cent in the case of France and 4·6 per cent for Benelux) whereas the other Member States increased their exports at a much higher rate (11·2 per cent for the Netherlands, 11·9 per cent for Germany and 14·7 per cent for Italy).': *Deniau Memorandum*, p. 11.

54. While in 1969 the EEC accounted for over 70 per cent of Associate exports, these represented approximately only 2 per cent of the EEC imports. Whatever diversification is achieved under a future agreement, it seems unlikely that this basic pattern will be quickly reversed.

55. In March 1973 Senghor informed the Commission that: 'We will continue to give to Europe the preferences she has enjoyed in our markets as much for considerations of human dignity as for commercial and juridical reasons.': *West Africa*, 9 Apr. 1973.

56. For a more detailed discussion of this point, see James Mayall, 'Funtionalism and international economic relations', in P. G. Taylor and J. Groom, eds., *Functionalism: Theory and Practice: International Relations*, London, 1975.

57. *West Africa*, 15 Oct. 1973.

58. *Financial Times*, 16 Oct. 1973.

59. The Agreement, which was reached at the joint ministerial meeting held in Kingston, Jamaica, 25–26 July 1975, specified that the new Convention would need to be framed in such a way as not to be challenged by third parties within GATT. Commission of the European Communities, *Information: Development and Cooperation, August 1974*, CEC, Brussels, 1974.

60. *West Africa*, 16 July 1973.

61. For text see US Department of State, *Bulletin*, lxviii, 1766, 30 Apr. 1973, pp. 513–22.

62. See, for example, the speech by Joseph Grunwald to the European Commission in February 1973, 'Europe can help by not overreacting. . . . It would be most helpful if the Community would continue to pursue the ideas brought up at the end of the year which were designed to move away from the so-called reverse preferences. . . . We recognise that for historical reasons the phasing out of old arrangements may take time but the important thing would be for both of us to be moving towards the same internationally agreed objectives.': United States Information Service, *Press, Release,*[21] Feb. 1973.

63. *Deniau Memorandum*, p. 7.

64. For text see C. Soames, 'The EEC's external relations', *World Today*, xxix, 5, May 1973, pp. 190–5.

65. For a discussion on this point, see E. Preeg, *Traders and Diplomats*, Brookings Institution, Washington, 1970, pp. 225–32.

66. Nicholas Hutton, 'Africa's changing relationship with the EEC', *World Today*, xxx, 10, Oct. 1974, pp. 426–35.

67. Commission of the European Communities, *Information: Development and Cooperation, June 1974*.

68. Curtin, 'Toward Eur-Africa?', p. 78.

69. The final STABEX scheme covered cocoa, cotton, copra, coconut and cake, groundnuts and groundnut-oil, palm products, hides and skins, timber and wood products, bananas, tea, sisal and iron ore.

    The EEC agrees to reimburse the exporting state when its earnings fall 7·5 per cent below the rolling average of the previous four years. Special treatment is to be given to certain commodities (sisal – 5 per cent) and the least developed of the ACP countries for which the figure is 2·5 per cent. For these states also there will be no repayment: *Financial Times*, 3 Feb. 1975.

70. Commission of European Communities, *Information: Development and Cooperation, August 1974*.

71. For the elaboration of this argument see Johan Galtung, 'A structural theory of imperialism', *Journal of Peace Research*, viii, 1, 1971, pp. 81–118.

72. J. Galtung, *The European Community: A Superpower in the Making*, Allen and Unwin, Oslo and London, 1973, pp. 134–5.

73. *Ibid.*, p. 85.

74. Arghiri Emmanuel, *Unequal Exchange: A Study of the Imperialism of Trade*, Monthly Review Press, New York, 1972.

75. Dharam P. Ghai, 'Concepts and strategies of economic independence', *Journal of Modern African Studies*, ii, 1, March 1973, pp. 41–2.

John F. Clark

13   Patterns of Support for International Organisations in Africa

In the past fifteen years Africa has been the scene of a significant proliferation of regional and sub-regional international governmental organisations (IGOs). Most have been formed for basically socio-economic purposes, but many have significant political functions as well. Despite the growing number of organisational efforts, however, African IGOs seem to have made little progress in solving the economic, social and political problems confronting African states. IGOs are formed, but they are provided with inadequate supportive resources to accomplish their assigned tasks. A vicious circle is typically formed in which IGOs are unable to produce substantive results, partly because of lack of support from members, and partly because members withhold support as a result of the lack of achievement. However, such a circle more clearly applies to the situation of some organisations more than to others.

As Wallerstein has noted in reference to the multiple memberships of African states, 'The more such alliances any one state is meaningfully involved in, the less total must be its commitment to any one given alliance.'[1] Commitment, or support, can be both tangible and intangible. In either form, support from members is both partly determinative and partly symptomatic of organisational success. Support from among members is not only necessary to enable an organisation to have a positive impact on its environment but also a result of an organisation's positive impact.

The primary purpose of this study is to explore the variations in support patterns among IGOs in Africa during the 1964–70 period, with a view to discerning determinants of support and the effect of multiple IGO commitments. Budget financing, secretariat staffing, participation in organisation conferences and other activities, hostships of meetings and headquarters, and

Table 13.1 Functional and Geographical Typology of Selected IGOs With African Members, 1964–70*3 (see Table 13.2 for explanation of abbreviations)

	Narrow Socio-Econ.	Broad Socio-Econ.	Broad Socio-Econ. + Polit.	Polit. + Broad Socio-Econ.	Solely political
Sub-Regional	UDEAO† Afr. Gr. C.† LACO† WARDA‡	L. Chad. B. C.† Niger R. C.† W. Afr. Cmty‡ Eco. Cmty of E. Afr.‡	EAC† Entente† Maghreb† OCAMM† OERS† UDEAC† OCCEAC‡ UEAC‡	CECAS‡ Tripoli C. Sts‡	
Regional	AFCAC‡	ADB† ECA†		OAU†	
Inter-Regional	UMOA UMAEC	EEC–EAMA	OAPEC	Arab League	
Particularist	Intern'l Coffee Organisation Cocoa prod. All. OPEC		Commonwealth 'Francophonie'		C. Non-al. Sts‡

Global	UNHCR	FAO WHO ILO UNESCO UNCTAD UNIDO IBRD UNDP	UN

* The functional category of 'Political plus Narrow Socio-Economic' is omitted in the table because no IGOs relevant to the African context meet the criteria for the category.

* Focus IGOs.

‡ IGOs with permanent secretariats.

verbal statements are used to indicate support patterns.[2] The results are intended to provide some indication of the kinds of organisations most likely to achieve the support necessary to enable them to make a positive impact on the problems facing African states. Secondly, it is hoped that the results will provide some insight into the question of whether the proliferation of IGOs enhances or detracts from member support and the overall ability of IGOs significantly to alter the African international environment.

Table 13.1 shows most of the IGOs to which African states belonged at the end of 1970. The typologies are based mainly on a framework devised by Wittkopf.[3] African sub-regional organisations are IGOs composed entirely of African states, but with the membership comprising less than 75 per cent of all African states, while African regional organisations are those in which all full members are African states and the membership comprises 75 ger cent or more of the total number of African states. Inter-regional organisations are IGOs with geographic membership criteria, and having one or more national members in two or more world regions, but in less than 75 per cent of the regions, while global organisations are those IGOs with almost world-wide membership. Particularist organisations are those which have no formal or informal geographical membership criteria, but which have members from two or more regions and require specific religious, cultural, political, or economic characteristics in order to qualify for membership.[4]

The functional categories are based on a typology related to scope of socio-economic activities (broad or narrow) and relative importance of socio-economic and political functions; the difference between broad socio-economic plus political and political plus broad socio-economic organisations is that in the former group, socio-economic functions have greater relative importance, while in the latter group, political functions are more important.

The focus organisations of this study, indicated (†) in Table 13.1, are those African regional and sub-regional IGOs in the 1964–70 period whose full memberships totalled three or more and which had permanent secretariats. Three African regional IGOs and eleven African sub-regional IGOs had permanent secretariats by the end of the period studied.

Table 13.2 English Names of the IGOs

ADB: African Development Bank
AFCAC: African Civil Aviation Commission
Afr. Gr. C.: African Groundnuts Council
Arab League
CECAS: Conference of East and Central African States
Cocoa Prod. All.: Cocoa Producers Alliance
Commonwealth
C. Non-al. Sts: Conference of Non-aligned States
EAC: East African Community
EADB: East African Development Bank
ECA: United Nations Economic Commission for Africa
Eco Cmty of E. Afr.: Economic Community of Eastern Africa
EEC–EAMA: Association of the European Economic Community and the Asso-
            ciated Afro-Malagasy States
Entente: Council of the Entente
FAO: Food and Agriculture Organisation
'Francophonie': The main institution of 'Francophonie' is the Agency of Tech-
            nical and Cultural Cooperation
IBRD: International Bank for Reconstruction and Development (World Bank)
ILO: International Labour Organisation
IACO: Inter-African Coffee Organisation
Intl. Coff. Org.: International Coffee Organisation
L. Chad B. C.: Lake Chad Basin Commission
Maghreb: Maghreb Permanent Consultative Committee
Niger R. C.: Niger River Commission
OAPEC: Organisation of Arab Petroleum Exporting Countries
OAU: Organisation of African Unity
OCAMM: Common African, Malagasy and Mauritian Organisation
OCCEAC: Common Organisation for Economic Co-operation in Central Africa
OERS: Organisation of Senegal River States
OPEC: Organisation of Petroleum-Exporting Countries
Tripoli C. Sts: Tripoli Charter States
UDEAC: Central African Customs and Economic Union
UDEAO: West African Customs and Economic Union
UEAC: Union of Central African States
UMAEC: Monetary Union of Equatorial Africa and Cameroon
UMCA: West African Monetary Union
UN: United Nations
UNCTAD: United Nations Conference on Trade and Development
UNDP: United Nations Development Programme
UNESCO: United Nations Educational, Scientific, and Cultural Organisation
UNHCR: United Nations High Commissioner for Refugees
UNIDO: United Nations Industrial Development Organisation
W. Afr. Cmty: West African Economic Community
WARDA: West African Rice Development Association
WHO: World Health Organisation

---

1. Financial Support

Financial support patterns provide one basis for delineating among international organisations to which African states belong. Contributions to IGO budgets are commonly recognised as an important measure of member support for international organisations,[5] and have previously been utilised in quantitative studies of member support for the United Nations.[6] In the case of African IGOs under consideration, member states did not in each year unilaterally determine the amount they would allocate to each organisation. Normally, agreements were reached according to which each state paid a fixed percentage of the total budget. The absolute amount contributed by each state for each year was determined by negotiations and/or voting to determine the total budget size for a given year. A state increased or decreased the amount allocated to a specific organisation not by directly increasing or decreasing its contributions, but by influencing the outcome of the bargaining over total budget size.

One indication, then, of the extent of success of an African organisation in achieving support from its members is the size of its budget; an indication of the extent of success of an inter-regional, particularist, or global organisation in the competition for financial resources from African members is the amount of the budget contributed by African members. However, absolute budget sizes are not particularly useful for purposes of comparison of commitment of members, due to the wide ranges in membership scope and financial resources of different memberships. Budget size as per cent of the combined GNPs of members provides an index which allows comparability of budgets of organisations with different geographic scopes and membership financial capabilities; this index is utilised to produce the results shown in Table 13.3.[7]

Among organisations for which data are available, the three organisations with greatest financial commitment from members, relative to members' GNPs, are the EAC, the Entente, and UDEAC, which were sub-regional, broad socio-economic plus political organisations. The EAC ranks highest in financial commitment when average annual subscriptions to the EADB are considered, and it ranks second to the Entente when the EAC budget minus EADB subscriptions is utilised for comparison.

Table 13.3 Financial Support of IGOs by African States[8]

	Annual budget funds provided by African states (000s of $)†	African-provided funds as % of combined GNPs‖ of African members
IGO*		
EAC* (incl. EADB)	7 580‡	0·3361
Entente*	2 377	0·1327
EAC* (excl. EADB)	1 980	0·0878
UDEAC*	886	0·0836
ADB*	16 325‡	0·0541
UN	10 017§	0·0315
OERS*	264	0·0193
Arab League	2 335	0·0178
OCAMM*	810	0·0135
OAU*	2 956¶	0·0092
Maghreb*	229	0·0032
L. Chad. B. C.*	151	0·0025
Commonwealth	201	0·0018
Niger R. C.*	58	0·0007

* Focus organisations.

† Figures shown are for 1970 calendar year or 1969 fiscal year. Exceptions are indicated in footnotes ‡ and §.

‡ Annual contributions to the EADB and ADB are calculated by computing an annual average from end-of-1970 paid subscrption total. The EADB figure is derived by dividing the total subscriptions by the three years of EADB operation, while the ADB average is derived by dividing the amount paid as of 31 May 1970 by 4, the number of years of ADB operation.

§ UN figures represent mean annual contributions during the 1965–69 period to the UN and all related agencies and programmes except UNRRA, IBRD, IBA, IFC, and IMF.

¶ OAU amount is total of regular budget and African Liberation Committee contributions for 1969–70.

‖ GNP figures are for 1965, except for Equatorial Guinea and Swaziland for which 1968 estimates are utilised.

The membership of the EAC, the Entente, and UDEAC did not overlap, and thus there was no competition among the three for financial resources; they do, however, compare very favourably with organisations with which they did overlap. Their members contributed considerably greater proportions of their incomes to the sub-regional organisations than they did to their nearest rivals, the ADB and the UN, and the financial burden assumed by OAU members was only a small proportion of the total IGO burden undertaken by the members of the three organisations receiving the greatest support. Other sub-regional organisations receiving significant financial commitments were the OERS and OCAMM. The OERS received a lower commitment than the ADB and the UN, but ranks higher than OCAMM and the OAU, which were also rivals for its members' commitments.. OCAMM ranks lower than four rivals – the Entente, ADB, UN, and OERS – but did generate greater financial support from its members than did the OAU. The relatively rich Maghreb states contributed larger proportions of their incomes to the competitors of the Permanent Consultative Committee for their support: the ABD, UN, Arab League, and OAU. The Lake Chad Basin Commission and Niger River Commission, socio-economic, sub-regional organisations with no political functions, generated the least financial support among focus organisations for which data were available.

Especially revealing are the relative rankings of the regional ADB, a broad socio-economic organisation, and the OAU, an organisation with political plus broad socio-economic purposes. While the ADB ranked only behind the EAC, Entente, and UDEAC, among possible competitors listed, the OAU generated less financial commitment than all major sub-regional organisations except the Maghreb organisation, less than the global UN, and less than the inter-regional Arab League. The only major organisation other than the Maghreb to score lower than the OAU on the financial support index was the Commonwealth, a particularist organisation with a budget similar to that of the OAU, but for which the thirteen African members were assessed only 15 per cent of the total.

The extent of membership overlap with other IGOs and the low financial support scores of the Lake Chad Basin Commission and the Niger River Commission reflect some of the problems encountered by sub-regional organisations which cut across Anglophone-Francophone boundaries. In crossing such barriers, the Chad Basin and Niger River organisations had to appeal for financial resources to states which looked in a multiplicity of directions for IGOs to achieve their extra-national goals. They overlapped not only with each other, but with the Entente, the OERS (Niger River Commission only), UDEAC and UDEAO (the latter not shown in Table 13.3 due to unavailability of data), as well as larger scope Francophone and Anglophone organisations (OCAMM and the Commonwealth). In restricting membership to states of similar linguistic and colonial background, some organisations not only avoid a number of mechanical problems and ensure greater community of interests, but they also restrict the number of possible competitors for financial and other types of support.

2. Personnel Support

Support of IGOs is also expressed by the contribution of personnel to work in the organisation secretariats. Each of the focus organisations maintained a permanent secretariat, staffed generally, but not always entirely, by nationals of the member states. The staffing of secretariats had important implications for the international organisations. Specific work programmes, although approved by governing bodies composed of national representatives, were normally formulated and executed by members of the secretariats. Attitudes of individuals towards organisations were in part determined by opinions of the competence of the secretariats. In general, the existence of a capable and productive secretariat was a necessary, though not sufficient, condition for significant expansion of task performance by an organisation; a capable secretariat was generally a basic internal goal of IGOs and achievement of such a secretariat affected ability to achieve external goals.

Typically, officials were nominated by their governments to serve in the secretariats, and they often were simply seconded from national civil service to the IGOs for a limited amount of time. In the case of all focus organisations, national government approval was necessary for an individual to serve in the secretariat of an organisation to which his government belonged. National governments weighed the relative value of organisations for achievement of national goals in determining whether to release nationals for international service at all, and, if so, to which organisations. The willingness of national governments to allow capable citizens to serve in international secretariats rather than work directly in national government service greatly affected the ability of the organisations to perform their tasks adequately. The ability of each organisation to attract capable staff personnel also depended on the interest of qualified individuals in working in the secretariat. Such interest was influenced, in addition to national government attitudes, by the ability of the organisation to provide attractive salaries and benefits, the attractiveness of the headquarters site, and the type and prestige of work performed by the organisation.

Development of an acceptable measure of the success of organisations in achieving personnel support is difficult for a number of reasons. One serious difficulty derives from the lack of availability of published information regarding the quality of secretariats. A second difficulty derives from the problem of determining exactly what should be measured, apart from the question of what can be measured. The size of secretariat might partly reflect personnel support from members, but this figure is probably more accurately a reflection of financial support, which has already been considered. Most likely financial considerations, along with the scope of tasks assigned to the IGO, determine the size of secretariats, and personnel support – as distinct from financial support – is then expressed in the willingness of individual members to part with nationals in quantity and quality. Thus, quantity of nationals in a secretariat may partly reflect an individual state's support of that specific IGO, but the total staff size is more accurately a reflection of members' total financial support, rather than personnel support. Given a fixed secretariat size the positions will generally be filled, but quality of personnel may vary.

One measure which might be useful in measuring varying personnel support patterns would be some kind of index of the quality of personnel permitted by members to serve in secretariats. If full information on each IGO were available it might be useful to measure, for example, education levels of secretariats and/or rank or salary level in national government positions before joining international secretariats. In any case, available published information does not permit a quantitative comparison of secretariat personnel quality. This study therefore presents, in lieu of a quantitative analysis, a descriptive analysis of relative recruiting strengths of some focus organisations, based on interviews conducted by the author and various documentary and secondary sources.

To a large extent, competition for secretariat personnel was between national governments and IGOs rather than among IGOs. In a majority of cases, the IGOs came out second in this competition, due both to national government attitudes and to national pay scales which were equal to or higher than IGO salaries. The major exception to this generalisation was the United Nations family, which had pay scales which were attractive in comparison with many African civil service compensatory arrangements. However, despite the favourable UN pay arrangements, the ECA, like the other two regional organisations ADB and OAU, and the global United Nations itself, found the major problem in staff recruitment in Africa to be the unwillingness of national governments to part with their highly qualified personnel, regardless of desires of individuals who might have chosen to serve in IGO secretariats.[9] Nevertheless, despite the common problem of competition with national governments, there was considerable variation among IGOs in Africa in their ability to obtain human resources from members.

ECA, being a United Nations entity with an all-African membership, had significant numbers of both Africans and non-African among its professional staff. An on-going controversy within ECA resulted from the attempt to further 'Africanise' the staff. The debate, like the more general UN debate over geographical distribution, was sometimes stated in terms of a conflict between representation from 'under-represented' countries and quality of personnel. Opinions regarding the validity of such a conflict vary greatly.[10] However, there probably was some accuracy in presenting the issue in such terms, due in large part to the previously noted unwillingness of many less developed countries to allow their most qualified personnel to participate in international service. Furthermore, a large proportion of the best qualified African personnel allowed by their governments to serve in the UN system were provided for fixed terms only, rather than on a career basis; the result was a high turnover of African personnel, making necessary a high degree of recruiting effort in Africa just to prevent reduction in the proportion of African personnel.

Among international organisations, the chief competitors of the ECA for personnel support were, above the sub-regional level, the other components of the United Nations system." Of the ECA professional staff at the end of 1968, 68 out of 109, or 62·4 per cent, were Africans. However, components of the United Nations other than the ECA employed 133 other Africans[12]; the United Nations attempted to maintain 'desirable ranges' of employment totals for each African country and the African region as a whole, and, in employing about twice as many Africans as ECA in components outside of ECA, provided significant competition to the ECA in its attempt to 'Africanise' without diluting the quality of its staff. Most of the non-ECA posts at which Africans were employed were in New York and Europe, sites which many Africans considered more desirable as places to live in than Addis Ababa.

ECA officials generally did not consider the ADB and OAU as competitors for professional staff. Although the ADB staff was 90 per cent African and the OAU staff was entirely African, these two organisations employed fewer numbers of Africans in professional positions than did the ECA; the OAU had a professional staff of 62 and the ADB employed 40 professionals, of which 36 were African. Both ADB and OAU had lower pay scales than ECA, which had the same pay scale as the rest of the UN components. As for site attractiveness, OAU was, like ECA, located in Addis Ababa. ADB's position in the somewhat more modern and cosmopolitan city of Abidjan may have offered a slightly more attractive residence site, but this advantage was at least partially offset by the higher cost of living in Abidjan, and less prominence, with resulting lower prestige, of the ADB on the African scene during the period studied. The ECA officials' lack of perception of competition with ADB and OAU may have been due to the ECA's success in competing with the other two organisations for qualified personnel.

The OAU was at a particular disadvantage in recruiting and maintaining staff due to its proximity to ECA headquarters, as well as the location of a number of other UN offices in Addis Ababa. OAU salaries were significantly lower than ECA salaries, and Administrative Secretary-General Diallo Telli saw this disparity in staff compensation as a major impediment to OAU efforts to recruit qualified personnel and to prevent the outflow of competent staff members.[13] There was general agreement among observers in Addis Ababa that the OAU secretariat was of low quality and that its deficiencies were in part due to the inferior OAU pay scale. Nevertheless, Telli's request for a significant increase in salaries was turned down in 1970. While various reasons were given for this opposition to higher pay for employees it appeared to be largely a manifestation of dissatisfaction with the organisation in general and its staff, including especially Telli, in particular.[14] The result of such opposition was to prevent the OAU from becoming stronger in comparison with ECA and other organisations in competing for personnel.

All three regional organisations had difficulty in competing with sub-regional organisations for personnel. As a high-ranking officer of the Personnel Section of ECA noted,[15] the sub-regional organisations were much closer to the states, and it was much easier for government officials to see their immediate benefits. Governments were therefore more willing to second civil servants to the sub-regional organisations than to the often far-away regional organisations, whose direct benefits to individual countries were often less than obvious. Most of the sub-regional staffs were relatively small and therefore probably had little effect on regional organisation recruitment, despite any preference which they might have received. However, EAC, UDEAC, and OCAMM had sizable numbers of professional-level officials,[16] and they thus may have had some adverse effect on the quality and quantity of regional organisation recruitment from countries which were members of one or two of the larger-staffed sub-regional IGOs. The main problem in recruitment for the sub-regional IGOs was, like that of the regional organisations, competition with the national governments and the need for persuading national governments to provide qualified personnel.

In short, there was some, but not much, competition among organisations in Africa for human resources. Capable African civil servants for employment outside national civil services were highly valued and fairly scarce, and some competition was therefore inevitable. Among focus organisations, sub-regional organisations seemed to have fared best in the competition, with the ECA being somewhat more competitively successful than the other two regional organisations, ADB and OAU.

3. Conference Participation

Another area of support for IGOs is conference participation. Many African organisations had for their governing authority conferences of heads of state, and the majority regularly convened meetings of ministers of economy, foreign affairs, and other ministerial-level delegates. Additionally, several inter-regional, particularist, and global organisations to which African states belonged often called together heads of state and other high-level officials. The heads of state and other upper-echelon officials thus had a multiplicity of multilateral conferences at which their attendence was requested, in addition to numerous bilateral interactions and domestic commitments. With such demands on their time and attention, top-level officials often had to choose whether to attend a conference, to send a lower-level representative, or not to be represented. It can be surmised that, in general, the conferences at which countries were represented by maximum-level delegations were those to which greater importance was attached by high-level officials.[17]

One index of member support for IGOs is, therefore, the frequency and rate of attendance by the maximum-level officials requested. The only attendance figures for which comprehensive published information is available are those for summit conferences, and the comparisons indicated in this section thus reflect only meetings of heads of state and government.

One measure of attendance support is absolute number of attendances by heads of state at multilateral conferences. The rationale for such a measurement is that heads of state are most likely to attend meetings of organisations whose activities and goals they most support, and that the organisations with more activity and support meet more often than those with less activity and support. Table 13.4 indicates total summit attendance per state for the period studied, with the organisations which met more often *and* which had high attendance rates showing higher scores than those for which the reverse was true. The average annual attendance per state is also shown in the table. This measurement is based on the same rationale as the score for average total attendance per state, with the difference being that the averages are based only on the years in the 1964–70 period for which each organisation was a multilateral group having a

Table 13.4. Average Summit Attendance Per Member, 1964–70[18]

IGO	1964	1965	1966	1967	1968	1969	1970	Total avg. head-of-state attendances per member	Avg. annual head-of-state attendances per member
Entente	0·75	4·00	2·40	2·60	4·80	1·00	2·80	18·35	2·62
EAC*	3·00	1·00	1·00	3·00	0	1·00	1·00	10·00	1·43
UDFAC*	—	1·80	0·80	1·00	2·00	1·00	1·00	7·60	1·27
OERS*	—	1·75	0	1·00	1·75	0	1·00	5·50	0·91
OCAMM*	0·43	1·50	0·86	0	0·93	0·71	0·60	5·03	0·72
OAU*	0·82	0·61‡	0·44	0·61‡	0·65‡	0·37	0·41	3·91‡	0·56‡
Commonwealth	1·00	0·89	1·00	0	0	0·77	0	3·66	0·52
CECAS†	—	—	0·87	1·30	0·64	0·43	0·29	3·53	0·71
Tripoli Ch. Sts†	—	—	—	—	—	1·00	2·00	3·00	1·50
Arab League	0·67	0·67	0	0·33	0	0·83	0	2·50	0·42
OCCEAC†	—	—	—	—	—	1·00	1·00	2·00	1·00
UEAC†	—	—	—	—	2·00	—	—	2·00	2·00
C. Non-al. Sts†	0·54	0	0	0	0	0	0·41	0·95	0·14
UDEAO*	—	—	—	—	—	—	0·88	0·88	0·88
W. Adr. Cmty†	—	—	—	—	0·50	0	0	0·50	0·17

* Focus IGOs.

† IGOs *without* permanent secretariats.

‡ Includes meetings of special commissions composed of selected heads of state.

conference of heads of state and government as its top decision-making body. Years during the period in which an organisation did not exist as a multilateral organisation governed by a body composed of heads of state and government do not lower an organisation's score. Thus, newer organisations, such as OCCMAC, and organisations which earlier had not convened heads of state, such as UDEAO, have relatively higher scores on this second measurement than on the measurement which reflects the aggregate for the entire seven-year period.

On both measurements, the Entente scores the highest among focus organisations and others convening heads of state and government. Despite the fact that most Entente states were also members of OCAMM, OAU, UDEAO, the West African Economic Community, and the Conference of Non-aligned States, heads of state and government of member countries attended an average of 2·62 conferences per year. Also scoring high are the EAC and its predecessors, whose meetings were attended an average of 10 times per member during the seven-year period, for an average annual attendance of 1·43. The third organisation scoring high on both indices is UDEAC, whose heads of state averaged 7·60 meetings for the period, for an average of 1·27 per year. By contrast, OCAMM and OAU chief executives attended an average of only 5·03 and 3·91 conferences, respectively, for the period, resulting in average attendance figures of 0·72 and 0·56 meetings per chief executive per year. Clearly, in the competition for participation at conferences by heads of state and government, the sub-regional organisations had a decisive advantage over the regional OAU, with OCAMM ranking between OAU and smaller sub-regional groups. CECAS, with scores of 3·53 and 0·71, ranks ahead of the OAU in annual average attendance, but behind in total average member attendance, while the Arab League, with figures of 2·50 and 0·42 for African members, ranks below the OAU on both scales. The broader-scoped Conference of Non-aligned States ranks at or near the bottom measurements. In general, the IGOs which were smaller in geographic scope achieved greater participation by heads of state and government than organisations with greater geographic scope.

It can be argued that total attendance is not the most significant attendance measure, because of the importance of number of meetings, in addition to rate of attendance at meetings, in determining the scores shown in Table 13.4. The validity of the Table 13.4 measures lies in the view that aggregate attendance is a more important measure of the extent to which an organisation successfully competes for heads of state participation than is percentage attendance. An alternative line of reasoning would hold that number of meetings is not highly significant; a smoothly-functioning organisation does not necessarily require several annual meetings of chief executives, and an organisation which is successful in competing for summit participation is one which simply has a high percentage rate of attendance at those meetings which it does hold. Percentage attendance rates are shown in Fig. 13.1. One result of such a measurement is high scores for some small organisations in existence for short periods

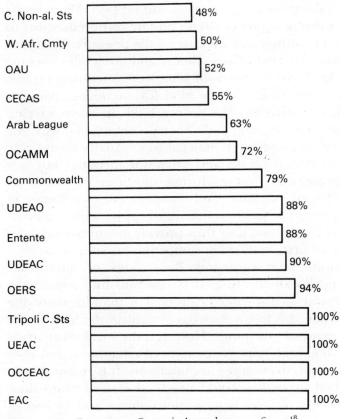

C. Non-al. Sts	48%
W. Afr. Cmty	50%
OAU	52%
CECAS	55%
Arab League	63%
OCAMM	72%
Commonwealth	79%
UDEAO	88%
Entente	88%
UDEAC	90%
OERS	94%
Tripoli C. Sts	100%
UEAC	100%
OCCEAC	100%
EAC	100%

Figure 13.1. Percentage Summit Attendance, 1964–70[18]

of time, such as the Tripoli Charter States, UEAC, and OCCEAC. Nevertheless, the main patterns discernible in Table 13.4 hold true for Fig. 13.1 also. Sub-regional organisations limited in geographic scope, such as EAC, OERS, UDEAC, and the Entente, show relatively high scores, ranging from 100 to 88 per cent, while larger sub-regional and inter-regional organisations, such as OCAMM, CECAS, and the Arab League, show lower attendance rates, ranging from 72 to 55 per cent. Ranking even lower are organisations to which all African states were eligible for membership, OAU and the Conference of Non-aligned States, with percentages of 52 and 48, respectively. Thus, not only does aggregate attendance vary inversely with the geographic scope of organisations, but the same is true for percentage rate of attendance.

It can also be argued, of course, that summit conference attendance is not a valid measure of organisation support. Many heads of state and government do not attend summit conferences due to political instability at home or because of the pressure of day-to-day internal and external affairs. Illness and other idiosyncratic variables also kept various heads of state from attending various meetings. Such arguments may be valid for attendance patterns for any single organisation, but do not hold up when varying attendance patterns are compared. They do not explain why, for example, President Senghor of Senegal was virtually always able to find time to attend OERS and OCAMM meetings but was usually on vacation in France during meetings of the OAU Assembly of Heads of State and Government. Variances in attendance patterns are partly reflective of support for organisations by heads of state, and they thus provide one measure of the relative success of organisations in competing for support.

A final consideration regarding the validity of attendance scores is the facility of meeting. It is easier to find a mutually agreeable date and site for three heads of state than for forty-one heads of state, and this factor may partly explain the high scores for small sub-regional groupings. However, the smaller organisations not only had high percentage rates of attendance, but they also met more often than larger organisations. It is reasonable to expect that chief executives could nearly as easily fit into their scheduled meetings of large organisations once a year or less, as they could find time for several meetings of smaller groups each year, *if* their priorities so dictated. Thus, low scores on all attendance measures are indicative of the low priority attached to the larger organisations by many heads of state and government.

Attendance patterns for meetings other than summits would also be useful for determining support patterns, but published data for representation at meetings below the heads of state level are not sufficiently complete to permit meaningful comparisons. The OAU, for example, was forced to eliminate and consolidate various ministerial-level commissions due to lack of sufficient attendance at meetings and because of sub-ministerial representation at conferences. Ministerial-level meetings of ECA, CECAS, and OCAMM were sometimes attended by lower-ranking officials, and meetings of the Niger River Commission were sometimes attended by very low-ranking officials or missed altogether. However, published data on sub-summit meetings normally describe representation, if at all, only in terms of countries, without names or positions of delegation heads. Data on attendance patterns at all levels of meetings would, nevertheless, be a useful supplement to summit attendance data.

4. 'General' Support

'Support' is, of course, far less tangible than has been suggested by the preceding discussion of support patterns deriving from financial resources, personnel, and representation at summit conferences. Support for international organisations is a state of mind among foreign policy decision-makers and influencers which determines the extent to which leaders will commit their attention and their resources to the collective goals of the membership as set forth in written guidelines for organisational performance and in the actions of individuals acting in the name of the organisation.[18] This state of mind could best be ascertained, of course, by in-depth interviews with the leaders and influencers in question and through examination of all relevant governmental foreign policy documents. Short of the ideal, one could examine indicators which are available in primary and secondary sources, and interview decision-makers and influencers who are accessible to the researcher. Table 13.5 represents an attempt to judge the degree of support by each state for each organisation by

Table 13.5 Organisational Support Levels of African States*[20]

	ADB	ECA	OAU	C. Non-al. Sts	Commonwealth	'Francophonie'†	EEC-EAMA	OCAMM	OERS	Entente	UDEAO	UDEAC	OCCEAC	EAC	Arab League	Maghreb	Tripoli G. Sts	OPEC	OAPEC	Afr. Gr. C.	IACO	CECAS	L. Chad B. C.	Niger R. C.	W. Afr. Cmy
Algeria	3	3	1	3	—	4*	—	—	—	—	—	—	—	—	2	2	—	2	3	—	—	—	—	—	—
Botswana	3*	3	3	3	2	—	—	—	—	—	—	—	—	—	—	—	—	—	—	—	—	—	—	—	—
Burundi	3	2	1	2	—	4*	2	3*	—	—	—	—	3	—	—	—	—	—	—	—	2	2	—	—	—
Cameroon	3	2	1	3	—	1	2	1	—	—	—	2	—	—	—	—	—	—	—	—	3	—	3	3	—
C. A. R.	3	3	2	2	—	3*	2	2	—	—	—	2	—	—	—	—	—	—	—	—	3	3	—	—	—
Chad	2	3	2	3	—	3*	3	1	—	—	—	3*	—	—	—	—	—	—	—	—	—	3	2	3	—
Congo-B.	2	3	2	2	—	2	2	3	—	—	—	2	—	—	—	—	—	—	—	—	3	3	—	—	—
Congo-K.	2	2	2	3	—	3*	2	2	—	—	—	—	2	—	—	—	—	—	—	3	3	3	—	—	—
Dahomey	2	2	2	3*	—	1	2	2	—	2	3	—	—	—	—	—	—	—	—	—	3	—	—	3	3
Equa. Guinea	3*	3	2	2	—	—	—	—	—	—	—	—	—	—	—	—	—	—	—	—	—	—	—	—	—

* 1 = high support   2 = medium support   3 = low support   4 = hostility

Table 13.5 (cont.)

	ADB	ECA	OAU	C. Non-al. Sts	Commonwealth	'Francophonie'†	EEC-EAMA	OCAMM	OERS	Entente	UDEAO	UDEAC	OCEAC	EAC	Arab League	Maghreb	Tripoli G. Sts	OPEC	OAPEC	Afr. Gr. C.	IACO	CECAS	L. Chad B. C.	Niger R. C.	W. Afr. Cmty
Ethiopia	2	1	1	1	–	–	–	–	–	–	–	–	–	–	–	–	–	–	–	–	2	1	–	–	–
Gabon	3*	3	3	3	–	2	2	1	–	–	–	2	–	–	–	–	–	–	–	–	3	–	–	–	–
Gambia	3*	3	2	3*	1	–	–	–	–	–	–	–	–	–	–	–	–	–	–	1	–	–	–	–	3
Ghana	1	2	2	3	3	–	–	–	–	–	–	–	–	–	–	–	–	–	–	–	–	–	–	–	2
Guniea	2	3	2	2	–	4*	–	4*	3	–	3*	–	–	–	–	–	–	–	–	–	–	–	–	3	3
Ivory Coast	1	2	3	3*	–	1	1	1	–	1	3	–	–	–	–	–	–	–	–	–	2	–	–	3	3
Kenya	1	2	1	3	2	–	2‡	–	–	–	–	–	–	1	–	–	–	–	–	–	3	1	–	–	–
Lesotho	3*	3	3	3	3	–	1	–	–	–	–	–	–	–	–	–	–	–	–	–	–	–	–	–	–
Liberia	2	1	1	3	–	–	–	–	–	–	–	–	–	–	–	–	–	–	2	–	–	–	–	–	2
Libya	3*	3	2	2	–	1	–	–	–	–	–	–	–	–	1	3*	1	1	2	–	–	–	–	–	–
Malagasy	3*	3	3	3*	–	1	1	1	–	–	–	–	–	–	–	–	–	–	–	–	2	3*	–	–	–

Table 13.5 (cont.)

	ADB	ECA	OAU	C. Non-al. Sts	Commonwealth	'Francophonie'†	EEC-EAMA	OCAMM	OERS	Entente	UDEAO	UDEAC	OCEAC	EAC	Arab League	Maghreb	Tripoli G. Sts	OPEC	OAPEC	Afr. Gr. C.	IACO	CECAS	L. Chad. B. C.	Niger R. C.	W. Afr. Cmty
Malawi	1	2	4	4*	2	–	–	–	–	–	–	–	–	–	–	–	–	–	–	–	–	3	–	–	–
Mali	2	3	1	2	–	3*	3	3*	2	–	2	–	–	–	–	–	–	–	–	2	–	–	–	2	3
Mauritania	1	3	1	1	–	3*	2	3*	1	–	3	–	–	–	–	–	–	–	–	–	–	–	–	–	3
Mauritius	3*	3	3	3*	2	.2	–	2	–	–	–	–	–	–	–	–	–	–	–	–	–	–	–	–	–
Morocco	3	3	3	3	–	3*	1‡	2	–	–	–	–	–	–	3	1	–	–	–	–	–	–	–	–	–
Niger	1	3	2	3	–	1	1	1	–	1	3	–	–	–	–	–	–	–	–	1	–	–	3	2	3
Nigeria	2	3	1	3	3	–	–	–	–	–	–	–	–	–	–	–	–	–	–	2	3	–	3	3	3
Rwanda	2	3	2	3	–	2	1	3	–	–	–	–	3	–	–	–	–	–	–	–	2	3	–	–	–
Senegal	2	1	3	3	–	1	2	2	1	–	3	–	–	–	–	–	–	–	–	1	–	–	–	–	3
Sierra Leone	1	2	3	3	1	–	–	–	–	–	–	–	–	–	–	–	–	–	–	3	3	–	–	–	3
Somalia	2	2	2	2	–	–	1	–	–	–	–	–	–	–	–	–	–	–	–	–	–	2	–	–	–

Table 13.5 (cont.)

	ADB	ECA	OAU	C. Non-al. Sts	Commonwealth	'Francophonie'†	EEC-EAMA	OCAMM	OERS	Entente	UDEAO	UDEAC	OCCEAC	EAC	Arab League	Maghreb	Tripoli G. Sts	OPEC	OAPEC	Afr. Gr. C.	IACO	CECAS	L. Chad B. C.	Niger R. C.	W. Afr. Cmty
Sudan	2	2	2	2	3*	—	—	—	—	—	—	—	—	—	1	—	2	—	—	—	—	2	—	—	—
Swaziland	3*	3	3	3	2	—	—	—	—	—	—	—	—	—	—	—	—	—	—	—	—	—	—	—	—
Tanzania	2	3	1	1	3	—	3‡	—	—	—	—	—	—	2	—	—	—	—	—	—	3	1	—	—	—
Togo	1	3	3	3	—	3*	2	2	—	3	3*	—	—	—	—	—	—	—	—	—	2	—	—	—	3
Tunisia	2	2	3	3	—	1	1‡	—	—	—	—	—	—	—	4	1	—	—	—	—	—	—	—	—	—
Uganda	2	3	2	2	2	—	2‡	—	—	—	—	—	—	2	—	—	—	—	—	—	2	2	—	—	—
U.A.R.	3	3	1	2	—	—	—	1	—	—	—	—	—	—	1	—	1	—	—	—	—	—	—	—	—
Upper Volta	2	3	2	3*	—	2	2	1	—	2	2	—	—	—	—	—	—	—	—	3*	—	—	—	3	3
Zambia	1	3	1	1	3	—	—	—	—	—	—	—	—	—	—	—	—	—	—	—	—	1	—	—	—

* Denotes score of states which fit the formal and informal objective criteria for membership, but resigned or never joined due to disagreement with and/or lack of interest in the organisation.

† States considered to be 'Francophonie' members are those which joined the Agency of Technical and Cultural Cooperation in 1970.

‡ Not a members of the Council of Association of the EEC and the Associated Afro-Malagasy States, but affiliated with the EEC through a separate agreement.

following such a procedure, and to derive 'general support' scores for each organisation, based on the average level of support of each member for each organisation.

Judgements reflected in Table 13.5 scores are based on a number of indicators analysed by the present writer. The most important are statements by decision-makers and influencers as expressed in interviews I have recorded in *Africa Research Bulletin* and various secondary sources, and views of various officials and scholars concerning support levels of states about whose foreign policies they are knowledgeable. The evaluations also utilise information, where available, concerning participation and non-participation in meetings below the summit level, as well as summit participation, chairmanships of organisations and hostships of conferences, non-payment of financial obligations, and level and extent of participation by nationals in IGO secretariats. An attempt is made to analyse long-term support patterns, but particular emphasis is placed on statements and activities in the final three years of the period studied. To the extent that support levels can be discerned as having changed over the period considered including in particular instances of changes in government, the greatest emphasis in assigning scores is placed upon the most recent indicators available to the end of 1970. Individual scores assigned are intended to have comparative validity both for each state over the range of organisations to which it belonged and for each organisation over the entire range of its membership.

Verbal support can have a number of meanings and can be translated into action in a number of ways. Obviously, the four-fold ordinal scale which is based to a considerable extent on oral expressions or attitudes blurs over many fine distinctions. However, an attempt is made in assigning scores to reflect at least some of the clearer distinctions. A state perceived to have both high support for an organisation in its current form and high support for expansion of task performance and authority of the organisation considered is assigned a high-support score for that particular organisation. The reverse is true for the low-support scores. A state perceived as having a high support for expansion and authority of an organisation, but low support for the organisation in its current form is assigned a '2', or medium-support score (an example is Guinea's score for the OAU).

Similarly, a state reflecting high support for an organisation in its current form, but low support for expansion of task performance and authority is also assigned a score of '2' (an example is the Ghanaian Government's attitude towards the OAU after Nkrumah). Finally, states indicating medium levels of both kinds of support are given medium-support scores. In borderline cases, such as medium level of one kind of support and high or low level of the other kind, scores are assigned according to relative intensities of the different kinds of support.

Table 13.6 shows the rank of organisations according to average support level of members, as derived from Table 13.5. Of the 25 organisations rated, six of the top nine are sub-regional organisations, all of which had both broad socio-economic and political purposes, with 2 of the others being particularist organisations and 1 being inter-regional. The highest scoring regional organisation is the ADB, ranked tenth, while the OAU ranks twelfth and the ECA nineteenth. Six of the seven lowest-ranking organisations are sub-regional organisations, and have no political purposes in addition to their socio-economic purposes. There thus seems to be a relationship between level of support for sub-regional organisations and range of organisational functions.

This relationship is more evident when only those organisations which were relatively permanent (i.e., those with permanent secretariats) are considered. Of the six broad socio-economic plus political, sub-regional organisations which are focus organisations, the lowest-ranking is UDEAC, which ranks twelfth with a 2·0 (medium) support score. Of the five focus, sub-regional organisations with only socio-economic purposes, only the African Groundnuts Council ranks higher than nineteenth. Regional, inter-regional, and particularist organisations ranging from narrow socio-economic to political plus broad socio-economic generally rank in the middle range of the support scale. A conclusion which may be inferrred from the information in Table 13.6 is that smaller organisations are likely to win over larger membership organisations in competition for support if they can perform a sufficiently wide range of functions to satisfy needs for which states look to multi-lateral cooperation. Conversely, there is strength in numbers (of members) for organisations with purposes limited to socio-economic functions only. Among regional, inter-regional, and particularist organisations, range of

Table 13.6 Average IGO Support Level by African Members*

Rank	Organisation	Support level
1	Maghreb†	1·3
1	Tripoli Charter States	1·3
3	'Francophonie'‡	1·5
3	OPEC	1·5
5	EAC†	1·7
5	OCAMM†	1·7
7	Entente†	1·8
7	OERS†	1·8
7	EEC–EAMA§	1·8
10	ADB†	1·9
10	African Groundnuts Council†	1·9
12	OAU†	2·0
12	UDEAC†	2·0
12	Arab League	2·0
15	CECAS	2·1
16	Commonwealth	2·2
17	Conference of Non-aligned States	2·4
18	OAPEC	2·5
19	ECA†	2·6
19	IACO†	2·6
21	UDEAO†	2·7
21	OCCEAC	2·7
23	Lake Chad Basin Commission†	2·8
23	Niger River Commission†	2·8
25	West African Economic Community	2·9

* 1 = high support   2 = medium support   3 = low support
4 = hostility.

† Focus IGOs.

‡ States considered to be 'Francophonie' members are those which
joined the Agency of Technical and Cultural Cooperation in 1970.

§ Average includes scores of African states associated with the EEC
outside of the EEC–EAMA arrangements, as well as those of EEC–
EAMA members.

functions seems to bear little relationship to degree of member
support.

Another variable which may be relevant is linguistic homogeneity of membership. The top nine ranked organisations are all
relatively homogeneous, while the ten linguistically hetero-
geneous organisations rank from tenth to twenty-fifth, including
five of the seven lowest ranked. It appears that, among African
sub-regional organisations, there is a positive relationship

between range of functions and support, and, among all IGOs with African membership, there is a positive relationship between linguistic homogeneity and support. It may be that while larger organisations are in a better position to provide collective benefits, smaller organisations with homogeneous memberships are in a better position to receive identitive member support. The small, homogeneous organisations which compensate for size with wide ranges of services receive the greatest support, while larger organisations, due to resource strength derived from numbers, maintain enough prominence to receive greater member support than small, limited-purpose organisations. In any case, linguistic homogeneity, range of functions, and size seem to be important influencers of organisational support, with linguistic homogeneity perhaps the most important of the three.[21]

One difficulty in using Table 13.6 to compare the success of organisations in competing for support is that only members' support scores are included in the support averages. One result of computing support scores on such a basis is that an organisation which actually loses a member exhibiting low support receives a higher support score than it would otherwise, while an organisation which succeeds in retaining the affiliation of a low-support member receives a lower score as a result. Similarly, an organisation insufficiently attractive to bring into its membership dubious states receives a higher score as a result, while an organisation which at least manages to affiliate formally a dubious, potential member receives a lower score than it would otherwise obtain. It can also be validly asserted that the important support average is not just that of members, but that of members and potential or previous members whose only reason for not belonging is that they choose not to belong. For example, the OAU was certainly no less successful in competing for the support of the Malagasy Republic, which was an OAU member with a support score of three, than was the ADB, which Malagasy chose not to join at all. Table 13.7 (derived from Table 13.5) provides comparisons of organisations' support-level averages based on scores of members and of states which fit the formal and informal objective criteria for membership, but resigned or never joined due to disagreement with and/or lack of interest in the organisation. Basically, the scores added for the averages in Table 13.7 are the scores for states which are former members of the respective

Table 13.7 Average IGO Support Level by African Members and Selected Non-members*

Rank	Organisation	Support level
1	Tripoli Charter States	1·3
2	OPEC	1·5
3	EAC†	1·7
4	Entente†	1·8
4	Maghreb†	1·8
4	OERS†	1·8
4	EEC–EAMA‡	1·8
8	African Groundnuts Council†	2·0
8	OAU†	2·0
8	OCAMM†	2·0
8	Arab League	2·0
12	ADB†	2·1
13	CECAS	2·2
13	UDEAC†	2·2
15	Commonwealth	2·3
15	'Francophonie'§	2·3
17	OAPEC	2·5
18	ECA†	2·6
18	IACO†	2·6
18	Conference of Non-aligned States	2·6
21	OCCEAC	2·7
22	Lake Chad Basin Commission†	2·8
22	Niger River Commission†	2·8
22	UDEAO†	2·8
25	West African Economic Community	2·9

* 1 = high support   2 = medium support   3 = low support
4 = hostility.

Scores of selected African non-members included in the averages for each organisation are for states which fit the formal and informal objective criteria for membership but resigned or chose not to join.

† Focus IGOs.

‡ Average includes scores of African states associated with the EEC outside of the EEC–EAMA arrangement, as well as those of EEC–EAMA members.

§ Average includes scores of all non-Arab, former French and Belgian colonies in Africa, as well as Mauritius.

organisations or were invited to join but refused acceptance. Potential members who were not members due at least in part to questions of acceptability by the incumbent members of the respective organisations are not included in those organisations' support averages.

Over all, the patterns of support evident in Table 13.6 are evident also in Table 13.7. The sub-regional organisations with socio-economic and political functions rank relatively low, and the regional, inter-regional, and particularist organisations generally occupy middle ranks. The most notable difference in the rank-orders concerns the OAU. Although in both tables the OAU ranks behind EEC–EAMA in support level, the scores in Table 13.7, in contrast to Table 13.6, place it at an even level of support with Francophone OCAMM and at a higher level of support than 'Francophonie'. 'Francophonie' has a poorer score in Table 13.7 due to the inclusion in its average of French-speaking states which decided against joining the Agency of Technical and Cultural Cooperation, created in 1970. Additionally, the ADB, which also is ranked ahead of 'Francophonie' in Table 13.7, in contrast to the rank-order of Table 13.6, shows a score in Table 13.7 lower than that of the OAU (but higher than ECA), due to inclusion of support scores for the nine African states which had not joined the ADB by the end of 1970.[22]

5. The Extent of Competition for Support

The analyses of different areas of support suggest that the form of cooperation which is most capable of achieving support from among African members involves sub-regional, linguistically homogeneous organisations which combine broad socio-economic cooperation with some political coordination as well, usually through meetings of heads of state. With regard to IGOs with broader memberships, the low support of ECA is probably partly due to lack of operational activities and the prominence that accompanies such activities. Other components of the UN in Africa conducted high-exposure operational activities, and it was anticipated that the ADB would conduct similar activities, although actual ADB operations to the end of 1970 were relatively sparse. The OAU, through its role as a forum for high-interest political issues, was provided with significant exposure, which at least partly compensated for its lack of more substantive activities.

So far, this chapter has delineated certain patterns of support for IGOs among African states. The purpose of this section is to explore the question of the extent to which the proliferation of

IGOs affects the ability of each IGO to achieve support from African states. Does, as Wallerstein suggests, commitment to many IGOs reduce commitment to each IGO? The same question was prominent in the mid-1960s in the controversy over whether or not sub-regional unity and regional (continental) unity are complementary, as Julius Nyerere argued, or conflicting, as Kwame Nkrumah believed.[23] The evidence presented in previous sections of this chapter suggests that certain forms of sub-regional unity generate greater commitment than do attempts at regional unity, but do the sub-regional schemes *cause* reduced commitment to regional organisations?

With regard to financial support, the available evidence provides no clear answer. African states contributed to a wide assortment of IGOs other than the ADB and the financially-plagued OAU, with the greatest member support being achieved by the Entente, EAC, and UDEAC. Did the revenue collected by other organisations decrease financial commitments to the ADB and OAU? The size of each government's financial resources pie at any given time was fairly fixed; an increase in the size of the slice going to any single IGO necessarily decreased, or limited, the amount of increase of the size of a slice being allocated elsewhere. The question is whether or not the slices being affected adversely by any particular IGO were the slices going to other IGOs. Would Cameroon have supported a larger OAU budget if it was not involved in UDEAC? On the basis of available evidence, the answer can only be guessed at. Cameroon and other members paid a fixed percentage of the OAU's budget, with the percentage scale, based on GNP, being seldom revised, but with the total budget being negotiated annually. It would be interesting to determine what correlation exists between votes to increase the OAU budget and other IGO commitments of states, but such information on OAU budget negotiations is not available. Similarly, the OAU keeps confidential the identity of states in arrears on assessed dues.

In my opinion, if African states had not, during 1969–70, contributed $10 017 000 to the UN system, $7 580 000 to the East African Community, $2 377 000 to the Entente, $2 335 000 to the Arab League and more to many other IGOs, they would have been rather more willing to increase the $2 956 000 allocation to the OAU, despite the fact that reluctance to support the organisation resulted from a number of other factors in addition to strictly financial considerations. The evidence presented in this study, however, offers no direct support for a conclusion, one way or the other.

With regard to personnel support, it was noted that the existence of other IGOs is unlikely to prevent an IGO from filling its staff, although competition from other IGOs could lower the quality of personnel recruited for any particular organisation. It is also possible that, in some very small states, provision of professional staff to several organisations by any given state could affect the quantity, as well as the quality, of that state's personnel support of a particular IGO. In general, however, the scarcity was in available *qualified* personnel, and available information does not permit a test of the proposition that the membership of African states in several IGO lessens the ability of some of the IGOs to obtain qualified personnel.

Summit conference attendance data provide more insight into the question of competition. EAC, OERS, UDEAC, Entente, and OCAMM all achieve a greater average amount of summit attendances per member for the 1964–70 period (Table 13.4) and had a higher percentage rate of attendance than did the OAU during the same period (Fig. 13.1). If competition from other IGOs was a factor in the relatively low OAU attendance figures, then one could expect that those heads of state involved in the more active and better-attended organisations would be less likely to attend OAU summits than would heads of state not involved in the more active organisations. As Table 13.8 (derived from Table 13.4) indicates, the twenty-one states belonging to one or more of the

Table 13.8. Per Cent Rate of Attendance by Groups at OAU Summits, 1964–70

	%
CCAMM members	43
Entente members	43
OERS members	50
EAC members	53
UDEAC members	61
21 members of one or more of above IGOs	47
20 members of none of above IGOs	57

better-attended sub-regional IGOs had a 47 per cent rate of attendance at OAU summits, while the twenty states which belonged to none of the above-named organisations had a 57 per cent rate of attendance. The evidence thus provides support for the view that the activity of sub-regional organisations does have an adverse effect on participation in, and perhaps commitment toward, OAU activities. Fuller information would indicate whether or not the participation problems which sometimes plague ministerial and lower-level meetings of the OAU and ECA are perhaps partly caused by sub-regional organisation competition, as Table 13.8 suggests is the case with summit level activity.

The final measure utilised in this chapter was the general support score, based upon the writer's evaluations. Because of the imprecise nature of the measure, conclusions deriving from its use must, of course, be highly tentative. Nevertheless, the same rationale which was applied to the attendance figures may also be applied to the support scores. If commitment is at least a partly-fixed sum for which IGOs compete, then it can be expected that the members of sub-regional IGOs receiving the most general support would be less supportive of regional IGOs than would non-members of well-supported sub-regional organisations. Were the lower scores of ADB, ECA, and OAU due to less support by states involved in relatively successful sub-regional organisations, or were the lower scores due to low support by states which were non-supportive of international organisations in general? Table 13.9 (derived from Table 13.5) provides no clear-cut answer, but it does suggest that states which are not members of well-supported sub-regional organisations are more supportive of OAU and ECA than are members of the best-supported sub-regional IGOs (see

Table 13.9. Average General Support Levels for ADB, ECA, and OAU

	ADB	ECA	OAU
Maghreb members	2·8	2·4	2·3
OCAMM members	2·1	2·6	2·3
OERS members	1·8	2·5	1·8
EAC members	1·7	2·7	1·3
Entente members	1·4	2·6	2·4
25 members of one or more of above IGOs	2·1	2·7	2·1
16 members of none of above IGOs	2·2	2·4	2·0

Table 13.6) – Maghreb, EAC, OCAMM, Entente, and OERS. However, the ADB, which least duplicates sub-regional organisation functions, is supported slightly more by members of the above-named sub-regional organisations than by non-members. Overall, the closeness of the average scores and the highly tentative nature of the data prevent any firm conclusion as to the possible adverse effect of commitment to sub-regional organisations upon support for regional, pan-African organisations.

6. Summary and Conclusion

Despite the popularity of 'pan-Africanism' as a general concept, this chapter suggests that genuine pan-African (regional) organisations, as well as other organisations cutting across Anglophone-Francophone-Arab lines, have been less successful in achieving support from among members than sub-regional, multi-purpose organisations composed of states with similar colonial backgrounds. This seems to be true of financial support, personnel support, and summit participation support, as well as 'general' support. Although this study is not conclusive about whether the proliferation of IGOs actually decreases support for individual IGOs it does suggest the possibility of such a relationship and provides some basis for the consideration of support as a good for which organisations compete. Although support cannot be viewed as a fixed amount within each state for which competition outcomes must be zero-sum, it is reasonable to regard such competition as variable-sum contests in which the support levels of any given IGO may be partly affected by the support levels of other IGOs. More research needs to be conducted on the compatibility, and/or incompatibility, of IGOs in Africa and the conditions in which international organisations on the continent can complement each other in making a favourable impact on the problems confronting African states.

Notes

Information for this chapter was derived from a doctoral dissertation study entitled *Relations among International Organizations in Africa* (Syracuse University, 1974). The chapter is based in part on information collected from a series of interviews conducted in Africa by the author during 1969–70. Notes referring to these interviews pertain to records on file with the dissertation in the Syracuse University Library, Syracuse, New York.

The author wishes to thank for financial support in the preparation of this study the International Relations Program at Syracuse University, the Center for African Studies at the University of Florida, and the Department of Political Science at the University of Florida.

1. Immanuel Wallerstein, *Africa: The Politics of Unity*, Random House, New York, 1967, p. 151.

2. Voting has sometimes been utilised as an indicator of member support of IGO activities. For example, see: John F. Clark, Michael K. O'Leary, and Eugene R. Wittkopf, 'National attributes associated with dimensions of support for the United Nations', *International Organization*, xxv, 1, Winter 1971, pp. 1–25; Hayward R. Alker, 'Supranationalism in the United Nations', *Peace Research (International) Papers*, 3, 1965, pp. 197–212; and Edward T. Rowe, *Strengthening the United Nations: a study of the member state commitments to the UN*, Sage Press, Beverly Hills, 1975. However, the lack of public records on voting positions at African IGO meetings and the common procedure of consensus decision-making make difficult the use of attitudes reflected by voting as indicators of support for African IGOs. Size of permanent delegations has been utilised as an indicator of United Nations support by: R. O. Keohane, 'Institutionalization in the United Nations General Assembly', *International Organization*, xxiii, 4, Autumn 1969, pp. 859–96; Clark, O'Leary and Wittkopf, 'National Attributes Associated with dimensions of support for the United Nations', and Rowe, *Strengthening the United Nations*. Such an indicator is not applicable to IGOs in Africa during 1946–70 because of the absence of permanent delegations accredited to African IGOs.

3. Eugene R. Wittkopf, 'A Statistical Classification of International Organizations: Preliminary Findings': Paper presented at International Studies Association Conference, Dallas, 1972.

4. See R. C. Angell, 'An analysis of trends in international organizations', *Peace Research Society (International) Papers*, 3, 1965, 186.

5. See: Mahdi Elmandjra, *The United Nations System: An Analysis*, Archon Books, Hamden, 1973, pp. 210–11; David Singer, *Financing International Organizations: the United Nations budget process*, Nijhoff, The Hague, 1961, p. 177; John Stoessinger, *Financing the United Nations System*, Brooking Institution, Washington, 1964, p. 22; and Keohan, 'Institutionalization in the United Nations General Assembly', p. 865.

6. Clark, O'Leary and Wittkopf, 'National attributes associated with dimensions of support for the United Nations'; Rowe, *Strengthening the United Nations*.

7. Because of differences in funding between development banks and other IGOs, various interpretations of Table 15.3 could be made. Subscriptions paid to development banks such as the ADB and the EADB were different in many ways from dues paid for operating expenses of organisations such as the OAU. The subscriptions, for example, could be returned to members upon withdrawal from bank participation, while withdrawal from the OAU would not bring back budget contributions for previous years. Nevertheless,

a state contributing funds to a development bank was forgoing direct use of the funds or interest income from holding them, just as it was forgoing use of funds provided to the OAU. The fact that a state may at some unknown time in the future regain use of funds contributed to a bank may make leaders less reluctant to participate, but the funds represent forgone alternative expenditures, just as did OAU contributions. The alternative expenditures were forgone, presumably, because of the perceived benefits to the collective good of the membership, in the cases of both the OAU and the development banks. In cases where benefits for the collective good were not perceived or were not highly valued, a state could have unilaterally decreased its financial participation – as was the case with such ADB members as the UAR and Dahomey, among others – or chosen not to obtain membership at all, as was the decision toward the ADB of some eligible states, including Libya and the Malagasy Republic. Figures in Table 13.3 for the ADB and EADB proportion of the EAC total represent average annual subscriptions paid, rather than just pledged, from the establishment of the banks until the end of 1970.

8. Sources for budgets include: *Africa Research Bulletin*; *Africa Contemporary Record*; *Europe Yearbook*; M. Margaret Ball, *The 'Open' Commonwealth*, Duke University press, Durham, 1971; Rowe, *Strengthening the United Nations*; and UDEAC data provided by Lynn Mytelka. Sources for GNP data include: *New York Times Encyclopedic Almanac, 1972* (for Equatorial Guinea and Swaziland); Donald George Morrison, Robert Cameron Mitchell, John Naber Paden, and Hugh Michael Stevenson, *Black Africa: a handbook for comparative analysis*, Free Press, New York, 1970 (for Botswana and Gambia); and Charles Lewis Taylor and Michael C. Hudson, *World Handbook of Political and Social Indicators*, 2nd edn, Yale University Press, New Haven, 1972 (for all others).

9. United Nations, *Report of the Advisory Committee on Staff Recruitment and Training* (UN Doc. E/CB. 14/CSRT/WP.9), United Nations, New York, 1969; African Development Bank, *Report by the Board of Directors of the African Development Bank Covering the Period from 1st January to 31st December 1967* (ADB/BG/IV/2), African Development Bank, Abidjan, 1968; Interview ECA-2, 4/7/70; Interview ECA-18, 12/11/69; Interview AD-6, 3/20/70.

10. James S. Magee, 'ECA and the paradox of African cooperation', *International Conciliation*, 580, Nov. 1970, pp. 30–2; United Nations, *Report of the Advisory Committee on Staff Recruitment and Training*, pp. 7 and 10–13; Interview ECA-17, 12/9/69; Interview ECA-18, 12/11/69; Interview ECA-19, 12/11/69; Interview AD-12, 1/6/70; Interview AD-19, 1/13/70.

11. United Nations, *Report of the Advisory Committee on Staff Recruitment and Training*, 12; Interview ECA-2, 4/7/70.

12. United Nations, *Review of the Organization and Functions of the Sub-Regional Groupings in Africa* (UN Doc. E/CN. 14/ECO/13), United Nations, New York, 1969, pp. 30–38.

13. Organisation of African Unity, *Introduction to the Report of the Administrative Secretary-General Covering the Period from September 1969 to February 1970* (CM/294, Part I), Organisation of African Unity, Addis Ababa, 1970.

14. J. Woronoff, *Organizing African Unity*, Scarecrow Press, Metuchen, N.J., 1970, pp. 188–92; Interview ECA-11, 12/16/69; Interview AD-9, 4/10/70; Interview AD-14, 4/15/70; Interview AD-17, 12/29/69; Interview AD-24, 1/9/70; Interview ND-9, 4/8/70.

15. Interview ECA-2, 4/7/70.

16. According to unpublished information supplied by their secretariats, the EAC headquarters in Arusha employed, in 1970, 37 Africans in professional-level posts, the EADB in Kampala employed about an additional 20, and OCAMM employed 18 Africans in professional-level positions. UDEAC, according to information supplied by Lynn Mytelka, had 47 upper-level employees, but the proportion of that 47 which is expatriate is not known.

17. Support on this point is provided by W. Scott Thompson and Richard Bissell, 'Legitimacy and authority in the OAU', *African Studies Review*, xv, 1, April 1972, p. 28; Woronoff, *Organizing African Unity*, p. 162; Magee, 'ECA and the paradox of African cooperation', p. 13; Interview OAU-34, 2/18/70; and Interview ND-1, 3/23/70. The problem of non-attendance at OAU meetings due to multiple IGO commitments of African government officials is also noted by Berhanykun Andemicael, 'UN-OAU Relations in the Economic and Social Field', paper presented at Sixteenth Annual Meeting of the African Studies Association, Syracuse, N.Y., 1973, p. 22.

18. (a) *African Research Bulletin*, (b) *Keasing's Contemporary Archives*, (c) *African Recorder*, (d) *New York Times*.

19. The tendency of IGO officials to appeal to member states for support when disputes arise over 'boundary' questions (overlapping jurisdictional areas) is noted by Robert W. Cox and Harold K. Jacobson, *The Anatomy of Influence: Decision Making in International Organization*, Yale University Press, New Haven, 1973, p. 385. The previous relative success of an IGO in the quest for general support can determine its success or failure in subsequent 'boundary' dispute outcomes.

20. (a) *African Research Bulletin*, (b) Interviews, (c) Secondary sources.

21. An additional issue which can be partly analysed on the basis of Table 13.6 is the question of French and British influence on the African unity movement in general. A number of observers allege that a major impediment to African regional unity is the competition from influence arrangements of France and Britain, pulling African states away from each other and toward their former colonial masters. This view is found, for example, in: Vincent Bakpetu Thompson, *Africa and Unity: The Evolution of Pan-Africanism*, Longman, London, and Humanities Press, New York, 1969, p. 295; R. H. Green and Ann Seidman, *Unity or Poverty? The Economics of Pan-Africanism*, Penguin Books, Baltimore, 1968, pp. 169–70; Interview ECA-10, 12/11/69; Interview ECA-13, 12/16/69; Interview AD-14, 4/15/70; Interview AD-15, 2/17/70; Interview AD-19, 3/19/70; and Interview OAU-34, 2/18/70. Table 13.6 offers some interesting evidence. The major organisational instrument of British influence in Africa, the Commonwealth, ranks ahead of the regional ECA in member support level, but behind the OAU and ADB. In contrast, 'Francophonie', OCAMM, and EEC–EAMA, which are all sometimes alleged to be instruments of French influence in Africa, rank higher

than their regional rivals for support among African states, ADB, OAU, and ECA. Francophone-centred organisations clearly have higher levels of support among their African members than do the three organisations comprised of all, or nearly all, African states.

22. Also noteworthy about Table 13.7 is the fact that the Commonwealth is ranked even with 'Francophonie' (although considerably behind EEC–EAMA and OCAMM), suggesting that although French ties with states that choose to retain close relationships with France are stronger than British ties with its former colonies in Africa that remain in the Commonwealth, the average, overall support level for institutional ties with the former colonial ruler among all former colonies is not significantly different between former colonies of France and those of Britain.

23. See: A. Mohiddin, 'Nyerere and Nkrumah on African unity', in University of East Africa Social Sciences Council Conferences 1968–69, *Political Science Papers*, Makerere Institute of Social Research, Kampala, 1969, pp. 200–11; Julius K. Nyerere, *Freedom and Unity*, Oxford University Press, Dar es Salaam, 1966, pp. 193–94; and Woronoff, *Organizing African Unity*, pp. 150–1 and 162–7.

Timothy M. Shaw

14 The Actors in African International Politics

The study of Africa's international politics has, over time, neglected both non-state actors and the development of the continental system. This chapter presents tentative typologies both of continental systems and actors as a contribution to remedying this neglect and to advance understanding of the dependence of African states.

In the mixed-actor systems[1] of Africa different types of actors have been dominant in various historical periods: in pre-colonial Africa nation-states were the primary actors; in the colonial period empires and foreign traders were dominant; the contemporary continental system is characterised by a rich variety of actors – African and non-African states, regional, continental, international and transnational organisations, African and global multinational corporations. An overview of developments in the structure and processes of the African international system over time is presented in this chapter. It concludes with a futuristic view of the emerging balance of power in Africa.

Although the Organisation of African Unity (OAU) celebrated its first decade in 1973, the African state system has existed for centuries rather than for decades. This chapter attempts to describe and explain contemporary African international relations by giving appropriate attention both to pre-colonial inter-state politics and to the impact of non-state actors. The approach is based on the premise that we cannot understand the development of the African system without the insights of oral history and political economy over time[2]; a multidisciplinary analysis should improve our explanations and predictions.[3]

1. Discontinuities and Continuities in the African International System[4]

The African international system has exhibited both change and stability over time. Its transformation has involved an evolution of its structure, processes and norms. As its component units have developed from traditional kingdoms into contemporary states so their inter-relations have changed; new rules have been devised to regulate relations. Because of the multiplicity and characteristics of African states the African inter-state system has been subsystem-dominant; its pattern of behaviour has been largely determined by national actors rather than by supranational institutions, except during the interlude of the imperial European order. However, although the OAU is clearly subordinate to the interests of its membership and so perpetuates this subsystemic dominance, over time the African international system has come to exhibit less dominance by national subsystems. Relations between traditional African nations were historically direct, limited and bilateral. In the colonial period (which is increasingly regarded as an interregnum) relations became more formal, extensive and multilateral. The present system is characterised by the emergence of new continental actors, such as the OAU, the Economic Commission for Africa (ECA) and a myriad of regional and transnational organisations, which have accelerated the trend towards multiple and frequent interactions. The growth of the influence and autonomy of these non-state institutions, with their potential for supranational action, has increased the complexity and interdependence of the African international system.

The analysis of regional subsystems and regional integration is one area of exciting theoretical and empirical discovery in the field of international politics. However, one of its deficiencies is its characteristic ahistorical approach. Zartman has suggested that an autonomous, subordinate African system exists.[5] We support this finding but suggest that identifiable sets of systems have existed for centuries.

However, Africa's subordination is recent in historical time. Until the protracted intrusion of traders, slavers, missionaries and administrators in the nineteenth century it was a continent of regional empires and clusters of state systems which were independent both of each other and of extra-African actors. The imperial era was the time of greatest dependence. The continent is now characterised by varying degrees of dependence according to national ideology and resources and the issue area of inter-action. This distinction between formal African independence and its real dependence or interdependence makes Africa's assertion of autonomy problematic.[6] Its geographic identity and its inter-state organisations give it a structure but it is still in the process of recovering the autonomy that was lost during the scramble for Africa. However, if we define the autonomy of a system in terms of change at one point leading to change in others, and in terms of the predominance of intrasystemic rela-tions over extraregional linkages, then Africa now has a greater potential for autonomy and control than at any time since its irregular early contacts with extra-African economies and reli-gions.

In pre-colonial times, Africa was a set of related regional subsystems; communications, technology and the scale of politics limited continental contacts except through the intermediaries of traders and religions. Now Africa has the potential to become a complex, multilateral international system. The system may be largely subordinate and dependent but it is now capable of self-transformation to reduce these inherited structures. In particular, strategies of regional integration in a pan-African context offer prospects of more self-reliant development.[7]

Our analysis supports Amin's periodisation of African history. He indicates that the era of formal colonisation was preceded by pre-mercantilist (up to the seventeenth century), mercantilist (seventeenth to nineteenth centuries) and preparatory (nineteenth century) periods.[8] These changes are reflected in the development of the structure and process of the African inter-national system. In the pre-mercantilist centuries, African politics were largely autonomous, although influenced at times by Islamic evangelism and European and Oriental capitalism. In the mercantilist decades, African politics were increasingly related to extra-continental developments, especially slavery, guns and exchange. In the preparatory century, European adventurers, traders and missionaries played an increasingly active and authoritative part in the making of African foreign policies. In the post-colonial era inherited structures which were permissive towards international capitalism began to be replaced.

The contemporary African system is increasingly non- or semi-capitalist and may be seen as a revival of the non-capitalist pre-colonial system. Strategies of state capitalism/socialism have transformed simple ties of dependence and have enhanced Africa's autonomy and identity. Colonial trading patterns and communications links are being replaced by more 'horizontal' African and Third-World structures, reviving some trans-Saharan and Indian Ocean pre-colonial relations. The African infrastructure of roads, railways, air routes and telecom-munications is now being developed to serve pan-African rather than Eur-African interests.

The development of states and international politics are inter-related in Africa; state structures were formalised in response to social conflict and external threat. Distinctive forms of class conflict predated colonialism in Africa and caused the develop-ment of states. Paradoxically, colonialism accentuated emergent class differences but created those classes which were to destroy it. Nevertheless, the ambitions of these groups also made a neo-colonial 'solution' possible because dependence on international capitalism and organisations would advance their interests and enable them to become the bureaucratic and entrepreneurial elites.[9] We need to adopt a critical linkage politics framework to explain the development of classes and states in Africa.[10] Africa's underdevelopment created significant, if limited, prospects for some indigenous groups. The adaptiveness of African regimes and groups to external threats and opportunities is an important continuity in the development of the African system.[11]

The new states of Africa exhibit different degrees of continuity and discontinuity with their historical antecedents. This chapter indicates some of the insights and problems of the 'discontinuities model' for the study of African international politics. Dis-continuities are both analytic and perceived. African leaders claim legitimacy and ideals from pre-colonial societies and myths; they selectively discard or ignore some historical precedents or analo-gies. We are interested in beginning to distinguish among such traditions.

Strategies of confrontation and collaboration in Africa have evolved over time to incorporate new technologies and ideologies; African military structures, for instance, have been and are related to the imperatives of expansionism and control.[12] African

leaders may use pre-colonial structures to legitimise contemporary policies; the 'golden age' of pre-colonial democracy and
tranquility serves to justify both one-party systems and informal
inter-elite support. The selective revival of African empires,
values and symbols reinforces the tenuous control of new regimes
on the continent. But reference to pre-colonial nations differs
between states.[13]

Increases in the scale of both pre-colonial and colonial
administration led to a decrease in the number of national actors
in Africa, as shown in Figure 14.1.[14] Post-colonial Africa contains
more national and multinational actors. Nationalism in Africa is
largely synthetic and anti-colonial. The creation and manipulation of new 'national' symbols is one strategy for creating
integration and preventing secession. Ethnic politics, or sub-
nationalism,[15] have their origins in arbitrary colonial boundaries
and the unwillingness of the new elites to redraw Africa's
inherited boundaries; they are incompatible with the enlarged
scale of African administration and problems. An extremely fluid
international system characterised by migrations, fragmentation,
incorporation, exchange and war, was prematurely ended by
colonial rule.

The rediscovery of African international history supports the
trend in African historiography towards oral as well as documentary sources and to a more balanced perspective on the transitory
nature of formal colonial rule.[16] African states and factions have
been able to exploit their ties with a variety of extra-African
powers over time, largely to enhance their prospects in bargaining
and competition with other African nations. Perhaps we should
be cautious in critically analysing contemporary African strategies
of collaboration with more affluent states and interests without
recognising their historical precedents. African diplomacy reveals
a continuing ability to reduce the impact of international
stratification and dependence over the course of time.

The scramble for Africa, which upset the pattern of informal
empire and coalition, was caused by a disturbance in the balance
of power in Europe rather than by the failure of African
diplomacy. Although Africa was not a central issue in the global
balance of power between the early 1900s and the rise of nationalism in the 1950s,[17] Africa's contemporary membership in global
organisations guarantees continued participation and visibility for

it in the international system. Bargaining by African states occurs now in the United Nations,[18] the Commonwealth, Francophonie and the non-aligned forums rather than in distant courts.

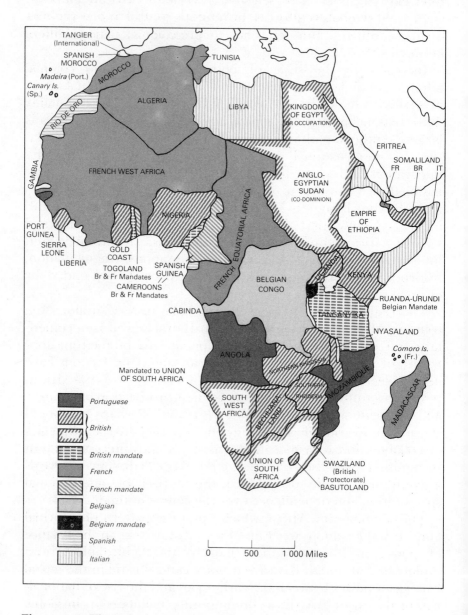

Figure 14.1. The Colonial System in Africa, 1924

2. Pre-colonial Africa: Intergovernmental Regional Subsystems

The international relations of traditional African nations were largely intergovernmental, although their scope was typically regional due to the primitive state of communications. The pattern of relations largely corresponded to Kaiser's model of an 'intergovernmental regional subsystem' in which 'the relations between national systems are handled and decided upon by elites located in governmental institutions'.[19] The scope of relations and the number of issue areas both increased over time as African societies became large and more complex. In the first millennium, African nation-states 'exchanged diplomatists and envoys, formed alliances either for attack or for defence, and carried on their external relations in much the same way as their European counterparts did about the same period'.[20]

The incidence of external trade opportunities is related to the development of two important international subsystems in the first millennium – Ghana in the sixth and seventh centuries and the Swahili city-states of the ninth century, the latter sharing unity of language, trade patterns, and a common faith in Islam.[21] Like the Chinese states and the Greek city-states in the fifth century B.C., there was no interaction between regional African systems at this time. Power was extremely diffuse.[22]

The growth of trans-Saharan, Atlantic and Indian Ocean trade in the second millennium produced political change in Africa. Trans-Saharan trade was in state necessities (gold and slaves to the north in exchange for cowries, salt and weapons) and luxuries (pepper, ivory and leather to the north in exchange for textiles, glassware and fancy goods). External trade produced a string of entrepots and a set of expatriate entrepreneurs. The development and articulation of economic interests dependent on imperialism promoted the expansion of European power. 'Interdependence was the basis of mercantilism: the power of the state was increased by measures designed to achieve a favourable balance of trade; at the same time particular interest groups sought to use state power as a means to private gain'.[23] Imperialism was advanced by the compatibility of interests between external groups in the metropole and domestic groups. Slavery may have been initiated and advanced by European plantations but it also depended on cooperative African leaders.[24]

European penetration initially required the cooperation of established entrepreneurial groups. These were later subordinated and were significant casualties of underdevelopment, but in the nineteenth century their contacts and skills were essential to European profitability.[25] The scale of traditional administration in Africa was enlarged to exploit the opportunities of long-distance trade. Regional empires arose based on conquest and/or incorporation. Disparate tribes were integrated into more defensible and profitable states. 'Nation-building' is not merely a mid-twentieth century phenomenon in Africa. However, extensive tributary relations and dependence on a monopoly of external trade both offered prospects and problems for a new generation of leaders. Middlemen were able to bypass imperial control and advance the fragmentation of empires. Yet, in the new environment, rejection of international trade was likely to lead to a coup.[26]

During the second millennium a set of substantial kingdoms rose, and in some cases fell, before colonial rule took over and momentarily stabilised the current balance of power. The succession of states included Ghana, Mali, Songhay and Bornu, the Guinea kingdoms and later the Fulani, Bunyoro, Baganda,[27] Lozi, Zulu, Ndebele and Ngoni. The surviving major African empires, along with European settlements, on the eve of partition are shown in Figure 14.2.[28] In response to the opportunities and threats of their changing environment, African states became more centralised and hierarchical. Modest structures of authority became complex political, military and economic systems.

Hopkins suggests that pre-colonial trade and manufacturing in West Africa allowed a small leisure class resources to develop their cultures.[29] Islam provided the necessary rules and structure for the conduct of trade, and traders were accorded an appropriate status. The network of long-distance trade routes thus gave West Africa a tenuous economic unity, linking and partially integrating different geographical zones and ethnic groupings, and crossing many state boundaries.[30] However, there were limitations to the development of a 'national' West African economy. The unity achieved through long-distance commerce was incomplete because the trade itself was restricted in volume and because its principal effects were felt by a minority of the total population. Despite the existence of regional currencies and capital markets pre-colonial Africa was not advancing towards industrialisation because of its under-

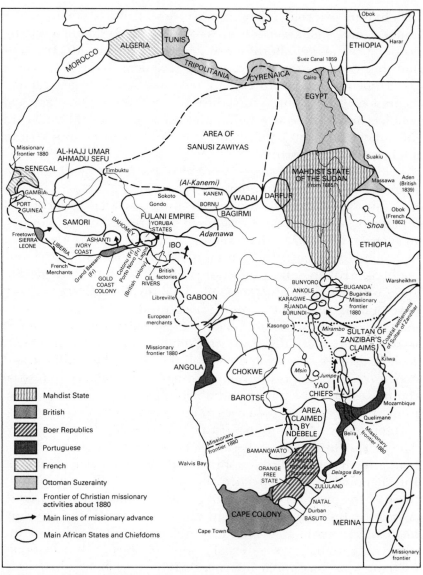

Figure 14.2. Map of African States on Eve of Colonial Partition

population and primitive transport technology. International trade was no 'engine of growth in West Africa'.[31]

The survival of a leader depended on his control over trade and tribute. The king had to control his warriors to both protect overland trade and to maintain the flow of taxes. In the second millennium external relations were essentially regional in the political and military issue areas and extra-continental in the economic issue area. Both sets of ties were controlled by the king and his court, although economic relations were less inter-governmental in structure than regional ties. Western capital, technology and values introduced new issues into factional conflicts in African courts although the more successful leaders in the nineteenth century remained ambivalent over non-African intentions and opportunities.[32]

Regional political relations were also developed by diplomacy. Boahen has drawn attention to the evidence of early trans-Saharan diplomatic relations. He suggests that pre-colonial diplomatic relations were organised by professional diplomats, such as the *Okyeame* of the Akan of Ghana: he was the equivalent of a modern Ministry of Foreign Affairs who also had inter-national privileges and protection and entered into strategic alli-ances with neighbouring states.[33] Ukpabi further suggests that the development of African empires also produced an evolution in military structures and strategies. Territorial armies, or *levées en masse*, were superseded by increasingly professional armies as state structures became more institutionalised, hierarchical and expansive.[34] Kingdoms developed their own 'military-industrial complexes' of blacksmiths and shield-makers, and came to use women, slaves and mercenaries as recruits as well as warriors.

International relations in Africa have essentially been inter-city. The urban-rural gap in Africa has its origins in the prospects for both growth and underdevelopment offered by external relations. International politics advance the interests of the elite, rarely those of the peasantry. Although certain inequalities appeared in African states before the advent of external trade, the develop-ment of classes was advanced by the institutionalisation of the state in response to external 'opportunities'.[35] International exchange produced new internal divisions of labour in Africa.[36]

Increased contact with international capitalism magnified domestic conflicts and advanced the interests of colonial powers concerned with efficient administration.[37] The formation of classes in Africa, a process which has accelerated with the oppor-tunities of independence, remains one of Africa's major problems. As we suggest in section 5 there is a relationship between domestic and international inequalities. Few African states have successfully attempted to revert to the pre-colonial policies of self-reliance.

Collaboration by Africans with external interests is a continuing issue for African leaders and critics. We cannot understand the impact of colonialism without an analysis of African responses to the opportunities and dangers of collaboration[38]; collaboration with external interests either reinforced or undermined the power of a ruler. The new African historiography has over-reacted to the neglect of African initiatives and voices by over-looking colonial influence; as Palmer suggests, outlawing the term does not make the phenomenon go away.[39] The Dar school of historiography prefers to ignore the central role of collaborators whereas the Dar approach to class formation in contemporary Africa attaches special importance to intermediary 'comprador' groups whose status is dependent on links with external finance.[40] Linkage politics focus on such continuities and discontinuities in Africa.

The dilemmas of external exchange also led to political change in the early Chinese and Greek systems. The Chou dynasts, like African kings, were unable to prevent the redirection of trade away from their central control. In the era of diffuse sybsystems,[41] African international politics were essentially concerned with war and diplomacy although extra-African relations began to generate structural changes.

So pre-colonial Africa was characterised by a diffuse, flexible balance of power between states or alliances of relatively equal power. But as Okoye notes, the pre-colonial 'international personality' of African states had not been recognised, at least until the present period of revisionist history.

> Admittedly these states were far more backward and primi-tive than fledgling European states that formed the centre of the international community. They lacked the capacity to exert serious diplomatic pressure or to engage in inter-national arbitration . . . however . . . African communities and states have for ages had contacts with the countries of Europe and Asia, and also frequently entered into relations among themselves which were generally regulated by commonly accepted usages and certain customary rules of international law. Treaties and agreements were entered into and meant to

be kept . . . international personality could not be denied to
the native states of that period.[42]

Holsti suggests, though, that over time all diffuse international
systems have been transformed into more polar-type structures.[43]
This generalisation is accurate for Africa, which evolved into an
artificial bipolar colonial system and is now developing into an
indigenous, multipolar continental system.

3. Colonial Africa: Transnational Imperial Subsystems

African nationalism rejected imperial rule; the success of pan-
African demands for independence makes the era of imperialism
one of illegitimate control by external regimes. The actors during
this interregnum were both foreign and unrepresentative. The
colonial period is, therefore, a deviant form of transnational
societal subsystem in which 'relations between national systems
are handled and decided upon by nongovernmental elites'.[44]
African relations were conducted by imperial administrations
supported by African collaborators and corporate interests. For a
time, the locus of African inter-colonial politics was Europe rather
than Africa. Most old regimes were not recognised actors in the
new imperial structures.[45] The development of African international relations was interrupted for half a century.

However, it is important to note the skill with which some
African leaders manipulated colonial and even settler interests,
particularly in southern Africa where the politics of white tribalism diverted imperial attention.[46] Eventually, though, as in the
development of the diffuse Greek city-state system, economic and
military redistribution led to bipolarity.[47] The rise of white power
in southern Africa created opportunities as well as conflicts for
the black states. Brown has commented that the confrontation
between Shaka and the Boers 'did not so much create internationl
relations in southern Africa as dramatically increase their scale
and intensity'.[48] We can neither understand African reaction to
the Bantustan scheme without considering diverse African
responses to the trek, nor can we comprehend the rejection of
'national' homelands without reference to the 'multi-tribal' states
of southern Africa which had developed before the white
intrusion.

Southern Africa displays two alternative modes of nation-building – the revolutionary and militaristic Zulu Mfecane form and the defensive strategies of the Swazis under Sobhuza and the Basuto under Moshweshwe. But both the latter nations lost territory to white farmers although their military positions enabled them to resist total defeat. The new white frontier was not always a threat to African states; for instance, the Zulu under Dingane attacked the Ndebele after a successful Boer raid. Although in pre-colonial times technological change was largely disadvantageous to the Africans, contemporary guerrilla tactics may reverse the imbalance. The Ndebele could not resist the settlers: 'The discovery of the Maxim gun had made the Ndebele fighting methods, so carefully perfected, hopelessly anachronistic.'[49] The guerrilla struggle of the liberation movement shows signs of reversing this strategic handicap,[50] and revising the memories of the Ndebele golden age under Mzilikazi.

White penetration into southern Africa generated an additional factor in the Ndebele's continuing battles; it was not resisted in any consistent or collective manner.[51] The great trek moved into the deserted gaps between divided African states whose pre-occupation was with the threat from the Ndebele and the Zulu rather than with the movements of the Boers, British and Portuguese. The resultant chequerboard pattern of population and political control was 'the result not of the action of white force on passive material but of a complex reaction between settler and Bantu societies. It was as much the work of Shaka and Mosheshe as of Pretorius and Retief'.[52] The traditions of the Mfecane are a rather neglected part of the basis of diverse African responses to white rule:

> The (black) leadership in Southern Africa differed in emphasis from African leaders north of the Zambezi river. They operated in the tradition of Moshoeshoe rather than Shaka, but more important they operated entirely within the legal and ideological limits established by the white community.[53]

The new black states in and around southern Africa from Zambia and Mozambique to the Transkei and Swaziland have begun to take advantage of the new balance of power and have ended the era of hopelessness in the region. Even before the discovery and extraction of Botswana's vast mineral reserves, President Khama drew attention to the historical continuities of his country's foreign policy and the regional scale of its international relations:

> the determination of the Batswana to preserve their independence is a continuous theme in our history since before the colonial period. Even in the nineteenth century before the establishment of the British protectorate our people recognised whence the real and long-term threat to their independence would come . . . we are determined to convert the almost total dependence of the colonial period into a dignified pattern of interdependence.[54]

Yet continental underdevelopment was the primary structural characteristic inherited by Africa after the colonial era.

4. Post-Colonial Africa: Towards a Comprehensive Continental Subsystem

Africa's recapture of its structures led to a revival of pre-colonial values and patterns of interaction as well as to novel forms of interstate interdependence. Traditional African empires were preoccupied with territory and sovereignty; the contemporary African system is also concerned with ideology and growth. African governments have reasserted themselves as the primary international actors on the continent. Informal trading relations and military alliances have been transformed into a rich variety of continental, regional and bilateral organisations covering the whole spectrum of issue areas. The diversity of political and functional institutions, inter-governmental and transnational relations, offer the prospect of a comprehensive continental subsystem eventually.[55] African unity is being advanced by a myriad African organisations, most of which are compatible and reinforcing.

Africa's economic dependence is a check on its political independence.[56] Although this dependence may be modified by state capitalism/socialism, regional and/or continental economic cooperation and autonomy are prerequisites for meaningful political control. As indicated in Table 14.1, Africa's continuing economic dependence limits continental and regional inter-dependencies in all other issue areas. Regional integration is only a partial solution while Africa as a whole remains part of the western economic system. An analysis of the political economy of regionalism reveals the main advocates and beneficiaries to be multinational corporations and local political and administrative elites.[57] While new continental and regional organisations may duplicate extra-continental and global structures at present, in time they may make inherited relations superfluous.

Table 14.1. Issue Areas, Mode and Scope of African Interactions

Issue area	Mode	Scope of interactions
Economic	Dependence	Regional and extra-continental
Political	Interdependence	Continental and extra-continental
Military	Interdependence	Regional and extra-continental
Societal	Interdependence	Regional and continental

However, economic integration does not necessarily involve disengagement from imperialism; indeed, among the leading advocates and supporters of regional integration are the US, Britain and France. To make integration compatible with dis-engagement, regional consumption must be satisfied by regional production. Regional planning for industrialisation and socialism are essential:[58]

Unless regional integration is firmly based on a new kind of political commitment to greater self-reliance and dis-engagement from international capitalism, it may not be a very substantial vehicle for economic development. Nor will it promote the objectives of development if the disengagement is not accompanied by very active and positive measures to undertake regional planning of production and demand.[59]

Africa's continuing economic dependence limits the develop-ment of inter-dependencies in the continent.[60] It perpetuates Eur-African ties, now symbolised by the spread of associate EEC status to most members of the OAU along with the continuance of ties within the French Community and the Commonwealth, and limits Africa's socio-political development. Moreover, military and economic ties with extra-African powers, including new links with rich Arab and Islamic states, have increased interstate inequalities in Africa. The feudal international system rewards compliant African states and condemns antagonistic regimes to an insignificant status within the world's peripheries.[61]

The international hierarchy is becoming more complex and fragmented as bipolarity is eroded. In a feudal international system

> Each of these rich metropolises dominates a poor area of the world as colonies or neo-colonies. The resulting picture is rather like an octopus, the head being the rich metropolis and the tentacles representing the ability of the metropolis to suck surplus out of the poor nations. Each tentacle is known as a 'sphere of influence'.[62]

However, within each 'tentacle' there may be limited prospects for upward mobility. In Africa there is a trend towards inequality based both on national power and on international association, as we indicate in the final section of this chapter. In a continental system characterised by growing inequalities the relatively equal distribution of power, similar to that of China, Greece and Renaissance Italy at certain periods, is unstable. The balance of power in Africa, characterised by shifting alliances of the pre-OAU era, is giving way to continental stratification and to a mixed-actor system.

The fallacy of 'indirect rule' has increased Africa's awareness of its vulnerability to 'informal penetration', especially to the activities of western economic interests. However, continued inter-state disagreements in Africa make strategic alliances with external actors still attractive. African statesmen have rarely benefited from unequal associations and the continued tolerance of transnational organisations undermines African authority and sovereignty. The Africanisation of certain transnational relations and the adoption of state capitalism/socialism is only a partial form of 'multinational regulation'. Nevertheless, we must recognise the new heterogeneity of actors in the African international system and complement the analysis of continental 'high politics' with attention to routine relations in other issue areas.

5. Actors in the African International System

The dominant and primary actors in Africa remain African states. However, one important discontinuity is the multiplication of actor types in the contemporary system. This evolution in the structure of the African system has produced new patterns of relations and new loyalties. Trading companies have been super-seded by multinational corporations; colonial continental institu-tions have been replaced by the OAU system; and a whole new set of African organisations has been established to service the functional and political needs of member states. The imperatives of nationalism now coexist with a variety of non-state actors which are accepted as legitimate participants in African international and national affairs. However, the trend towards multinational politics in Africa should be distinguished from the growth of interdependence in the Atlantic Community.[63] International relations in Africa are still dominated by intergovernmental poli-tics. Nevertheless, the plurality of inter-state and transnational organisations makes possible a transition towards a more complex comprehensive structure.

Associated with the process of development and the rise of multinational actors is the growing complexity of national struc-tures. The post-independence era in particular has been charac-terised by a proliferation of state organisations concerned with external relations – parastatal bodies, ministries of planning and development, a variety of military institutions – as well as the characteristic offices of the president and foreign affairs.[64] The colonial powers initiated the development of continental functional organisations, such as the Commission for Technical Cooperation in Africa.[65] However, the explosion of continental and regional organisations is essentially a post-independence phenomenon.

Integration in Francophone, east and southern Africa was advanced before independence. But in the 1960s multiple attempts were made to form ideological, political or economic groupings and to widen the impact of established organisations. The transitional era of a plurality of ideological groups – the Monrovia, Casablanca and Brazzaville 'blocks'[66] – has been superseded by a decade characterised by the increasing organisa-tional pre-eminence of the OAU as the exclusive continental

Table 14.2. Membership of Regional Organisations in Africa

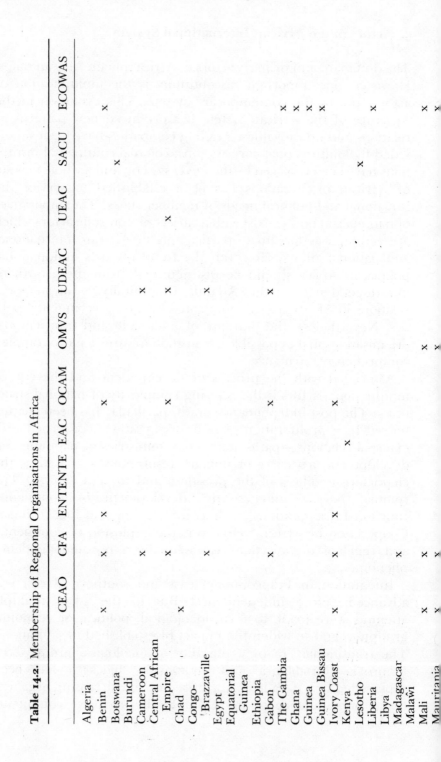

	CEAO	CFA	ENTENTE	EAC	OCAM	OMVS	UDEAC	UEAC	SACU	ECOWAS
Algeria										
Benin		x	x		x					x
Botswana									x	
Burundi										
Cameroon		x					x			
Central African Empire		x			x		x	x		
Chad		x								
Congo-Brazzaville		x					x			
Egypt										
Equatorial Guinea										
Ethiopia										
Gabon		x			x		x			
The Gambia										x
Ghana										x
Guinea										x
Guinea Bissau										x
Ivory Coast	x	x	x		x					x
Kenya				x						
Lesotho									x	
Liberia										x
Libya										
Madagascar										
Malawi										
Mali	x					x				x
Mauritania	x					x				x

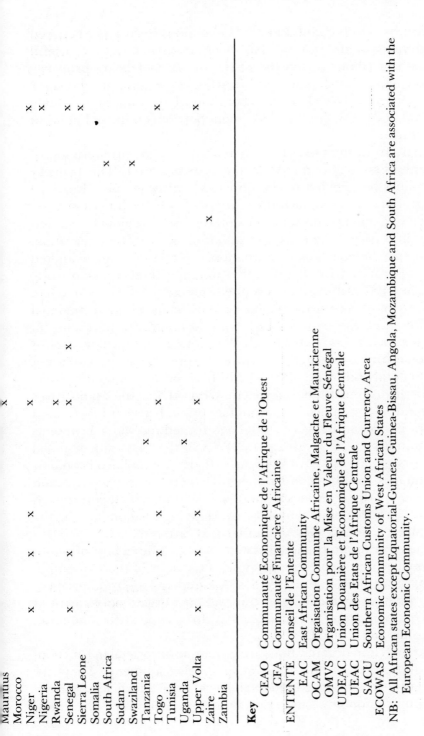

Mauritius
Morocco
Niger
Nigeria
Rwanda
Senegal
Sierra Leone
Somalia
South Africa
Sudan
Swaziland
Tanzania
Togo
Tunisia
Uganda
Upper Volta
Zaire
Zambia

Key

CEAO	Communauté Economique de l'Afrique de l'Ouest
CFA	Communauté Financière Africaine
ENTENTE	Conseil de l'Entente
EAC	East African Community
OCAM	Orgaisation Commune Africaine, Malgache et Mauricienne
OMVS	Organisation pour la Mise en Valeur du Fleuve Sénégal
UDEAC	Union Douanière et Economique de l'Afrique Centrale
UEAC	Union des Etats de l'Afrique Centrale
SACU	Southern African Customs Union and Currency Area
ECOWAS	Economic Community of West African States

NB: All African states except Equatorial-Guinea, Guinea-Bissau, Angola, Mozambique and South Africa are associated with the European Economic Community.

African political organisation.[67] The tenuous coexistence between 'moderates' and 'radicals' has been translated into a useful division of labour within the OAU, the former being primarily concerned with mediation and functional cooperation, the latter group more involved in the liberation of the continent.[68] Only OCAM detracts from the OAU monopoly of continental political structures.

Apart from the OAU/ECA system, the major proliferation of organisations has occurred at the regional level. The primacy of politics has yielded to the imperative of economics. Regional integration is a characteristic reponse to an inheritance of poverty. Table 14.2 presents data on the rise of regional organisations in Africa. These exhibit different degrees of integration, from specific functional organisations (OMVS)[67] and a limited free trade area (CEAO), through common markets which provide for some redistribution of revenue (Entente, UDEAC, SACU), to Africa's most advanced region (EAC). Many of these regional organisations have developed from colonial arrangements in former British East and French West Africa and include a set of regional functional agencies. More recently, however, a series of multilateral and bilateral structures have been proposed to overcome this colonial inheritance. In West Africa, the Mano River Declaration announced an economic union between Liberia and Sierra Leone, and Nigeria and Togo forged the wider Economic Community of West Africa (ECOWAS), the first trans-regional grouping in West Africa. Clearly there are politico-economic advantages for the leading states of Ivory Coast, Senegal and Nigeria in these proposals and we may anticipate protracted rounds of bargaining before the overlapping relations among the Entente, CEAO, ECOWAS and UDEAC are resolved.

The African international system now includes a host of multinational actors; Table 14.3 proposes a typology of these organisations, using the dimensions of scope and function as variables. Both intergovernmental and transnational organisations exist at the continental and regional level in three issue areas – political, economic and societal.[70]

Most African organisations are economic or societal in function, one indication of the imperative of development. They are concentrated at the continental level, thus advancing African identity, autonomy and development. However, the most important organisations in terms of both development and integration are continental political organisations and regional economic communities. So, although there are some thirty continental economic institutions and over seventy continental societal associations, the most influential are the four continuing common markets and their associated regional organisations.[71] The impact on behaviour and structure within a subsystem of a regional economic organisation like the EAC or UDEAC is much greater than the limited function of a continental societal institution, such as the All-African Conference of Churches, the Supreme Council for Sport in Africa, or the Association of African Universities.

Table 14.3. A Typology of Multinational Organisations in Africa[72]

Scope	Function	Examples of organisations
Continental	Political	OAU
Continental	Economic	ECA
Continental	Societal	All Africa Games
Continental	Transnational	All African Conference of Churches
Regional	Political	OCAM
Regional	Economic	Entente
Regional	Societal	East African Literature Bureau
Regional	Transnational (P)	Mulungushi Club
Regional	Transnational (E)	Anglo-American Corporation
Regional	Transnational (S)	West African Science Association
Bilateral	Economic	Tanzania–Zambia Railway Authority

Our findings, using African data, are thus generally supportive of Nye's hypotheses about the relatedness of scope of the regional grouping to the primary functional issue area:

> ... military security organisations tend to be of the low contiguity macro-regional type and quasi-regional in membership. Political organisations seem to be divided between macro- and micro-regions, but tend to be regional rather than quasi-regional. ... Economic organisations involved in promoting high levels of trade integration or common services among their members tend to be 'micro-regional', with high geographical contiguity.[73]

We use the terms 'continental' and 'regional' instead of Nye's more rigorously defined categories of 'macro-regional' and 'micro-regional' respectively.[74] It is noticeable in Table 14.2 that military cooperation does not occur at either level, an indication of the limited symbolic and territorial roles played by African armies. Finally, close bilateral relations between Tanzania and Zambia are a notable exception to the characteristically multi-lateral patterns of cooperation in Africa.

This tentative typology is not exhaustive because of the novelty and fluidity of African international structures. The OAU system includes its commissions and the Liberation Committee, which is both intergovernmental and transnational in membership and operations; the Committee extends recognition, assistance and services to the liberation groups. The movements have trans-national ties among themselves, notably within the 'Khartoum alliance' and CONCP. The ECA system includes regional offices, the African Institute for Economic Development and Planning and the African Development Bank and Fund; it is the 'African' part of the UN system and has close relations with international agencies such as UNDP and IBRD. Other continental functional agencies include the Association of African Airways and the Inter-African Coffee Organisation; these are characteristically composed of national institutions controlled by each government.

The demise of regional political organisations, because of their potential incompatibility with the OAU, means that the only other remaining grouping in this category is the Conference of Heads of State of East and Central Africa, with its core in the 'Mulungushi Club' of the parties of eastern Africa – TANU–UNIP–FRELIMO–BDC–MPC. This constitutes the modest successor institution to the Pan-African Freedom Movement for East, Central, and Southern Africa (PAFMECSA) which disbanded after the formation of the OAU in 1963. It operates as a ginger group within the OAU and originates proposals, such as the 1969 Lusaka Manifesto and the 1975 Dar es Salaam Declaration. It has a more modest structure and goal than OCAM, is more compatible with the OAU and has served as the basis for the grouping of front-line states in Southern Africa.

The growth of the number and complexity of actors in the African international system suggests the gradual and relative demise of the state in Africa despite the imperatives of national-ism. The state-centric view is increasingly inaccurate and inappropriate as regional and functional cooperation and inter-dependencies erode even the tenuous sovereignty of the new states. Nationalism must now confront multinationalism rather than colonialism. Africa has evolved from a uni-actor to a mixed-actor system; its autonomy depends on continental control over the rich variety of intrusive pressures, which must first be identified.

The growth of political scale in Africa has produced changes in the impact of the system's dominance by subsystems. The basis of political order has evolved from nation-states through the colonial period to a complex pattern of interaction between a variety of actors, especially the continent's great powers and continental and regional organisations. The rules of the system have begun to evolve to accommodate these new and intermediate levels of interaction. Discontinuities will continue until overlapping subsystems are eliminated and rendered compatible but meanwhile the interests of the new actors are challenging customary African procedures.

The mixed-actor system[75] in Africa opens the prospect of a new set of loyalties and values. The rise of nationalism reinforced traditional notions of state sovereignty, territoriality and identity. Although the African inter-state system remains essentially conservative and protective of the status quo, this chapter suggests that we should be sceptical of the inherited, monist, state-centric view. The tenuous authority of new regimes in Africa is threatened not only by ethnic nationalisms and regional inequalities from within but by non-state actors from without. The linkage politics of ethnicity and investment are particularly subversive of regime control.

International relations in Africa are now of three types – inter-state, inter-non-state actors, and between state and other actors. The latter pattern includes domestic linkage politics as well as transnational relations. We suggest that continental law and organisations have yet to respond fully to this variety of hetero-geneous actors and that the ruling elites of African states must deal with this range of targets and influences if the state system is to be preserved. The vulnerability of control exercised by African regimes is threatened both by domestic integration and by the variety of international actors. The impact of corporate invest-ment on the development strategies and performance of African states is of particular significance.

Corporations in Africa have learned to live with a variety of forms of state intervention but they still possess considerable leverage in perpetuating conservative factions within the ruling class and in advancing certain types of regional integration.[76] Profit and national development may coexist rather than lead to confrontation because dependence relationships benefit a few indigenous members of the elite; cooption may perpetuate their 'power'. Domestic and inter-state inequalities undermine the bargaining strategies advocated for African states by Curry and Rothchild.[77] Improved bargaining positions based on regional or global concerns have thus far not advanced African interests significantly in either the EEC or UNCTAD as the feudal world structure erodes such collective advocacy.

Confrontation with the structures of dependence by Africa demands recognition of the heterogeneity of international actors and the design of strategies to minimise their interference. The assertion of independence in all issue areas requires different tactics for different states in Africa. African international law is being rewritten to advance these claims. Pan-Africanism and the notion of 'we are all Africans' constitute the revival of African law and rules after the era of colonialism. The oral traditions of pre-colonial inter-state diplomacy have been recalled and updated in contemporary African international forums. Pan-Africanism and racial consciousness are expressed in symbols and identities rather than in effective supranational constitutions and structures.

Africa displays a characteristic ambivalence about the acceptability of global norms and institutions. In practice, it recognises two levels of international law and organisation: the global system symbolised by the UN; and a distinctive continental and racial order in which African law takes precedence.[78] Notions of 'good neighbourliness' are the beginning of African regional law in which ideological diversity is tolerated in the interests of economic integration and growth. The rules which ordered pre-colonial interstate politics have been selectively adapted to provide criteria for acceptable behaviour now. Mazrui notes that African law is particularly concerned with control, racial representativity, legitimate assumption of power and regime authority. Africans recognise three levels of diplomatic identity – racial, continental and 'national' – which are comparable to the levels of analysis perceived by students of international politics – global, regional and state.

The principle of African continental jurisdiction is expressed in the concept of 'try OAU first'. The numerical dominance of the African states in the UN, as well as the general impact of the new states on the content of international law,[79] has made the UN and OAU largely compatible organisations.[80] The multiplicity of national actors and the associated fragmentation of the global system have enhanced the role of regional organisations in mediation. Peaceful settlement of local disputes is now a function of continental institutions rather than the Security Council. However, the OAU has been involved in border disputes[81] and internal conflicts as well as in the liberation of minority regimes.[82] It is the centre of a multinational coalition involving international organisations, non-aligned or radical states, liberation movements, and support groups whose activities reinforce the demands and prospects for change in southern Africa.[83] It is more effective in advancing the normalisation of difficult relations than it is in removing the causes of tensions. It has employed a variety of commissions and leaders to bring rapprochements but has insufficient resources to undertake extended peace-keeping or problem-solving operations.

The emphasis on mediation is not only a reflection of the OAU interest in continental order. It is also a revival of pre-colonial African norms in which compromise was preferred to confrontation.[84] African states advocate necessary force to bring about political change in southern Africa; but they collectively oppose violence in intra-African affairs.

The variety of tactics open to national actors has increased dramatically in the last century. Earlier African inter-state relations were conducted through wars or orthodox dipolomacy; more sophisticated instruments of statecraft such as exchange rates and sanctions were unavailable. However, advocates of liberation on the continent have not limited their attention to the overthrow of white regimes; ethnic irredentism and ideological purity have also been causes of inter-state conflict between black States. The African system will increasingly reflect the tensions as well as opportunities of its mixed-actor structure. The contemporary complexity of African international relations stands in contrast to the relatively simple politics of pre-colonial Africa.

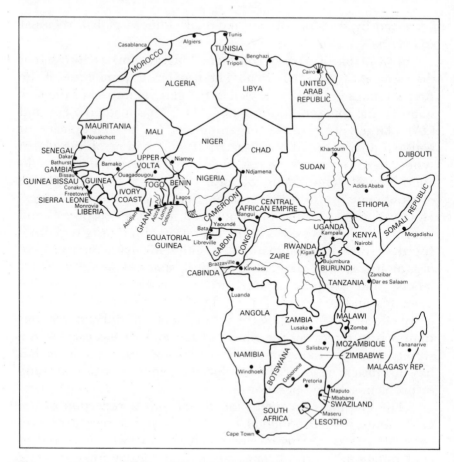

Figure 14.3. Contemporary African State System[85]

6. A Preview of Post-Independence Africa: Unity and/or Inequality

International relations in Africa have always posed dilemmas – expansion with the prospect of exploitation, growth with the possibility of underdevelopment. The rise and fall of African kingdoms is a function of continual inequality. Uneven patterns of development have been magnified by the unequal distribution of benefits in a hierarchical international system. Our preview of a trend towards national inequalities in Africa is compatible with the regionalisation of global politics. This is an alternative regional framework to that proposed by Amin. He advances a distinction between three politico-economic regions in black Africa: colonial economy (West Africa); concession-owning companies (Congo River Basin); and labour reserves (Eastern and Southern Africa). Rather, we suggest that within each region of Africa there is a core to which most of the benefits of regional integration flow. National elites and multinational corporations within these are the primary beneficiaries of the regionalisation of Africa. Of course, these states may in turn be semi-dependent on the international capitalist system (Kenya, Ivory Coast, South Africa, Zaire) or on international commodity markets (Libya, Nigeria, Algeria, Zambia).

In a feudal global system, characterised by scarce resources and rewards, a few states will be able to develop. In Africa, these 'semi-peripheral'[86] states will increasingly achieve positions of super-ordination in relation to their neighbours. So while the prospects for continental development are discouraging, a few African states may be able to exploit their control over scarce global resources and over regional markets. The counter-dependence strategies of these states involve the paradox of causing regional dependence among neighbouring countries. However, their collective behaviour may contain potential autonomy for the African system, albeit at the cost of increased differentials among African states.

Sub-imperial roles might be in the interests of either pan-Africanism or of extra-continental powers. They will have an increasing impact on the rate of development and autonomy in Africa. Regional powers are tolerated by the superpowers so long as they are compatible with imperial interests. The United States, the Soviet Union, Europe, China and Japan are permissive of such secondary, regional structures while their own politico-economic interests are protected. Imperial spheres of influence have developed since the fifteenth century, but the present system is complicated by both conflict between the great powers and the growth of local hegemonies.[87] Paradoxically, the cores of African regions are themselves dependent on imperial metropoles.

We suggest that inter-state politics in Africa will increasingly reveal the impact of the 'atimic process' – the growing gap between formal equality and real inequality.[88] The difference between national attributes and control of states in Africa is heightened by the development of a mixed-actor continental system in which non-state actors may be more powerful over some dimensions than poor national units. Zartman points to the low level and diffuse distribution of power in Africa; this represents a continuity of its structure over time. However, we suggest that the unequal distribution of resources in Africa, combined with fluctuations in world demand for commodities, will increase inequalities among African states. States which possess minerals in great demand or which are able to maintain spheres of influence through regional institutions are likely to be influential African actors in the next decade – Libya, Zambia, Nigeria, Zaire in the first category, Kenya, Ivory Coast, Senegal in the second; significantly, South Africa is the only state to appear in both categories. These states are diplomatic centres, have large GDP's, armies and populations, receive aid from a variety of sources, especially from the US, and are host to the largest number of corporate subsidiaries; conversely, their balance of trade is most dependent on regional exchange.[89] They are also host to the most headquarters or regional offices of African and global organisations.[90]

Africa's rediscovery of *realpolitik* is a function of its developing continental inequalities. Ideological alliances of the pre-OAU era are decreasing as diverse strategies of development and regional cooperation produce a variety of growth rates and structures. One indicator of Africa's maturity is the decline of ideological conflicts and the advocacy of political coexistence among the independent states on the continent. Africa's leaders are increasingly preoccupied with the interrelated politics of international dependence and domestic class formation. They recognise the diversity and dilemmas of Africa and accept the fluidity of continental leadership and organisations.

The feudal nature of the global system and the international politics of scarcity offer prospects of upward mobility for only a few states in Africa. The possession of strategic materials or valuable minerals, along with being the core of a region, are crucial capabilities in the exercise of power on the continent. The new balance of power in Africa will not involve kingdoms or empires but the exploitation of minerals, commodities or regions. In the permissive era of formal superpower withdrawal, the status of a state in Africa is partially dependent on the interests of a variety of extra-African actors, such as the EEC, Japan and China. Nevertheless, ideological inventiveness will no longer produce changes in political behaviour as readily as the manipulation of economic power. The choice of a 'realist' or 'idealist' foreign policy is no longer a dilemma for most African states; their economic and political resources determine their tactics.

The poverty of Africa is not equally distributed. Africa in general may be dependent and subordinate, but a few African states are increasingly powerful in global as well as in continental affairs because of their resources. Their influence constrains the foreign policy choices of other states both within and outside the continent. Although the impact of the African caucus on issues like southern Africa and underdevelopment is essentially based on moral influence and appeal, the emerging power of some African states reflects their real, rather than merely charismatic, resources.[91]

The activities of Africa's 'middle powers' have the potential to disturb the present pattern of continental relations. They may revive images of conquering African states, like the Zulu and Ndebele kingdoms, and replace the present indulgent atmosphere of tolerance and coexistence, more reminiscent of benign Lozi or Swazi rule. They could challenge the informality and interdependence which characterise African politics in the OAU system. Moreover, the withdrawal of colonial powers has increased the prospects for African spheres of influence by major African states. In southern Africa it has permitted South Africa to practise an 'outward policy' of dialogue and detente thus complicating and diverting the continent's advocacy of majority rule in the region.[92]

The bases of power in Africa have been remarkably consistent over time; they are still defined in terms of material and human resources, military capabilities and geo-political position. Of course, the content of each of these variables has changed: petroleum reserves are now more important than salt, educated personnel are more valuable than slave markets, military strength is calculated according to jet fighters not warriors, and air routes are now as important as ports and railway connections. Leadership and institutionalisation continue to be important factors.

Zartman points to 'the presence of subregional constellations within the continental pattern'.[93] However, we suggest that the subsystemic dominance of the African system is characteristic of all its historical periods except for the brief period of African nationalism and the early years of the OAU. Continental coexistence is still maintained by the desire to expand the scope of free Africa to the perimeter of the continent. Colonial inheritance, trade patterns and political transactions all suggest the development of regional rather than continental integration in Africa.

Nevertheless, we should be cautious in treating kaleidoscopic patterns of African interstate factionalism as indicative of new trends and alliances. In his monograph on the impact of the Uganda coup on African international politics Mittelman suggests that

> The scenario of fluctuating alignments and counteralignments, the nuclei being composed of Uganda–Kenya–Zaire and Tanzania–Zambia–Somalia, bears resemblance to Africa's 'protobalance of power' period (roughly 1959–1963): a mobile pattern of alliances and counteralliances in which no one group of states is able to dominate the system.[94]

Such diplomatic maoeuvres may have little lasting impact on the underlying structures of continental relations and are in any case subject to environmental constraints and changes.

Regional hegemonies may be secured if the ECA proposal of five subregions leads to a decline in the number of overlapping regional units. Kenya's dominance in eastern Africa would be enhanced by an expansion of the EAC to the limits of the ECA sub-region; half the non-members have already applied to join the Community.[95] The Economic Community of West Africa (ECOWAS) includes all the sub-region's fourteen members and will probably be dominated by the triumvirate of Nigeria, Senegal and the Ivory Coast.[96] An appreciation of the structure of international inequality and collective association with the EEC has encouraged such wide, sub-regional integration. If ECOWAS plans are implemented then it will mark one stage in the obliteration of the colonial inheritance; it includes Francophone, Anglophone and Lusophone states; those who rejected Eur-Africanism (Guinea) or accepted it (Ivory Coast and Senegal); states with a long (Liberia) or short period of independence (Guinea-Bissau); and several military as well as democratic regimes. If Zaire joins it would include two emergent black great powers (Nigeria and Zaire) and three important trading states (Ghana, Ivory Coast and Senegal). Zaire did propose a Union of Central African states (with CAE and Gabon) and had been interested in long-term ties with Zambia, Gabon, Burundi, Rwanda and liberated Angola and Zimbabwe; it may yet become the industrial link between those two groupings. In any case, it clearly dominates the designated ECA Central African sub-region.[97]

The North African sub-region includes the Maghreb grouping and two members of the proposed Federation of Arab States.[98] The Southern African sub-region is ill-defined but after political change would include the present members of the Southern African Customs Union, plus Zimbabwe, Namibia. Angola and Mozambique. Some established regional organisations already reinforce this ECA continental plan; others could be expanded or modified. Nevertheless considerable conflict is likely to occur over states which exist between these macro-regions; should Mozambique, Zambia and Malawi be in Southern or in Eastern Africa?

Regional integration may threaten continental autonomy unless the OAU modifies its structure and style to recognise regional and other non-state actors. The emerging middle powers in Africa are likely increasingly to dominate African organisations and erode the real, if not formal, equality of African states. Conflict in Africa in the next decade is likely to be centred on alternative definitions of spheres of influence; overlapping sub-systems may be terminated. The 'second scramble' for Africa is not so much by the multinational corporations as between a small group of important African states with their international advocates. Although the dialogue and détente debates raised the prospects of a renewed conflict over values, the era of ideological alliances has passed. As national interests become more defined and less flexible so Africa will re-enter the world of *realpolitik*. In historical perspective, the first decade of OAU was an era of transition; we suggest that on the basis of present trends, the African inter-state system will in future be characterised more by continuity than by discontinuity with its historical antecedents. The new diversity of actors in Africa will be made compatible with the interests of the leading African states. A new balance of power is evolving on the continent.

Notes

An earlier version of this chapter was presented at a Political and Administrative Studies Seminar in the University of Zambia in December 1973, and at a conference of the Canadian Association of African Studies in Halifax in February 1974. I am grateful for comments received in both Zambia and Canada and for the support of both the University of Zambia and Dalhousie University. I would like to express my appreciation of the criticism and stimulation provided by Robert Molteno, Neil Parsons and Robin Palmer of the University of Zambia and to members of both the Centre for African Studies and the Centre for Foreign Policy Studies at Dalhousie University.

1. On the complexities of African international politics see Timothy M. Shaw, 'Discontinuities and inequalities in African international politics', *International Journal*, xxx, 3, Summer 1975, pp. 369–90.

2. On the need for such understanding see I. Wallerstein, 'Africa in a capitalist world', *Issue*, iii, 3, Fall 1973, pp. 1–11. On the characteristic violence of African culture – which is now expressed in internal and international conflict as well as conciliation – see Adda B. Bozeman, *Conflict in Africa: concepts and realities*, Princeton University Press, 1976. This is an innovative interdisciplinary 'social anthropology' of pre- and post-colonial African international norms, law and behaviour.

3. This is a positive response to Elias's plea for more comparative and reflective research on Africa's contribution to international law. He insists that this requires an acquaintance with 'the political, the commercial and the diplomatic history of the more significant of African states and kingdoms during the Middle Ages. It is only against this background that Africa's place in international law and relations can be understood'. (T. O. Elias, *Africa and the Development of International Law*, Sijthoff, Leiden, 1972, p. 6.) For complementary pleas for comparative and historical studies of war and diplomacy see: Bethwell A. Ogot, 'Introduction' in his collection, *War and Society in Africa: ten studies*, Frank Cass, London, 1972; A. Adu Boahen, 'Fanti diplomacy in the eighteenth century' in K. Ingham, ed., *The Foreign Relations of African States*, Butterworth, London, 1974, pp. 25–49; and A. K. Mensah-Brown, 'Introduction' and 'Notes on international law and pre-colonial legal history of modern Ghana' in his collection, *African International Legal History*, UNITAR, New York, 1975, pp. 1–7, 107–24. For a review of studies of pre-colonial war see G. N. Uzoigwe, 'Precolonial military studies in Africa', *Journal of Modern African Studies*, xiii, 3, Sept. 1975, pp. 469–81.

4. This mode of analysis is derived from the stimulating writing and teaching of Oran R. Young; see his 'Political discontinuities in the international system', *World Politics*, xx, 3, Apr. 1968, pp. 369–92; reprinted in Richard A. Falk and Saul H. Mendlovitz, eds., *Regional Politics and World Order*, Freeman, San Francisco, 1973, pp. 34–48.

5. See I. William Zartman, 'Africa as a subordinate state system in international relations', *International Organisation*, xxi, 3, Summer 1967, pp. 545–64; reprinted in Marion E. Doro and Newell M. Stultz, eds., *Governing in Black Africa: perspectives on new states*, Prentice-Hall, Englewood Cliffs, 1970, pp.

324–41. See also Zartman's 'Africa', in James N. Rosenau, Kenneth W. Thompson and Gavin Boyd, eds., *World Politics: an introduction*, Free Press, New York, 1976, pp. 569–94. For comparable analyses see George Shepherd, *Nonaligned Black Africa: an international subsystem*, Heath-Lexington, Lexington, 1970; Paul Saenz, 'The OAU in the subordinate African regional system', *African Studies Review*, xiii, 2, Sept. 1970, pp. 203–25; W. Scott Thompson and Richard Bissell, 'Legitimacy and authority in the OAU', *African Studies Review*, xv, 1, Apr. 1972, pp. 17–42, revised version in *Polity*, v, 3, Spring 1973, pp. 335–61; and B. David Meyers, 'Intra-regional conflict management by the OAU', *International Organization*, xxviii, 3, Summer 1974, pp. 345–73.

6. On the political interdependence and economic dependence of Africa see Ali A. Mazrui, 'African diplomatic thought and supra-nationality', in Ali A. Mazrui and Hasu H. Patel, eds., *Africa in World Affairs: the next thirty years*, Third Press, New York, 1973, pp. 121–33.

7. On the problems of regionalism in Africa see Timothy M. Shaw, 'Regional cooperation and conflict in Africa', *International Journal*, xxx, 4, Autumn 1975, pp. 671–88 and 'International stratification in Africa: subimperialism in eastern and southern Africa', *Journal of Southern African Affairs*, ii, 2, April, 1977, pp. 145–165.

8. See Samir Amin, 'Underdevelopment and dependence in Black Africa: historical origin', *Journal of Peace Research*, 21, 1972, pp. 105–19, especially 105–7; reprinted as 'Underdevelopment and dependence in Black Africa – origins and contemporary forms', *Journal of Modern African Studies*, x, 4, Dec. 1972, pp. 503–24.

9. See: Samir Amin, *Neo-colonialism in West Africa*, Penguin, Harmondsworth, 1973, and 'Accumulation and development', *Review of African Political Economy*, 1, 1974, pp. 9–26; and Bonnie Campbell, 'Social change and class formation in a French West African state', *Canadian Journal of African Studies*, viii, 2, 1974, pp. 285–306.

10. See Timothy M. Shaw, 'The political economy of African international relations', *Issue*, v, 4, Winter 1975, pp. 29–38.

11. See A. G. Hopkins, *An Economic History of West Africa*, Longman, London, 1973, p. 288.

12. See Claude E. Welch, 'Continuity and discontinuity in African Military organization', *Journal of Modern African Studies*, xiii, 2, June 1975, pp. 229–48.

13. See Nehemia Levtzion, *Ancient Ghana and Mali*, Methuen, London, 1973, p. 219.

14. V. B. Thompson, *Africa and Unity*, Longman, 1969.

15. See: Victor A. Olorunsola, ed., *The Politics of Cultural Sub-nationalism in Africa*, Anchor, New York, 1972; and M. Crawford Young, 'Nationalism and separatism in Africa', in Martin Kilson, ed., *New States in the Modern World*, Harvard University Press, Cambridge, Mass., 1975, pp. 57–74.

16. For a critical, if exaggerated, review of the problems of forcing continuities in the nationalist struggle see Donald Denoon and Adam Kuper, 'Nationalist institutions in search of a nation: the "new historiography" in Dar es Salaam', *African Affairs*, lxix, 277, Oct. 1970, pp. 329–49.

17. Roland Oliver and J. P. Fage, *A Short History of Africa*, Penguin, Harmondsworth, 1966, especially pp. 182, 196.

18. See, for instance, Berhanykun Andemicael, *The OAU and the UN*, Africana for UNITAR, New York, 1976; Thomas Hovet, 'Effect of the African group of states on the behaviour of the United Nations', in Yassin El-Ayouty and Hugh C. Brooks, eds., *Africa and International Organization*, Nijhoff, The Hague, 1974, pp. 11–17; and David Kay, 'The impact of African States on the United Nations,' *International Organization*, xxiii, i, Winter 1969, pp. 20–49.

19. Karl Kaiser, 'The interaction of regional subsystems', *World Politics*, xx, 10, Oct. 1968, p. 92.

20. Elias, *Africa and the Development of International Law*, p. 32. See also his 'International relations in Africa: a historical survey', in Mensah-Brown, ed., *African International Legal History*, pp. 87–103.

21. See G. S. P. Freeman-Grenville, 'The external relations of the East African Coast: before 1800', in Ingham, ed., *The Foreign Relations of African States*, pp. 69–83. See also: C. S. Nicholls. *The Swahili coast: Politics, Diplomacy and Trade on the East African Littoral, 1798–1856*, Africana, New York, 1971; and K. Ingham, 'East Coast trading treaties of the precolonial era', in Mensah-Brown, ed., *African International Legal History*, pp, 167–151.

22. On the analogous early Chinese and Greek state systems see K. J. Holsti, *International Politics: a framework for analysis*, Prentice-Hall, Englewood Cliffs, 1972, especially pp. 29–53; on early South Asian international politics see George Modelski, 'Kautiliya: foreign policy and international system in the ancient Hindu world', *American Political Science Review*, lviii, 3, Sept. 1964, pp. 549–560.

23. Hopkins, *An Economic History of West Africa*, p. 92.

24. *Ibid.*, p. 106. On the Oyo Kingdom see E. J. Alagoa, 'The Niger Delta states and their neighbours, 1600–1800', and I. A. Akinjogbin, 'The expansion of Oyo and the rise of Dahomey, 1600–1800', in J. F. Ade Ajayi and Michael Crowder, eds., *History of West Africa*, vol. 1, Longman, 1971, pp. 269–303, and 304–43.

25. See, for instance, Fola Soremekun, 'The rise and fall of Ovimbundu trade', and Neil Parsons, 'The economic history of Khama's country in Botswana, 1844–1930', in Robin Palmer and Neil Parsons, eds., *The Roots of Rural Poverty: in Central and Southern Africa*, Heinemann, London, 1977, pp. 82–95, 113–143.

26. See Richard Gray and David Birmingham, eds., *Pre-Colonial African Trade: essays on trade in central and eastern Africa before 1900*, OUP, London, 1970.

27. See Kenneth Ingham, 'Foreign relations of the kingdoms of Western Uganda', in Ingham, ed., *The Foreign Relations of African States*, pp. 161–87; and Semakula Kiwanuka, 'The diplomacy of the lost counties question: its impact on the foreign relations of the kingdoms of Buganda, Bunyoro and the rest of Uganda, 1900–1964', *Mawazo*, iv, 2, 1974, pp. 111–41.

28. *Africa South of the Sahara, 1973*, Europa, London, 1973, p. 13.

29. Hopkins, *An Economic History of West Africa*, especially pp. 8–77.

30. See J. O. Hunwick, 'Songhay, Bornu and Hausaland in the sixteenth century', and R. A. Adeleye, 'Hausaland and Bornu 1600–1800', in Ajayi and

Crowder, eds., *History of West Africa*, pp. 202–39, 485–530. See also Godwin-Collins, K. N. Onyeledo, ' "International law" among the Yoruba-Benin and the Hausa-Fulani', in Mensah-Brown, ed., *African International Legal History*, pp. 153–64 and Robert Smith, 'Peace and palaver: international relations in pre-colonial West Africa', *Journal of African History*, xiv, 4, 1973, pp. 599–621.

31. Hopkins, *An Economic History of West Africa*, pp. 122–3. See also Lars Sundstrom, *The Exchange Economy of Pre-Colonial Tropical Africa*, Hurst, London, 1974.

32. See, for instance: Andrew D. Roberts, *A History of the Bemba: Political Growth and Change in North-Eastern Zambia before 1900*, Longman, London, 1973; and Bridglal Pachai, 'Ngoni politics and diplomacy in Malawi: 1848–1904' in his collection, *The Early History of Malawi*, Longman, London, 1972, pp. 179–214.

33. See A. A. Boahen, 'Traditional African diplomacy and diplomatic techniques', Third International Congress of Africanists, Addis Ababa, Dec. 1973, and 'Fanti diplomacy in the eighteenth century', in Ingham, ed., *The Foreign Relations of African States*, pp. 25–49. See also Adamou Noam Njoya, 'Sociology of African diplomacy', *Mawazo*, iv, 3, 1975, pp. 7–22; Graham Irwin, 'Precolonial African diplomacy', *International Journal of African Historical Studies*, viii, i, 1975, pp. 81–96; and J. F. Ade Ajayi, 'Recent studies in West African diplomatic history', *Nigerian Journal of International Affairs*, i. 1, July 1975, pp. 39–46.

34. See S. C. Ukpabi, 'The military in traditional African societies', Third International Congress of Africanists, Addis Ababa, Dec. 1973. For a very stimulating introduction to the pre-colonial international relations of West Africa see Robert S. Smith, *Warfare and Diplomacy in Pre-Colonial West Africa*, Methuen, London, 1976; see also his 'Peace and Palaver: international relations in pre-colonial West Africa', *Journal of African History*, xiv, 4, 1973, pp. 599–621.

35. See Abdul M. H. Sheriff, 'The dynamic of change in pre-colonial East African Societies', Universities Social Science Conference of the East African Universities, Dar es Salaam, Dec. 1973.

36. See Basil Davidson, *The Africans: an entry to cultural history*, Penguin, Harmondsworth, 1973, p. 224. For a synthetic history of this process see J. Forbes Munro, *Africa and the International Economy 1800–1960*, Dent, London, 1976.

37. On factionalism, collaboration and dependence in Uganda see Jan J. Jorgensen and Timothy M. Shaw, 'International dependence and foreign policy choices; the political economy of Uganda', Canadian Association of African Studies Conference, Ottawa, February 1973.

38. See Anthony J. Dachs, 'Politics of collaboration – imperialism in practice', in Bridglal Pachai, ed., *The Early History of Malawi*, Longman, London, 1972, pp. 283–92.

39. See Palmer's critique of the exclusion of colonial, administrative history, 'Johnston and Jameson: a comparative study in the imposition of colonial rule' in *ibid*, pp. 293–322; for a supportive attack see Denoon and Kuper

'Nationalist institutions in search of a nation: the "new historiography" in Dar es Salaam'.

40. See, for instance, Giovanni Arrighi and John S. Saul, *Essays on the Political Economy of Africa*, Monthly Review, New York, 1973; and Lionel Cliffe and John S. Saul, eds., *Socialism in Tanzania*, vols. 1 and 2, East African Publishing House, Nairobi, 1972 and 1973.

41. See Holsti, *International Politics*, p. 93.

42. F. C. Okoye, *International Law and the New African States*, Sweet & Maxwell, London, 1972, p. 5.

43. Holsti, *International Politics*, p. 95.

44. Kaiser, 'The interaction of regional subsystems'.

45. See Elias, *Africa and the Development of International Law*, p. 19.

46. On the complex regional politics of Southern Africa see Timothy M. Shaw, 'International organisations and the politics of Southern Africa: towards regional integration or liberation?', *Journal of Southern African Studies*, iii, 1, October 1976, pp. 1–19, and 'Southern Africa: cooperation and conflict in an international subsystem', *Journal of Modern African Studies*, xii, 4, Dec. 1974, pp. 633–55. For a lucid account of one African leader's skilful regional diplomacy see Leonard Thompson, *Survival in Two Worlds: Moshoeshoe of Lesotho 1786–1870*, Clarendon Press, Oxford, 1975.

47. Holsti, *International Politics*, p. 47.

48. Richard Brown, 'The external relations of the Ndebele kingdom in the prepartition era', in Leonard Thompson, ed., *African Societies in Southern Africa*, Heinemann, London, 1969, p. 260.

49. J. D. Omer-Cooper, *The Zulu Aftermath: a nineteenth-century revolution in Bantu Africa*, Longman, London, 1966, p. 154.

50. See Timothy M. Shaw, 'South Africa's military capability and the future of race relations', in Mazrui and Patel, eds., *Africa in World Affairs*, pp. 37–61.

51. See M. V. Jackson Haight, *European Powers and South East Africa: a study of international relations on the south-eastern coast of Africa 1796–1856*, Routledge and Kegan Paul, London, 1967; and E. Stokes and R. Brown, eds., *The Zambesian Past*, Manchester University Press, 1966.

52. Omer-Cooper, *The Zulu Aftermath*, p. 179. For more on the early state systems of Central Africa, including their impact on contemporary internal and regional relations, see T. O. Ranger, ed., *Aspects of Central African History*, Heinemann, London, 1968.

53. Donald Denoon *et al.*, *Southern Africa since 1800*, Longman, London, 1972, p. 227.

54. President Seretse Khama, *Botswana and Southern Africa*, Government Printer, Gaborone, 1970, pp. 2, 4.

55. See Shaw, 'Discontinuities and inequalities in African international politics'.

56. On the dilemmas of balkanisation and dual economies see *inter alia*, Reginald H. Green and Ann Seidman, *Unity or Poverty? The Economics of PanAfricanism*, Penguin, Harmondsworth, 1968; and Ann Seidman, *Comparative Development Strategies in East Africa*, EAPH, Nairobi, 1972.

57. See Timothy M. Shaw and Terry L. Evans, 'The international environment and African development: case studies from East Africa', Canadian Asso-

ciation of African Studies Conference, Waterloo, Feb. 1972 and 'Towards a comparative analysis of regional integration in southern and eastern Africa', African Studies Association, Philadelphia, Nov. 1972; this approach is supportive of that advanced by Lynn Krieger Mytelka in her plea for research on 'The salience of gains in Third World integrative systems', *World Politics*, xxv, 2, Jan. 1973, pp. 236–50.

58. See Kassim Guruli, 'Towards an independent and equal East African Common Market', *East Africa Journal*, viii, 9, Sept. 1971, pp. 25–32.

59. Mark D. Segal, 'Development and integration', Third International Congress of Africanists, Addis Ababa, Dec. 1973, p. 48.

60. See Oran R. Young, 'Interdependencies in world politics', *International Journal*, xxiv, 4, Autumn 1969, p. 726. Compare T. dos Santos, 'The crisis of development theory and the problem of dependence in Latin America', in Henry Bernstein, ed., *Underdevelopment and Development: the Third World today*, Penguin, Harmondsworth, 1973, p. 76.

61. See Immanuel Wallerstein, 'Dependence in an interdependent world: the limited possibilities of transformation within the capitalist world economy', *African Studies Review*, xvii, 1, Apr. 1974, pp. 1–26.

62. Robin Jenkins, *Exploitation: the world power structure and the inequality of nations*, MacGibbon and Kee, London, 1970, p. 84.

63. Cf. Edward L. Morse, 'The transformation of foreign policies: modernization, interdependence and externalization', *World Politics*, xxii, 3, Apr. 1970, pp. 371–92.

64. See, for instance, Timothy M. Shaw, 'The foreign policy system of Zambia', *African Studies Review*, xix, 1, Apr. 1976, pp. 31–66.

65. See Isebill V. Gruhn, 'The Commission for Technical Cooperation in Africa, 1960–1965', *Journal of Modern African Studies*, ix, 3, Oct. 1971, pp. 459–69.

66. See *inter alia*, Thompson, *Africa and Unity*, especially pp. 141–77; and Adekunle Ajala, *PanAfricanism: evolution, progress and prospects*, Andre Deutsch, London, 1973.

67. See Immanuel Wallerstein, 'The early years of the OAU: the search for organizational pre-eminence', *International Organisation*, xx, 4, Aug. 1966, pp. 774–87, and 'The role of the OAU in contemporary African politics', in El-Ayouty and Brooks, eds., *Africa and International Organization*, pp. 18–28; Yashpal Tandon, 'The OAU: forum for African international relations', *The Round Table*, 246, Apr. 1972, pp. 221–30; Cervenka, 'Major policy shifts in the OAU, 1963–1973', in Ingham, ed., *The Foreign Relations of African States*, pp. 323–42; Timothy M. Shaw, 'OAU: prospects for the second decade', *International Perspectives*, Sept.–Oct. 1973, pp. 31–4; S. C. Ukpabi, 'The genesis of the OAU and the problems of African unity', African Studies Association Conference, Chicago, Oct. 1974; and Jan Woronoff, 'The OAU and sub-Saharan regional bodies', in Yassin El-Ayouty, ed., *The Organisation of African Unity: Comparative Perspectives*, Praeger, New York, 1975, pp. 62–78.

68. See Patricia Berko Wild, 'Radicals and moderates in the OAU: origins of conflict and bases for coexistence', in Paul A. Tharp Jr., ed., *Regional International Organisations/Structures and Functions*, St. Martins, New York, 1971,

pp. 36–50; and Colin Legum, 'Africa's contending revolutionaries', *Problems of Communism*, 2, Mar.–Apr. 1972, pp. 2–15.

69. On the over-politicisation of OERS and its more pragmatic, functional successor see Parbati K. Sircar, 'International waters, multi-national cooperation and regional development in Africa', Third International Congress of Africanists, Addis Ababa, December 1973.

70. See Shaw, 'Regional conflict and cooperation in Africa'.

71. For data on regional and continental organisations in Africa see *Yearbook of International Organisations*, Union of International Associations, Brussels, 1972, 14th edn, especially p. 781; and *Africa South of the Sahara, 1973*, Europa, London, 1973, 3rd edn., pp. 90–146. See also Andemicael, *The OAU and the UN*, pp. 21–3.

72. For a set of alternative typologies of interstate organisations on the continent see Louis B. Sohn, 'The organs of economic cooperation in Africa', *Journal of African Law*, xvi, 3, Autumn 1972, pp. 212–19. This issue also contains other papers presented at the August 1972 Uppsala conference on legal mechanisms of economic cooperation in African international organisations.

73. Joseph S. Nye, *Peace in Parts: integration and conflict in regional organisation*, Little Brown, Boston, 1971, p. 10.

74. See *ibid* and his 'Regional institutions', in Cyril E. Black and Richard. A. Falk, eds., *The Future of the International Legal Order, 4: The Structure of the International Environment*, pp. 425–47, Princeton University Press, 1972; reprinted in Falk and Mendlovitz, eds., *Regional Politics and World Order*, pp. 78–92.

75. For general critiques of state-centric assumptions see *inter alia*: Oran R. Young, 'The actors in world politics', in James N. Rosenau, Vincent Davis and Maurice East, eds., *The Analysis of International Politics*, Free Press, New York, 1972, pp. 121–44; Arnold Wolfers, *Discord and Collaboration: essays in international politics*, Johns Hopkins, Baltimore, 1962; and Richard W. Mansbach, Yale H. Ferguson and Donald E. Lampert, 'Beyond conservatism in the study of global politics', in their *The Web of World Politics: non-state actors in the global system*, Prentice-Hall, Englewood Cliffs, 1976, pp. 1–45.

76. See Timothy M. Shaw, *Dependence and Underdevelopment: the development and foreign policies of Zambia*, Ohio University Papers in International Studies, Africa Series Number 28, 1976, and 'Zambia: dependence and underdevelopment', *Canadian Journal of African Studies*, x, 2, 1976, pp. 3–22. See also Henry Bretton, 'Patron-client relations: middle Africa and the powers', and 'Direct foreign investment in Africa: its political purpose and function in patron-client relations', General Learning, New York, 1971 and 1976.

77. See Robert L. Curry and Donald Rothchild, 'On economic bargaining between African governments and multinational companies', *Journal of Modern African Studies*, xii, 2, June 1974, pp. 173–89. See also John Cartwright, 'Multinational corporations and political leadership', *Canadian Political Science Association*, Quebec City, June 1976.

78. See Ali A. Mazrui, *Towards a Pax Africana: a study of ideology and ambition*, Weidenfeld and Nicolson, London, 1969, p. 118.

79. See S. P. Sinha, *New Nations and the Law of Nations*, Sijthoff, Leyden, 1967, pp. 11–79, 137–45; Elias, *Africa and the Development of International Law*; and Okoye, *International Law and the New African States*.

80. See Leon Gordenker, 'The OAU and the UN: can they live together?' in Mazrui and Patel, eds., *Africa in World Affairs*, pp. 105–19; and Andemicael, *The OAU and the UN*. Compare Minerva M. Etzioni, *The majority of One: towards a theory of regional compatibility*, Sage, Beverly Hills, 1970: 'By compatibility we mean that the relationship between two organisations is such that the activities of one do not undermine those of the other and vice versa', p. 18.

81. See *inter alia*: Saadia Touval, *The Boundary Politics of Independent Africa*, Harvard University Press, Cambridge, Mass., 1972, and Carl Gosta Widstrand, ed., *African Boundary Problems*, Scandinavian Institute of African Studies, Uppsala, 1969.

82. See Saenz, 'The OAU in the subordinate African regional system'; Berhanykun Andemicael, *Peaceful Settlement Among African States: roles of the UN and OAU*, UNITAR, New York, 1972; and Ernst Haas, Robert L. Butterworth and Joseph S. Nye, *Conflict Management by International Organisations*, General Learning, Morristown, 1972.

83. See Shaw, 'International organisations and the politics of southern Africa'.

84. See Okoye, *International Law and the New African States*, p. 211.

85. Moore and Dunbar, *Africa Yesterday and Today*, pp. x, xi.

86. See Wallerstein, 'Dependence in an interdependent world'.

87. See Michael Barratt Brown, 'Imperialism in our era', *The Spokesman*, 24/25, Winter 1972–73, pp. 66–89; Vladimir Dedijer *et al.*, *Spheres of Influence and the Third World*, Spokesman, Nottingham, 1973; George Lichtheim, *Imperialism*, Pelican, Harmondsworth, 1974; and Pierre Jalée, *Imperialism in the Seventies*, Third Press, New York, 1972, especially pp. 178–210.

88. For a definition of 'atimia' see Gustavo Lagos, *International Stratification and Underdeveloped Countries*, University of North Carolina Press, Chapel Hill, 1963, p. 24. For other analyses of international inequality see: Marshal R. Singer, *Weak States in a World of Powers*, Free Press, New York, 1972; Steven L. Spiegel, *Dominance and Diversity: the international hierarchy*, Little Brown, Boston, 1972; David Vital, *The Inequality of States: a study of the small power in international relations*, Oxford University Press, London, 1968; Ronald P. Barston, ed., *The Other Powers: studies in the foreign policies of small states*, George Allen and Unwin, London, 1973; Tamas Szentes, *The Political Economy of Underdevelopment*, Akademiai Kaido, Budapest, 1973; P. J. Lloyd, *International Trade Patterns of Small Nations*, Duke University Press, Durham, 1968; and Jenkins, *Exploitation*.

89. For supportive data see Timothy M. Shaw, 'The development of international systems in Africa', Third International Congress of Africanists, Addis Ababa, Dec. 1973.

90. See *Yearbook of International Organisations*, pp. 734–5, 880.

91. C. F. Okwudiba Nnoli, 'The bases for realism in African foreign policy', Social Science Conference of the Universities of East Africa, Dar es Salaam, Dec. 1973; Olajide Aluko, 'Nigeria's role in inter-African relations with

special reference to the OAU', *African Affairs*, lxxii, 287, Apr. 1973, pp. 145–62, and Ibrahim Agboola Gambari, 'Nigeria and the world: a growing internal stability, wealth and external influence', *Journal of International Affairs*, xxix, 2, Fall 1975, pp. 155–69.

92. See Timothy M. Shaw, 'The political economy of technology in Southern Africa', in Shaw and Heard, eds., *Cooperation and Conflict in Southern Africa*, pp. 365–379; and with Agrippah T. Mugomba, 'The political economy of regional détente: Zambia and Southern Africa', *Journal of African Studies*, iv, 4, Winter 1977/78, pp. 392–413; and 'Zambia: dependence and détente', in J. Seiler, ed., *Southern Africa Since the Portuguese Coup* (forthcoming).

93. Zartman, 'Africa as a subordinate state system', p. 333.

94. James H. Mittelman, 'The Uganda coup and the internationalisation of political violence', *Munger Africana Library Notes*, 14, Sept. 1972, pp. 25–6.

95. The ECA Eastern African sub-region includes EAC members (Kenya, Uganda, Tanzania); EAC applicants (Zambia, Ethiopia, Somali and Burundi); and other states (Madagascar, Malaŵi, Mauritius and Rwanda).

96. The ECA West African sub-region includes Benin, Gambia, Ghana, Ivory Coast, Liberia, Mali, Mauritania, Niger, Nigeria, Senegal, Sierra Leone, Togo, Upper Volta and Guinea. Guinea-Bissau, the OAU's 42nd member, will presumably be added.

97. The ECA Central African sub-region includes Cameroon, Chad, Congo, Gabon and Zaire. For an alternative scenario of a 'Federal Republic of Africa' see Ajala, *PanAfricanism*, pp. 332–6.

98. The ECA North African sub-region includes Morocco, Algeria and Tunisia, Libya and Egypt, and the Sudan. For details of the structures and processes of regional organisations in Africa see B. W. T. Mutharika, *Towards Multinational Economic Cooperation in Africa*, Praeger, New York, 1972; Louis B. Sohn, *Basic Documents of African Regional Organisations*, Oceana, for Inter-American Institute for Legal Studies, Dobbs Ferry, NY, 4 vols, 1971–72; Peter Robson, *Economic Integration in Africa*, George Allen and Unwin, London, 1968; James H. Mittelman, 'The development of post-colonial African regionalism and the formation of OAU', *Kroniek van Afrika*, 2, 1971, pp. 83–105; A. M. P. Ramolefe and A. J. G. M. Sanders, 'The structural pattern of African regionalism', *The Comparative and International Law Journal of Southern Africa*, iv, 2, July 1971, pp. 155–92; iv, 3, Nov. 1971, pp. 293–323; v, 1, Mar. 1972, pp. 1–55; v, 2, July 1972, pp. 171–188; v, 3, Nov. 1972, pp. 299–338; and vi, 1, Mar. 1973, pp. 82–105; and Economic Commission for Africa, *Directory of Intergovernmental Cooperation Organisations in Africa*, Addis Ababa, 6 June 1972, E/CN 14/CEC/1.

Index

Note: References in italics are to the figures and tables

Abraham, Willi, 167
Achebe, Chinua, *A Man of the People*, 153, 166
Africa Research Bulletin, 342
Africanisation: civil service, 51–3, 141, 143, 173; of dependence, 54; IGO secretariats, 329–30
Algeria, 193, 195, 282–3
Allen, Christopher, 15
Amin, President Idi, 39, 64, 153
Amin, Samir, 11, 95, 99, 102–3, 359, 383
anarcho-syndicalism, 9
Anglin, D. G., 132
Angola, 195, 200–2, 204
apartheid, 126
Arrighi, G., 99, 101–2, 124
Arrighi, G. and Saul, J., 10, 31–2

Bailey, F. G., 233
balance of power, 382–7
Balewa, Tafawa, 288
Banda, Dr Hastings, 132, 161, 164–5, 170–6
Bembello, M., 292
Bienen, H., 171
Bodenheimer, S., 45
Botswana, 73, 126
'bourgeois objectivity', 6
bourgeois social science, 99–100
bourgeoisie, 29–31
Burundi, 160

Canada, aid to Africa, 217–18, 247–63, 255
capitalism, 24–5, 44, 64, 97–104, 225, 360, 366
Cartwright, John, 131
Casalis, Eugene, 119
centre-periphery model of dependence, 74–6, 310–11
Chad, 73
Chipenda, Daniel, 204–5
Chodak, S., 27–30, 32

Clark, J. F., 266–7
class analysis, 2, 7–12, 19, 82; 'classical' classes, 7–8; metropolitan/satellite relationship, 10–11; objectifying subjective attitudes, 8–9; production modes and class, 11–12; subterranean classes, 9–10
class solidarity, 8, 12–13, 25–6; *see also* labour movement
class stratification: complexity, 23; consolidation, 26; economic development and, 24, 43, 48, 59; and politics, 49–50, 53, 59, 166, 360, 366; and revolutionary activity, 10, 32–3; schemes, 27–8; trans-ethnic, 34; transitional phenomena and, 24
Cohen, Robin, 2, 26–9
confrontation, 9–10
Cooperstock, Henry, 2
Cuba, 224, 226

de Kiewet, C. W., 120
dependence, 77–8; cultural, 82; definition, 44–5, 74–6; and foreign aid, 217–18, 223–8, 231; and migration, 79–82, *89*; structural, 44–7, 54; and underdevelopment, 85–8, *89*, 223
dependence theory, 39–41; centre-periphery model, 74–5, 310–11
development, 77–8; definition, 73–4; goals, 74; problems of, 1
Diane, General Lanfane, 294
diplomatic exchange, 265, 269–83; and change of government, 270; interregional, 279–81, *280*; statistics, 272–9, *273–5*; uses, 271
dos Santos, T., 44

Easton, David, 132; *A Systems Analysis of Political Life*, 154–9, 164, 174
economic cooperation, 285–312
economic development: capitalism, 24–5, 44, 64, 97–104, 225, 360, 366; and class

continued—economic development
stratification, 24, 43, 48, 59; and
foreign aid, 234, 248–50; labour
reserve economy, 97–104; and
migration, 83; 'Open Door' policy,
145–6; and public support, 155,
175–6; state control, 43, 53–8, 62
Egypt, 265, 282
Ehrlich, Cyril, 52
Ekangaki, Mr, 293, 304
elections, 168–70
elite *see* political-administrative elite
Emmanuel, Arghiri, 311
Engels, Friedrich, 7, 13, 99
Ethiopia, 282–3
ethnic loyalties, 28, 34, 142–3, 147
European Economic Community, and
Africa, 232, 266, 285–312;
neo-colonial aspects, 287–95, 298;
reciprocity, 302–9; socialism and,
309–12; Yaoundé Conventions, 290–1,
295–302

Fanon, Frantz, 9
foreign aid, 43, 47, 55, 80, 107, 217–18;
application, 252–60; criteria for,
248–52, 256; dependence and, 217–18,
223–8, 231; dimensions, 228–30, *228*,
254–6, *255*; and economic
development, 234, 248–50; programme
v. project, 236–7, 252–3; recipients'
viewpoint, 230–42, 260–2; technical
assistance as part, 229, 236, 238–41,
252–3, 258–9; *see also* Canada
foreign investment, 145–6, 232, 288
France, and Upper Volta, 79–80

Gaddafi, Colonel, 289
Galtung, Johan, 74, 310
Gambia, 14–15
Ghai, Dharam, 311
Ghana, 75–6, 80, 83–4, 89; coup, 1966,
153, 270; diplomacy, 282–3
Gold Coast, 14, 16; labour unrest, *17*
Goody, Jack, 153, 160
Gowon, General, 293
Gregory, J. W., 40
Guinea, 288, 294

Harberger, A. C., 222
Hassan, King of Morocco, 194
Helleiner, G. K., 217–18
Hirshman, A. O., 231
history, African: African view, 5–6;
imperialist view, 5; Marxist view, 6–7;
reorientation, 6; significant questions,
12–14; *see also* systems
Hochet, Jean, 82

Hodder-Williams, Richard, 132
John Holt & Co, 13
Hopkins, A. G., 7, 11
Hughes, A., and Cohen R., 14, 16
human rights, 166
Hyden, G., 166–7

Iliffe, John, 12, 14
import substitution, 43, 46, 55–6;
personnel, 241
income redistribution, 44, 50, 54, 59–61,
64–5
inequality among states, 382–7; *see also*
diplomatic exchange
Ingle, C. R., 167
integrated economy, 43–4, 53–5, 64–5
International Governmental
Organisations (IGOs), 319–51, *320–1*,
323, 358, 373–81, *377*; competition
among, 347–51; conference
participation, 332–7, *333*, 335,
349–50, *349*; financial support for,
324–7, *325*, 348; 'general' support for,
337–47, *338–41*, *344*, *346*, 350–1, *350*;
personnel support for, 327–31, 349;
regional organisations, *374–5*;
secretariats, 327–8
Ivory Coast, 75–6, 79–80, 83–5, 89

Jackson, R. H., 25, 27, 30, 32, 34
Johns, D. H., 265–6
Johnson, President L. B., 304
Johnson, I. T. A. Wallace, 14
Jonathan, Chief Leabua, 105, 115, 117
Jørgensen, J. J., 39–40

Kabaka Edward Mutessa II, 48
Kaiser, Karl, 363
Kakonge, John, 47
Kapwepwe, Simon, 184, 201
Kariuki, J. M., 35
Kasfir, Nelson, 62
Kaunda, President Kenneth, 132,
188–91, 193–4, 198–202, 204–5, 210;
and gun-running, 209; pacifism, 186;
and Rhodesian UDI, 191, 198–9
Kenya, 165–6, 169–71; and bourgeoisie,
29–31; and capitalism, 25; Kariuki
assassination, 1975, 35
Kenyatta, President Mzee Jomo, 35–6
Keyta, Ceyda, 294
Khama, President Seretse, 370
Kitching, Gavin, 175
Kiwanuka, Benedicto, 49

labour movement, 12–13; action *15*,
16–17, *17*; analysis, 18; consciousness,
17–19; organisation, 14–16; trade
unions, 14–15, 33, 98

labour reserve economy (Marxist), 97–104
112; dualism, 98–100, 108–10; proletarianisation in, 100–2
law, African, 380–1
leadership styles, 138–9
Lesotho, 40, 73, 95–126; dependence on South Africa, 95; economic background, 104–7; exports, *114*; industrial development, 105–6, 108–10, 117–18; labour reserve economy, 97–104, 112; migration of labour, 95–126; 'non-development', 108–18; political economy of underdevelopment, 118–26
Lewis, W. A., 97, 99
Leys, C. T., 30–2, 40, 166
liberation movements, 131–2, 183–213, *187, 189, 196–7*; administrative and financial assistance, 190–1; disunity, 195–205; operational facilities, 192–4; radio propaganda, 191–2; recognition, 188–90, 195; restrictions on, 205–13; training camps, 193
Libya, 270–1
Lloyd, P. C., 27

Mair, Lucy, 161
Malaŵi, 126, 131–2, 160–77; elections, 161, 170; national identification, 163–4; political structure, 173; stability, 176
Mali, 73
Margai, Sir Albert, 131, 135, 142–9
Margai, Sir Milton, 131, 135, 142–7
Marx, Karl, 7, 25–6, 99; *Das Kapital*, 99; *Zur Kritik der Hegelschen Rechtsphilosophie*, 18–19
Marxism, 6–7, 9, 286, 289, 310; labour reserve economy, 97–104; modes of production, 11–12
Mayall, James, 266
Mazrui, Ali, A., 59, 291, 380
migration of labour, 40, 76–85, *77–8*, 88–9, 95–126, *111–13, 124, 163*; and dependence, 79–82, *89*; earnings, *106*; and 'non-development', 110–14; structural and opportunity costs, 102–4; structure, 123–4; and underdevelopment, 83–5, *89*
Miliband, R., 24
Mobutu, President, 202
Mokhehle, Ntsu, 115–16
Morocco, 270–1
Moshweshwe, Chief, 118–19
Mozambique, 126, 195, 200–1
Muzorewa, Bishop A., 200

nationalism, 131, 163, 361, 379; economic, 311; *see also* liberation movements
neo-colonialism, 54, 76, 79–81, 131, 266, 360; *vis-à-vis* EEC, 287–95, 298
Neto, Agostinho, 204–5
Neustadt, Richard, 135
Niger, 73
Nigeria, 13–16, 153, 159, 165, 232, 289; diplomacy, 265, 282, and EEC, 288, 292–3, 295, 307; and foreign aid, 256
Nixon, President R. M., 305
Nkomo, Joshua, 198, 200
Nkosolo, Mukaka, 206
Nkrumah, Kwame, 153, 184, 270, 288–9, 348
'non-development', 108–18; industrial development strategy, 108–10; migrant labour and, 110–14; and political development, 114–16
Nye, J. S., 377
Nyerere, President Julius, 161–2, 190, 198, 202, 225, 289, 294, 303, 348

Oberschall, A. R., 166
Obote, President Apolo Milton, 39, 153–4, 166, 270; economic policy, 47–65
Okuda, Kenji, 217–18
'Open Door' economic policy, 145–6
Organisation of African Unity (OAU), 163, 184–5, 188, 190–1, 194–5, 198–201, 204–5, 265, 269, 282, 287, 289–90, 357, 373–4, 378, 387; Economic Charter, 292–4; and law and order, 381; support for, *see* International Governmental Organisations
Ossowski, S., 9
Ougadougou, 80

patron-client networks, 28–9, 34–6, 49, 157–8
peasantry, 27, 31, 34, 59–60, 168; proletarianisation, 100–2
political-administrative elite, 27–9, 48–53, 61–4, 79, 131, 157, 169; local, 171
political economy: influences on, 45; of underdevelopment, 118–26
political interaction, 157–8
politics: approach to, 1, 165–6, 288–9, 359–60; international, 357–87
Portugal, 200, 202
power, balance of, 382–7
production modes (Marxist), 11–12
proletariat, *see* working class
public support, 153–77; politically relevant, 156–7; and stability, 174–7

radicalism, 133
regional integration, 371, 374–5, 376–8, 380, 383, 386–7
revolutionary activity: class structure and, 10, 32–3; theatre of, 193–4
Rhodesia, 188, 192, 210: Arrighi's study, 101–2; UDI, 191, 198–9, 209, 211; see also Zimbabwe
Roberto, Holden, 201

Sandbrook, R., 25, 28, 34
Saul, J. S., 170
Savimbi, Dr Jonas, 201–2, 210
Seers, Dudley, 73, 222
Sekondi, 14
Sékou-Touré, President, 288
Selwyn, Percy, 108–9
Senegal, 103, 283
Senghor, President Léopold, 290, 292, 302, 336
Shaw, T. M., 266–7
Sierra Leone, 131, 135–49; political environment, 141–2; rail strikes, 16; trade unionism, 14
Sipalo, Mr, 198
Sithole, Ndabaningi, 198, 200
Smith, Ian, 186, 191, 210
Soames, Sir Christopher, 306
social criteria for foreign aid, 251, 253–4
social science methodology, 6, 100; Lesotho, 95–6; survey research, 8–9
socialism, 48, 53–4, 225; and EurAfrican trade relations, 309–12; ujamaa, 160, 162, 167
society, modern and residual sectors, 139–40
South Africa, 40, 185; and Lesotho, 95–126; and Malawi, 171–2
state, role of, 24–5; control of economy, 43, 53–8, 62
structural dependence, 44–7, 54; and Obote regime, 47–65
Sudan, 283
Swaziland, 73
systems, political: colonial, 368–70, 362; 362; discontinuities and continuities, 358–62; post-colonial, 370–2; post-independence, 382–7; pre-colonial, 363–8, 365; see also Easton, David

Tanzania, 161–2, 165–70, 175, 193, 195, 208, 232; and capitalism, 24–5; and foreign aid, 226, 230
technical assistance see under foreign aid
Telli, Diallo, 330–1

Thompson, E. P., *Making of the English Working Class*, 7–8, 18
trade strategy, 226–7; pre-colonial trade, 363–4; see also European Economic Community
trade unions, 14–15, 33, 98

Uganda, 39, 43–65, 165–6, 172, 250; Constitution, 1962, 62; coup, 1971, 153–4, 270, 386; economic reform, 43–4, 53–8; elite, 169; social and political structure, 48–53
ujamaa, 160, 162, 167
underdevelopment: and dependence, 85–8, 89, 223; and dualism, 98–100; and migration, 83–5, 89; political economy of, 118–26
United Kingdom: and Rhodesian UDI, 211; trade with Uganda, 47
United States: social and political science, 99–100; trading policy, 304–6
Upper Volta, 40, 73–90; agriculture and industry, 85–8; France and, 79–80
urbanisation, 76, 89

Vorster, John, 200

wages, determination of, 101, 124
Wallerstein, I., 24, 319, 348
Wallman, Sandra, 111
Ward, Michael, 107
Weisfelder, R. F., 115–16
Williams, J. C., 110–11
Wilson, Harold, 186
Wittkopf, E. R. 322
Woddis, Jack, 7
work, history of, 12–13
working class (proletariat), 31–3; creation, 100–2; identity, 7–8, 18, 33
World War I, 79
World War II, 15, 79, 88, 110

Yaoundé Conventions, 290–1, 295–302

Zaire, 195, 201, 232; diplomacy, 265, 282
Zambia, 132–3, 165, 167, 169, 183–213; controls on freedom fighters, 194–211; liberation support, 185–94; risk-taking, 207–8, 207; and terrorism, 210
Zanzibar, 166
Zartman, I. W., 358, 384–5
Zimbabwe, 133, 191, 195–201, 203–4; see also Rhodesia